Praise for *Regulating Digita*

"In this book, Mark MacCarthy takes on the most challenging problem in today's digital world—how can the public enjoy the enormous benefits of digital platforms without ceding to these companies control of our digital lives? With scholarly precision, MacCarthy shows that decades of reliance on 'self-regulation' and existing consumer protection laws have created a world in which a handful of mammoth digital platforms exercise outsized control over how we do everything from looking for work and shopping for goods and services to receiving our daily news that shapes our opinions and our democracy. Fortunately, MacCarthy presents a workable solution to give us back control of our digital lives—creation of a new federal agency with both the expertise and the regulatory power to restore our online autonomy and protect our democratic institutions from the current flood of disinformation and harassment. This approach has worked before and can work again—if policymakers find the political will to follow the proposals in this book and make it happen."

—**Harold Feld**, senior vice president, Public Knowledge

"MacCarthy astutely points out the key ways in which current US law fails to address the enormous economic and social harms caused by dominant digital platforms and then provides a cogent and comprehensive solution: a public oversight body up to the task of reining in digital market abuses. By reviving the time-tested sector regulatory model updated to reflect today's market realities, MacCarthy delivers a challenge for lawmakers that must be addressed to preserve our democratic institutions and competitive marketplace principles."

—**Gene Kimmelman**, senior research fellow, Mossavar-Rahmani Center for Business and Government Harvard Kennedy School; senior policy fellow, Yale's Tobin Economic Policy Center; former deputy associate attorney, General Department of Justice

"MacCarthy's decades of experience in government, the private sector, and academia are reflected in a work of great importance, certain to influence the ongoing policy debates surrounding the incalculable benefits and substantial costs attributable to the digital sector. MacCarthy's proposed solution, a dedicated digital regulatory agency with sufficient legal authority and relevant expertise, is designed to protect the benefits while minimizing the costs.

"*Regulating Digital Industries* describes the digital business models and the reasons that today's legal and regulatory institutions have not been successful in addressing market power, privacy protection, and 'information disorder' issues that have emerged from those business models. By going beyond admiring the problems and offering a practical (if long-term) solution, MacCarthy has made a material contribution to one of the most important policy debates of our time."

—**Phil Verveer**, former deputy assistant secretary of state for international communications and information policy; first lead counsel on *United States v. AT&T* and senior counselor to the chairman of the FCC

"MacCarthy has produced a clean, clear, and thought-provoking analysis of the challenges of the digital platform economy. While the problems of privacy invasion, competition destruction, and misinformation are well documented, the solutions are not. MacCarthy's solution: the revival of government's recognition that new technologies require new kinds of oversight. This book belongs on every policymaker's desk."

—**Tom Wheeler**, visiting fellow, Governance Studies, Center for Technology Innovation, Brookings Institution; former chairman of the Federal Communications Commission

"With the idea of a regulator for AI gaining traction, Professor MacCarthy's blueprint for sectoral digital regulation is timely and important. He explains why and how decades of experimentation in an unregulated digital sphere produced the predicted results of undue concentration, information disorder, and commercial surveillance. AI looks ready to supercharge these problems. But regulation is difficult. Professor MacCarthy has been providing thought leadership on how to stand up digital regulation for years, and his work has never been more important."

—**Ellen P. Goodman**, distinguished professor, Rutgers Law School

"MacCarthy has a remarkable knack for focusing on the right questions, at the right time. In a field too often dominated by handwaving and yelling, he provides the thing we really need: lucid, thoughtful, and timely analysis."

—**Daphne Keller**, director, Program on Platform Regulation, Stanford Cyber Policy Center

"To begin to address the damage neoliberalism and tech-utopianism have wrought, MacCarthy offers big, creative solutions, rooted in history but designed for current challenges. He recognizes that guardrails can mitigate societal harms while enhancing innovation. It is a handy guide for policymakers and citizens alike eager for practical options."

—**Karen Kornbluh**, managing director, Digital Innovation and Democracy Initiative, German Marshall Fund; former US ambassador to the Organisation for Economic Co-operation and Development

"It took Progressive-era reforms to tame the Gilded Age. Professor MacCarthy, a skilled Washington insider as well as an accomplished scholar, explains how to reinvent both competition and privacy protection to tame today's second Gilded Age."

—**Peter Swire**, Liang Chair of Cybersecurity and Policy, Georgia Tech; first person to have US government-wide responsibility for privacy policy

Regulating Digital Industries

How Public Oversight Can Encourage Competition, Protect Privacy, and Ensure Free Speech

Mark MacCarthy

BROOKINGS INSTITUTION PRESS
Washington, D.C.

Published by Brookings Institution Press
1775 Massachusetts Avenue, NW
Washington, DC 20036
www.brookings.edu/bipress

Co-published by Rowman & Littlefield
An imprint of The Rowman & Littlefield Publishing Group, Inc.
4501 Forbes Boulevard, Suite 200, Lanham, Maryland 20706
www.rowman.com

86-90 Paul Street, London EC2A 4NE

The Brookings Institution is a nonprofit organization devoted to research, education, and publication on important issues of domestic and foreign policy. Its principal purpose is to bring the highest quality independent research and analysis to bear on current and emerging policy problems.

British Library Cataloguing in Publication Information Available

Library of Congress Cataloging-in-Publication Data
Names: MacCarthy, Mark, author.
Title: Regulating digital industries : how public oversight can encourage competition, protect privacy, and ensure free speech / Mark MacCarthy.
Description: Washington, D.C. : Brookings Institution Press, [2023] | Includes bibliographical references and index. | Summary: "This book calls for a single industry regulatory agency to promote competition, privacy and free speech in digital industries"— Provided by publisher.
Identifiers: LCCN 2023016357 (print) | LCCN 2023016358 (ebook) | ISBN 9780815740155 (cloth) | ISBN 9780815739814 (paperback) | ISBN 9780815739821 (epub)
Subjects: LCSH: Electronic industries—Law and legislation. | Social media—Law and legislation. | Online social networks—Law and legislation. | Privacy, Right of—Data Processing.
Classification: LCC K564.C6 M33 2023 (print) | LCC K564.C6 (ebook) | DDC 343.09/99—dc23/eng/20230713
LC record available at https://lccn.loc.gov/2023016357
LC ebook record available at https://lccn.loc.gov/2023016358

∞™ The paper used in this publication meets the minimum requirements of American National Standard for Information Sciences—Permanence of Paper for Printed Library Materials, ANSI/NISO Z39.48-1992

This book is dedicated to Representative John D. Dingell Jr. of Michigan, who taught me the vital importance of regulating industry in the public interest

Contents

Preface

This book is an exercise in historical retrieval. It revives the once revered and now reviled ideal of a sectoral regulatory agency. It argues that a digital regulator is the best hope for bringing under social control the companies engaged in search, social media, electronic commerce, mobile app infrastructure, and ad tech. These lines of business collectively form the core digital industries of our time. Their discontents are well known and growing—industrial concentration that has dissipated the benefits of once-vigorously competitive markets, privacy invasions of truly massive dimensions, and information disorder that threatens our ability to govern ourselves and to respond to public health crises like the COVID-19 pandemic. A sectoral regulator with expert knowledge of the industry is the best institutional response to these well-known digital challenges.

Well over 150 years ago, US policymakers devised the institution of an expert regulatory agency to exercise governmental control over the new giant corporations that were changing the nature of economic activity. These companies were using the new advanced technologies of their day in electronic communications and transportation to upend the local and regional economies of small- and medium-sized companies and establish a new economic order controlled by a new organizational innovation, the giant corporation. At first, policymakers had no idea how to respond to this development, but they quickly devised an institutional mechanism of their own to govern the technological giants of their day—the expert regulatory agency. In the 1980s, business historian Thomas McCraw wrote a Nobel Prize–winning history of this long period of institutional experimentation and reform.[1]

State railroad commissions in the 1870s were the first example of this innovative governance structure. Then in 1887, Congress established the Interstate Commerce Commission (ICC) to regulate railroads that crossed state borders. These commissions established the first principles of regulated industrial activity: transparency of rates; availability to all on nondiscriminatory terms and conditions; fair, reasonable, and affordable rates; and interconnection among competing service providers. Early progressive reformers dreamed that regulatory controls should properly apply in all major business sectors, creating an ordered, harmonious economic world.

Policymakers so thoroughly embraced this ideal to deal with technological and business innovations that, when a new technology arose, their natural impulse was to regulate it. Indeed, without regulation, new technology often seemed unable to make the transition from interesting invention to sustainable business. In the 1920s, broadcasting was a popular novelty, apparently able to bring music, sports, news, and political conventions into the home from a distance. But unlicensed stations interfered with each other's signals so often that they could not effectively reach an audience. The industry itself asked for public regulation to restore enough order in the use of the radio spectrum to permit the development of a stable industry. Congress created the Federal Radio Commission (FRC) in 1927 as a sectoral regulator of the broadcasting industry that used broad licensing authority to end spectrum disorder. Congress merged the agency into the larger Federal Communications Commission (FCC) in 1934, giving it full authority to regulate the interlinked communications industry that provided electronic communications by wire or cable. Under regulation, the broadcasting and telecommunications industry flourished in the United States for generations.

When commercial aviation became a genuine possibility in the 1930s, the first thought in the mind of policymakers was to establish a regulatory structure to bring the technology to market in an orderly way. In 1938, Congress established the Civil Aeronautics Board (CAB) to govern entry and exit of aviation firms from the industry, allocate routes, and set rates for the emerging industry. Through the succeeding decades, the industry grew spectacularly under this regulatory supervision.

Throughout the economy, regulatory agencies expanded to cover communications, gas, electricity, water, securities exchanges, banks, insurance companies, stockbrokers, shipping, trucking, and inland waterways. Everywhere consumers turned they encountered businesses whose economic activity was supervised and governed by regulatory agencies. The details differed, but the sectoral regulatory agency was accepted and welcomed by the policymakers and the public alike as a tool for effective economic and technological governance.

Through a historical accident, this model of social control never applied to the computer industry. When the industry developed in the 1950s, it was essentially a provider of machinery and services to large corporations with no connection to the ordinary individual consumer. In the early days of the industry, individual consumers would no more own their own computers than they would own their own electric generating plant. Probably because individual consumers never directly saw or felt the presence of the growing computer industry and because it was a piece of infrastructure that could be used in a broad range of industries, it never attracted the attention of policymakers as needing its own regulatory structure.

Instead, it was the computer industry as applied to specific economic activities that became the object of regulation. When the mainframe computer allowed credit reporting agencies to digitize, maintain, and analyze systems of records relating to people's creditworthiness, it sparked the first attempt to regulate the applied computer industry. In 1974, Congress passed the Fair Credit Reporting Act, giving consumers legal rights to fair treatment and requiring credit reporting agencies to protect these rights. It gave enforcement power to the Federal Trade Commission (FTC), an economywide agency with the general authority to protect competition and consumers. In effect, this general-purpose agency took on the additional task of serving as the sectoral regulator of the credit reporting agencies.

But the computer industry itself escaped regulatory control. When the personal computer industry arose in the late 1970s to provide the new computing technology to the general public for the first time, it might have been possible to throw a regulatory net around the emerging consumer-focused computer industry at that time. But by then the tide had turned against the very idea of a regulatory agency.

This major shift in governing philosophy occurred in the mid-1970s. Policymakers increasingly turned against the ideal of sectoral regulation. Some of the criticism was detailed and specific—too often it seemed a particular regulation was poorly thought out and imposed burdensome processes on business with no discernible gain for the public. Another criticism was that the agencies had been captured by the industries they regulated; they protected the industries rather than the public. But the most fundamental criticism of all was that the agencies were not needed. In the new approach, the normal forces of competition would protect the public better than the obscure workings of bureaucrats ever would.

Following this new thinking, the FCC began to promote competition in the 1970s. These efforts formed a part of the movement in the courts and Congress to break up the integrated phone company in the 1980s and 1990s and deregulate the communications industry. The hope of the reformers was to generate robust competition throughout the industry. Regulatory reform in aviation was even more thorough. Under Alfred Kahn in the late 1970s, the agency deregulated as fast as it could. Congress endorsed this move away from airline regulation, passing regulatory reform legislation that eventually shut down the CAB in 1985 and left us with the unregulated airline industry we have today.

This movement against sectoral regulation was part of the general revolt against government. From the time of President Ronald Reagan in the 1980s to the present, government was seen as the problem, not the solution. Often, regulatory officials under both Democratic and Republican administrations seemed to think their major task was to reduce the footprint of the government itself. The common deregulatory approach was to establish new legal requirements only sparingly, as a last resort, and only after demonstrating that the use of government power to address a real problem would do more good than just leaving the problem to work itself out.

In that context, it is not surprising that the digital successors of the computer industry—search engines, social media, electronic commerce, mobile apps—all grew up in a world where a sectoral regulator seemed to be a relic of the forgotten industrial past. In that climate of opinion, it was unthinkable to establish a new regulatory agency to usher in this new technology, the way the FCC had for broadcasting and the CAB had for aviation. Every attempt to impose even the slightest public control on digital industries was derided as outmoded, an unthinking extension of a governance model fit, perhaps, for the slow-moving technologically static industries of the nineteenth century but totally unable to respond to the fast-moving pace of today's digital tornados.

The underlying premise of this book is that this deregulatory governing philosophy has had its day. A forty-year natural experiment in leaving industries alone to govern themselves has produced the results we face in today's digital industries: concentration in each digital sector, massive privacy invasions, and a distorted public information sphere.

The movement to restore social control to digital industries has begun. Beginning in 2021, policymakers began to consider new laws to reform competition policy for digital companies and to establish strong privacy rules and content moderation guidelines. The movement will not happen all at once, and it may encounter setbacks and false starts. No major reform movement, especially one upending an entrenched policy consensus, can accomplish its results quickly. But it is the new direction for digital policymaking.

As part of this reform effort, this book seeks to rehabilitate the ideal of a sectoral regulator for the digital world. Rather than argue the point in the abstract, it attempts to show in case after case how the necessary measures to protect competition, preserve privacy, and establish good content moderation practices can be administered most effectively by a sectoral regulator.

The good news is that Congress is moving in its slow, siloed way toward such a regulatory solution. In a way, today's movement toward digital regulation might recapitulate the movement of other independent regulatory agencies that were initially housed in established agencies and then spun off into their own separate administrative structure. Proposed legislation to reform competition law for digital industries authorizes the FTC to administer the new procompetition measures. Proposed privacy and content moderation laws also designate the FTC as the enforcement agency. These separate decisions amount collectively to a congressional determination to designate the FTC as the nation's digital regulator.

This move toward digital regulation under the FTC would be a very large step in the right direction. A second or even a third step might be needed to refine the most effective regulatory structure. A digital regulator is awkwardly housed in the FTC, which is primarily an economywide law enforcement agency, not an industry-specific regulatory agency. Just as Congress separated the FCC from the ICC and the Securities and Exchange Commission (SEC) from the FTC, Congress should eventually spin off digital regulatory responsibilities to one or more separate digital agencies as the need for increasing expertise requires expanded resources and more focused staff with expert knowledge and experience.

An entirely new regulatory structure for digital industries will not be created in one legislative measure or even in one session of Congress. It will come in stages over a period of many years, not all at once. But the time to start is now. My hope is that this book can serve as one of the guideposts along the way.

NOTE

1. Thomas K. McCraw, *Prophets of Regulation: Charles Francis Adams, Louis D. Brandeis, James M. Landis, Alfred E. Kahn* (Cambridge, MA: Harvard University Press, 1984).

Acknowledgments

Regulation has been in retreat for most of my professional life. I first learned this fact when I joined the Occupational Safety and Health Administration in 1978 as a regulatory analyst, where President Jimmy Carter's new Regulatory Analysis Review Group demanded proof that a proposed regulation's benefits would exceed its costs. This requirement that all regulations pass a cost-benefit test was later enshrined in executive orders that apply to this very day.

In the 1980s, I was a professional staff member of the Committee on Energy and Commerce of the US House of Representatives, chaired by the formidable John D. Dingell Jr. of Michigan. It was an almost perfect institutional setting to witness and participate in the growing bipartisan deregulatory mood, including breaking up AT&T and deregulating the cable TV industry. In 1987, the FCC repealed the broadcast Fairness Doctrine and President Ronald Reagan vetoed Chairman Dingell's attempt to codify it. This triumph of the new deregulatory philosophy turned that generations-old safeguard for political pluralism into a historical relic.

In my later public policy work for industry, the task was almost entirely focused on repealing old regulations or blocking new ones. For Capital Cities/ABC, the job was to loosen radio ownership rules and repeal the financial interest and syndication rules. For the clients of the public policy advocacy firm Wexler/Walker, AT&T and Comcast, the task was to tear down the regulatory barriers that prevented them from entering the local telephone industry as part of the 1996 Telecommunications Act. For Visa, the assignment was to ward off antitrust suits and regulations aimed at lowering merchant interchange fees. At the

Software & Information Industry Association, the project was to resist new national legislation in consumer privacy, data security and breach notification, encryption, Section 230 reform, and cybersecurity.

In writing this book, I benefited from the experience accumulated in these senior public policy positions. My basic takeaway, however, was that the deregulatory impulse had run its course after forty years or so of ascendancy in Washington, DC, policy circles. It was time to return to an older tradition of public oversight of business in general and the tech industry in particular.

In this effort of regulatory revival, I have learned much from the advice, counsel, and comments of my colleagues at the Brookings Center for Technology Innovation. Nicol Turner Lee, Darrell West, and Tom Wheeler welcomed me as a nonresident senior fellow in 2020 and encouraged me to pursue a book project on digital regulation. Tom and Alex Engler provided thoughtful comments on an initial draft. The regular interchange with the scholars and the discipline of writing regular tech policy commentaries for the CTI blog *TechTank* helped me develop and sharpen the ideas in this book.

I'd also like to thank Paul Ohm and Julie Cohen for bringing me on as a nonresident senior fellow in 2019 at the Institute for Technology Law and Policy at Georgetown Law Center. I'm especially grateful to then–executive director of the Tech Institute Alexandra Givens for organizing a workshop in May 2019 that allowed me to gather reactions to my initial paper on a consumer protection approach to content moderation regulation. I've also learned much from the criticisms of Julie and Paul on the limits of transparency rules as a way to promote social media accountability.

As senior vice president for global public policy at the Software and Information Industry Association from 2011 to 2019, I was privileged to meet and work with many officials and representatives of the tech industry. I'm grateful to them for the experiences and expertise they shared with me during my time at SIIA. Colleagues at SIIA, including Ken Wasch (the founder and former CEO), Carl Schonander, and David Leduc, also guided my thinking on tech policy and provided insightful comments on an initial draft of this book.

I am likewise grateful to my colleagues at Georgetown's Communications, Culture & Technology Program, especially the former program director Linda Garcia, who hired me almost twenty-five years ago, and Meg Leta Jones and David Lightfoot, who encouraged me to pursue a book project on digital regulation. Meg and my longtime friend and professional colleague Jonathan Band shared their mixed experiences in academic publishing and warned me of the inevitable snags and delays involved in such a project.

I want to express a particular word of thanks to the many graduate and undergraduate students I have taught at Georgetown. Especially in my classes over the last four years, as the ideas in this book took shape, their sharp questions and comments on tech policy issues have been an unending source of inspiration.

Many other friends and colleagues contributed in different ways to the ideas expressed in this work, including David Rubashkin, Karl Kronebusch, Seth Carus, Andrew Jay Schwartzman, Phil Verveer, and Edmond Chibeau. I'm grateful for the care and time they devoted to commenting on early drafts.

I owe a special debt of gratitude to my son Colin, who pushed me to write this book and provided invaluable guidance and support as I was writing it.

For all the rest, I thank my beloved wife Ana Maria Espinoza. She gave me the unstinting love, support, and encouragement without which this book—and many other things—would not have been possible.

Chapter 1

Digital Industries and Their Discontents

"Policymakers need to disaggregate the Big Tech debate into its constituent parts and give greater focus to the digital age's novel challenges."

—Oren Cass[1]

"The reason that we are now in the early stages of a great debate about regulating the Internet is that a quarter century ago just about everyone, including liberals, assumed that an unregulated Internet would be a good idea."

—Nicolas Lemann[2]

Introduction

In a speech following his victory in the 2020 Democratic senatorial primary, US Senator Ed Markey announced triumphantly, "The era of incrementalism is over."[3] His call to "think big and take bold action" is part of a growing wave of policy innovation sweeping over Washington, DC. After a forty-year hiatus, during which the dominant slogans were to let the private sector lead and to rely on industry self-regulation instead of rigid government rules, proposals for significant expansion of government regulation are back on the national policy agenda.

This new consensus in favor of a stronger role for government is bipartisan. Republican Senator Marco Rubio has called for vigorous government intervention in the economy to promote "common-good capitalism."[4] Former Republican presidential candidate and current senator from Utah Mitt Romney has proposed a Family Security Act that would provide increased government cash support to all families with children.[5]

This return to regulation is especially evident in connection with the digital businesses that are rightly the source of substantial and increasing public concern and scrutiny. The major tech companies dominate their business environment in a way not seen since the growth of the trusts in the late nineteenth century, making a mockery of the lax antitrust enforcement practices of the last forty years. Their power is evident in the vast troves of information they collect about their users and the complete inability of users to exercise any effective control over how this personal data is used to make inferences about their most sensitive traits. Their failure to control hate speech, misinformation, and disinformation on their systems has damaged the nation's process of political governance and crippled its ability to counteract the COVID-19 pandemic—the worst infectious disease crisis in more than one hundred years. The calls to respond to these tech challenges are bipartisan.

New ideas for digital governance are flourishing. Some relate to new procompetition tools to supplement traditional antitrust actions to restore competitive vigor to the core digital industries now dominated by one or only a few suppliers. New directions in privacy law and regulation are being considered to meet the challenges of ubiquitous online information collection and analysis. The need to contest information disorder on social media services, especially the hate speech and disinformation present on the largest platforms, has given rise to innovative proposals. Some of them challenge the twenty-five-year-old policy consensus that online companies deserve the highest level of protection from government regulation and should not be held responsible for the information provided by their users.

This book is a sustained argument that the three challenges of promoting competition, protecting privacy, and ensuring online safety must be addressed through a single coherent system of regulation. Adequate solutions will require new legislation that establishes a sector-specific regulatory agency to supervise digital industries. Unlike other books, white papers, and scholarly articles that have documented the unfair business practices, privacy abuses, and information disorder in digital industries, the approach here largely assumes the existence of these problems. The issue it addresses is not whether the country has urgent challenges in these areas, but what policymakers ought to do about these well-known and widely recognized problems.

Concentration in digital industries is undeniable. A few digital companies dominate the essential services of search, social networking, electronic commerce, and mobile apps. This tendency toward economic domination is driven by the exceptionally strong network effects in digital markets. The lack of genuine alternatives to these providers of essential services exposes dependent businesses and customers to abuse and exacerbates other significant problems in digital markets.

The loss of privacy in digital industries is also evident. The same dominant digital companies have amassed large databases of personal information about their users, and the lack of competitive alternatives, omnipresent information externalities, and the inherently relational character of digital data mean individuals are powerless to act on their own to restore their lost digital privacy. Information disorder is rampant in core digital industries, especially social media platforms that have allowed their systems to become infested with hate speech, terrorist material, material harmful to children, and disinformation. This information disorder threatens the nation's ability to choose its political leaders, to protect its children, and to respond to emergencies like the COVID-19 pandemic, but it arises from deep roots in social media technology itself, the advertising model used to fund these systems, and the external nature of harms it produces.

To meet these diverse challenges, legislators will need to provide a digital regulatory agency with a range of different tools. Privacy intrusion is not the same problem as hate speech, and both differ from the use of concentrated economic power to exploit dependent users and merchants. But a measure conceived as a remedy to one of these problems almost always has implications—either positive or negative—for the other two. Voluntary data portability, for instance, might further competition and privacy, but mandatory data sharing would advance competition at the expense of user privacy. End-to-end encryption preserves privacy, but it makes it difficult to detect and stop hate speech and other online abuse.

The best visual model for the digital policy space of competition, privacy, and content moderation is a Venn diagram with three intersecting circles, where measures in the overlaps either help to attain the different policy goals or interfere with each other (see figure 1.1). The metaphor is not original. Former chairman of the FCC Tom Wheeler suggested this visual model in conversation, and he has incorporated it into his book titled *Techlash: Who Makes the Rules in the Digital Gilded Age?* (2023). In a 2021 article, Stanford University legal scholar Daphne Keller wrote that in her platform regulation class every year she draws "a Venn diagram on

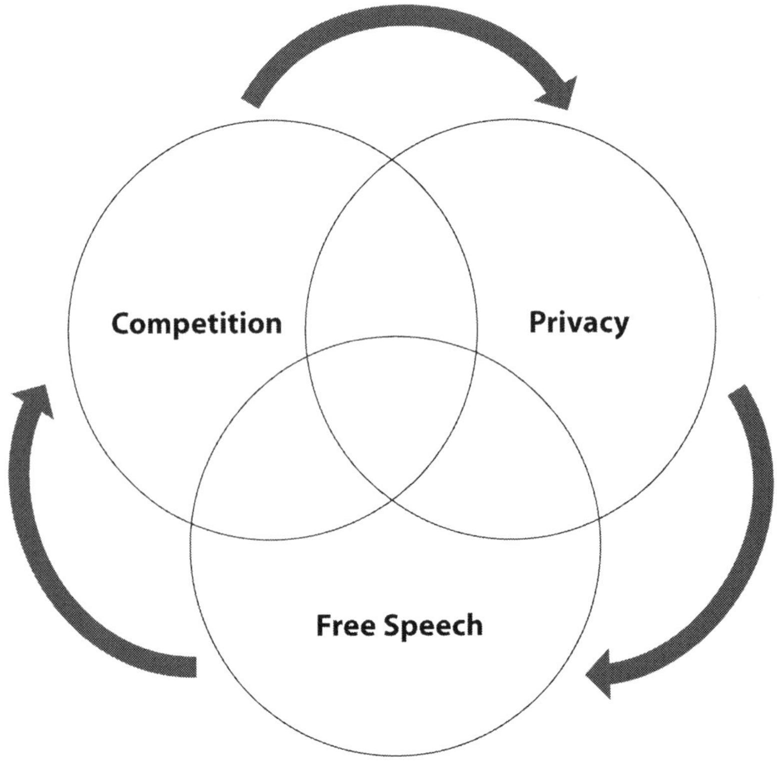

Figure 1.1.

the board with three interlocking circles: privacy, speech, and competition. Then we identify all the issues that fall at the intersection of two or more circles."[6]

Largely because personal data is such a key resource in digital industries, almost the entire digital policy space is in areas of overlap. The existence of these synergies and tensions is one reason to centralize the missions of promoting competition, protecting privacy, and ensuring online safety in a single industry-specific regulator. A single regulator would be best positioned to seek out synergies and to avoid or mitigate regulatory conflicts.

How to design the shape and functions of a regulatory agency capable of promoting competition, protecting privacy, and preserving information order in digital industries is a genuinely hard problem. To preserve autonomy from partisan interference, it should be structured as a traditional independent regulatory commission. This institutional form is less efficient than an agency led by a single administrator, since its membership can consist of a bare majority from the same political party, and it can act only by majority vote, but it has substantial leadership independence and so has greater autonomy from current administrations.

The agency should have sufficient regulatory authority to advance and balance sometimes conflicting policy goals and to adapt to changes in digital industries. However, it must still be accountable to Congress, the courts, and the public, and to prevent partisan abuse, its authority to regulate content should be restricted. In addition, the rules surrounding its operation should be structured carefully to minimize the risks of capture by the industries it seeks to regulate.

Despite these challenges, the time to begin the struggle for such fundamental reform is now. Congress has the opportunity not simply to react to today's critical issues but to put in place the adaptable institutional mechanisms the country will need to address tomorrow's digital challenges in competition, privacy, and content moderation. The rest of this chapter introduces these challenges and outlines the approach to address them that will be covered in the rest of the book.

Dominance in Digital Industries

The key consumer-facing lines of business in today's digital economy are social media, search, electronic commerce, and the operating systems, browsers, and app stores that make up the mobile app infrastructure. A few companies dominate these digital industries: Google in search, Amazon in electronic commerce, Google and Apple in mobile app infrastructure, and Facebook in social media. The digital ad industry is also a key element of the digital economy, and a few companies—principally Google, Facebook, and Amazon—dominate it. I will cover the ad industry to some degree in what follows, but my primary concern in this book is with the companies that dominate the core consumer-facing digital lines of business.

Google dominates today's general search market in the United States with an 88 percent market share, followed by Bing with about 7 percent, Yahoo! with less than 4 percent, and DuckDuckGo with less than 2 percent. Google's share has been increasing over time. According to Google's own estimates, it controlled 68 percent of the market as of July 2007, and 77 percent of the market on computers by June 2013. That grew to 79 percent on computers and 93.5 percent on mobile by April 2018. As of September 2020, Google accounted for almost 90 percent of all general search engine queries in the United States and almost 95 percent of queries on mobile devices.[7]

Amazon is the leading retailer in the world outside China, online or offline, surpassing Walmart in August 2021.[8] It dominates the US online retail sales market. In 2020, the House Judiciary Committee's report on its investigation into digital markets said, "Although Amazon is frequently described as controlling about 40 percent of US online retail sales, this market share is likely understated, and estimates of about 50 percent or higher are more credible."[9] The complaint in the antitrust suit filed against Amazon by the attorney general of the District of Columbia says, "Amazon is estimated to have between 50 to 70 percent of the market share of the online retail sales market. By contrast, the next two largest retail platforms—Walmart.com and eBay—have only around 5 percent of the market each. . . . Sixty-six percent of consumers start their search for new products on Amazon, and a staggering 74 percent go directly to Amazon when they are ready to buy a specific product."[10]

Apple and Google together control the US mobile app infrastructure through dominance of the operating systems that power mobile devices, the mobile browsers that enable internet access, and the distribution services that allow device owners to download applications that work on these operating systems.[11] Apple's iOS mobile operating system has about 60 percent of the US market, and Google's Android system has about 40 percent. The two companies have shared control of this market since 2011. Google's Chrome browser and Apple's Safari control the mobile browser market with Safari at 54 percent market share and Chrome at 38 percent.[12] They control the app distribution system as well. The only way to obtain an app that works with an iOS device is through Apple's App Store, and the dominant way to obtain an app that works on a Google Android system is through Google's Play Store. Both companies charge app developers up to 30 percent of the fees the developers charge their users. About $38.8 billion was spent in the Play Store and $72.3 billion was spent in Apple's App Store in 2020, according to industry research firm Sensor Tower Inc., generating billions of dollars of revenue to both companies.

Facebook dominates the personal social network market. During a Senate hearing in 2018, when Senator Lindsey Graham (R-SC) asked whether there was an alternative to Facebook in the private sector, Mark Zuckerberg struggled to name a single Facebook competitor.[13] Basic statistics tell the story of Facebook's dominance. It has 256 million daily active users in the United States and Canada, and 73 percent of them use Facebook at least once a day; seven in ten Americans use Facebook; about one-third of them get their news from Facebook; it dominates the amount of time people spend on social media with thirty-eight minutes a day; together with its subsidiaries, Facebook accounts for three-quarters of all time spent on social media.[14]

In October 2021, Facebook rebranded itself as Meta to reflect its commitment to the "metaverse," the new technology of virtual reality and enhanced reality. By October 2022, however, things looked bleak in its core social media business. User growth stalled and even declined in absolute numbers for one quarter of 2022. Advertising revenue fell, reflecting an industry-wide slump after Apple allowed users to opt-out of ad tracking on its mobile devices. And its share value plummeted 60 percent from its 2021 peak of $1.1 trillion.[15]

None of this means, however, that Facebook faces robust competition in social media, and competition authorities can walk away and let the market do its work. Measured by the key social media metrics, Facebook still dominates its core business.

In its amended complaint against Facebook, filed in August 2021, the FTC uses time spent on social networking services, daily active users, and monthly active users as indicators of Facebook's dominant position in the US market for social networking services. It alleges that every year since 2012, Facebook's share of time spent on social media platforms has exceeded 80 percent, its share of daily active users has exceeded 70 percent, and its share of monthly active users has exceeded 65 percent.[16] In a later filing, the FTC claimed that from September 2012 through December 2020, Facebook's share of time spent by users of social media apps in the United States averaged 92 percent per month. The combined shares of other apps, including Snapchat, Google+, MeWe, and Friendster, didn't exceed 18 percent in any month during that period.[17]

There are social media alternatives to Facebook for news and information, but only a small minority of the population uses them. In late 2022, the Pew Research Center reported that only 6 percent of adults say they regularly get news from one of seven alternative social media sites—BitChute, Gab, Gettr, Parler, Rumble, Telegram, and Truth Social.[18] These sites do not pose a genuine threat to Facebook's dominance.

What about the rise of TikTok and the decline of Facebook among teenagers? Pew Research Center reported in 2022 that some 67 percent of teens say they use TikTok, while teen usage of Facebook has plummeted from 71 percent in 2014–2015 to 32 percent today. Pew also reported that 95 percent of teens use YouTube. Doesn't this show that Facebook no longer has market power?[19]

Facebook has been losing share among teens for more than a decade and is unlikely to regain its popularity with teens. Still, Facebook remains dominant in social media for two reasons. First, even though TikTok and

YouTube compete for ad dollars with Facebook, they do very different things. TikTok and YouTube enable one-way broadcasting from creators to consumers; Facebook is a genuinely interactive communications platform. So, users who need communications services such as a cancer support group or a neighborhood exchange or just keeping up with family and friends cannot use TikTok or YouTube as alternatives. Second, Facebook is still the most popular platform among the general US population, even though YouTube and TikTok are more popular among teens. Advertisers seeking to reach the public with a new campaign cannot simply ignore Facebook and work with TikTok instead.[20]

The digital ad industry is dominated by Google, Facebook, and Amazon. In 2020, Google had 28.9 percent of the digital ad revenue, Facebook had a 25.2 percent share, and Amazon broke 10 percent for the first time with 10.3 percent, up from 7.8 percent in 2019.[21] There are hundreds of other companies providing services in the largely invisible ad-tech world, but these three companies garner the lion's share of the revenue and hold gatekeeper power over advertisers seeking to reach an audience. In addition, Google holds a commanding position in the complex ad-tech space with dominant positions in the publisher-facing ad server business, the advertising exchange business, and the brand-facing demand-side platforms.[22]

A major question is why these markets have tipped to a single or a small number of suppliers. The key factor is network effects—the tendency of a product or service to become more valuable to consumers when more people use it.[23] Network effects were first noticed in the communications industry and made famous by Ethernet founder Robert Metcalfe's rule of thumb that the value of a network is roughly proportional to the square of the number of its users.[24] Network effects exist throughout the economy and are a driving force in some industries such as communications networks and payment card networks. But they are uniquely pervasive and powerful in digital industries, where their strength impels consumers to choose and stay with the largest provider of a specific digital service.

A social network is more valuable when many people are on it because it provides the greatest opportunities to connect with family, friends, business associates, and an audience of strangers with whom users want to share ideas and experiences, and to expand these relationships through new connections. The result is that people want to join and remain in the largest social media platform because that is where their friends, family, business associates, and audiences are.

An online marketplace is more valuable to merchants when there are many customers on the same platform, and more valuable to customers when there are many merchants offering them a variety of goods and services. As a result, merchants and buyers want to join the largest online marketplace and to stay there because that is where they have the best chance of making a successful transaction.

A search engine is more valuable to users when many other people use it because the more data fed into a search engine, the better it is at returning accurate search results. It is more valuable to website owners when many people use the search engine because it increases the chances that people will find their site through a search. Internet users want to use the largest search engine because the larger the volume of search requests, the better the search algorithm is at finding the information they seek.

App developers want to write for a limited number of mobile app systems with the largest potential user base because that gives them the greatest chance of successfully locating users. Users pick one of the mobile app infrastructures in part because that is where they can find the largest number and variety of usable apps, and then they face prohibitively high switching costs that lock them into their chosen ecosystem.

In digital ad markets, the companies that can compile the most detailed, personalized profiles of their users can appeal to the broadest range of advertisers. The huge user bases for Google, Facebook, and Amazon provide a rich treasure trove of data for analysis and allow them to create the most efficient mechanisms for advertisers to target their messages to those most likely to be receptive to them. In addition, algorithms designed to infer characteristics of users from observed interactions with websites work more efficiently with larger volumes of data. Companies that achieve an initial advantage are likely to keep it unless a new entrant can offer something dramatically better. Amazon was able to gain traction in the digital ad market after initially ignoring it because it had reliable access to information about what customers purchase.

In the digital ad-tech industry, network effects operate as well. An advertising exchange linking internet publishers and advertisers for the sale of digital ad space is more valuable to both publishers and advertisers when it services many users of both types, creating a tendency for only a few large digital ad exchanges to develop and maintain themselves. Using this chokepoint, a dominant exchange can leverage strong positions in the supply-side ad server market and the advertiser's demand-side market.

Because of these strong network effects, the real role of competition in digital markets is competition *for* the market, rather than competition *within* a market. For many, perhaps most digital industries, and certainly for the four core digital industries of search, social media, electronic commerce, and mobile apps, one company is going be the dominant player. The business question is which company that will be. In the beginning stages, the competition is often fierce and perhaps even cutthroat as companies jockey for position to aggregate a large enough consumer base to take full advantage of network effects and emerge as the winner with durable control over the market. Over time as the competition proceeds, a single company gets a small advantage of size, gradually builds an insuperable lead, and comes to dominate the market.

Once a market tips, network effects operate as a barrier to entry. Existing users would face enormous switching costs to move to a new provider and leave the old one behind. To move to a new Facebook, users would have to convince their current network to move with them, a coordination challenge beyond the resources of individual users. Merchants fleeing Amazon's online marketplace would give up access to Amazon's enormous customer base—as of December 2019, there were an estimated 112 million US Amazon Prime subscribers—about 66.4 million of the 120 million US households.[25] People would be reluctant to abandon Google's search engine because rival search engines are less able to return the search results they want, since they operate at much smaller volume.

In assessing dominance, the key question is not just whether another vendor of a similar service is available but also whether it is a substitute—not whether users can access another provider of a key digital service easily but whether they can ever leave the dominant provider. Users can often multihome by using several providers of the same service at the same time. People can easily use Bing or DuckDuckGo in addition to Google. It is often convenient for merchants to sell through their own website or list on Shopify or eBay as well as on Amazon. The key question is not just whether it is easy for users to use a different provider but also whether the scale and resulting attractiveness of the dominant provider make it impossible for them to leave if they are not satisfied. Dominant players such as Amazon often try to limit the attractiveness of other platforms by, for instance, restricting the price they can charge on other platforms relative to the price they charge on Amazon. However, such business restrictions increase (but do not create) the intrinsic advantages of platform scale. For users of the dominant providers of key digital services, exiting is not an option. As K. Sabeel Rahman says, "Google is indispensable for search, as is Amazon for retail and Facebook for information flows."[26] And this lack of real alternatives is what gives these companies their extraordinary power over their users.

This tendency toward concentration in digital markets is often hidden from view because the initial stages of a new digital market are often so vibrantly competitive, with early leaders displaced by newcomers, who are in turn displaced by still more vigorous rivals. But vigorous competition is just a stage in the development of the industry, not its permanent condition or a result it naturally tends toward. Facebook initially competed against Myspace and Friendster—companies that preceded them in social media. Yahoo! was the leading search firm for years, but Google displaced it and other rivals, including WebCrawler, Lycos, AltaVista, Ink Tomi, and Ask Jeeves. eBay was the leading online market for years until Amazon entered and became the unquestioned market leader. Apple jumped into a mobile phone market dominated by Nokia phones with the Symbian operating system and Blackberries. In a few short years, Apple and Google had replaced them all. A cycle appears repeatedly in these industries—an initial burst of robust competition resulting from a new application of technology, followed by a period of concentration and then an equilibrium stage of a durable monopoly, where the industry is stable and concentrated.[27]

Having established itself as the paramount supplier of a digital service, a company can use this network effects barrier to enjoy a durable position of dominance. Left to itself, such a market will not automatically generate new rivals and will tend to crush the rivals that do emerge. It is crucial to recognize that this tendency toward concentration does not arise simply from the ability of tech companies to buy potential rivals, which could be mitigated by better controls on anticompetitive mergers. Network effects mean rivals do not really have a chance to topple a company that has achieved dominant status in its line of business. The ability to absorb rivals can exacerbate this underlying drive to concentration but does not create it.

The challenge for competition policy is how to restore competitive conditions in digital industries without also destroying the consumer benefits that come with large networks. One major theme of this book is that only a digital agency with a mission to promote competition and ongoing supervisory authority can inject competition into an industry where it would not naturally flourish and maintain this competition over time.

CENTRALITY OF DIGITAL SERVICES

Before moving on to the other challenges of privacy and content moderation, it is important to discuss another feature of digital industries often confused with the economic dominance of individual companies. The digital industries of search, social media, electronic commerce, and mobile apps have become central to the economic, social, political, and cultural life of the United States in the twenty-first century. The costs of avoiding these core digital services have become so high that people without access to them have effectively been excluded from full participation in contemporary life. It is virtually impossible to find or keep a job, to stay in regular contact with friends, family, and business associates, to retrieve the information needed to shop, work, seek housing or health care or financial services without relying on these services. The COVID-19 pandemic brought home to the country the extent of this dependence, as many people withdrew to their homes and relied on digital services to work, shop, relate to friends and family, and receive health care, and those who could not access these digital services fell farther and farther behind.

Not every line of business achieves this kind of centrality in contemporary life. The fashion industry, for instance, seems less than central to the nation's public life, even though it provides services many people cherish. But telecommunications, health care, housing, financial services, and energy are all essential to how people live in today's world. Core digital services have this kind of centrality today and will keep it into the foreseeable future.

When a line of business achieves this degree of centrality, government supervision of some kind becomes necessary to advance and protect the public interest, even when no one company dominates the provision of these essential infrastructure services. As we have seen, however, in each of the core digital lines of business, one company, or a handful of them, have come to control the bulk of the business. Regulation of core digital services seems even more important when only a few companies provide these essential services.

Because of the twin characteristics of dominance and centrality, these core digital companies have become extraordinarily powerful. When Facebook and Twitter banned President Donald Trump from their systems following the Capitol Hill riot on January 6, 2020, Trump virtually vanished from public view. In the first quarter of 2023, he used his newly restored Facebook page to fundraise off his indictment by a New York grand jury, raising almost $19 million in a few days.[28] A merchant that has no or diminished access to Amazon's large consumer base or who appears on the second page of Google's search results or who is banned from Apple's App store or Google's Play Store will not have a significant online business for very long. As public interest advocate Harold Feld notes, the few powerful companies providing core digital services "can bankrupt businesses, sway federal elections, and change the ways we think and feel about ourselves and others without our even realizing it."[29]

This centrality of these digital lines of business means that companies with durable dominant positions in providing these services have enormous, unchecked power to influence the shape and direction of the life of the nation. Nathan Robinson, editor of the progressive magazine

Current Affairs, spoke for the entire news industry when he said in 2018, "The sharing of our articles on social media is the engine of our growth. Without it, I don't know how anybody would find us."[30]

The dependence of younger people on social media for news is even more pronounced than it is for the general public. A poll conducted by Morning Consult in April 2022 found that "68% of Gen Z adults turn to social media for news at least once a week." No other outlet comes even close. This centrality of social media to news consumption for younger people adds to the power of social media to influence discussion of public policy issues and exacerbates the dependence of news outlets on access to social media platforms as essential distributors of their content.[31]

In 2022, Pew Research Center found that social media is now a "need" for many teenagers, as 53 percent of them say it would be hard or very hard for them to abandon these services. With 95 percent of American teenagers using YouTube and 67 percent of them using TikTok, it is easy to see that social media has become central to their lives. As a YouTube employee said, "How do you boycott electricity?"[32]

Combining the centrality of digital services with the dominance of companies providing these services means business decisions by five or six companies can make or break a political candidate, a newspaper, a book, a movie, or a product launch. Data derived from interactions on a small number of digital platforms can determine a person's credit rating, employment prospects, and insurance rates.

A variety of commentators have reflected on this feature of centrality using slightly different terminology. Harold Feld notes the increasing social and economic "costs of exclusion" from digital services.[33] Laura Moy observes that these services are largely "unavoidable" for people seeking to live life in the twenty-first century.[34] K. Sabeel Rahman asserts that they have become "informational infrastructures" that control access to vast areas of social, political, consumer, and business life.[35] They are all getting at the same phenomenon that is a commonplace of everyday discourse—the extent to which these core digital services have become as essential to contemporary life as the traditional essential services such as energy, transportation, food, water, banking, housing, and medicine.[36]

When an industry achieves this kind of centrality, regardless of whether it exhibits failures of competition, it is typically the object of regulatory supervision to ensure that the public interest is protected. This is what lawmakers did in setting up earlier regulatory agencies such as the FCC for broadcasting and telecommunications, the banking agencies for the financial services industry, the SEC for stockbrokers and exchanges, and the Food and Drug Administration (FDA) for the pharmaceutical industry.

It is critical to realize that the agencies supervising businesses with a central role in the nation's life do more than foster competition and protect dependent businesses. The FCC has a strong procompetitive mission in telecommunications and an array of rules to control horizontal and vertical integration and cross-ownership in the broadcasting and cable industry. But it is also responsible for pursuing other public policy objectives under the broad rubric of protecting the public interest in the industries it regulates, including the promotion of a media landscape that allows the public access to information from "diverse and antagonistic sources."[37] It pursues this additional mission through overseeing the content on broadcast outlets and defining and enforcing public interest responsibilities of broadcasters. It has an additional role of protecting privacy in the telecommunications, broadband, and cable industries. It needs to balance these different policy objectives in making its regulatory determinations.

The US banking industry is concentrated, but not nearly as much as the core digital industries. The regulatory regime for the financial services industry includes some procompetitive measures to preserve this unconcentrated industry structure, such as a rule preventing banking mergers that would give a depository institution control of more than 10 percent of the national market.[38] Yet public policymakers do not entrust the stability, safety, and soundness of the financial system and the protection of financial consumers to the forces of competition. In addition to their procompetitive role, federal agencies ensure that the financial services companies follow safe practices designed to forestall systemic risk and protect financial consumers from potentially ruinous harm. Prior to its repeal by the Gramm-Leach-Bliley Act in 1999, federal law prevented banks from engaging in the securities and insurance business so as to preserve system stability.[39] In the wake of the 2008–2009 financial crisis, Congress adopted new legislation to tighten and extend regulatory requirements to mitigate collective risks to financial institutions of systemic importance and to establish a new regulatory agency, the Consumer Financial Protection Bureau (CFPB), to protect financial consumers from unfair, deceptive, or abusive practices.[40]

Companies providing essential core digital services share with the large financial institutions this characteristic of systemic importance to the whole economy. As with other agencies seeking to regulate centrally important firms, regulation of these vital digital services must go beyond attempting to create and maintain a competitive market structure in digital services. It must also focus on protecting and preserving other important social values and interests. Chief among these additional challenges are the protection of privacy and the furtherance of effective content moderation. These challenges to other important values are exacerbated, but not created, by the lack of competition. They cannot be met solely, or even predominantly, by restoring competition.

Privacy Challenges

To address the privacy challenges endemic in digital industries, policymakers will have to create a legal framework that regulates how companies providing core digital services are permitted to collect, share, and use the personal information of their users. The United States has a myriad of sector-specific privacy statutes covering financial services, health care, education, and cable television, to name a few. But nothing except a smattering of comprehensive state privacy laws and residual consumer protection authority at the FTC applies to digital industries.

A national comprehensive privacy law might provide the needed legal basis, but, as in financial services, health care, and education, the way digital companies collect and use data is idiosyncratic and differs in crucial ways from its use in other parts of the economy. It is often the driver of its business model and key source of competitive advantage. It is the basis of the personalization and targeted advertising that creates the tendency toward information disorder that is so prevalent in these industries. As a result, the best way to protect users from abusive data practices in digital industries is through a dedicated industry regulator that either applies its own sector-specific privacy law or enforces a comprehensive privacy law.

New digital privacy rules must move beyond the theory that lies behind traditional privacy law. The animating idea built into traditional privacy laws is that consumers have inadequate information and restricted opportunities to make informed choices about collection and use of their personal data. Privacy law, in this theory, protects vital privacy interests by ensuring that businesses follow proper procedures for informing consumers about how they collect and use personal data and for providing them with an opportunity to accept or reject these uses.

This reliance on consumer control as the legal weapon against privacy abuse gave rise to the key measure in traditional privacy law—a requirement that companies should send privacy notices to individuals describing their data collection and use practices and providing some mechanism for consumers to accept or reject these practices. Jessica Rich, former head of the Bureau of Consumer Protection at the FTC, summarizes years of criticism of this model of privacy regulation when she observes that "overreliance on 'notice-and-choice' to protect privacy places an enormous and impossible burden on consumers to read the privacy policies of hundreds, even thousands, of companies that collect their data, and then make privacy choices for each of them."[41]

Privacy as individual control was meant to restore the imbalance of power and knowledge between individuals and giant institutions. But any attempt to remedy the informational imbalance between data collectors and data subjects by requiring notice and choice will overwhelm users with too many choices to manage and too little understanding of what they are being asked to agree to. Privacy notices are widely ignored, not the basis for informed decisions. An old but well-known study from 2008 showed they would also be astonishingly costly to read—the time spent reading internet privacy notices would cost the economy $781 billion per year.[42]

This burden of too much choice in too little time will lead data subjects to accept whatever default is offered or to affirmatively agree to just about anything to get on with using the service. By burdening the user with the responsibility to make sensible choices, notice and choice measures have allowed companies to evade their responsibility to provide privacy protective data practices. For this reason, cutting edge privacy advocates have called for relying on individual consent to the least extent possible in national privacy legislation.[43]

But reliance on consumer control to address privacy abuse is especially unlikely to be effective in digital industries where the forces of competition have limited effect. Users of digital services cannot try to satisfy their privacy preferences by shopping around. If users feel that Google collects too much information about them, they are powerless to vote with their feet because doing so would mean abandoning the improved search results Google provides. If Facebook collects third-party website information and shares it with its affiliated businesses Instagram and WhatsApp to construct detailed advertising profiles, users have no viable alternative that might have less privacy-intrusive practices. If Amazon snoops on their merchants' activity and uses the information to develop its own private label brands or to decide whether to provide the same product through its vendor program, merchants really have no choice if they want access to Amazon's huge customer base.

As a result, digital industries collect vast treasure troves of information about the daily activities of ordinary citizens. Google provides a vast array of interlocking digital services—search, the Chrome browser, its email service Gmail, Drive, Calendar, Photos, Maps, YouTube, the Play Store. Google collects and integrates information from its users across these different services, assembling it into profiles that include location data, search history, web browsing history, video watching preferences, and mobile app purchases. It adds data from outside sources to complete these profiles and uses advanced data analysis techniques on this treasure trove of personal data to infer user preferences and interests to personalize more effectively the services it provides to its users. Personal data helps Google to improve search results, for example, or to recommend videos its YouTube users are likely to enjoy. In addition, it uses some of the personal information it collects and analyzes to create advertising profiles that power its $100 billion digital ad revenue business.[44]

Facebook records everything its users do on its site. That includes all its users' posts, who or what they search for, what groups they belong to, their entire social network of friends and family, business associates and audience, and their messages exchanged on Messenger. In addition, it tracks its users around the internet and combines that information with its on-site usage data to form profiles it uses to recommend content, friends, and groups that might interest its users. External datasets are also used to complete these profiles. Its off-site information is especially helpful for advertisers seeking to confirm that users made a purchase after viewing an ad. It plans to integrate data from its core social media and messaging service with WhatsApp and Instagram data.[45]

Amazon collects data from its users as they browse its site, including what its users buy and how much time they spend viewing each page. It knows the address of each of its users and can make inferences about their demographics based solely on this information. It combines this on-site information with information from external data sources to form a fuller picture of its buyers. It uses this information to power an effective recommendation engine that suggests what products its users might like based on what products similar people have chosen. On the merchant side, it tracks what each independent merchant sells and has used this information to power its own choice of products to sell.

The massive datasets collected by dominant digital industry companies call to mind privacy scholar Paul Ohm's nightmare of a "database of ruin." Ohm asks people to imagine "the data from all of the databases in the world together into one, giant, database-in-the-sky" and then to consider what their "worst enemies" could do with that information. The danger is more than "embarrassment or inconvenience." It is "blackmail, discrimination, harassment, or financial or identity theft" or other legally cognizable harm. He conceives of privacy rules as measures designed to protect people against this kind of risk of an indefinite range of harm from excessive data collection. The gigantic databases in the hands of monopoly digital companies create privacy risks of similar magnitude.[46]

The extent of this data collection also suggests that consumer choice is not effective in these markets. Dina Srinivasan, the former digital advertising executive turned Facebook critic, makes the point clearly.

"Who the heck consents to having a company track them across the internet," she asks. "They [the digital companies] could only do it because they had monopoly power to do something that clearly goes against consumer interests."[47] The resigned acquiescence with which many users receive digital services that invade privacy may not reflect genuine autonomous choice so much as the recognition that they do not have any real choice, that there is nothing much they can do about a company's data practices if they want to continue to use the service, and that there are no really acceptable substitute services.

Individual control alone is unlikely to be an effective way to protect privacy in digital markets for reasons beyond the lack of consumer alternatives and choice fatigue. Information externalities are present in these markets to an unusually high degree. They occur when the choice by some people to reveal sensitive information about themselves has implications for other people who have chosen not to reveal this about themselves. For decades, marketers have used demographic and sales information about people to make predictions about their tastes, preferences, interests, and personalities. An entire consumer scoring industry has developed based on the extent to which data about some individuals can be used successfully to make reliable inferences about others.[48]

To see how information externalities worked in predigital marketing, recall the initial conversation in the pilot episode of the NBC television series *30 Rock* between Jack Donaghy, the network executive played by Alec Baldwin, and Tina Fey's character, Liz Lemon, the head writer and creator of the sketch comedy show *The Girlie Show*. Donaghy tells Lemon she is "a New York third-wave feminist, college-educated, single-and-pretending-to-be-happy-about-it, over-scheduled, undersexed, buys any magazine that says 'healthy body image' on the cover and every two years takes up knitting for . . . a week." It's all accurate, even the knitting. When asked how he knows this, Baldwin answers, "Market research."[49] Liz Lemon did not tell anyone in a marketing research firm about her knitting, but the rest of her demographic made it very likely that she would take it up (and abandon it regularly).

Information externalities existed well before the internet, but they are especially prevalent in digital industries. The case of Cambridge Analytica illustrates how information externalities work in the online world.[50] The company obtained sensitive information from a few hundred thousand Facebook users through an online contest and gained access to their Facebook accounts and those of their contacts. They built up psychological profiles of these users based on the online quiz and their interactions with others on Facebook. Using this model, they were able to predict the psychological characteristics of tens of millions of other Facebook users who had never revealed this information to anyone online. The company was then able to use these profiles to target political ads.

Reforms at Facebook might prevent a reoccurrence of this precise privacy intrusion, but similar information externalities are everywhere online. Digital companies are like online detectives examining all aspects of the behavior of their users, as vividly detailed in the 2020 Netflix documentary *The Social Dilemma*.[51] Everything people do online is open to the gaze of these omnipresent digital detectives that use the information gathered from this surveillance to personalize the digital services they provide and to display ads narrowly targeted to individuals or thinly segmented groups. As a result, online behavior can reveal ethnicity, religious preferences, political views, gender, and sexual orientation as well as detailed consumer tastes, even if a user never reveals this information to anyone online.

Commentators and reporters often note these externalities and seem to consider them to be odd, freakish marginal cases. In fact, they are the central privacy feature of the online world. Ubiquitous online data collection and algorithmic inferences means that these information externalities are omnipresent, massive, and unavoidable in social media, search, electronic commerce, and the use of mobile systems. The devastating implication of this central fact for traditional public policy aimed at protecting users from information abuse is this: *even fully informed individual choices in digital markets will fail to protect user privacy.*[52] This is so because what a company knows about a particular user depends on its background knowledge, including its evolving models of user behavior and what other people have revealed to the company, neither of which users can control through their own choices, no matter how well informed.

The model of individual control is less adequate for privacy regulation in the digital world for still a third reason. This feature of the online world was pointed out in a 2019 report about data portability from New York University School of Law. "The data on social networks," the report said, "is inherently relational, and platforms must create a perimeter between where one user's data ends and another's begins."[53] But this is true more generally beyond just social media. Information used in digital industries is almost always relational. It concerns a plurality of data subjects. A consumer's online purchase information is also an online business's sales data. An online picture of a group of people is "about" all of them. An online conversation among several people on social media concerns each of them.

The inherently relational nature of data implies that records of someone's activities almost always concern other people, and this feature of data holds throughout the economy. A person's employment status at a company is part of the company's personnel records. A person's membership in a church's congregation puts him or her on its list of congregants. Marriage, home ownership, loan repayments, home and car rental agreements, vacation destinations, schools attended—all of this and more is information about many people, not simply a single data subject.

But inherently relational data records that concern several people or institutions are especially pervasive in digital industries. Social media services, of course, are inherently relational. The entire point is to connect people and to allow exchanges of ideas, pictures, experiences, and information that create and sustain a web of relationships among family, friends, and complete strangers who share interests. Mobile apps often link individuals in game playing, purchasing, and sending and receiving specialized information. Search engines typically link individuals to organizations and enterprises they are seeking to learn more about. Online stores provide transaction services connecting merchants and customers.

The vast databases that record the myriad online interactions cannot be reduced to atomistic individual records that concern only each user taken one at a time. Each of these core digital industries creates records that are the shared history of many users. Each user has a genuine interest in what is done with these records, and, of course, the companies creating and maintaining these records have their own legitimate interests as well.

Many privacy analysts have noted the inherently relational nature of data records in today's digitized world. But as in the case of information externalities, the full implications of this obvious-once-pointed-out fact have not been fully appreciated. With many data subjects involved in just about all interesting data records in digital industries, there is no legitimate basis to provide a unique legal right to control what is done with these records. Privacy rules for the digital industry cannot be based on ownership by the data subject or, more broadly, on providing data subjects with individual control over their digital data.[54]

The key privacy challenge in digital markets is what additional privacy protections are needed to protect users in the face of choice fatigue, limited competition, pervasive information externalities, and the almost universal tendency of digital data to concern more than one data subject.

Content Moderation Challenges

Information disorder on social media consists of several interrelated problems. The first is the extent to which terrorists, racists, hackers, thieves, gamblers, child pornographers, purveyors of defamatory or obscene material, fraudsters, and others use the facilities of online platforms to carry out their illegal activities or to conspire to carry them out in the offline world. Some of this illegal activity is based on the content of information circulated on social media sites such as defamatory information, incitements to violence, stolen financial credentials, or child pornography images.

A second problem is the extent to which social media users engage in harmful but legal activities online or use social media facilities to prepare for objectionable but legally permissible conduct in the real world. This category includes hate speech and organized efforts to intimidate, ridicule, and humiliate women and members of minority groups, to silence or drive them offline, or to incite others to treat them as less than full members of society. It also includes the material that drives teens, especially teenage girls, to mental health crises characterized by loss of self-confidence, feelings of loneliness and despair, and clinical depression.

Often the dividing line between illegal conduct and harmful but legal activity is hard to draw. Cyberbullying, stalking, revenge porn, and online harassment, for example, are so often matters of context that only a court looking at an extensive factual record can determine whether a law has been broken.

The third aspect of the online information disorder problem is the widespread transmission of disinformation or misinformation about matters of significant public importance such as political or medical information. Misinformation and disinformation campaigns fall into the harmful but legal category, but they have such large social and political implications they deserve special attention. The problems of much illegal or harmful speech online are largely individual in character—a particular person has been injured by the harmful online activity. But large-scale disinformation campaigns do their damage at the social level. They impede public health campaigns and eat away at the smooth operation of the US system of governance. Getting the facts wrong concerning elections and disease mitigation and prevention on a large scale on social media can have significant adverse consequences for public health and effective political governance.

The existence of hate speech, misinformation, material harmful to kids, terrorist material, and other information disorders on social media is not really in question. Commentators such as Tarleton Gillespie, Siva Vaidhyanathan, and Kate Klonick have documented them in great detail.[55] Nor is there really much doubt that this disorder has produced extensive individual and social harm. In connection with misinformation about COVID-19, for instance, the surgeon general concluded in 2021 that "many people have also been exposed to health misinformation: information that is false, inaccurate, or misleading according to the best available evidence at the time. Misinformation has caused confusion and led people to decline COVID-19 vaccines, reject public health measures such as masking and physical distancing, and use unproven treatments."[56]

The questions are why information disorder is so prevalent on these platforms, and why, despite years of substantial effort, the companies have not been able to deal with it satisfactorily. The *Wall Street Journal*'s series of reports in the fall of 2021, based to a large degree on material leaked from Facebook, examined these issues in great detail.[57] The reasons go to the heart of what digital companies do, how they fund themselves, the external nature of the harms connected to online information disorder, and what role policymakers want them to play in the media landscape.

The tendency toward social media information disorder arises in part from the technical capacities of social media systems and the algorithms that power them. At the heart of their promise as new information distribution systems is the ability of social media systems to allow people with the same interests to find each other, even if they have no ordinary social relationship. Isolated people with idiosyncratic approaches to art, entertainment, recreation, religion, earning a living, or politics can display these interests through their activities on social media platforms. What they post, what they read, what they like, and what groups they join form a pattern that turns out to have similarities to the pattern exhibited by other people on the network. Social media technology identifies these patterns and brings together like-minded strangers.

This capacity is a genuine advance in information distribution systems. It means self-selected groups of people can find each other and share information they know will be of mutual interest. It is a halfway house between mass distribution of information to an undifferentiated audience and the one-to-one messaging typical of mail and telephone calling. It has a vital place in the overall media ecosystem that needs to be preserved and encouraged.

But this capacity has a fatal flaw: it is content-neutral. There is nothing in the system that knows what it is that the people it brings together have in common. They could share an interest in stamps, old movies, or birdwatching. The technology does not know or care, and neither, at first, did the companies furnishing this technology. All that matters is that linking these people seems to increase their engagement with the system and provides even more clues about what interests and preferences they might have. The system creates a virtuous cycle whereby engagement breeds more engagement, all without any understanding or judgment upon the underlying content or activity that brings the system users together.

The downside of giving people the connections suggested by their online behavior is that people with dangerous, racist, misogynistic, homophobic, or terrorist interests can find each other as easily as the isolated stamp collectors can. The system of engagement works just as well for harmful and illegal content as it does for harmless amusements. In fact, the matchmaking technology seems to work even better for much illegal and harmful material because such material often has the emotional charge that encourages engagement. As a result, dangerous and inflammatory content spreads like wildfire on social media platforms, creating a mechanism for radicalization and the growth of violent terrorist networks.

Of course, this tendency toward online filter bubbles predated social media. Eli Pariser noted the problem of filter bubbles years ago, and early internet critics such as Cass Sunstein deplored the drift toward the Daily Me, a narrowing rather than an expansion of horizons that resulted from ability of users to select only what fit their preconceived interests rather suffer exposure to unanticipated, unchosen encounters and a range of shared experiences.[58] But the advanced social media technology of engagement puts such personalizing tendencies of the presocial media internet on steroids.

The same technological tendency that produced hate speech online leads to the prevalence of misinformation on social media platforms. As social media companies grew, people began to rely on them for more than just casual entertainment and amusement. The platforms began to distribute news and political information. By 2020, according to the Pew Research Center, 36 percent of US adults "regularly" got news from Facebook and 23 percent from YouTube.[59] But unlike legacy media that relied on human editors to make a judgment about the truth and news value of the material they published, social media engagement algorithms had no way of telling accurate news from deliberate falsehoods. All they knew was what engaged their users, and misinformation could do that as well as truth. Indeed, as in the case of hate speech, false but inflammatory news stories engaged viewers even more than true but boring stories. Also, as in the case of hate speech, the misinformation problem feeds on itself, since the way current recommendation algorithms are set up on social media ensures that if users start interacting with misinformation, they will get more and more of it.[60]

This intrinsic tendency of the technology itself to breed information disorder would persist, even if social media companies did not fund their business through advertising. But the need to please advertisers makes the problem even worse. Every time users pay attention to something on social media, they reveal something about themselves that is of interest to advertisers. The more time on a social media platform, the more opportunity for exposure to advertising. This gives social media companies an incentive to foster engagement far beyond what users themselves would autonomously want based solely on the users' own interests. No one wants to spend all their time online, even when the topic is of interest. But social media companies seek to reward users psychologically for each extra minute they devote to online activities, using specially designed techniques to generate dopamine hits for each new follower, like, or response. The result is the oft-observed addictive quality of online activity, a feature that is primarily a result of the need to gain a fuller perspective on users to build more detailed advertising profiles and to increase the number of advertisements to which users are exposed.

This advertiser-driven need to encourage online interactions leads to ever more engagement with emotionally laden but false, misleading, or harmful material. Engagement with this dangerous material generates even more ad revenue and creates even more detailed profiles. The natural incentives of a technology of engagement combine with the advertiser-based revenue model to produce a perfect storm leading to ever more harmful material online.

Because emotional valence counts for more than other features of content such as truth or racial respect, social media systems of engagement work to foster an online atmosphere of content disorder. Social media companies knew this early on and began to temper their algorithms with efforts to curate their material based on its content, not merely its effect on engagement. Their systems of content controls developed from very general standards such as a ban on pornography to very specific content rules proscribing hate speech and other unacceptable content. They did this, as many observers noted, not out of sense of civic duty but out of business necessity. Their systems would rapidly become unusable for both ordinary users and advertisers if harmful material was allowed to flourish unchecked.[61]

Even with the best will in the world, content moderation is hard. Formulating content rules for the online world creates thorny legal and policy challenges. Figuring out processes to enforce them is even harder, and administering these processes, even with the aid of high-powered machine-learning algorithms, is expensive, time consuming, and labor intensive. Facebook says it employs an army of fifteen thousand content moderators to screen the material on its system and to make split-second (and traumatizing) decisions about whether material violates any of the myriad content rules that have grown up in the company over the last fifteen years.[62]

Companies must and will invest resources in content moderation to protect their business and their brand. But content moderation resources will not be deployed indefinitely. Their internal efforts will cease where the costs of content moderation exceed the long-term financial harm done to the company from content disorder, considering the brand benefits and the public relations gains from keeping their systems orderly.

The point at which financial incentives compel them to stop their efforts to promote information order is not, however, the point where their systems adequately protect their users and society from harm. Part of the reason is that much of the harm that is done by information disorder on their systems is external. Facebook faced no direct or even indirect financial repercussions for allowing its system to be used to organize offline harms such as ethnic cleansing in Myanmar, but the Rohingya suffered a great deal. The spread of political and medical misinformation on its system does not directly cost the company money, even though the cost to its users and to the public is considerable. Bad public relations and hostility from policymakers can go only so far in correcting for the lack of any direct financial costs to the company from content disorder on its systems.

Another reason that company content moderation efforts fall short is that they can reduce advertising revenue. Too much content moderation can reduce user engagement, a key metric of their financial success.

Cutting back on this harmful material would mean not just fewer minutes of engagement with the service but also less accurate advertiser profiles. In the short term, advertisers have few alternatives to the larger digital companies—Google, Facebook, and Amazon. But in the longer term, advertisers have some choice as to where to spend their ad dollars. If a digital company reduces the accuracy of its user profiles through vigorous content moderation measures, this situation will lead to less productive advertising campaigns. Other digital companies that are not so vigorous in content moderation will produce greater returns for advertising dollars, and over time advertisers will move there. No digital company on its own has an incentive to push its content moderation efforts past the point where advertisers begin to leave.

Finally, company content moderation efforts to control information disorder raise profound issues of information diversity and political pluralism that can only be addressed by a national decision on the proper role of social media within the nation's information ecosystem. A real resolution of information disorder on social media awaits the resolution of this national debate on social media's role.

The companies themselves are uncertain about the role they should play within the information ecosystem. They have a business commitment to allowing voice from their users, which reinforces their self-conception and the widespread public perception that they are a neutral platform for the speech of others. They do not see themselves, and are largely not seen, as publishers of their own material in the same way that traditional newspapers and broadcasters are. This puts them closer to traditional common carriers like telephone companies and providers of broadband internet access. But content moderation has them performing a function like that of traditional publishers, promoting or downplaying content based on their own standards. They play both roles at the same time: they carry the speech of others the way common carriers do, and they edit the material on their system the way broadcasters and newspapers do. So, what are they?

This is not a decision that the companies can make for themselves. It is a matter for law and public policy. Even if the digital companies think they should be accorded full First Amendment rights, but without traditional publisher responsibilities, ultimately legislatures and courts will determine whether the law should treat them that way. The role they ought to play in the information ecosystem is ultimately one for determination by national policymakers, not the digital companies. Policymakers established a legal system for the new information distribution companies in the late 1990s at the dawn of the internet. But that traditional answer is up for reconsideration and is at the heart of the content moderation debates in Congress.

The internet policy that developed in the late 1990s had three pillars. One was the 1997 Supreme Court decision in *Reno v. ACLU* that granted to internet companies the fullest possible First Amendment freedoms. The court recognized that by providing cheap and virtually unlimited capacity for others to reach an audience, these companies allowed everyone to be a publisher, not just the fortunate few companies that owned a printing press, a broadcast station, or a movie studio. To preserve this role as enabler of the speech of others, the court ruled that government attempts to restrict what speech these platforms would allow their users to post on these systems would have to pass the strictest First Amendment test.[63]

This optimistic Supreme Court vision was complemented by another somewhat darker perspective that emerged from the 1996 Communications Decency Act. Under this vision, there were indeed some dangerous corners to the internet where harmful material flourished. Policymakers thought internet companies should be encouraged to control voluntarily the distribution of this harmful material on their system. Section 230 of the Communications Decency Act said that internet companies should not be treated as the publishers of material posted by their users. Their users could be held liable for posting illegal material on internet sites, but the internet companies themselves had legal immunity. The purpose of this grant of immunity from the legal consequences of what their users posted was to encourage them to act like publishers and to purge their systems of objectionable material without becoming liable for the illegal material on their system.[64]

Together the *Reno v. ACLU* case and Section 230 created an extraordinary position for internet companies under the law. For purposes of the

First Amendment, they enjoyed full protection against government regulation just as traditional publishers did. But for purposes of legal accountability, they were not treated as the publisher of what they allowed others to put on their systems. Creating a zone free from government regulation *and* free from the normal constraints against transmitting illegal material gave internet companies substantially more leeway than any other element in the information ecosystem.

These two pillars of early internet policy were soon joined by a third, a "notice and takedown" system established in the 1998 Digital Millennium Copyright Act (DMCA). It provides a safe harbor from copyright infringement for internet companies that act to remove infringing material upon notification.[65] While neither content owners nor platforms are completely satisfied with this system of notice liability, it has provided a workable system that protects both copyright interests and the freedom of platforms to operate their business.

The other two pillars, however, are under assault. Scholars, advocates, and even a Supreme Court justice are urging changes to the libertarian First Amendment jurisprudence that appears to leave social media companies beyond government regulation.[66] Congress has already carved out an exception from Section 230 immunity for sex trafficking and more are under consideration.[67] Bipartisan legislative proposals have been introduced to regulate the content moderation processes at social media companies.[68] In the spring of 2023, the Supreme Court considered and then rejected interpretations of Section 230 that would have significantly narrowed it. Congress, however, is considering a myriad of Section 230 reform proposals.[69]

These challenges facing policymakers in recrafting the content moderation rules of the road for social media companies are substantial, requiring them to renegotiate the internet policy that has dominated the tech industry since the late 1990s.

The Regulatory Solutions

Policymakers confront three interconnected challenges of competition, privacy, and free speech in seeking to regulate today's digital industries. How can they design a system of governance that promotes competition without losing the scale advantages of large networks? How can they structure privacy rules to respond to the lack of consumer alternatives, the information externalities, and the relational character of data in digital industries while still allowing beneficial uses of personal information? How can they set content moderation rules to control illegal and harmful online material while still preserving its role as a vibrant medium for public discussion?

For reasons that will emerge more fully throughout the book, the traditional self-regulatory modes of governance for the tech industry will not suffice to meet these challenges. One example makes the point. In 2016, tech companies agreed to a European Union code of conduct on online terror and hate speech. The companies pledged to remove from their systems any material that incited hatred or acts of terror. They promised to review precise and substantial complaints about terrorist and hate content within twenty-four hours of receiving them and cut off access to the content, if required.[70]

But progress under the code proved to be unsatisfactory to European policymakers. No one was responsible for enforcing this code except the individual companies themselves. As a result, in 2018 the European Commission proposed a measure to require tech companies to take down terrorist material within an hour of receiving a complaint from a competent European authority. The measure received final approval from the European Parliament in April 2021 and went into force in June 2021.[71]

Time after time, purely voluntary self-regulation has proven to be a failure and has largely been abandoned in Europe. US policymakers reluctant to resort to government mandates might be tempted to consider a halfway house that moves beyond individual company self-regulation but not so far as full government regulation. They might consider an industry-wide regulatory approach, where enforcement of industry standards is lodged with an external industry organization with the power to sanction an individual company for failure to comply with industry norms. But without enabling legislation, digital industry companies are unlikely to use their existing trade associations to create binding codes of conduct that could address the competition, privacy, and content moderation challenges. And if they did, such cooperation might very well be illegal under the antitrust laws.

Companies will not voluntarily or collectively agree to abandon monopoly power, so self and industry regulation to promote competition is a nonstarter. The privacy challenges also involve the exercise of monopoly power and economic externalities that are beyond the self-organizing capacities of companies themselves to address. Self-regulation has been the default policy mode for dealing with content disorder since the late 1990s—surely a sufficient time for this natural experiment to have revealed its inadequacies to any fair-minded observer.

Bill Baer, former head of the Department of Justice's Antitrust Division, summed up the consensus rejection of the laissez-faire theory at the heart of all forms of tech self-regulation: "The four-decade dilution of the power of the federal government to tame capitalism's worst instincts that began during the Reagan era needs to come to an end."[72]

The only viable option is some form of mandatory government action. Self-regulation and industry regulation might help but cannot do the job alone. One possibility for a more active government role is enhanced enforcement of the antitrust laws. It is certainly worth a try to ramp up enforcement efforts, given the sad state of antitrust enforcement since the rise of the internet economy. The cases filed at the state and federal level in the last several years show that this option is very much alive. With antitrust activists Lina Khan heading the FTC and Jonathan Kanter leading the Antitrust Division, this approach is likely to have as good a test in the Biden administration as it will ever have.

Still, there are good reasons to be skeptical that this path will be sufficient. In 2018, longtime antitrust practitioner and government official Phil Verveer warned against dealing with the problems of tech by bringing more big antitrust cases, citing a raft of practical and doctrinal obstacles.[73] In 2020, Verveer, along with the former chair of the FCC Tom Wheeler and consumer advocate and former Department of Justice (DOJ) official Gene Kimmelman, published a report for the Shorenstein Center repeating that warning. This report noted that "it would be a serious mistake to rely on antitrust enforcement as the sole mechanism for securing our society's interest in the workings of the ever more critical digital platforms."[74]

One doctrinal limitation is that antitrust law as currently conceived and practiced countenances durable monopolies and does not generally allow remedies like a duty to deal with competitors to overcome an entrenched incumbent's monopoly position. Such arrangements can be prescribed by regulators authorized by Congress but not generally under today's antitrust law. One famous Supreme Court case upheld congressional authority to require a duty to deal with competitors in the telecommunications industry but rejected it as a possible remedy for monopolization under antitrust law. It even endorsed the lure of monopoly profits unconstrained by a duty to aid competitors as the engine of innovation.[75] Other difficulties and obstacles in increasing enforcement efforts under existing antitrust law are described in chapter 2 on remedies for the competition policy challenges in digital industries.

The failures of self-regulation and the limits of existing antitrust law mean that legislated antitrust reforms targeted at the tech industry are a needed step toward bringing the tech industries under control. A series of bills passed by the US House Judiciary Committee in June 2021 provided an interlocking set of tools designed to jump-start competition in the tech industry. These bills put in legislative language many of the reforms that had been proposed by scholars and advocates over the last several years. The Ending Platform Monopolies Act would prohibit a large platform from owning a line of business that utilizes the platform "for the sale or provision of products or services."[76] The ACCESS Act of 2021 would impose data portability and interoperability requirements on these platforms.[77] The American Choice and Innovation Online Act would impose various nondiscrimination and access requirements on platforms.[78] The Platform Competition and Opportunity Act of 2021 would prohibit the largest online platforms from engaging in mergers that would eliminate competitors or potential competitors.[79] These measures would be enforced through the existing antitrust agencies, with traditional review by the courts.

In 2022, the Senate Judiciary Committee passed the Open App Markets Act that would constrain the power of the Apple and Google app stores to discriminate against and abuse app developers.[80] The Senate Judiciary Committee also adopted a version of the American Choice and Innovation Online Act that imposed nondiscrimination and access duties on digital companies.[81]

These legislative proposals are a good start to mitigate unfair practices in digital industries, but they are a strong departure from antitrust law as currently understood and practiced. The US Chamber of Commerce opposes all of them, but the business lobbying organization is not wrong when it notes the contrast with current antitrust law: they are written for specific industries, they do not rely on a showing that business conduct produces more harm than good for consumers, and hence they are "regulatory efforts disguised as changes to the antitrust laws."[82]

The measures that the enforcing agencies are authorized to take are underspecified in the legislation itself and require substantial interpretation to be made relevant to particular lines of business. The legislation gives the enforcing agencies wide discretion to do this. One logical implementation strategy for electronic commerce, for instance, would be to start with a nondiscrimination rule as set out in the America Choice and Innovation Online Act and move to the more restrictive measures such as a separation requirement or a line-of-business prohibition outlined in the Ending Platform Monopolies Act if the less restrictive measures fail to control unfair practices. If properly implemented, these measures would go a long way toward restoring competitive conditions in these industries, at least to the extent that it is possible to do so through determined government action. I discuss the strengths and limitations of these procompetition measures in chapter 2.

Despite strong efforts by their sponsors and high hopes that the antimonopoly moment had come, none of these bills passed Congress in 2022. In the larger picture this is not surprising. Fundamental policy reforms rarely succeed in Congress on the first attempt. The antitrust reform movement will have to lengthen its time horizon and look to a longer struggle to implement its agenda for digital industries.

In any case, procompetition measures do not really address the privacy and content moderation issues that are at the heart of increasing public concern about digital industries. The hope that more competition in these industries will automatically generate good privacy and content moderation practices is misplaced. More social media alternatives, for example, might increase privacy abuses as the social media rivals seek to outdo each other in exploiting consumer data to serve advertisers more effectively. More social media platforms might make it more difficult for them to enforce good content moderation rules if the alternatives have lax content moderation practices.

As the antitrust economist and former official in the Department of Justice's Antitrust Division Carl Shapiro has said, "Indeed, it is not even clear that more competition would provide consumers with greater privacy, or better combat information disorder: unregulated, competition might instead trigger a race to the bottom, and many smaller firms might be harder to regulate than a few large ones."[83]

To fully protect the public, policymakers will need to legislate new privacy and content moderation rules in addition to new competition policy laws. National privacy legislation would provide a framework to preserve privacy in all economic sectors. But as noted before, the model of individual consumer choice that is embedded in standard privacy law would be especially ineffective in noncompetitive digital industries where personal information almost always concerns more than one individual user and where what a digital company knows about one user depends on what other users have revealed. Enhanced privacy duties are needed for dominant companies in the digital industries.

One such enhanced privacy duty, derived from the European Union's General Data Protection Regulation, would require digital companies to demonstrate a legal justification for data collection and use based on consumer consent, necessity for providing the service, or legitimate interest.[84] In addition, digital monopolists would be required to live under digital age versions of the traditional principles for data minimization and limited secondary use.

Another duty, based on recent scholarly work by Woodrow Hartzog, would require digital companies to refrain from using technology designs that are unreasonably deceptive, abusive, or dangerous.[85] A third enhanced privacy requirement, based on Jack Balkin's work on information fiduciaries, would require digital companies to fulfill special duties of care, loyalty, and confidentiality toward their customers.[86] Finally, some limits on data use might have to be established directly to fully protect the public from privacy abuses that cannot be controlled with these behavioral restrictions of company data practices. Chapter 3 discusses these enhanced privacy duties for dominant digital companies.

In 2022, Congress made some progress on passing a national privacy law but fell short. The House Energy and Commerce Committee adopted a compromise bill that addressed the twin challenges of private rights of action and state preemption that had been preventing forward movement of the legislation. But leading privacy advocates criticized the House bill as inadequate compared to the California privacy law it would preempt. Partly as a result, the House and the Senate failed to act. Into this vacuum stepped the FTC, which opened a privacy rulemaking proceeding that could go a long way toward establishing a national policy without, however, creating the uniform approach that preempting state laws would allow.[87]

Neither competition rules nor enhanced privacy duties by themselves fully address the problems of online information disorder. Legislators must also create new rules to respond to this separate challenge. These rules fall into several groups. Policymakers must determine the extent to which social media companies are liable for the illegal material posted on their systems by their users, which involves reform of Section 230. One approach might be a system of notice liability modeled after the notice and takedown safe harbor system established for online copyright violations.[88]

Policymakers must also decide where in the media landscape digital companies belong. Proposals for treating social media companies as common carriers are a nonstarter because the common carrier requirement to carry all legal traffic would leave them powerless to deal with information disorder on their systems. But neither should the dominant social media companies be treated like newspapers with full First Amendment freedoms because they essentially distribute the material of their users and possess bottleneck economic power in this role.[89] Instead, policymakers should treat them like broadcasters, subject to significant public interest obligations but otherwise free to moderate content on their own systems as they see fit.[90]

Chief among these public interest obligations would be a system of transparency and accountability. A regime of mandated disclosures would provide social media users with due process rights to make sure the content moderation systems treat them fairly. Additional transparency requirements should be imposed to make available data for regulators and researchers to determine the extent of harmful information on their systems and the efficacy of social media efforts to control it. These transparency and accountability measures will give social media companies an additional incentive to discourage damaging but legal material on their systems, especially the misinformation that does so much social harm. Congress and the states have also been considering and in some cases passing new laws to protect kids online.[91] Chapter 4 discusses these issues in further detail.

Chapter 4 details the First Amendment challenges to these measures and the possible defense against these challenges based on the *Turner Broadcasting* and the *Red Lion* cases, which rely on a more positive conception of the First Amendment than the libertarian jurisprudence that has dominated court opinions in the last decades.[92] It also addresses the possibility of a public interest responsibility to provide for a diversity of political opinion and duties connected to advertising by political candidates. A major challenge in crafting such nondiscrimination and fairness rules is to account for the special characteristics of the new information distribution systems and to address First Amendment issues.

In 2022, state legislatures began to take on the challenges of content moderation. That year, California passed a law imposing various transparency and disclosure requirements on social media companies.[93] Also in 2022, Texas and Florida passed legislation restricting the ability of platforms to act in a politically discriminatory way in their content moderation activities. These laws also imposed various disclosure duties. They have been challenged in court. As of 2022, courts have upheld the Texas law and blocked the Florida law. A Supreme Court resolution of the First Amendment issues at stake is likely to be forthcoming in 2024.[94]

Policymakers often look at the diverse challenges posed by digital industries through separate policy silos. Antitrust reform proceeds on one congressional track, privacy regulation on another, and constraints on the discretion of platforms to engage in content moderation move through still other congressional committees. Legislators and regulators work within established jurisdictional boundaries that often prevent them from seeing the implications of measures pursued in their areas of responsibility for outcomes in other policy areas.

However, measures to address tech policy challenges almost always have implications across multiple policy areas. This is primarily because these industries are so heavily reliant on personal information, and company control over personal information is a key component of the policy challenges in competition, privacy, and content moderation. Mandated data sharing, for instance, might improve competition in digital industries but create additional privacy concerns for consumers. However, overly stringent privacy or content moderation laws might disadvantage struggling start-ups and further entrench established incumbents. As political scientist Francis Fukuyama and his co-authors point out, "Just as we do not want measures such as requiring data sharing that promote competition but harm privacy interests, we do not want privacy laws to harm competition."[95]

Other examples of the tensions among the policy areas are not hard to find. Interoperability might jump-start competition to Facebook but make it harder to moderate content. Transparency rules might improve content moderation but impinge on privacy. Privacy measures to dispense with web tracking cookies might solidify Google's dominance in the ad-tech space. Data portability is aimed at promoting both privacy and competition, but if it is not done right, it could damage privacy rights of those who do not want their data moved to another provider. As law scholar Erika Douglas says, data privacy law is "a distinct area of doctrine that, at times, pursues interest at odds with the antitrust goal of promoting competition."[96] Some conscious effort to overcome this non-complementarity is needed. Digital regulatory measures must overcome these tensions to achieve synergy and can only do so through conscious attention to ways in which policy measures can conflict.

Substantive harmonization among competing goals cannot be achieved entirely within the legislation that establishes a framework for addressing competition, privacy, and content moderation issues. The tensions and overlaps are too many, too varied, and too dependent on context to resolve within authorizing legislation. And if the legislation got the balance right for today's world, it would soon be out of date for tomorrow's very different tech landscape. The best that can be done is prescribe a general standard similar to the public interest standard that allowed the FCC to apply its regulatory authority to new technologies that were undiscovered at the time the Communications Act of 1934 was enacted.

Instead, the answer to policy tensions must lie in the creation of an institutional structure within which these overlapping tensions and synergies can be accommodated, where commonalities can be amplified, and conflicts mitigated or avoided. After noting the tension between efforts to protect privacy by allowing dominant digital companies to lock up personal data behind corporate walls, which solidifies their dominant position, and damage to privacy by allowing personal data to flow to competitors, the Shorenstein report concludes, "A new agency would be well positioned to balance privacy and competition."[97]

While mechanisms for regulatory cooperation among separate agencies charged with separate missions to promote competition, privacy, and online safety might work, a more efficient way to harmonize the missions is to put them in the same administrative agency.

The Digital Regulator

Policymakers facing challenges in improving competition, privacy, and content moderation in digital industries cannot rely on self-regulation or enhanced enforcement of existing law to do the job. Legislators need to put in place a new regulatory regime to address these digital industry challenges. Given the omnipresent synergies and tensions among policy measures in an industry heavily reliant on data, the most promising institutional structure is a single administrative agency. To set up such an agency, legislators need to pass authorizing legislation that specifies the nature of the regulator, its internal structure, the mechanisms for independence, accountability, and restricted authority, its jurisdiction, and its powers and duties.

Studies and legislative proposals for a digital regulatory agency have proliferated in recent years. A report for the government of the United Kingdom by the former chair of the US Council of Economic Advisers Jason Furman and colleagues argued for a new digital markets unit in the UK government empowered to create special procompetitive rules for platforms with strategic market position.[98] Harold Feld's report for Public Knowledge argues for a dedicated agency to regulate dominant digital platforms with authority to establish and enforce procompetitive and information diversity rules.[99] Yale University economist Fiona Scott Morton and her colleagues authored a report for the Stigler Center urging the creation of a Digital Authority, a specialist regulator with authority over digital platforms with bottleneck power and able to prescribe a variety of procompetitive rules for these companies.[100]

The Shorenstein Center report, cited earlier, proposes an innovative institutional structure consisting of a new three-person federal regulatory commission called the Digital Platform Agency (DPA) and a Code Council with equal membership from the industry and the public. The division of responsibilities—the Code Council drafts "enforceable behavioral rules for the affected companies" and the DPA approves and enforces them—is meant to provide the agility needed for regulation to keep pace with the technological and business developments in a rapidly evolving industry.

More recently, Martha Minow, who is the former dean of Harvard Law School and daughter of Newton Minow—the renowned FCC chair in the 1960s who coined the phrase "vast wasteland" to describe the TV landscape of his time—published a less detailed recommendation for a digital public utility regulator. Her proposal seems less focused on fostering competition. For instance, she would authorize a digital regulator to "oversee market entry, exit, and expansions; standards and terms of service; and disputes and complaints by users." The agency would require reports, guard against unfairness, and ensure due process and transparency, while still leaving the platforms able to "restrict hate speech, clickbait articles, or inflammatory or untrustworthy news."[101]

The approach developed in this book draws on these legislative proposals. Perhaps the best way to introduce it might be as a contrast to the United Kingdom's emerging regulatory structure for digital industries. The United Kingdom has proposed the creation of a digital markets unit inside its traditional competition agency, the Competition and Markets Authority (CMA), with a mandate to promote competition in digital markets. While Parliament did not act on this proposal in 2022, the UK government announced it is still government policy to do it "in due course" and "when Parliamentary time allows."[102]

The UK government has also proposed an Online Safety Act, which would authorize the traditional media regulator, the Office of Communications (Ofcom), to regulate digital companies to prevent online harms. Despite concerns from some online companies that the revised bill would outlaw encrypted messaging, it appeared poised for final action in the second quarter of 2023.[103]

The United Kingdom is not proposing any new data protection laws for the digital industry, but it has in place a long-standing comprehensive data protection law parallel to the European Union's Data Protection Regulation. An established privacy regulator, the Information Commissioner's Office (ICO), enforces comprehensive privacy rules covering all companies, including digital companies.

To deal with the conflicts and synergies arising from the overlaps of competition, privacy, and content moderation law, the United Kingdom has created a nonstatutory digital regulator cooperation forum consisting of these three agencies and a financial regulator—the Financial Conduct Authority—to approach online regulation in a uniform and harmonized way.[104]

This regulatory structure covers the three policy areas of interest and has a mechanism for handling the tensions and synergies arising from their overlap. While the approach of coordination among distinct regulatory agencies each with their own generic mission might be an appropriate structure for other jurisdictions, where separate regulators have been established for decades, it needs to be modified in several key respects to make it work more effectively for the United States context.

The digital regulator in the United States should be a single agency with three regulatory functions. One reason for doing this is the creation of industry expertise. Privacy regulators and competition authorities are spread thin, constantly trying to monitor and regulate business practices throughout the economy. The media regulator already has its hands full with the traditional media industries. Specialization in the tech industry would enable the development of the industry expertise to monitor industry practices, devise and implement solutions, and upgrade them in the face of changing industry conditions.

A further rationale for a single digital agency with multiple missions is that the synergies and tensions among competition, privacy, and content moderation are likely to be commonplace, rather than rare or isolated corner cases. The Venn diagram of three intersecting circles that is our visual model of the policy spaces in digital industries would consist almost entirely of overlapping areas. Almost any measure that promotes competition implicates privacy and content moderation. And the same is true for all the other policy tools—they all implicate the other policy areas. As a result, a coordinating mechanism that relies on consultations among independent regulators with no common decision maker would be less likely to result in balanced measures that give each policy area its due.

A second contrast is that an effective digital agency should be sector-specific, focused just on digital industries and covering the three different policy spaces. ICO is a single policy agency, responsible just for data protection but covering the entire economy. Its actions might have an outsized effect on digital companies because these companies rely so heavily on data collection and use. But in principle it is an economywide agency focusing on privacy issues wherever they occur. CMA is also a single-mission agency with an economywide mission to protect the competitive process in all sectors. Within it, the proposed digital markets unit would have a procompetitive mission focused on digital platforms, but it would have no authority over privacy or content moderation. Ofcom has had an industry focus, aiming to regulate just the traditional media industry. Under the proposed online safety law, it would extend its jurisdiction to cover digital media, but it would focus on illegal and harmful online material and have no role in promoting privacy or competition.

In addition, an agile and flexible digital agency should be a new institution, not a traditional agency with an expanded mandate to deal with digital industries. This approach would increase the initial set-up costs but has a better chance of allowing a fresh approach unfettered by agency traditions to meet the evolving challenges of digital industries. The Shorenstein report makes this point on the need to set up a new institution, saying, "Rather than bolt on to and dilute an existing agency's responsibilities, it is preferable to start with a clean regulatory slate and specifically established congressional expectations." In 2022, Senator Michael Bennet introduced legislation setting up a new digital platform commission mirroring the recommendations of the Shorenstein report. Also in 2022, Representative Peter Welch—now Senator Welch—introduced a companion digital commission bill into the House of Representatives. On May 18, 2023, Senators Bennet and Welch reintroduced the Digital Platform Commission Act.[105]

An agency able to do the job of regulating today's digital industry and flexible enough to keep up with tomorrow's challenges must be a new sector-specific institution with policy mandates in all three policy areas of competition, privacy, and content moderation. This choice, however, concerns the relationship between the new agency and existing antitrust agencies. The enabling legislation could leave the existing authority of the antitrust agencies unchanged through a savings clause. This is the approach recommended in the Shorenstein report. It is also adopted in the House-passed legislation authorizing existing antirust agencies to take additional steps to promote competition in tech. This approach, however, risks creating exactly the kind of unresolvable conflict among policy objectives that the choice of a single agency was designed to avoid.[106]

Alternatively, the enabling legislation could remain silent on the question of the assignment of regulatory jurisdiction and leave the matter up to the vagaries of court application of the doctrine of implied consent, under which regulated companies can sometimes gain immunity from enforcement actions by the antitrust agencies. This course is unsatisfactory and would do more harm than good by prolonging uncertainty since it would just turn the question over to the judiciary rather than have Congress answer it.

Finally, the enabling legislation could expressly reserve exclusive antitrust authority to the new digital agency. The need to avoid policy conflicts among competition, privacy, and content moderation favors this last alternative as the best way to prevent competition authorities from acting at cross-purposes with the new digital agency. Still the issue poses substantial political and policy challenges and is explored further in chapter 5 on the nature of the digital regulator.

The enabling legislation that establishes this new sectoral agency must also provide for independence, accountability, and restricted authority. It is urgent to get these details of administrative structure right because the agency will be making decisions closely related to the content and diversity of information distributed to the public through digital outlets.

Independence is especially important as a safeguard against partisan abuse of the regulatory function, such as through an order to a social media company to carry or delete certain material in the hopes of securing partisan electoral advantage. Court review of agency action might ultimately block such a move, but it might be better to provide the digital agency with substantial independence to resist such partisan pressure and even to ensure that it does not have such censorship authority to begin with.

One way to bolster agency independence is to ensure that its leaders cannot be removed by the existing government—except for cause, such as neglect of duty or malfeasance in office. But instituting such leadership independence is complicated by a recent court case involving the CFPB.[107] As a result of this decision, a trade-off now exists in administrative law between a multimember commission whose members can be removed only for cause and a single-administrator agency, whose leader serves at the will of the president. Multimember commissions are less agile and less efficient but more independent. The ideal might be the efficiency of a single administrator and the independence of a multimember commission, which is how the CFPB was originally organized. But the court case rules out this possibility.

The fact that the agency will be so close to the content decisions of digital companies prioritizes the need for independence to minimize the risk that the agency could be used to impose a partisan bias on the content judgments of digital companies. Given the court-imposed trade-off, this means the digital agency would have to be structured as a commission, like the FTC or the FCC. As a traditional regulatory commission, the agency would be led by five commissioners, each nominated by the president and confirmed by the Senate, with no more than three from the same political party.

As an extra precaution to prevent partisan abuse, the authorizing legislation must also restrict agency authority. One model is a key provision of a proposed social media bill, making it clear that the bill would not authorize the regulatory agency to "review any action or decision" by a social media company related to the application of its content standards.[108] Such an anticensorship provision would keep the digital regulator from second-guessing the content decisions of companies in the digital industries.

The legislation should also determine the jurisdiction, powers, and duties of the digital regulator. To future-proof the agency against failure to deal with a new problem, the potential jurisdiction of the agency should be broad. The enabling legislation would focus its authority in the areas of greatest need, defining the jurisdiction by enumeration as consisting of companies providing social media, search, electronic commerce, ad-tech, or any of the mobile app infrastructure services (browser, operating system, or app store). However, digital industries change quickly, and new challenges in competition, privacy, and content moderation can emerge outside these designated industries. Video communications services, for instance, expanded dramatically during the COVID-19 pandemic. To allow the agency to respond quickly to these new challenges without needing to go back to Congress for additional powers, the enabling legislation should authorize it to extend its jurisdiction, considering changed circumstances in the industry. By rulemaking after providing for notice and comment and after providing a report to Congress, the agency would be authorized to extend its authority to include any website, online or mobile application, or online service.[109]

Some proposals for a digital regulatory agency limit its jurisdiction to digital platforms—that is, to digital companies that link one or more independent users. But this narrowing might leave many online lines of business uncovered such as electronic retailers and streaming services. Moreover, this limitation on jurisdiction would inevitably hamper agency flexibility in responding to the evolution of online services. To provide this needed flexibility, as part of its residual authority to expand its jurisdiction, the agency should be able to reach companies that do not use a platform business model.

Other proposals limit the jurisdiction of the agency to companies with some measure of market power such as firm size, market share, or strategic market status. It is true that some measures might be especially suited to restrain the power of dominant companies, and the agency should have powers to craft special rules for such companies. But to allow the agency to fulfill its triple mission, its jurisdiction should extend to all players in the digital marketplace, not just to those with a dominant position. A comprehensive data portability or interoperability rule, for instance, might be intended to constrain the power of dominant companies, but it would need to include nondominant digital companies to be effective.

The agency would have standard rulemaking authority as provided for under the Administrative Procedure Act (APA). This would require them to publish notices of proposed regulatory action and allow time for interested parties to comment before taking a final action. Agency actions would be subject to court review to ensure due process, consistency with statutory authority, and a rational relationship between the measure adopted and the policy objectives sought. The agency should be empowered to issue injunctions, assess financial penalties up to a statutory limit, and seek judicial enforcement. It should also possess the authority to inspect books and records as necessary to carry out its responsibilities under the act. It should also preempt inconsistent state laws to make sure the country has a single, uniform national policy in this vital area.

Finally, it is worth building on the suggestion in the Shorenstein report that the rules of the digital road should be developed in concert with the industry itself. This is one way to ensure the agility and flexibility needed to adapt rules to the rapidly changing nature of digital companies. Enabling legislation should authorize the digital industries to form self-regulatory organizations, modeled on the private sector associations that regulate stock exchanges and the broker-dealer industry. Just as that participatory regulatory scheme is supervised by the SEC, so the self-regulatory organizations (SROs) in the digital world would be overseen by a digital regulator.[110]

The agency would have a size based on the budget and personnel of agencies with comparable missions. The federal privacy agency proposed by Representatives Anna Eshoo and Zoe Lofgren has a $550 million yearly budget with about 1,600 employees. The 2021 proposed budget of the FTC is $390 million and 1,250 employees; the Department of Justice's Antitrust Division has a proposed budget of $188.5 million with 782 employees; the FCC's proposed budget is $389 million with 1,550 employees; and the CFPB, a recently created and comparable sector-specific federal agency, has a proposed budget of $618 million and 1,560 employees.[111] The Build Back Better Act, passed by the House of Representatives on November 19, 2021, would provide $500 million to the FTC through September 30, 2029, to "create and operate a bureau, including by hiring and retaining technologists, user experience designers, and other experts" that focuses on "unfair or deceptive acts or practices" relating to "privacy, data security, identity theft, data abuses, and related matters." Although this proposal was never adopted, it provides some indication of the resources legislators think would be needed just to handle digital privacy issues.[112]

An initial estimate of the agency's proposed size would therefore be roughly the same as the size of the proposed privacy agency—$550 million and 1,600 employees. Senator Bennet funds his Digital Platform Commission at $500 million starting in 2027.[113] This is also comparable to the size of the proposed expanded FTC. The actual resources needed to do the job will depend on experience with the agency's efforts to supervise digital companies. The sticker shock of new federal outlays might be mitigated to the extent that the industry's self-regulatory organization can take on much of the regulatory work and fund itself through service fees on industry members.

Coda: From Here to There

The good news is that legislation is moving forward to promote competition in digital industries, protection of privacy, and fair and effective content moderation on social media. The bills are on separate legislative tracks, even to the extent of being considered by different congressional committees. Senator Bennet's legislative proposal for a new digital platform commission would set out a desirable institutional structure, but it is probably not the direction Congress will choose. Reform measures will become law (if at all) separately, not as part of a comprehensive legislative package. Given the lack of final passage of any of these bills in 2022, it is likely that the progress of reform will be slow over the next several years, as is typical of any effort to reform a policy area.

The movement of these reform measures as separate bills creates some danger of incoherence, of Congress working against itself. This is precisely the danger this book is intended to guard against. The good news, however, is that through a series of separate choices, Congress appears to have chosen the same agency, the FTC, to administer the separate digital competition, privacy, and content moderation statutes. Many of the concerns about regulatory inconsistency, of competition measures working against privacy and content moderation measures and vice versa, can be addressed when the same administrative agency has responsibility for all three digital policy areas.

The political prospects are good for moving forward with this ambitious reform agenda, even though it will take some time to complete the legislative process. Progressives, moderates, and conservatives share the view that the large online companies have too much power. Despite the partisan gridlock paralyzing much of Washington, DC, policymaking, this is a rare moment of agreement in principle. To be sure, their common concern with overweening tech power might mask different emphases. Conservatives tend to emphasize the power tech companies have to censor conservatives. But this concern over content censorship and the rise of a social media centrist monoculture is shared by progressives too, from Black Lives Matter activists to democratic socialists. Both might find an area of commonality in a requirement for political pluralism on social media.

To take a different issue, reform of Section 230 is a bipartisan issue. Legislation to exempt sex trafficking from Section 230 immunity passed with an overwhelming bipartisan majority of 97–2 in the Senate. Other proposals for piecemeal reform have also received backing from senior Democrats and Republicans. A proposal for notice liability to make social media companies liable for illegal content if they fail to remove it expeditiously upon receiving an appropriate notice might garner bipartisan support.

Progressives like Tim Wu and Lina Khan want to revamp antitrust enforcement to promote competition in digital industries, but so do conservatives. Attorneys general from Republican-controlled states have taken the lead on several groundbreaking antitrust cases against the tech giants, and Republican House members are among the leaders of measures to reform the antitrust laws to deal more effectively with the power of tech companies.

National privacy laws have been stalled because of traditional disagreements between liberals and conservatives on the preemption of state laws and a private right of action to enforce privacy duties. But privacy itself has always been a bipartisan issue, and so the urgent need to constrain the ability of dominant tech companies to extract data from their users is common ground on the left and right and might overcome unrelated disagreements.

All sides of the political spectrum are looking for ways to throw a regulatory net around companies in the digital industries. The constellation of political forces in Washington presents a once-in-a-lifetime opportunity to make fundamental reform. The ongoing debate concerns the structure, the details, and the timing of this coming regulatory regime, not whether it is coming. This book is aimed at contributing to that important conversation.

Notes

1. Oren Cass, "Curtailing Big Tech Requires Much More than Breaking It Up," *Financial Times*, May 30, 2021, https://www.ft.com/content/4d3df1d9-971f-4e1d-ad45-b73881dcd965.

2. Nicolas Lemann, "The Last Battle Over Big Business," *New Yorker*, May 31, 2021, https://www.newyorker.com/magazine/2021/06/07/the-last-battle-over-big-business.

3. John Nichols, "Ed Markey Has a Message for Democrats: 'The Age of Incrementalism Is Over,'" *The Nation*, September 3, 2020, https://www.thenation.com/article/politics/ed-markey-progressive-aoc/.

4. Senator Marco Rubio, "Catholic Social Doctrine and the Dignity of Work," The Catholic University of America, November 5, 2019, https://www.rubio.senate.gov/wp-content/uploads/_cache/files/6d09ae19-8df3-4755-b301-795154a68c59/C58480B07D02452574C5DB8D603803EF.final---cua-speech-11.5.19.pdf.

5. "The Family Security Act," February 4, 2021, https://www.romney.senate.gov/wp-content/uploads/2021/02/family-security-act_one-pager.pdf.

6. Daphne Keller, "The Future of Platform Power: Making Middleware Work," *Journal of Democracy* 32, no. 3 (2021): 168–172, https://muse.jhu.edu/article/797795.

7. "Complaint, US Department of Justice v. Google, Inc.," US Department of Justice, October 20, 2020, https://www.justice.gov/opa/press-release/file/1328941/download, par. 92 and 93.

8. Karen Weise and Michael Corkery, "People Now Spend More at Amazon than at Walmart," *New York Times*, August 17, 2021, https://www.nytimes.com/2021/08/17/technology/amazon-walmart.html.

9. US House of Representatives, Committee on the Judiciary, Investigation on Competition in Digital Markets, Majority Staff Report and Recommendations, 2020 (House Competition Report), https://permanent.fdlp.gov/gpo145949/competitionindigitalmarkets.pdf, p. 15.

10. "Complaint, District of Columbia v. Amazon.com, Inc.," Office of the Attorney General for the District of Columbia, May 25, 2021, https://oag.dc.gov/sites/default/files/2021-05/Amazon-Complaint-.pdf, par. 16.

11. See UK Competition and Markets Authority, "Mobile Ecosystem Market Study," June 15, 2021, https://assets.publishing.service.gov.uk/media/60c8683a8fa8f57cef61fc18/Mobile_ecosystems_-_statement_of_scope_.pdf.

12. "Browser Marketshare Worldwide," Statcounter, May 2021, https://gs.statcounter.com/browser-market-share/mobile/united-states-of-america/#monthly-200901-202105; "Mobile Operating System Market Share United States of America," Statcounter, May 2021, https://gs.statcounter.com/os-market-share/mobile/united-states-of-america/#monthly-200901-202105.

13. Sarah Jeong, "Zuckerberg Struggles to Name a Single Facebook Competitor," The Verge, April 10, 2018, .

14. Gary Henderson, "How Much Time Does the Average Person Spend on Social Media?" *Digital Marketing Blog*, August 24, 2020, https://www.digitalmarketing.org/blog/how-much-time-does-the-average-person-spend-on-social-media; "Frequency of Facebook Use in the United States as of 3rd Quarter 2020," Statista, January 27, 2021, https://www.statista.com/statistics/199266/frequency-of-use-among-facebook-users-in-the-united-states; Matthew Johnston, "How Facebook Makes Money," Investopedia, January 30, 2021, https://www.investopedia.com/ask/answers/120114/how-does-facebook-fb-make-money.asp; John Gramlich, "10 Facts About Americans and Facebook," Pew Research Center, June 1, 2021, https://www.pewresearch.org/fact-tank/2021/06/01/facts-about-americans-and-facebook; Ben Mattison, "Facebook's Dominance Is Built on

Anti-Competitive Behavior," *Yale Insights*, June 18, 2020, https://insights.som.yale.edu/insights/facebook-s-dominance-is-built-on-anti-competitive-behavior.

15. "How Much Trouble Is Mark Zuckerberg In?" *The Economist*, October 16, 2022, https://www.economist.com/business/2022/10/16/how-much-trouble-is-mark-zuckerberg-in.

16. "Amended Complaint," FTC v. Facebook, August 19, 2021, 65–66, https://www.ftc.gov/system/files/documents/cases/ecf_75-1_ftc_v_facebook_public_redacted_fac.pdf.

17. David McLaughlin, "US Antitrust Cops Unveil Data Backing Facebook Monopoly Case," *Bloomberg*, September 8, 2021, https://www.bloomberg.com/news/articles/2021-09-08/u-s-antitrust-cops-unveil-data-backing-facebook-monopoly-case.

18. Galen Stocking et al., "The Role of Alternative Social Media in the News and Information Environment," Pew Research Center, October 6, 2022, https://www.pewresearch.org/journalism/2022/10/06/the-role-of-alternative-social-media-in-the-news-and-information-environment.

19. Emily A. Vogels et al., "Teens, Social Media and Technology 2022," Pew Research Center, August 10, 2022, https://www.pewresearch.org/internet/2022/08/10/teens-social-media-and-technology-2022; Mark Jamison, "Pew Research Center Study Contradicts Federal Trade Commission's Cases Against Meta," American Enterprise Institute, August 15, 2022, https://www.aei.org/technology-and-innovation/pew-research-center-study-contradicts-federal-trade-commissions-cases-against-meta.

20. Matt Stoller, "Yes, Facebook Is Still a Monopoly," *BIG*, February 11, 2022, https://mattstoller.substack.com/p/yes-facebook-is-still-a-monopoly.

21. Alexandra Bruell, "Amazon Surpasses 10% of US Digital Ad Market Share," *Wall Street Journal*, April 6, 2021, https://www.wsj.com/articles/amazon-surpasses-10-of-u-s-digital-ad-market-share-11617703200.

22. "Amended Complaint," Texas AG and other State AGs v. Google, March 15, 2021, https://www.texasattorneygeneral.gov/sites/default/files/images/admin/2021/Press/Redacted%20Amended%20Complaint%20FILED%20(002).pdf.

23. Carl Shapiro and Hal Varian, *Information Rules: A Strategic Guide to the Network Economy* (Boston: Harvard Business School Press, 1998), especially chapter 7 on networks and positive feedback; Michael Katz and Carl Shapiro, "Systems Competition and Network Effects," *Journal of Economic Perspectives* (Spring 1994): 93–113, http://faculty.haas.berkeley.edu/shapiro/systems.pdf; Joost Rietveld and Melissa A. Schilling, "Platform Competition: A Systematic and Interdisciplinary Review of the Literature," *Journal of Management* 47, no. 6 (July 1, 2021): 1528–63, https://doi.org/10.1177/0149206320969791.

24. Metcalfe's Law, Wikipedia, July 31, 2021, https://en.wikipedia.org/wiki/Metcalfe%27s_law.

25. "Number of Amazon Prime Members in the United States as of December 2019," Statista, https://www.statista.com/statistics/546894/number-of-amazon-prime-paying-members; "Total Number of Households in the United States with an Amazon Prime Subscription from 2018 to 2022," Statista, https://www.statista.com/statistics/861060/total-number-of-households-amazon-prime-subscription-usa.

26. K. Sabeel Rahman, "Regulating Informational Infrastructure: Internet Platforms as the New Public Utilities," *Georgetown Law Technology Review* 2, no. 234 (2018): 241, https://pdfs.semanticscholar.org/3c2f/9fbb07719d29287b26643edb7dc283b607d2.pdf.

27. See Paul Starr, *The Creation of the Media* (NewYork: Basic Books, 2004); Tim Wu, *The Master Switch: The Rise and Fall of Information Empires* (New York: Random House, 2010); Deborah Spar, *Ruling the Waves: From the Compass to the Internet* (New York: Harcourt, 2001); and Eli Noam, "The Dynamics of Media Concentration: A Model," in *Media Ownership and Concentration in America* (New York: Oxford University Press, 2009), 33–39.

28. Brian Schwartz, "Trump Campaign Uses Newly Restored Facebook Page to Fundraise Off Indictment," CNBC, April 4, https://www.cnbc.com/2023/03/31/trump-indictment-campaign-uses-facebook-to-fundraise.html; Alex Isenstadt, "Indictment Turbocharges Trump's Fundraising," *Politico*, April 15, 2023, https://www.politico.com/news/2023/04/15/trump-fundraising-indictment-data-00092176.

29. Harold Feld, "The Case for the Digital Platform Act: Market Structure and Regulation of Digital Platforms," Roosevelt Institute, May 8, 2019, https://rooseveltinstitute.org/publications/the-case-for-the-digital-platform-act-market-structure-and-regulation-of-digital-platforms.

30. Nathan Robinson, "Why I Love Mark Zuckerberg and Can Never Say a Word Against Him," Current Affairs, January 3, 2018, https://www.currentaffairs.org/2018/01/why-i-love-mark-zuckerberg-and-can-never-say-a-word-against-him.

31. Kevin Tran, "Trust Isn't Everything When It Comes to Gen Z News Consumption," Morning Consult, June 22, 2022, https://morningconsult.com/2022/06/22/gen-z-trust-social-media-news-consumption.

32. Vogels et al., "Teens"; Kevin Lozano, "How YouTube Created the Attention Economy," *New Yorker*, October 4, 2022, https://www.newyorker.com/books/under-review/the-overlooked-titan-of-social-media.

33. Feld, "The Case for the Digital Platform Act," 41–48.

34. Laura Moy, "Statement of Laura Moy, Before the US Senate Committee on Commerce, Science, and Transportation, Hearing on Consumer Data Privacy: Examining Lessons from the European Union's General Data Protection Regulation and the California Consumer Privacy Act," Georgetown Law Center on Privacy and Technology, October 10, 2018, 16, https://www.commerce.senate.gov/services/files/baf68751-c9bc-4b15-ab0f-d4a5f719027c.

35. Rahman, "Regulating Informational Infrastructure."

36. For further discussion of centrality, see Mark MacCarthy, "Enhanced Privacy Duties for Dominant Technology Companies," *Rutgers Computer & Technology Law Journal* 47, no. 1 (2021), esp. part III, https://ssrn.com/abstract=3656664.

37. Associated Press v. United States, 326 US 1 (1945), https://supreme.justia.com/cases/federal/us/326/1.

38. Bank Holding Company Act of 1956, 12 U.S.C. § 1842(d)(2), Cornell Law School Legal Information Institute, https://www.law.cornell.edu/uscode/text/12/1842.

39. Lina M. Khan, "The Separation of Platforms and Commerce," *Columbia Law Review* 119, no. 973 (2019), https://scholarship.law.columbia.edu/faculty_scholarship/2789.

40. Dodd-Frank Wall Street Reform and Consumer Protection Act of 2010, Pub. L. 111-203, 124 Stat. 1376 (2010), https://www.govinfo.gov/content/pkg/PLAW-111publ203/pdf/PLAW-111publ203.pdf.

41. Jessica Rich, "After 20 Years of Debate, It's Time for Congress to Finally Pass a Baseline Privacy Law," *TechTank*, Brookings Institution, January 14, 2021, https://www.brookings.edu/blog/techtank/2021/01/14/after-20-years-of-debate-its-time-for-congress-to-finally-pass-a-baseline-privacy-law.

42. Aleecia McDonald and Lorrie Faith Cranor, "The Cost of Reading Privacy Policies," *A Journal of Law and Policy for the Information Society* (2008), http://lorrie.cranor.org/pubs/readingPolicyCost-authorDraft.pdf.

43. Woodrow Hartzog, *Privacy's Blueprint: The Battle to Control the Design of New Technologies* (Boston: Harvard University Press, 2018), 21–56; Cameron F. Kerry, John B. Morris Jr., Caitlin T. Chin, and Nicol E. Turner Lee, "Bridging the Gaps: A Path Forward to Federal Privacy Legislation," Brookings Institution, June 2020, https://www.brookings.edu/wp-content/uploads/2020/06/Bridging-the-gaps_a-path-forward-to-federal-privacy-legislation.pdf.

44. For background, see Zak Doffman, "Why You Shouldn't Use Google Chrome After New Privacy Disclosure," *Forbes*, March 20, 2021, https://www.forbes.com/sites/zakdoffman/2021/03/20/stop-using-google-chrome-on-apple-iphone-12-pro-max-ipad-and-macbook-pro/?sh=449838ec4d08; David Nield, "All the Ways Google Tracks You—And How to Stop It," *Wired*, May 27, 2019, https://www.wired.com/story/google-tracks-you-privacy; "Study of Google Data Collection Comes amid Increased Scrutiny over Digital Privacy," Vanderbilt University, November 2018, https://engineering.vanderbilt.edu/news/2018/study-of-google-data-collection-comes-amid-increased-scrutiny-over-digital-privacy.

45. Mike Isaac, "Mark Zuckerberg Plans to Integrate WhatsApp, Instagram, and Facebook Messenger," *New York Times*, January 25, 2019, https://www.nytimes.com/2019/01/25/technology/facebook-instagram-whatsapp-messenger.html.

46. Paul Ohm, "Broken Promises of Privacy: Responding to the Surprising Failure of Anonymization," *UCLA Law Review* 57, no. 1701 (August 18, 2010): 1748, https://www.uclalawreview.org/broken-promises-of-privacy-responding-to-the-surprising-failure-of-anonymization-2.

47. Daisuke Wakabayashi, "The Antitrust Case Against Big Tech, Shaped by Tech Industry Exiles," *New York Times*, December 12, 2020, https://www.nytimes.com/2020/12/20/technology/antitrust-case-google-facebook.html.

48. Pam Dixon and Bob Gellman, "The Scoring of America: How Secret Consumer Scores Threaten Your Privacy and Your Future," World Privacy Forum, 2014, https://www.worldprivacyforum.org/2014/04/wpf-report-the-scoring-of-america-how-secret-consumer-scores-threaten-your-privacy-and-your-future.

49. Abigail Charpentier, "How Tina Fey Made Waves with 30 ROCK," Broadway World, March 6, 2020, https://www.broadwayworld.com/bwwtv/article/How-Tina-Fey

-Made-Waves-with-30-ROCK-20200306; and "30 Rock Pilot (Episode Highlights)," https://www.youtube.com/watch?v=aYGbfKuBBBk.

50. See the *New York Times* coverage at https://www.nytimes.com/2018/04/04/us/politics/cambridge-analytica-scandal-fallout.html; and Alvin Chang, "The Facebook and Cambridge Analytica Scandal, Explained with a Simple Diagram," *Vox*, May 2, 2018, https://www.vox.com/policy-and-politics/2018/3/23/17151916/facebook-cambridge-analytica-trump-diagram.

51. *The Social Dilemma*, directed by Jeff Orlowski-Yang (Netflix, 2020), https://www.netflix.com/title/81254224/.

52. See Mark MacCarthy, "New Directions in Privacy: Disclosure, Unfairness and Externalities," *A Journal of Law and Policy for the Information Society* 6, no. 425 (2011): https://ssrn.com/abstract=3093301; Simeon de Brouwer, "Privacy Self-Management and the Issue of Privacy Externalities: Of Thwarted Expectations, and Harmful Exploitation," *Internet Policy Review* 9, no. 4 (2020): https://doi.org/10.14763/2020.4.1537.

53. Gabriel Nicholas and Michael Weinberg, "Data Portability and Platform Competition: Is User Data Exported from Facebook Actually Useful to Competitors?" NYU School of Law, November 2019, https://www.nyuengelberg.org/outputs/data-portability-and-platform-competition/.

54. See Mark MacCarthy, "Privacy Is Not a Property Right in Personal Information," *Forbes*, November 2, 2018, https://www.forbes.com/sites/washingtonbytes/2018/11/02/privacy-is-not-a-property-right-in-personal-information/?sh=7d896652280f.

55. See, for instance, Tarleton Gillespie, *Custodians of the Internet: Platforms, Content Moderation, and the Hidden Decisions that Shape Social Media* (New Haven, CT: Yale University Press, 2018); Siva Vaidhyanathan, *Antisocial Media: How Facebook Disconnects Us and Undermines Democracy* (New York: Oxford University Press, 2018); Kate Klonick, "The New Governors: The People, Rules, and Processes Governing Online Speech," *Harvard Law Review* 131, no. 6 (April 2018): 1598–1670, https://harvardlawreview.org/wp-content/uploads/2018/04/1598-1670_Online.pdf.

56. "Confronting Health Misinformation: The US Surgeon General's Advisory on Building a Healthy Information Environment," US Department of Health & Human Services, 2021, https://www.hhs.gov/sites/default/files/surgeon-general-misinformation-advisory.pdf.

57. "The Facebook Files," *Wall Street Journal*, September/October 2021, https://www.wsj.com/articles/the-facebook-files-11631713039?mod=series_facebookfiles.

58. Eli Pariser, *The Filter Bubble: What the Internet Is Hiding from You* (New York: Penguin, 2011); Cass R. Sunstein, *Republic.com 2.0* (Princeton University Press, 2007).

59. Elisa Shearer and Amy Mitchell, "News Use Across Social Media Platforms in 2020," Pew Research Center, January 12, 2021, https://www.journalism.org/2021/01/12/news-use-across-social-media-platforms-in-2020.

60. Roddy Lindsay, "I Designed Algorithms at Facebook. Here's How to Regulate Them," *New York Times*, October 6, 2021, https://www.nytimes.com/2021/10/06/opinion/facebook-whistleblower-section-230.html.

61. See Klonick, "The New Governors," for more detail on the growth of content moderation.

62. Casey Newton, "For Facebook Content Moderators, Traumatizing Material Is a Job Hazard," interview by Terry Gross, *Fresh Air*, NPR, July 1, 2019, https://www.npr.org/2019/07/01/737498507/for-facebook-content-moderators-traumatizing-material-is-a-job-hazard.

63. Reno v. American Civil Liberties Union, 521 US 844 (1997), https://supreme.justia.com/cases/federal/us/521/844.

64. Communications Decency Act of 1996, 47 U.S.C. § 230 (1996), https://www.law.cornell.edu/uscode/text/47/230; Jeff Kosseff, *The Twenty-Six Words That Created the Internet* (Ithaca, NY: Cornell University Press, 2019).

65. Digital Millennium Copyright Act of 1998, 17 U.S.C. § 512 (1998), https://www.law.cornell.edu/uscode/text/17/512.

66. Tim Wu, "Is the First Amendment Obsolete?" Knight First Amendment Center at Columbia University, September 1, 2017, https://knightcolumbia.org/content/tim-wu-first-amendment-obsolete; Adam Candeub, "Bargaining for Free Speech: Common Carriage, Network Neutrality, and Section 230," *Yale Journal of Law and Technology* 22, no. 391, https://yjolt.org/bargaining-free-speech-common-carriage-network-neutrality-and-section-230; Biden v. Knight First Amendment Institute, 593 US ___ (2021), https://www.supremecourt.gov/opinions/20pdf/20-197_5ie6.pdf.

67. Allow States and Victims to Fight Online Sex Trafficking Act of 2017, Pub. L. No. 115–164, 132 Stat. 1253 (2018), https://www.congress.gov/115/plaws/publ164/PLAW-115publ164.pdf; Protecting Americans from Dangerous Algorithms Act, H.R. 2154, 117th Cong. (2021), https://www.congress.gov/117/bills/hr2154/BILLS-117hr2154ih.pdf.

68. PACT Act, S. 797, 117th Cong. (2021), https://www.congress.gov/117/bills/s797/BILLS-117s797is.pdf.

69. Twitter, Inc. v. Taamneh, ___ US ___ (2023), https://www.supremecourt.gov/opinions/22pdf/21-1496_d18f.pdf; Gonzalez v. Google, 598 US ____ (2023), https://www.supremecourt.gov/opinions/22pdf/21-1333_6j7a.pdf.

70. Natalia Drozdiak, "US Tech Firms Agree to EU Code of Conduct on Terror and Hate Content," *Wall Street Journal*, May 31, 2016, https://www.wsj.com/articles/u-s-tech-companies-sign-up-to-eu-code-of-conduct-on-terror-1464689959.

71. European Parliament, "New Rules Adopted for Quick and Smooth Removal of Terrorist Content Online," press release, April 28, 2021, https://www.europarl.europa.eu/news/en/press-room/20210422IPR02621/new-rules-adopted-for-quick-and-smooth-removal-of-terrorist-content-online.

72. Bill Baer, "The Biden Administration Takes an Overdue First Step to Foster Competition," *Washington Post*, July 10, 2021, https://www.washingtonpost.com/opinions/2021/07/10/biden-administration-takes-an-overdue-first-step-foster-competition.

73. Phil Verveer, "Platform Accountability and Contemporary Competition Law: Practical Considerations," Shorenstein Center on Media, Politics and Public Policy, November 20, 2018, https://shorensteincenter.org/wp-content/uploads/2018/11/Phil-Verveer-Practical-Considerations-Nov-2018.pdf.

74. Tom Wheeler, Phil Verveer, and Gene Kimmelman, "New Digital Realities; New Oversight Solutions, Shorenstein Center on Media, Politics and Public Policy,"

Shorenstein Report, August 20, 2020, https://shorensteincenter.org/new-digital-realities-tom-wheeler-phil-verveer-gene-kimmelman.

75. Verizon Communications Inc. v. Law Offices of Curtis V. Trinko, 540 US 398 (2004), available at https://supreme.justia.com/cases/federal/us/540/02-682/opinion.pdf.

76. Ending Platform Monopolies Act, H.R. 3825, 117th Cong. (2021), https://www.congress.gov/117/bills/hr3825/BILLS-117hr3825ih.pdf.

77. ACCESS Act of 2021, H.R. 3849, 117th Cong. (2021), https://www.congress.gov/117/bills/hr3849/BILLS-117hr3849ih.pdf.

78. American Choice and Innovation Online Act, H.R. 3816, 117th Cong. (2021), https://www.congress.gov/117/bills/hr3816/BILLS-117hr3816ih.pdf.

79. Platform Competition and Opportunity Act of 2021, H.R. 3826, 117th Cong. (2021), https://www.congress.gov/117/bills/hr3826/BILLS-117hr3826ih.pdf.

80. Open Markets Act, S. 2710, 117th Cong. (2021), https://www.congress.gov/bill/117th-congress/senate-bill/2710.

81. American Innovation and Choice Online Act, S. 2992, 117th Cong. (2021), https://www.congress.gov/bill/117th-congress/senate-bill/2992.

82. Chamber of Commerce of the United States, Letter to House Judiciary Committee Chairman Jerrold Nadler and Ranking Member Jim Jordan, June 22, 2021, https://www.uschamber.com/assets/archived/images/210622_antitrustmarkup_housejudiciary.pdf.

83. Carl Shapiro, "Protecting Competition in the American Economy: Merger Control, Tech Titans, Labor Markets," *Journal of Economic Perspectives* (June 12, 2019), https://ssrn.com/abstract=3405501.

84. "Lawfulness of Processing," General Data Protection Regulation, Article 6(1)(f) http://www.privacy-regulation.eu/en/article-6-lawfulness-of-processing-GDPR.htm.

85. Hartzog, *Privacy's Blueprint*.

86. Jack M. Balkin, "Lecture, Information Fiduciaries and the First Amendment," *UC Davis Law Review* 49, no. 1183 (2016), https://lawreview.law.ucdavis.edu/issues/49/4/Lecture/49-4_Balkin.pdf.

87. Kristin L. Bryan, "Passage of Federal Privacy Bill Remains Possible This Year, Remains a Continued Priority," *National Law Review*, September 30, 2022, https://www.natlawreview.com/article/passage-federal-privacy-bill-remains-possible-year-remains-continued-priority; Federal Trade Commission, Advanced Notice of Proposed Rulemaking, "Trade Regulation Rule on Commercial Surveillance and Data Security," August 22, 2022, https://www.federalregister.gov/documents/2022/08/22/2022-17752/trade-regulation-rule-on-commercial-surveillance-and-data-security; Mark MacCarthy, "Why the FTC Should Proceed with a Privacy Rulemaking," *TechTank*, Brookings Institution, June 29, 2022, https://www.brookings.edu/blog/techtank/2022/06/29/why-the-ftc-should-proceed-with-a-privacy-rulemaking.

88. See Mark MacCarthy, "Back to the Future for Section 230 Reform," *Lawfare Blog*, March 2, 2021, https://www.lawfareblog.com/back-future-section-230-reform.

89. See Genevieve Lakier and Nelson Tebbe, "After the 'Great Deplatforming': Reconsidering the Shape of the First Amendment," *Law and Political Economy*, March 1, 2021, https://lpeproject.org/blog/after-the-great-deplatforming-reconsidering-the-shape-of-the-first-amendment; Robert Post, "Exit, Voice, and the First Amendment Treatment

of Social Media," *Law and Political Economy*, April 6, 2021, https://lpeproject.org/blog/exit-voice-and-the-first-amendment-treatment-of-social-media; Ramya Krishnan, "The Pitfalls of Platform Analogies in Reconsidering the Shape of the First Amendment," *Law and Political Economy*, April 19, 2021, https://lpeproject.org/blog/the-pitfalls-of-platform-analogies-in-reconsidering-the-shape-of-the-first-amendment.

90. Philip M. Napoli, *Social Media and the Public Interest* (New York: Columbia University Press, 2019).

91. Mark MacCarthy, "Transparency Requirements for Digital Social Media Platforms: Recommendations for Policy Makers and Industry," Transatlantic Working Group, February 12, 2020, https://ssrn.com/abstract=3615726.

92. Red Lion Broadcasting Co. v. FCC, 395 US 367 (1969), https://supreme.justia.com/cases/federal/us/395/367.

93. "California Assembly Bill 587, Approved by Governor," California Legislative Information, September 13, 2022, https://leginfo.legislature.ca.gov/faces/billTextClient.xhtml?bill_id=202120220AB587.

94. Mark MacCarthy, "The Eleventh Circuit's Acceptance of a Consumer Protection Approach to Social Media Regulation," *Lawfare Blog*, June 10, 2022, https://www.lawfareblog.com/eleventh-circuits-acceptance-consumer-protection-approach-social-media-regulation.

95. Francis Fukuyama et al., "Report of the Working Group on Platform Scale," Program on Democracy and the Internet, Stanford University, October 6, 2020, 29, https://fsi-live.s3.us-west-1.amazonaws.com/s3fs-public/platform_scale_whitepaper_-cpc-pacs.pdf.

96. Erika Douglas, "The New Antitrust/Data Privacy Law Interface," *Yale Law Journal* Forum, January 18, 2021, 658, https://www.yalelawjournal.org/pdf/DouglasEssay_pv1pt6ak.pdf.

97. Shorenstein Report, p. 49.

98. Jason Furman et al., "Unlocking Digital Competition: Report of the Digital Competition Expert Panel," United Kingdom, Chancellor of the Exchequer, March 13, 2019 (UK Report), https://assets.publishing.service.gov.uk/government/uploads/system/uploads/attachment_data/file/785547/unlocking_digital_competition_furman_review_web.pdf.

99. Feld, "The Case."

100. Fiona Scott Morton et al., "Stigler Committee on Digital Platforms, Market Structure and Antitrust Subcommittee: Final Report," Stigler Center for the Study of the Economy and the State, September 16, 2019, 23–138, https://research.chicagobooth.edu/stigler/media/news/committee-on-digital-platforms-final-report.

101. Martha Minow, *Saving the News* (New York: Oxford University Press, 2021), 123.

102. UK Department for Digital, Culture, Media & Sport and Department for Business, Energy & Industrial Strategy, "Response to the CMA's Market Study into Online Platforms and Digital Advertising," November 27, 2020, https://www.gov.uk/government/publications/government-response-to-the-cma-digital-advertising-market-study; UK Department for Digital, Culture, Media & Sport and Department for Business, Energy & Industrial Strategy, "A New Pro-Competition Regime for Digital

Markets," July 2021, https://assets.publishing.service.gov.uk/government/uploads/system/uploads/attachment_data/file/1003913/Digital_Competition_Consultation_v2.pdf; Secretary of State for Digital, Culture, Media & Sport and the Secretary of State for Business, Energy & Industrial Strategy, "Government Response to the Consultation on a New Pro-Competition Regime for Digital Markets," May 2022, https://assets.publishing.service.gov.uk/government/uploads/system/uploads/attachment_data/file/1073164/E02740688_CP_657_Gov_Resp_Consultation_on_pro-comp_digital_markets_Accessible.pdf.

103. UK Department for Digital, Culture, Media & Sport, "Online Safety Bill," January 18, 2023, https://bills.parliament.uk/bills/3137/publications; Mark MacCarthy, "UK Government Purges 'Legal but Harmful' Provisions from Its Online Safety Bill," *TechTank*, Brookings Institution, December 21, 2022, https://www.brookings.edu/blog/techtank/2022/12/21/u-k-government-purges-legal-but-harmful-provisions-from-its-revised-online-safety-bill/; Chris Morris, "What Is the U.K.'s Online Safety Bill—And Why Are So Many Tech Companies Opposing It?" Fast Company, April 18, 2023, https://www.fastcompany.com/90883733/uk-online-safety-bill-whatsapp-signal.

104. UK Competition and Markets Authority, "The Digital Regulation Cooperation Forum," March 10, 2021, https://www.gov.uk/government/collections/the-digital-regulation-cooperation-forum; Digital Regulation Cooperation Forum, "Plan of Work for 2022–2023," April 28, 2022, https://www.gov.uk/government/publications/digital-regulation-cooperation-forum-workplan-2022-to-2023/digital-regulation-cooperation-forum-plan-of-work-for-2022-to-2023.

105. Wheeler et al., "New Digital Realities," 20; Digital Platform Commission Act, S. 4201, 117th Cong. (2022), https://www.congress.gov/bill/117th-congress/senate-bill/4201; Digital Platform Commission Act, H.R. 7858, 117th Cong. (2022), https://www.congress.gov/bill/117th-congress/house-bill/7858?r=1&s=1; Office of Senator Michael Bennet, "Bennet-Welch Reintroduce Landmark Legislation to Establish Federal Commission to Oversee Digital Platforms," press release, May 18, 2023, https://www.bennet.senate.gov/public/index.cfm/2023/5/bennet-welch-reintroduce-landmark-legislation-to-establish-federal-commission-to-oversee-digital-platforms.

106. Wheeler et al., "New Digital Realities," 36; Section 7 of American Choice and Innovation Online Act, H.R. 3816.

107. Seila Law LLC v. Consumer Financial Protection Bureau, No. 19–7, June 29, 2020, https://www.supremecourt.gov/opinions/19pdf/19-7_n6io.pdf.

108. PACT Act, S. 797, 117th Cong. (2021).

109. See, for instance, the definition of "online platform" in American Choice and Innovation Online Act, H.R. 3816.

110. See Mark MacCarthy, "A Dispute Resolution Program for Social Media Companies," *TechTank*, Brookings Institution, October 9, 2020, https://www.brookings.edu/research/a-dispute-resolution-program-for-social-media-companies.

111. See budget proposals for the FTC at https://www.ftc.gov/system/files/documents/reports/fy-2022-congressional-budget-justification/fy22cbj.pdf, FCC at https://docs.fcc.gov/public/attachments/DOC-372853A1.pdf; CFPB at https://files.consumerfinance.gov/f/documents/cfpb_performance-plan-and-report_fy21.pdf; Antitrust Division at

https://www.justice.gov/doj/page/file/1246781/download; and the Eshoo-Lofgren proposal for a Digital Privacy Agency, https://www.congress.gov/bill/116th-congress/house-bill/4978/text.

112. Build Back Better Act, H.R. 5376, 117th Cong. (2021), passed by the House of Representatives, November 19, 2021, https://www.congress.gov/bill/117th-congress/house-bill/5376/text.

113. Digital Platform Commission Act, S. 4201, 117th Cong. (2022).

Chapter 2

Competition Rules for Digital Industries

"These are the richest and most powerful companies in the world, they have no regulation on them. Wow, that's fantastic. You know, they're virtual monopolies in many cases, and marketplaces, and no regulation who gets to do that, you know, sign me up for that."

—Kara Swisher[1]

"Determining what is anti-competitive behavior . . . is the relatively easy part. Deciding how best to fix that problem . . . is the difficult part."

—Mark Scott[2]

Introduction: The Antimonopoly Moment

In the first six months of his presidency, Joe Biden looked like a trustbuster. He made antitrust activist Lina Khan head of the FTC; nominated big-tech foe Jonathan Kanter to lead the Antitrust Division in the Department of Justice; and gave Tim Wu, the progressive neo-Brandeisian cheerleader-in-chief, a key leadership post in the White House. In June 2021, the White House issued a sweeping executive order promoting competition throughout the economy.

Also in June 2021, the House Judiciary Committee capped two years of investigation and the issuance of a major report on competition in digital markets by passing six interlocking bills aimed at breaking up the economic power of big tech. It was an antimonopoly moment not seen since the heady days of the antitrust revival under Franklin Roosevelt's Antitrust chief Thurmond Arnold in the late 1930s.[3]

In this chapter, we'll look at how this antimonopoly moment happened, and how it is part of a global reaction against the power of tech companies. We'll also make the case that ongoing regulation, not one-time antitrust action, is needed to maintain tech competition and to protect dependent businesses from abuse by dominant companies in the core digital industries.

In his speech introducing his June 2021 procompetitive executive order, President Biden blamed the Chicago School of antitrust for the failure to maintain competition in the economy. "Forty years ago," he said, "we chose the wrong path, in my view, following the misguided philosophy of people like Robert Bork and pulled back on enforcing laws to promote competition." He did not quite say that the consumer welfare standard for antitrust action was the villain, but it was clear he wanted to use the powers of his administration to push all sectors of the economy toward a less concentrated market structure, without needing to demonstrate in any empirical detail that this would lower consumer prices or improve the quality of consumer products and services. Structural antitrust was back in all but name.

In her justly famous 2017 article called "Amazon's Antitrust Paradox," Khan made clear this difference between the traditional approach and economic structuralism. The approach of economic structuralism, she said, holds that "concentrated market structures promote anticompetitive forms of conduct." And so antitrust law should aim to promote "markets populated with many small- and medium-sized companies."[4] In contrast, the consumer welfare approach shows no preference for one market structure over others. The only reasonable standard for antitrust, said Bork in a mantra picked up by generations of antitrust scholars, practitioners, enforcers, and judges, is "the maximization of consumer welfare."

While it is commonly thought that this turn to consumers as the touchstone of antitrust was the invention of Bork and the Chicago School, in fact the crucial turn took place much earlier, and it was accomplished by one of the legendary antitrust enforcers, Arnold, Roosevelt's second-term head of the Department of Justice's Antitrust Division. The debate over firm size is, Arnold wrote scathingly, "like arguing whether tall buildings are better than low ones or big pieces of coal better than small ones." He welcomed the economic efficiencies brought by scale and had no Brandeisian attachment to small businesses as such. Consumers, he argued, "are unwilling to lose the advantages of a machine age because of a sentimental attachment to the ideal of little business." They will support antitrust solely because of their interest in lowering "the price of pork chops, bread, spectacles, drugs and plumbing."[5]

This switch from the interest of the producer to the interest of the consumer is precisely what the neo-Brandeisian antitrust reform movement is seeking to reverse. The consumerist mantra from Arnold through Bork and to today's antitrust practitioners has been that antitrust seeks to protect competition, not competitors. The rarely noted corollary of this mantra is that antitrust enforcers should tolerate markets without any competitors at all unless it could be shown that consumers would be better off by actively promoting the interests of competitors. Even more traditional economists such as Jason Furman, the head of the Council of Economic Advisers under President Barack Obama, have recoiled from this implication. "Ensuring that competition is vibrant," he commented in 2019, "requires ensuring that there are competitors."[6]

The new goal of the antitrust reformers is explicitly structural. Antitrust enforcement should foster markets with many small- and medium-sized firms throughout the economy and especially in the consumer high-tech markets that have come to be dominated by a few large firms in the last decade.

The neo-Brandeisian reformers prefer markets with many competitors, in part for cultural and political reasons. As with their philosophic heroes, Louis Brandeis and Woodrow Wilson, they endow trustbusting with an ethical value and conceive of reform as a kind of moral awakening. As Harvard philosopher Michael Sandel put it, their concern is not only (or even primarily) with consumer prices, "but rather with an economy of small, independent producers and with the qualities of character—of enterprise, initiative, and responsibility—that this system ideally called forth."[7]

A decentralized economy of small independent producers develops the personal character essential for self-government and prevents the accumulation of ungovernable, private economic power. Small firms are the natural home for self-reliant citizens capable of independent judgment; they are amenable to control by local and national governments that are themselves of limited size and power. A key goal for cultural antitrust is the devolution of power from inaccessible and antidemocratic large firms toward the individual and smaller humane institutions.[8]

In addition, antitrust reformers think small- and medium-sized firms are drivers of innovation and economic growth. Small companies in competitive markets must keep prices low and quality high and constantly improve their products because if they do not, strong, capable rivals will do it. Except in a few rare cases of natural monopolies, where regulation might be appropriate to protect the public, reformers think giant corporations have grown beyond the scale needed for efficient operations, achieving their outsized market position primarily through unfair methods of competition.[9]

For this reason, some antitrust reformers such as Sandeep Vaheesan, the legal director for the antitrust reform group Open Markets Institute, would explicitly add to the mission of antitrust the idea that not all competition is beneficial. Competition through unfair means should be rejected because competition as such is not the goal. Fair competition is the goal, and unfair competition is the enemy.[10]

The neo-Brandeisian reformers share Brandeis's view that generally bigness is an unnecessary curse in business. "If it were possible today," said Brandeis in the 1930s, "to make the corporations act in accordance with what doubtless all of us would agree should be the rules of trade, no huge corporation would be created or if created would be successful." Today's reformers share this skepticism of the claim that bigness and monopoly in business is efficient. They always look at markets with a monopolistic structure with suspicion and aim either to destroy the monopoly or to regulate it in the public interest.[11]

For these mixed social, political, and economic reasons, their view is that the default national policy should be to promote competitive market structures throughout the economy. In passing the antitrust laws, they think, Congress resolved the argument of centralization versus decentralization in favor of decentralized, fragmented industries and markets.

A lot of commentary on the new progressive approach to antitrust misidentifies this crucial issue. In moving away from the consumer welfare standard for antitrust action, the reformers have not moved away from the goal of antitrust to maintain fragmented markets with many small, independent producers. They have not asserted that antitrust enforcers should act against companies for reasons unrelated to this procompetitive goal. They do not think that antitrusters should directly promote privacy, free speech, economic equality, environmental protection, or a political process freed from the corrupting influence of big business. They recognize that these worthwhile missions are not part of their own procompetitive mission. The confusion about this might stem from the fact that the reformers think promoting competition and maintaining fragmented markets will help to achieve these other public policy objectives, and they do not hesitate to argue for this connection in attempting to build public and political support for their antimonopoly agenda.[12]

What about the network effects that are the natural forces of concentration in tech markets? The last chapter illustrated how network effects created enormous scale advantages in digital markets that do not seem to "run out" the way supply-side economies of scale sometimes do. The current tech giants made strategic use of these network effects to climb to the top of an initially competitive market. If network effects are destiny, this goal of promoting tech competition is a chimera. The nation could waste a lot of resources pursuing a competitive goal that, no matter how attractive in principle, is simply unattainable in practice.

The reformers have a response. In tech markets, they argue, the network advantages of scale are real. But clever remedies, many of which we will examine in this chapter, can allow many small companies to provide the key digital services while still allowing consumers to reap all the advantages of scale. If it is feasible to have deconcentrated tech markets that provide consumers all the benefits of scale, then the default national policy of competition demands that policymakers should give it a fair run for its money in tech.

The underlying theme of this chapter is that the pursuit of competition in digital industries is worth an extended experiment. An additional theme is that competition in digital markets does not automatically sustain itself; it must be consciously and continuously engineered, fostered, and protected. If policymakers can get there, without harming other important values that we hold dear, they should do it. The policy tools that have been proposed to accomplish this objective, which we will examine in detail in this chapter, are plausible candidates for fostering competition. They have been used before with some success in other markets and have a reasonable prospect, if used properly, to create competition in this market.

The problem is how to give these tools a fair chance to do their work. A major flaw in the neo-Brandeisian program of promoting tech competition is that it is inconsistent with current antitrust jurisprudence. At their core, neo-Brandeisian reformers oppose giant corporations, including the tech giants, not solely because of their origins in unfair competitive practices, but simply because of their size and power. In contrast, current antitrust enforcers act against firms only when these firms seek to obtain or maintain a monopoly position through unfair means, something other than competition on the merits. Antitrust law is made almost entirely by the courts that can and have rejected broad antitrust actions brought by enforcing agencies. Under the current judicial interpretation of the law, the courts will simply reject enforcement actions from antitrust agencies based on the premise that they are needed simply to break up a monopoly position, even the monopolies as transparent and entrenched as the ones in tech today.

Another way to state the consumer welfare standard that dominates current antitrust jurisprudence is that there is nothing wrong with a company having a durable monopoly when prices are low and products are of high and continually improving quality. Trying to break up a monopoly without showing in detail that the monopoly is hurting consumers, which is the underlying premise of the neo-Brandeisian movement, is a nonstarter for today's antitrust courts.

The consumer welfare standard seems to mean that the current tech companies are largely immune from antitrust enforcement actions. They all have monopoly or dominant positions in their lines of business, but they do not seem to satisfy the conditions for antitrust action. Amazon's prices and service quality are unbeatable. Google does not charge a price, and its service is the best in the search market. Facebook also charges a zero price, and its enormous and stable user base suggests a group of satisfied customers. Apple and Google run their duopoly in ways that please a large and growing number of app users, who pay a small charge or nothing at all for a spectacular array of innovative mobile services.

There is one escape hatch for reformers seeking to use current antitrust law to break up tech monopolies. If they could show that a company obtained its monopoly or maintained it by anticompetitive or unfair means, as is required under current judicial interpretations of antitrust law, then remedies would be available, and one of these remedies might be to end its monopoly. Doing this need not involve showing directly that consumers are harmed by the current monopolist; instead, the required showing might be that the state of the market would have been competitive but for the unfair tactics of the current monopolist. Anticompetitive conduct, not network effects or competition on the merits, created the monopoly and deprived consumers of market choices.

Given their belief that monopolies arise or are maintained almost always from unfair business practices, neo-Brandeisian antitrust enforcers should usually be able to find anticompetitive conduct at the heart of any monopoly structure. The job of the antitrust enforcer under current law, according to the neo-Brandeisian enforcers, is to find that conduct, bring it to the attention of the courts, and ask for relief. The only way to prevent a recurrence of the anticompetitive conduct that led to or maintained a monopoly, they could argue to the court, would be measures to dismantle the monopoly and create an opening for the emergence of genuine alternatives to the incumbent monopolist.

This escape hatch might be harder to take advantage of than the current optimistic antimonopoly moment is allowing for. Experienced antitrust enforcers such as Phil Verveer, who worked on the case that led to the breakup of AT&T as a young Antitrust Division lawyer and has held senior positions at the FTC and the FCC, have emphasized that making a monopolization case is a long uncertain and resource-intensive process. Due process requirements take years to move through the trial courts, and still more years for appeals. Given the novel nature of the tech monopolies, the chances of success in all the cases of tech monopoly are vanishingly small. Moreover, enforcement agencies are unlikely to have the resources to conduct more than a few of them.[13]

This argument concerning the practical difficulties of big monopolization cases seems correct to me. Economist Fiona Scott Morton, a dedicated opponent of tech monopolies, has warned those who were enthusiastic when the first antitrust case against Google's search monopoly was filed by the Department of Justice in October 2020 not to expect quick action. "Don't get too excited," she has said, "because these things take years. We aren't even going to trial until 2023." She agrees with the central thrust of this book, that antitrust is an "unwieldy" tool and that policymakers need "regulation to complement it."[14]

But in this chapter, I have different fish to fry. My main argument is that the remedies needed to introduce and maintain a market structure of small- and medium-sized tech companies are beyond the antitrust laws. So also are the measures that would be needed to regulate a monopoly in the public interest to prevent it from abusing its captive customers and dependent businesses. Antitrust agencies and the courts are ill-suited to the daily ongoing supervision of tech industry practices that is needed to sustain a competitive market or to ensure that a monopolized market protects the public and dependent businesses.

The rest of this chapter attempts to show this in some detail by looking at some of the antitrust cases that have been brought against the tech giants in the United States and showing how in each case the remedies that would respond to the problems identified are unavailable to antitrust enforcers. For instance, one court has already ruled that the remedy of interoperability for Facebook, which would give other social media companies access to Facebook's huge user base or allow app developers open access to Facebook's app platform, is not allowed under the antitrust laws, even if Facebook is a proven monopolist.[15]

One and all, the measures needed to restore competition in tech or protect dependent businesses require the ongoing supervision of a sector regulator with a statutory mission to end monopoly and monopoly abuses in digital industries.

It is important to be clear-eyed about this project of promoting tech competition. The key digital industries might very well be natural monopolies, and demand-side scale effects might prove to be unremovable, even with fullest use of procompetitive tools. The competitive phase of the tech industry might just have been a transition to its natural equilibrium of a single or small number of providers. This is certainly the lesson of the decades-long attempt to introduce competition into the telephone industry.

But if so, all is not lost. There is still a role for a digital regulator with a procompetition mission. If tech companies are natural monopolies, then, as Khan says, it is appropriate to apply elements of public utility regulation to "limit how a monopoly may use its power."[16] In this chapter, we'll look at ways even a durable tech monopoly can be prevented from abusing business customers or leveraging its monopoly into another dominant position in adjacent markets.

This continuing role is needed because the harms of monopolization are not just felt by the direct end-user of the digital services provided by the tech monopolist. Other businesses depend on these services for their lifeblood of customer access. Providers of vertical search services rely on the general search services that Google monopolizes. Independent third-party merchants depend on Amazon to reach their customers. News outlets need access to Facebook and Google search to attract readers and so advertisers. App developers have no business without having a presence on either Google's Play Store or Apple's App Store or both.

These businesses depend on a monopolist that they cannot avoid. They are open to a variety of abuses because of this lack of competition. One abuse is the usual problem of monopoly pricing. Amazon can charge its merchants virtually whatever it wants for use of its marketplace platform, up to the point where its charges would make it unprofitable for merchants to use the service. Google and Apple can take whatever portion they want of the price an app developer charges its end-users as their fee for access to their app stores. Facebook and Google do not even need to pay news publishers for using their news stories in news feeds and search results, much less provide them with fair compensation for the value of their news product.

A second potential way that monopoly tech platforms might abuse dependent businesses arises because the platforms often provide the same products and services as their business users on the platform they operate. The monopoly platforms compete directly with their own dependent business users. This conflict of interest together with their monopoly power gives them the incentive and ability to act unfairly. They could treat their own services better than they treat the competing service provided by a company that uses its platform to reach its customers. Google can return general search inquiries that list its own travel, shopping, and review services ahead of the similar services provided by the vertical search companies that rely on Google's search engine to reach their own users. Amazon can see the prices its independent merchants are charging and what their sales volume is and set its own prices and product offerings accordingly. Google and Apple might want their own apps like Google Maps or Apple Music to be more easily accessible on their app stores than similar popular apps provided by competitors.

So, a further task is to ensure that tech monopolists cannot abuse their monopoly position either by charging excessive prices or by leveraging its platform monopoly into an improved position in an adjacent market. As before with the task of promoting competition to the platforms themselves, the remedies for monopoly pricing and abuses of a monopoly position are often beyond contemporary antitrust laws. For instance, the most obvious remedy for overcharging app developers in app stores is ongoing price regulation, one of the normal functions of a public utility regulator. That is why these functions were traditionally entrusted to a sector regulator charged with preventing the industry monopolist from abusing its monopoly position.

There is a fix to the problem that needed remedies seem to be beyond the scope of current antitrust law. Instead of relying on current antitrust law, reformers should look at rewriting the antitrust statutes to address the problem of tech monopolies. The needed remedies are beyond current law. So current law must change.

This is the direction taken by members of the House Judiciary Committee in passing digital antitrust reform legislation in June 2021 and by the European Commission in its Digital Markets Act, and by the United Kingdom in its proposal to create a new digital markets unit in its competition authority. In the United States, the agency charged with implementing these antitrust reforms is primarily the FTC.

By a happenstance, this move to provide new competitive powers over digital industries to the FTC might prove to be just the right thing. Other legislative initiatives in the United States to promote privacy and good social media content moderation also house regulatory authority in the FTC. The FTC as a single administrative entity charged with competition, privacy, and content moderation goals would be well positioned to manage the tensions that will inevitably arise among these disparate missions. In a second legislative effort in the future, Congress could move to separate out the responsibilities to regulate digital industries to promote competition, privacy, and content moderation, and place them in a sector-specific independent digital regulator.

This dual mission of a digital regulator to seek competitive outcomes and to prevent monopoly abuses might unite the long-sundered strands of the progressive antitrust movement. It fits with the program of Brandeis and Wilson whose New Freedom movement in the 1912 presidential election sought to create an agency that turned out to be the FTC, to regulate to promote competition and prevent unfair methods of competition. But it also fits with the New Nationalist program of Teddy Roosevelt that would regulate monopolists, thinking that the best way to deal with proven monopolists was "controlling them in the interests of public welfare."[17]

The chapter proceeds this way. We start with a discussion of the two big monopolization cases since the early 1980s—the breakup of the Bell Telephone System in the 1980s, and the antitrust case against Microsoft in the 1990s—and derive from these cases some lessons for how to promote competition in tech. Then we turn to some of the current reform proposals to get a sense of the regulatory tools that are being considered to promote competition and to protect dependent businesses.

To illustrate how these remedies might work and why they are beyond current antitrust law, we look at their possible applications to Amazon's dominant position in electronic commerce, Google's control of search and ad-tech, the Google-Apple duopoly in app infrastructure, and Facebook's control of social media. The digital regulator, we will find, might have to apply some of these tools to all companies in the key digital industries, while it might need to apply others only to dominant companies, and forbear from applying them to the smaller firms in the industry. Along the way we'll identify a series of tensions and synergies with privacy and free speech issues in the various tools needed to promote tech competition and protect dependent businesses.

Promoting Competition in the Telephone Industry

The attempt to promote competition in the telecommunications industry from the 1970s through the 1990s has important lessons for promoting tech competition today. In particular, the tools used to foster competition among different suppliers of telephone service and to protect companies in adjacent markets from abuse by dominant telephone companies can be reimagined for similar purposes in the tech industry. Tools to promote alternative service suppliers include requirements for access, interconnection, unbundling of essential facilities, and sharing of competitively important data. Tools to protect dependent businesses include divestitures, nondiscrimination rules, and line-of-business restrictions. In this chapter, we'll see how these tools were used with varying degrees of success in the telephone industry.

The telephone industry developed in the United States in the late nineteenth century as a monopoly based on the patents obtained by Alexander Graham Bell in 1876. Bell's company successfully defended its patents against challenges, reached a settlement with the existing provider of telegraph services—Western Union—that had independent patents for telephone equipment, obtained a controlling interest in the major equipment supplier of telephone equipment—Western Electric—and operated or licensed companies to build and operate local telephone companies in major cities throughout the country. The company also provided long-distance service connecting the cities. Collectively, the local and long-distance operations were known as the Bell system.

After the patents expired in 1893, this integrated Bell system made strategic use of scale economies and network effects to survive an early competitive challenge from independent companies. The challenge took the form of system competition, a rivalry between two separate, closed communications networks, whose subscribers could not communicate with each other. Competition took this form because current law did not compel interconnection, the Bell system saw no reason to help its rivals by allowing them to reach its larger consumer base, and the independents, for their part, did not seek to coexist with the larger existing network but to displace it.

The Bell system's strategic use of network effects dramatically weakened its independent rivals. It then bought out the weakened, independent companies in a far-reaching acquisition program that attracted the attention of the Department of Justice, which considered it an attempt to monopolize in violation of the Sherman Act.

In 1913, AT&T resolved the Department of Justice's concerns through the Kingsbury Agreement that brought its acquisition program to a close. But by then the industry had consolidated, moving from the fragmented but competitive telephone industry of 1907 into a single national system composed of noncompeting local companies largely controlled by AT&T.[18]

For more than seventy years, the integrated company provided local, long-distance, and customer-premises equipment under pervasive state and federal regulation. The company was first brought under federal regulation in the 1910 Mann-Elkins Act, which granted regulatory authority over telephone rates to the Interstate Commerce Commission (ICC), which regulated railroad rates. In 1934, its interstate operations were brought under the regulatory control of the FCC, which was given extensive authority to regulate long-distance service and connection of devices to the national network. Together with state public utility regulators, the FCC established a national policy of universal service that included long-distance rate averaging, business to residential subsidies, and long-distance subsidies for local service. The company owned its own equipment supplier, Western Electric, which produced network equipment and the customer-premises equipment that connected to the network. It also operated one of the world's most advanced and productive research institutions, Bell Labs.

In the 1950s, the FCC began to open this integrated but closed network. In 1956 it ruled that AT&T could not block the mechanical attachment of devices to the network. In the 1960s, it ruled that the company had to allow electrical interconnection with devices that linked the network to other services provided they did not cause harm to the system. These rulings opened the door to later innovations such as competitive supply of telephones, answering machines, fax machines, and modems for internet access. In 1969, the FCC authorized MCI's application to provide private microwave service between Chicago and St. Louis, thereby inaugurating an extended period of long-distance competition. By the 1970s, this switch in regulatory philosophy from traditional public utility regulation to the promotion of competition through regulation was well established. The FCC fostered competitive supply of customer-premises equipment and promoted independent long-distance competition.[19]

At the same time, the FCC strove to keep AT&T from dominating the growing market for computer services such as data processing. In a series of computer inquiries beginning in 1966, it first kept AT&T out of these services; then, in the late 1970s, it allowed AT&T to provide such services (now called enhanced services) on an unbundled basis and only through a separate subsidiary; finally, in the mid-1980s, it permitted the company to provide unbundled enhanced services without a separate subsidiary if it adopted various accounting safeguards to prevent cross-subsidization and adopted comparably efficient interconnection for its own enhanced service and those of competitors using its network.[20]

A Justice Department monopolization suit began in 1974, alleging that AT&T had resisted the new push for competition through various anticompetitive tactics. The parties reached a settlement in 1982. The 1984 Modified Final Judgment (MFJ) broke apart the integrated Bell system. Long distance was treated as competitive since there were already three facilities-based suppliers—AT&T, MCI, and Sprint.

AT&T retained this long-distance business, the research arm Bell Labs, and the manufacturing company Western Electric. The local service providers were reorganized into seven Regional Bell Operating Companies (RBOCs) and were treated as regulated monopolies. They were required to provide all competing long-distance carriers with equal access to their local system and were prohibited from entering other lines of business including long-distance, information service, and telecom equipment manufacturing.

The rationale behind the divestiture, which the Department of Justice had sought in its original complaint, was that it was the only effective way to promote competition in long-distance, consumer-premises equipment, and information services that relied on monopoly local telephone systems. The local service provider's monopoly gave it the incentive and opportunity to seek to extend its monopoly into these adjacent markets, and no amount of regulatory supervision would prevent it from exercising this monopoly power. If the country wanted competition in these services, the local regulated monopoly providers could not be part of it.

The key role for these local telephone companies was to reorganize their local systems to accommodate the needs of the competitive long-distance carriers. They had been organized to pick up and deliver the traffic of a single long-distance network. When long-distance competition began, the companies dragged their feet in providing the same quality of access service to the new carriers. Now they would be under a regulatory obligation to provide access service that was equal in type, quality, and price to each of the long-distance rivals, including their former affiliate AT&T.

The trial court judge, Harold Greene, administered the consent decree for twelve years, presiding over increasingly strident attempts by the RBOCs to extract waivers or a repeal of the line-of-business restrictions. But that structure of the telephone industry—a regulated monopoly core constrained to provide only regulated local services and exchange access service separated from a competitive periphery of long-distance service providers and equipment manufacturers—was maintained for this entire time. The enduring idea from this period is the strategy of requiring a monopolist to provide equal access to its services and confining it to certain narrowly defined functions to preserve competition in adjacent markets. This ideal is now a model for much cutting-edge thought in tech regulation.[21]

Twelve years after the Bell system breakup, however, Congress took a second step in the process of promoting competition in the telephone industry. In the 1996 Telecommunications Act, it deliberately undercut the idea of a local regulated telephone monopoly by mandating that the local market had to be open to competition from any provider, especially to the local cable operators whose electronic distribution system was already in the ground providing video service. In this approach, everyone in telecommunications should be able to get into anyone else's business. As a transition carrot, the Bell companies were allowed to get into long-distance service only after they had satisfied regulators that they had sufficiently opened their local market to rivals through taking several required steps, including number portability, resale, interconnection, and unbundling requirements. These telecom rules are also models for measures like data portability and interoperability to jump-start competition in the tech industry.[22]

This story of the attempt to promote the telephone industry is a cautionary tale, however. The 1996 Act spurred massive investment in local competition and a gold-rush of additional investments in long-distance capacity. As more companies offered to provide local service as either resellers or facilities-based carriers, the FCC and state regulators gradually approved the entry of the Bell companies into long-distance service. But it soon became clear that long-distance and local were not separate markets. Consumers seemed to want one provider to give them local, long-distance, and cell phone service in one package.

Moreover, with the line-of-business restrictions gone, the legal barriers against consolidation in the industry were also gone. The RBOCs began to merge with each other and with long-distance companies. In 1997, Bell Atlantic merged with NYNEX and later acquired the independent telephone company GTE and changed its name to Verizon. In 2006, it bought the remains of the long-distance company MCI WorldCom. In 1997, SBC (formerly Southwestern Bell) acquired Pacific Telesis. Two years later, in 1999, it acquired Ameritech, and in 2005 it bought the long-distance company AT&T and took its name. In 2006, it bought BellSouth. In place of an integrated Bell monopoly, there emerged an integrated AT&T–Verizon duopoly.[23]

The great telecoms crash of the early 2000s cannot be forgotten, either. Half a million people lost their jobs, telecom stocks lost $2 trillion in value, and many of the new entrants went bankrupt. This included WorldCom, the owner of long-distance pioneer MCI, which collapsed in what was then the biggest bankruptcy in US history, amid stories of accounting fraud and insider deals. The crash challenged the policy consensus at the time that the telecom industry could be transformed into markets with large numbers of firms generating innovation and growth.

The result of a decades-long effort to instill competition into an industry formerly considered to be a natural monopoly is that the telephone industry reintegrated into two giant end-to-end service providers, Verizon and AT&T, neither of which is regulated to any significant degree as to price or service quality.[24]

A largely unanswerable question persists as to the causes of this failure to introduce significant competition. Certainly, the fundamental economics of the industry—high fixed costs, low marginal costs, and network effects—meant the drive to instill competition was moving against natural marketplace forces. But it is also likely that bad conduct on the part of the industry incumbents helped to bring the procompetitive effort to a standstill.

One lesson from this history is crucial for our current purpose. It is the importance of a regulatory agency in introducing competition into an industry. The classical view was that regulation was an alternative to antitrust. Former Supreme Court justice Stephen Breyer encapsulates this view in his mantra that "antitrust is not another form of regulation. Antitrust is an alternative to regulation and, where feasible, a better alternative." For deregulatory czar Alfred Kahn, who rejected regulation as the enemy of competition, "the antitrust laws are not just another form of regulation but an alternative to it—indeed, its very opposite."

In contrast to this view that regulation is the enemy of competition, the lesson from the telecommunications industry is that efforts to promote competition work through regulation. Antitrust scholars

Joseph Kearney and Thomas Merrill describe this reversal as the great transformation of regulated industries law. Antitrust activist and scholar Tim Wu generalizes the approach beyond telecommunications, calling it "antitrust via rulemaking." The key is that regulators are assigned the task, not of maintaining industry monopoly, but of implementing regulations designed to establish and maintain competitive conditions.[25]

The FCC did this through decades of managing the activity of the companies it regulated. It mandated equal access requirements to promote long-distance competition, and together with state regulators oversaw the process of introducing competition into the local loop. None of the methods of introducing competition and protecting dependent businesses were self-enforcing decisions that could be made once by an antitrust court and then never revisited. They were tools that had to be used on an ongoing basis through supervision of the industry. Even the MFJ, which apparently relied on a nonregulatory structural separation mandates and line-of-business restrictions, had to have ongoing court supervision, which would not have been practical without the backdrop of a regulatory agency. As antitrust scholar Al Kramer put it, for telecommunications competition to flourish, "both a sector-specific regulator and antitrust enforcers were needed."[26]

But even with the determined efforts of state and federal regulators to support competitive entry, competition failed to take hold in telecom. This is not a cause for celebration. Still for policymakers looking for guidance on what to do about tech monopolies, the lesson is clear. Without industry regulators, this effort to promote telecom competition could not have even gotten off the ground. A project to instill competition into the tech industry will need to rely on a similar role for regulation. While the telephone industry already had a stable regulatory environment, which had to be reoriented from public utility regulation to promoting competition through regulation, the tech industry is not now supervised by its own sector regulator. The most important lesson from the telephone experience is this: the first course of business in promoting competition in the tech industry is to create a sector regulator that can manage this process of seeking to introduce and maintain competition.

Preventing Monopolization in Computer Software

An independent software market for personal computers was needed to service the new personal computer market that had grown up in the late 1970s to challenge the integrated mainframe computer industry dominated by IBM. The earlier computer industry focused on providing hardware and software for large enterprises in government, business, and other large institutions. Small businesses and home users were not the industry's target market.

The personal computer pioneered by Apple sought to fill that gap by providing sufficient computing power in a small, inexpensive desktop device to satisfy the diverse computing needs of the small user market. It integrated its operating system with its hardware, but it still needed software programmers to write the programs that would make the devices usable. By making the application programming interfaces generally available for all developers to use and exercising no control over the pricing and distribution of the application software, it encouraged entrepreneurs to enter the field. They did in astonishingly large numbers, and in the early 1980s, the industry was a young, vibrant field full of innovation, driven by improving technology, changes in business models, and evolving consumer preferences.

IBM had a choice to make in the face of this challenge to its dominance. It could enter the industry, and thereby help to undermine its own market position in the mainframe business, or it could double down on what it did best in serving the large enterprise market. In the fall of 1980, it chose to enter the field in a hurry to prevent Apple from achieving a position of insuperable dominance. It designed its own personal computer and picked Intel as the provider of the chips that powered it and Microsoft as the provider of the operating system that would interface with the applications programs. Fatally for itself, but fortunately for the future of the computer it designed, IBM allowed others to manufacture compatible computers using the Intel chips and the Microsoft operating system.

The story of how the rivalry between Apple and the IBM-compatible computer played out is well known. Apple's integration strategy produced a high-quality hardware platform and associated operating system that was technically better because of the integration. But it did not license its hardware or operating system and was the sole provider of the integrated device to the public. This situation led to limited-scale economies in production, higher manufacturing costs, higher prices for consumers, and lower sales volume. As a result, application developers began to first develop software for the cheaper, slightly more prevalent IBM-compatible computers and then port their programs over to the Apple platform later. Consumers who bought IBM-compatible computers thereby had access to the latest, most innovative software ahead of owners of Apple computers. In addition, Microsoft, the operating system provider, encouraged independent programmers to develop a large number and a wide variety of business and entertainment applications that could stimulate demand for IBM-compatible computers, while Apple focused more on the in-house development of a small number of applications. By the early 1990s, the number of applications available for Apple computers was a small fraction of that for the IBM-compatible device. Slowly but surely Apple lost ground, and the IBM-compatible computer came to dominate the personal computer market. By 2006, Apple had only 5 percent of the market.

Microsoft rode the growth of the IBM personal computer to become a giant. It charged developers very little for access to its operating system platform to encourage their active participation in the development of software for the platform. It made almost all its money through the licensing of its operating system to equipment manufacturers and to end-users. As the IBM PC market grew, Microsoft became fabulously successful.

No equipment manufacturer had to use the Microsoft operating system. They were free to use any other system they thought would work with the underlying hardware—and to offer it as an option on the computers they sold. But the availability of a large number and variety of compatible programs meant that an operating system challenger would have to enter with a substantially equivalent body of programs to offer to the public. It looked for a time as if IBM's OS/2 operating system might become a serious alternative, but the application barrier to entry warded off this substantial challenge. By the early 1990s, Microsoft enjoyed an undisputed position as the dominant provider of personal computer operating systems.

From the beginning, Microsoft did more than provide operating systems to equipment manufacturers. It also created its own application programs for end-users. It was, in other words, also in the same business as the developers it relied on to construct its application barrier to entry. It competed with its own customers. The core of its programming business was office productivity software for enterprises and home users, including word processing, spreadsheets, graphics programs, presentational applications, and small databases. Microsoft was not the first to enter this office productivity business, and for many years it was not alone in it. There was intense rivalry, a period of fierce competition, and constant innovation and upgrades as companies sought to improve their business software to serve the market more effectively.

Throughout the 1980s and early 1990s, a series of category leaders in office productivity software arose and were replaced by newer competitors. But gradually Microsoft products came to dominate each category. In word processing, WordStar was replaced by WordPerfect, and then replaced by Microsoft's Word in 1993. VisiCalc first dominated spreadsheets, to be followed by Lotus 1-2-3. Then came Borland Quattro Pro, and finally in 1993 Microsoft's Excel became the market leader. In a similar way, Microsoft came to dominate small database products and presentational software.[27]

This dominance caught the attention of the antitrust authorities. The US Justice Department's 1998 antitrust suit against Microsoft was aimed at preventing Microsoft from maintaining its operating system monopoly through anticompetitive conduct involving internet browsers. The DOJ had negotiated a consent decree with Microsoft in the early 1990s that dealt with its earlier anticompetitive concerns, and this consent decree barred Microsoft from tying the licensing of one of its products to the licensing of other products. Then, in 1995, Microsoft began requiring computer manufacturers that sought to license its Windows operating system to install its Internet Explorer browser as well. The DOJ thought this was barred by the consent decree, but when it tried to enforce the consent decree, the courts disagreed with this interpretation. As a result, it filed a larger complaint alleging Microsoft had engaged in a broad pattern of anticompetitive conduct seeking to maintain its operating system monopoly.

The DOJ alleged that Microsoft had targeted Netscape Navigator, the pioneer internet browser, in anticompetitive ways. It did this to prevent the emergence of a rival platform for software developers who might write programs for an independent browser. The browser would then handle the mechanics of interfacing with the computer's operating system. Software developers could ignore the underlying operating system. The browser would become the key interface for programmers, bypassing Microsoft's application barrier to entry that was based on its dominant operating system.

The anticompetitive conduct focused on the two main avenues for the distribution of browser software—computer equipment manufacturers and internet service providers. Microsoft sought to condition access to its operating system on agreements by these companies to limit the distribution of competing browsers and to favor the distribution of Microsoft's own browser, Internet Explorer. It even technically integrated its browser with its operating system so it could not be removed without causing the operating system to malfunction. The scheme worked. By 1998, when the DOJ filed its case, Microsoft's Internet Explorer had replaced Navigator as the leading internet browser.

In June 2000, the trial court found that Microsoft violated the antitrust laws in seeking to squash an emerging competitive threat. The trial court sought to break up the company into an applications software entity and an operating system company that would be subject to line-of-business restrictions designed to prevent reintegration of the application and programming function. Microsoft appealed. In July 2001, the District Court of Appeals for the DC Circuit reversed that order and remanded the case to a new trial judge. A new Justice Department team put in place by a new Republican administration did not pursue a structural remedy but proposed instead a variety of disclosure, licensing, and other behavioral requirements that were approved by the new trial judge in 2002 and the appeals court in 2004.

The settlement's remedies proved to be ineffective if the goal was to reduce the power of Microsoft derived from its premier position in operating systems. They were behavioral obligations and prohibitions aimed to prevent the anticompetitive conduct that Microsoft used in the browser wars. Moreover, they were imposed six years after the beginning of the case, an eternity in a fast-moving industry like computer software. They did nothing to weaken the application barrier to entry, which remained in place. Microsoft continues its dominance of personal computer operating systems and associated productivity software to this day.[28]

Many of the allegations against today's tech companies mirror the charges against Microsoft, and so the failure of the case to achieve its objective suggests the limits of pursuing another big monopolization case against the tech giants. But several other important lessons might be learned from the Microsoft experience.

The first lesson is that courts have affirmed antitrust enforcement action that targets companies that seek to maintain a strong market position by thwarting the rise of nascent or potential competition from companies in adjacent markets. Harm to innovation counts as an antitrust harm, the courts affirmed, even under the consumer welfare standard.

The second lesson is that even failed antitrust action might modify corporate behavior, teaching targeted companies to treat emerging competitive threats with greater respect. Microsoft's unwillingness to take on Google, Facebook, Amazon, and Apple in any serious way suggests the antitrust action might have persuaded Microsoft's senior management to be more circumspect in their business practices.

The third lesson is that if the structural separation and line-of-business restrictions used in the AT&T case proved to be only temporary barriers to reintegration of the telephone industry, conduct remedies enforced by the courts and a generalist antitrust authority fared no better in dislodging a durable monopoly.[29]

The New Procompetitive Tools

The limits of existing antitrust law as illustrated by the mixed results from these two high-profile cases have persuaded antitrust reformers that legislation targeted at the tech industry is needed to bring the tech industries under control. These proposed legislative reforms would provide competition authorities with a clear mandate and the regulatory tools they need to promote a competitive market structure in tech and would prevent durable tech monopolists from abusing dependent business users.

In June 2021, building on the recommendations from a House Judiciary Committee staff report and proposals from Senator Elizabeth Warren, the House Judiciary Committee approved several interlocking bills authorizing antitrust agencies to use these tools to promote competition in the tech industry. The Ending Platform Monopolies Act would prohibit a large platform from owning a line of business that utilizes the platform "for the sale or provision of products or services." The ACCESS Act of 2021 would impose data portability and interoperability requirements on these platforms. The American Choice and Innovation Online Act would impose various nondiscrimination and access requirements on platforms. The Platform Competition and Opportunity Act of 2021 would prohibit the largest online platforms from engaging in mergers that would eliminate competitors, or potential competitors, or that would serve to enhance or reinforce monopoly power.[30]

The US Senate also joined the antitrust reform movement. In 2022, the Senate Judiciary Committee passed the Open App Markets Act that would constrain the power of the Apple and Google app stores to discriminate against and abuse app developers.[31] The Senate Judiciary Committee also adopted a version of the American Choice and Innovation Online Act that imposed nondiscrimination and access duties on digital companies.[32]

The limitation on all these reform bills, as economist Fiona Scott Morton has pointed out, is that they lack a regulator. "It's regulation done through the courts," she says. When digital platforms violate the new laws, she points out, "they have to be sued in court by the FTC or the DOJ. Again, we're back to that slow litigation process." Still, these reform bills provided a significant improvement in antitrust standards for addressing tech monopolies.[33]

Despite strong efforts by their sponsors and high hopes that the antimonopoly moment had come, none of these bills passed the US Congress in 2022.[34] As if to signal the drawing to an end of this antimonopoly moment, procompetitive White House advisor Tim Wu returned to his academic position at Columbia Law School at the end of 2022.[35] In the larger picture, this outcome is not surprising. Fundamental policy reforms rarely succeed in Congress on the first attempt. The US antitrust reform movement will have to lengthen its time horizon and look to longer struggle to implement its agenda for digital industries.

The United States is not the only jurisdiction looking at competition policy reform for digital industries. The European Union has finalized its Digital Markets Act that would impose a series of ex-ante duties and prohibitions on tech companies. It would apply to digital companies with gatekeeper status, including electronic marketplaces, app stores, search engines, and social media companies. Among its duties, it would require a designated gatekeeper to allow third parties to interoperate with the gatekeeper's own services in certain specific situations, allow their business users to access the data they generate in their use of the gatekeeper's platform, allow companies advertising on their platform to carry out their own independent verification of their advertisements hosted by the gatekeeper, and allow their business users to tell their customers about the possibility of doing business outside the gatekeeper's platform. Among other prohibitions, it would not allow a gatekeeper to treat services and products offered by the gatekeeper itself more favorably in ranking than similar services or products offered by third parties on the gatekeeper's platform, to prevent consumers from linking up to businesses outside their platforms, or to prevent users from uninstalling any preinstalled software or app if they wish to do so.

On March 24, 2022, the European Parliament and the Council of Europe (representing the twenty-seven EU member states) reached a political agreement on the Digital Markets Act. The final text was adopted by the European Parliament and the Council on September 14, 2022, and was published in the *Official Journal of the European Union* on October 12, 2022. The legislation became applicable on May 2, 2023.[36]

In March 2019, Jason Furman (the former head of the Council of Economic Advisors under President Obama) and a team of competition policy experts issued a report requested by the UK government on unlocking digital competition. It recommended a code of conduct to promote fair digital competition to be developed and enforced by a new, specialized digital markets unit. Picking up on these recommendations from the *Furman Report*, the United Kingdom has proposed a digital markets unit to be housed in its competition agency, the Competition and Markets Authority, which would be responsible for regulating digital companies to promote competition. In July 2021, it issued a consultation on legislation to establish and empower this new digital regulator.

The digital markets unit would develop or enforce a code of conduct for digital companies with strategic market status. The code would consist of general regulatory principles, more specific regulatory objectives, and guidance for companies seeking to live up to the code. The objectives would relate to fair trading, open choices, and trust and transparency, and the regulatory principles would be more specific rules such as a general duty to trade on fair and reasonable terms and to provide clear, relevant, accurate, and accessible information to users. The guidance might specify that a default contract term would be unfair if compared to alternatives it imposed costs on the digital company's business customers that exceeded its benefits to them.

In addition, the digital markets unit would have the power to implement procompetitive interventions designed to open digital markets to greater competition. The digital markets unit would have broad discretion to devise and implement these interventions and would not be constrained to a specific list of remedies set out in legislation. These measures might include an affirmative duty for covered digital companies to interoperate with competitors or a functional separation to remedy conflicts of interest arising from a company engaging in commerce on the same platform it operates. The government recognizes that some of these procompetition tools such as mandating access to data, enforcing greater interoperability, changing choices and defaults for consumers, and imposing separation remedies come with significant policy and implementation risks.

The proposal goes beyond existing law by giving the digital markets unit the ability to engage in ongoing and proactive oversight of the industry. It includes the ability for the digital markets unit to enforce these measures through agreements with digital companies, directives to companies, financial penalties, and court orders.[37]

While the UK Parliament did not act on this proposal in 2022, the UK government announced that it is still government policy to do it "in due course" and "when Parliamentary time allows." In April 2023, the United Kingdom introduced the Digital Markets Competition and Consumer Bill, which contains these procompetitive reforms and would create and empower the Digital Markets Unit in the Competition and Markets Authority to implement and enforce them.[38]

Not much is to be gained by talking about these procompetitive measures in the abstract. Interoperability, for instance, would mean one thing applied to social media companies and something very different applied to electronic commerce marketplaces. So, the following discussions are focused on how to use these tools to address specific competitive problems as they arise in the core digital industries that are dominated by Amazon, Google, Apple, and Facebook.

Amazon's Antitrust Troubles

Even though Lina Khan had written a justly famous and previously cited law review article attacking Amazon's monopoly practices, and despite rumors of a possible case, she has not (as of 2023) taken advantage of her position as head to the FTC to pursue a case against Amazon.[39] But state attorneys general have.

In May 2021, the attorney general for the District of Columbia brought a case, alleging that Amazon's restrictions on merchant pricing on other marketplaces kept prices artificially high and hurt consumers. In 2022, the trial judge dismissed the case. The DC attorney general, with support from the US Department of Justice, has filed an appeal. In September 2022, Rob Bonta, California's attorney general, brought a similar case against Amazon, noting that Amazon's restrictions on merchant pricing practices on other websites would cost Californians "more for just about everything." The case is still at the trial stage.[40]

The European Commission is also concerned about Amazon's business practices. In November 2020, the European Commission sent a statement of objections to Amazon in connection with the company's use of its merchants' data to benefit its own retail sales operations. In July 2022, Amazon offered to restrict its use of merchant data and provide Amazon merchants with easier ways to reach its customers.[41]

Are these cases the best way to constrain Amazon's economic power? That depends on the problem to be solved. If the goal is to restrict the power that Amazon can accumulate by being a leading provider of services in several overlapping and adjacent markets, a full breakup into separate companies might be needed. This might very well require a complete overhaul of the company, requiring Amazon to separate out its different functions as retailer, marketplace, logistics provider, and cloud computing firm.[42]

A more focused problem is the conflict of interest that arises because Amazon is a merchant on its own marketplace platform. This conflict can play out in several ways: Amazon could give preference to its own products in search results, recommendations, and website design. It could use information from a third-party vendor's sales to plan its own product development strategy. It could pressure independent merchants to sell their operations to Amazon by undercutting their price and limiting their availability on the site until they accept a hostile buyout offer. It could give more favorable treatment to merchants who use its warehouse and delivery services.

So far, the antitrust cases in the United States and Europe have focused narrowly on Amazon's restrictions on merchant pricing flexibility and its use of merchant data. And the remedies suggested are simply to require that Amazon stop the offending anticompetitive practices. But, as we shall see in more detail below, broader measures that go closer to the heart of Amazon's power might be needed.

One of the broader solutions attacks the conflict of interest between Amazon's role as a platform and its role as a merchant on its own platform. Former Democratic presidential candidate Senator Elizabeth Warren wants to bar Amazon from being a merchant on any marketplace it operates. Khan also endorsed this approach, and it is contained in legislation passed by the House Judiciary Committee. Economist Hal Singer wants nondiscrimination rules instead, and they are embodied in another House bill. If both bills passed, the United States would be in the position of India, which has put in place both safeguards! Harold Feld has proposed strong data rules to prevent Amazon's abuse of its merchants. In this section, we'll review these proposed remedies to Amazon's conflict of interest. We will see how they are aimed at preventing abusive treatment of dependent businesses, rather than the creation of a new marketplace to compete directly with Amazon's marketplace, and how they all would require ongoing supervision of the company to prevent it from abusing its market position.

The structural separation approach, as described both by Senator Warren and in the House Judiciary Committee's bill, Ending Platform Monopolies Act, is less extreme than the full breakup aimed at controlling market power spread across several interlinked markets. The functional separation approach would prevent Amazon from being a merchant on the electronic commerce platform it operates. But this statement of the remedy is ambiguous. Its requirement could be interpreted in different ways: as a ban on selling store brands, as a requirement for separate operation of an online marketplace and an online store, or as a full separation or divestiture requirement.

Under the "store brand" interpretation of the separation rule, an operator of an e-commerce marketplace would be allowed to sell goods on its platform, but not its own store brands. The "separate operations" interpretation of the separation requirement would prohibit a platform from selling anything at all on the platform; it could not even be a vendor of other people's products on its own platform. But it could be an online merchant separately from the marketplace it operates—through its own distinct website, for instance, or by selling on another marketplace. A line-of-business restriction would be the strictest form of separation. It would be an absolute ban on a marketplace operator being a vendor anywhere; it would not be allowed to operate its own online store at all. If Amazon wanted to operate its own online retail store, it would have to sell its marketplace.

These interpretations differ in the level or strength of separation required and all have some basis in the text of Senator Warren's proposal and the House Judiciary Committee bill. But there is a trade-off: the level of protection from unfair business practices increases as the stringency of separation goes up, but so does the loss of the business efficiencies that motivated the combination. When these business efficiencies are dissolved, the losers might very well be the online merchants that the separation requirement is designed to benefit.

The danger of the separation requirement for independent vendors is the potential loss of Amazon's customer base. Much of the value of the Amazon Marketplace for independent merchants is access to Amazon's retail customers. Amazon's thriving digital marketplace is seamlessly integrated with its main retail shopping experience, which is regularly used by more than 115 million Amazon Prime shoppers. When merchants come to the Amazon Marketplace, they often see their sales double or triple. That is why they are flocking to Amazon. Amazon has 1.5 million active third-party vendors. More than 450,000 merchants joined Amazon in the first months of 2021, at which rate more than 700,000 merchants would join by the end of 2021. In the second quarter of 2021, 56 percent of paid units for the combined retail store and marketplace were sold by third-party sellers. These merchants would lose significant sales volume from a separation requirement that prevents them from accessing Amazon's customer base. If the price of protection from Amazon's predation is the loss of Amazon's customers, it might be too high a price for them to pay.[43]

For this reason, some antitrust practitioners such as Singer have urged a remedy of nondiscrimination rules to bar platforms from using their control of platform features to abuse dependent merchants. Under this standard, modeled after the statutory nondiscrimination rules for vertically integrated cable operators, a third-party merchant would not have to prove that Amazon's conduct caused a product price, quality, or output effect. It would have to prove only that it was discriminated against by the platform based on its lack of affiliation and, as a result, was materially impaired in its ability to compete effectively. This nondiscrimination proposal has a significant drawback, however. It would rely on expensive and uncertain case-by-case enforcement before a tribunal, where relief from abuse might arrive too late, if it arrives at all.

In contrast, the American Choice and Innovation Online Act would establish ex-ante rules barring specific discriminatory practices and would turn enforcement over to the FTC. It would impose a nondiscrimination standard on the larger electronic marketplaces, making it unlawful for them to advantage their own products or services, disadvantage those of another business user, or discriminate among similarly situated business users. The act would also bar a specific list of other discriminatory activities. The FTC would be empowered to enforce the requirement through a new bureau of digital markets, similar in concept to the United Kingdom's digital markets unit.[44]

A new nondiscrimination rule might be needed to guard against Amazon's ability to use a specific business user's sales data to choose what products to sell on its own. Reports that Amazon has done this are widespread and have prompted an investigation and a statement of objections from the European Commission. The American Choice and Innovation Online Act would specifically bar using sales data to support the offering of the dominant platform operator's own products or services. Public interest advocate Harold Feld proposes to ban the practice as one of the special data rules for digital platforms, modeled after the telecommunications privacy rules established in the Telecommunications Act of 1996.

But such a data rule must be crafted with some care. Amazon follows the common industry practice of using information about the sales in its stores to determine which products it wants to produce as private-label brands. If the company is allowed to sell private-label brands on its own marketplace, it should be allowed to engage in this routine practice that often provides consumers with less-expensive versions of everyday products. Retail giants such as Walmart produce private-label brands, and to a much greater extent than Amazon does. Fifteen percent of Walmart's revenue is from its private-label brands versus 1 percent for Amazon. Feld's ban on using consumer information to support sales planning appropriately contains an exception for the use of aggregated information.

But Feld applies the rule to all online marketplaces, Etsy, Shopify, and eBay, as well as the dominant one operated by Amazon, while the House bill applies it only to the large dominant marketplaces, not to the smaller platforms seeking to compete with the entrenched incumbent. An asymmetric version of that rule might apply only to Amazon, leaving other marketplaces free to negotiate arrangements with its vendors that might allow the data-sharing practice and give it a competitive advantage.[45]

The nondiscrimination approach has the advantage of flexibility and case-by-case adjudication and continues to allow Amazon and its merchant customers to enjoy the benefits of integration. But it risks enforcement difficulties. Even if the agency can bring cases on its own motion, to avoid putting too much of a burden on small merchants, the resources needed to police all possible complaints of abuse are likely beyond the feasible budgets of any digital regulator. The extent of day-to-day regulatory oversight might make it very difficult for the enforcing agency to thwart determined efforts to discriminate.

This leads to the pure separation requirement as a remedy for the enforcement difficulties of a nondiscrimination rule. It is often thought that a pure separation requirement has little or no need of regulatory supervision and, in that way, has an advantage over a nondiscrimination requirement. Senator Warren reflected this common view when she defended her structural separation fix by saying, "When you've just got a bright-line rule, you don't need the regulators. At that point, the market will discipline itself."[46]

Although that is a common view of structural separation as an antitrust remedy, it is wishful thinking. As we saw in the case of the AT&T breakup, structural separation and line-of-business restrictions need a specialist regulator for effective enforcement. This was also the case for the separation between commerce and banking and the separation of banking, securities, and insurance before the passage of the 1999 Gramm-Leach-Bliley Act.

The need for a regulator to supervise any structural separation requirement is especially strong in the case of Amazon. One problem is that after a separation under which Amazon kept its online store but sold its marketplace, Amazon and the new fully divested marketplace operated by a different company would have the same incentives to cooperate they had when they were affiliated and seamlessly integrated. They could recreate a mutually advantageous customer-sharing arrangement and its potential conflict of interest by contract instead of by administrative fiat. Regulators would have to determine whether the mandated separation of functions rules out or permits, for instance, the use of a common landing page and search function. The companies could devise a myriad of other possible business arrangements that might have consumer benefits but also create the same conflicts of interest the separation was designed to avert. Regulators would have to determine whether that was permitted or banned under the separation requirement.

India approached this question of whether to require separation or nondiscrimination by answering not either/or, but rather both/and. In its 2018 policy on foreign investment in e-commerce, India has put in place both the nondiscrimination approach and the separation approach. It prohibits e-commerce marketplaces from engaging in e-commerce on their own platform, and it also requires them to provides service to their vendors in a "fair and nondiscriminatory manner."[47] The idea of having a "belts and suspenders" approach is to ensure that the separated companies cannot collude to recreate the conflict of interest the separation was designed to avoid. If the United States combines the different antitrust reform bills into a single coherent reform package, it would be able to mimic this approach.

But a more cautious approach might be called for than requiring both remedies. The danger that separation would lose the benefits of integration to the detriment of both consumers and merchants is real. Why go there unless less drastic measures have failed? The UK government suggests its Digital Markets Unit should have the "flexibility to implement remedies in an incremental, proportionate, and coherent way," starting with "smaller interventions and considering their effectiveness before implementing more interventionist remedies where needed to address an adverse effect on competition."[48] This incremental approach would counsel, starting with nondiscrimination rules and then moving on (if necessary) to structural rules. Once it became clear that nondiscrimination was insufficient, a cautious way to impose structural separations would be careful sequencing. This cautious approach would first impose a bar on private-label brands, then structural separation between platform and commerce, and finally a full line-of-business ban being both a retail outlet and an operator of a marketplace. Climbing the ladder of increased stringency from nondiscrimination to full line-of-business restriction keeps in place the lower-level protections and adds to them as experience shows that the less stringent rules are ineffective at preventing abuse.

Reform legislation should give the enforcing regulatory agency the flexibility to mount the ladder of increasing controls rather than mandating a one-size-fits-all response in the legislation itself. Only with that kind of flexibility will the enforcing agency be able to craft rules responsive to the ever-changing dynamics of an industry still in the stages of rapid technological and business evolution.

A different competitive concern is that Amazon dominates the entire field of electronic commerce. Shouldn't antitrust aim at creating new competitors to Amazon, the way telecom regulation in the 1980s and 1990s aimed at creating competition to incumbent telephone companies? As of June 2022, Amazon accounted for 37.8 percent of the US e-commerce market. The distant second is the e-commerce outlet of Walmart, with a 6.3 percent share.[49] Merchants think of access to Amazon's huge customer base as a "must-have" condition of a successful online business. More alternatives are needed to give consumers and merchants genuine choices. Interoperability is a standard remedy in network industries to give users the benefit of network size and the advantage of choice among rivals.

While a common element of telecommunications regulation, interoperability is not generally available as a remedy for anticompetitive conduct or monopolization under the antitrust laws.[50] If policymakers want to require it for tech companies, they will have to pass legislation authorizing a regulatory agency to implement it. The House Judiciary Committee's bill, the ACCESS Act of 2021, would impose interoperability requirements on large online platforms, including electronic marketplaces.[51] The details are left to the FTC and its technical advisory committee. But any system of interoperability for electronic marketplaces would require extensive ongoing regulation if it is to have any chance of jump-starting competition to the Amazon Marketplace itself.

Interoperability for electronic marketplaces might mean that consumers looking for products on Amazon's marketplace would also be able to see offerings from merchants on other marketplaces, even though these merchants were not Amazon merchants. For merchants thinking that Amazon's conditions for using its platform are too onerous, this kind of interoperability would mean they could leave Amazon, join a new electronic marketplace, and still have access to Amazon's enormous consumer base.

But how would this kind of interoperability work in practice? How is Amazon supposed to get paid for providing marketplace services? Why would vendors become Amazon merchants—where Amazon takes up to 15 percent of the selling price as a commission—if they could join a different marketplace and sell on Amazon's marketplace without paying Amazon's fee? In principle, this matter of compensation could be handled through payments between the marketplaces. That is, each marketplace would set its own merchant fees, and then the marketplaces themselves would work out an arrangement for compensation when one of their merchants made a sale on the other's marketplace. This is roughly how telecommunications and internet backbone providers handle the exchange of their traffic. But Amazon, of course, has no interest in stimulating competition to itself, just as AT&T saw no reason to interconnect with its early telephone rivals. In the absence of regulation, Amazon would simply set an interoperability or interconnection price that was so high no one would take it.

Then there is the matter of what features would be available to non-Amazon merchants. Would they be part of Amazon's recommendation system? Could they advertise on Amazon's web page? Would they be eligible for Amazon's fulfillment and warehouse storage services? Could they use Amazon's one-click payment system? There is also the question of innovation. If Amazon discovers a new mechanism for bringing merchants and customers together, would it automatically be made available to non-Amazon merchants? These issues could be left to negotiations among the marketplaces, but once again Amazon would have no interest in setting the terms and conditions of access to these features in a fair and workable manner. Only a regulator could prevent the company from gaming the system and defeating the purpose of the regulation, which is to give alternative marketplaces a fair shot at competing with Amazon.

It is important to be realistic about the extent of the challenge in creating new competitive alternatives to Amazon itself. It might be that regulated interconnection among competing marketplaces is just too complicated even for a specialized, expert, and well-funded regulatory agency.[52] It might be that the digital regulator will, as a practical matter, be limited to defending the interests of dependent merchants relying on a dominant marketplace to reach their customers. This would be an invaluable and urgent service for the government to supply to these dependent merchants. But in either case, whether the goal is to jump-start competition to Amazon or to defend dependent merchants, it can be accomplished, if at all, only through the supervision and vigorous actions of a digital regulator.

The Google-Apple Mobile App Duopoly

Apple introduced the iPhone on January 9, 2007, at a time when the cell phone device market was led by Nokia and Research in Motion, the makers of the Blackberry. At first Apple did not operate an app store. Some apps were preinstalled on the iPhone, and users had access to apps that ran on the web through the Safari browser that Apple preinstalled. The App Store opened in 2008. Google quickly followed Apple into the mobile business, launching its own mobile operating system, associated browser, and app store in 2008. Soon, the two dominated the market. They also control the app distribution system as well, with both companies charging app developers up to 30 percent of the fees the developers charge their users.

Antitrust complaints allege that both companies use their control over their distribution outlets to raise prices to app developers and favor their own apps over rivals. Solutions include nondiscrimination rules, mandated sales through outside app stores or sideloading (downloading apps available on the web), and structural separations that would force the companies to choose between providing apps and running an app store.[53]

Competition authorities outside the United States are acting against this duopoly in mobile app infrastructure. In April 2021, the Australian Competition and Consumer Commission released an extensive report on the app marketplaces, concluding that Apple and Google have market power and recommending a series of improvements, including that consumers have the ability to change any preinstalled default app on their device, that app developers be allowed to provide consumers with information about alternative payment options, and that information collected by Apple and Google in their capacity as app marketplace operators be ring-fenced from their other operations.[54]

In June 2021, the UK Competition and Markets Authority began an investigation into whether Google and Apple's duopoly over the mobile ecosystem could hurt businesses and consumers. It covers operating systems (iOS and Android), app stores (App Store and Play Store), and web browsers (Safari and Chrome). In October 2021, it announced that it was launching a market study on the streaming music business focused on how mobile app stores and music streaming giants like Apple Music and Spotify operate in the United Kingdom. In June 2022, it concluded that Apple and Google have "an effective duopoly on mobile ecosystems" through their stranglehold on mobile operating systems, app stores, and web browsers on mobile devices. It is focusing on interventions related to mobile browsers and access to cloud gaming on mobile devices.[55]

In June 2020, in response to a complaint from the music streaming service Spotify concerning Apple's 30 percent commission on in-app purchases, the European Commission opened an investigation into Apple's use of its Apple Pay payment system. The investigation focused on the mandatory use of Apple's Apple Pay, its proprietary in-app payment processing system for the distribution of paid digital content (which comes with a 30 percent commission fee on in-app payments), and restrictions on app developers' ability to inform users of alternative payment outside the app. Apple considers these rules to be "anticircumvention" measures. In May 2022, the Commission sent a statement of objections to Apple in connection with these restrictions on payment alternatives. Separately, on April 30, 2021, the Commission sent a statement of objections to Apple over its treatment of music streaming services. The objections focus only on streaming music services and allege discriminatory treatment of competing apps. "They want all the benefits of the App Store but don't think they should have to pay anything for that," Apple said in a statement.[56]

Some countries have already acted to constrain the duopoly. In August 2021, South Korea passed a law requiring companies that operate app stores to let users pay for in-app purchases using a variety of payment systems.[57]

In September 2021, Apple settled an antitrust case in Japan against its bar on apps communicating with their users. In an agreement with Japan Fair Trade Commission (JFTC), Apple will allow subscription developers such as Netflix to tell users that they can sign up and manage service subscriptions through an external website.[58]

In December 2021, the Dutch Competition Authority ordered Apple to provide avenues for dating apps to use payment systems of their choice. After the competition authority fined Apple for noncompliance over a period of months, the agency accepted an adjustment of Apple's practices that satisfied its order in June 2021.[59]

Antitrust action against the app duopoly has taken place in the United States as well. In July 2021, a group of state attorneys general filed an antitrust complaint against Google, alleging that Google's technical and contractual restrictions on consumer access to apps through competing app stores and through independent sideloading were an illegal attempt to monopolize and maintain a monopoly in the app distribution market. The suit alleges that this market dominance allows Google to charge higher commissions on app store sales. The remedy sought is a court injunction to prevent this illegal conduct. Google responded that there are lots of alternatives outside Google's Play Store, and its rates are reasonable, comparable to other rival digital stores.[60]

Apple has not escaped antitrust scrutiny in the United States, either. In August 2021, Apple announced a handful of changes coming to the App Store in response to a class-action lawsuit from US developers. The key change is that developers can now communicate with users about alternative payment solutions outside of their applications.[61]

In 2021, the game developer Epic, maker of the popular game Fortnite, filed a private antitrust suit against Apple in the United States, alleging a variety of anticompetitive abuses centered on how Apple maintained its control over what apps are loaded onto its mobile devices through bans on sideloading and the use of other app stores, restricting what payment systems developers could use for in-app payments and constraining the ability of app developers to communicate payment alternatives to their users. In September 2021, the trial court exonerated Apple from most of the charges, including the allegation that it had a monopoly. But the court did find Apple's constraints on app developer communications with their users violated California state law, and it required Apple to allow app developers to link within the app to an outside payment method, without allowing alternative payment methods to be used within the app. The trial judge refused to stay this injunction during the appeals that both parties filed. The Department of Justice asked and received permission to present during the oral argument in October 2022, apparently concerned that the trial court's ruling, if left in place, could imperil the antitrust against Apple that it is reportedly preparing. But in April 2023, the Ninth Circuit Court of Appeals upheld the trial judge's ruling in its entirety, including its requirement under California law to allow app makers to direct customers to payment services outside of the App Store. Apple claimed a "resounding victory" in its campaign to show that its app store practices did not violate national antitrust laws.[62]

Despite these antitrust challenges to the anticircumvention rules that both Google and Apple use, they have a serious procompetitive business purpose. They prevent app developers from pretending falsely to be a free app on the app stores, thereby escaping any app store fees. App developers would very much like users to download their app for free from these stores, only to be told later through a link to a sign-up page, for instance, that there is a fee for using the app and they should go elsewhere to pay. If app developers could do this, they could pretend to be a free app for purposes of downloading the app and so escape any app store commission, when in fact they provided only a for-fee service. They would use the Google and Apple app stores for free to distribute their app and then collect an in-app payment through other means. The app stores anticircumvention rules prevent this outcome.

Banning these rules through US antitrust action would require distinguishing this case from an earlier Supreme Court decision that upheld Amex's similar anti-steering rule, which prevented merchants from urging customers to use a cheaper payment method. But this might not be very hard. The Amex decision was restricted to the transactions market where Amex cardholders received a tangible benefit from the anti-steering rule in the form of rewards for using the card. It is hard to see how the app consumer benefits from Apple's anti-steering rule.[63]

It is easy to see why app developers want to end-run the restrictions and fees imposed by the app stores. From the perspective of the app developers, the app stores are monopolists. As a practical matter, developers have to build apps for both Android and iOS if they want to reach more than half their potential users. An iOS app is essential to reach a large slice of the population. And an Android app is needed to reach the rest of the potential user base. App developers have no choice but to use both stores for distribution of their products. From the perspective of the users, the stores are also monopolist. They became locked into one of the two distribution services from the moment they chose their devices.

But that is not the way US courts appear to analyze the markets. The court decision in the *Epic v. Apple* case, for instance, clearly stated that Apple has no monopoly and, by implication, neither does Google. The trial court concluded, "The App Store competes against other platforms for both consumers and developers . . . neither consumers nor developers are 'locked-in' to the App Store for digital mobile game transactions—they can and do pursue game transactions on a variety of other mobile platforms and increasingly other game platforms." The idea is that the availability of the other app store means that neither app store has a monopoly.[64]

These antitrust complaints concerning the monopoly abuses of app distributors face a high hurdle of proof in today's antitrust courts. Moreover, remedies that would improve things for app developers might be hard to craft in a way that the courts would approve. Policymakers in Congress have introduced bills that would avoid this limitation of current antitrust law. One of the bills passed by the House Judiciary Committee, the Ending Platform Monopolies Act, would prohibit a large platform from owning a line of business that utilizes the platform "for the sale or provision of products or services." The implication is that both Google and Apple would have to either get rid of their app stores or stop producing apps that work on their mobile platform. This bill faces all the concerns described in the previous section on electronic commerce marketplaces and, in addition, faces privacy and security hurdles described below. As a result, the various nondiscrimination rules in another House Judiciary Committee bill—the American Choice and Innovation Online Act—might be a better way to start. This bill would require the app store companies to permit the use of competing app stores and sideloading.[65]

Legislation specifically targeting the app store duopoly is also under consideration. In August 2021, a bipartisan group of senators introduced legislation—the Open App Markets Act—that would require Google and Apple to allow their mobile operating system users to choose another app store, to install apps through means other than their app stores, and to delete any app or app store that they preinstall. In addition, the bill would prevent Apple and Google from requiring apps to use their own payment systems to collect their in-app fees, from requiring that in-app prices on its app store be equal to or less than the prices charged elsewhere, and from taking any punitive action against app developers if they use a different payment system and charge a lower price using it. Moreover, under the bill, Apple and Google are not allowed to prevent app developers from communicating with their users inside the app. It further bars them from using any nonpublic information to compete with app developers that use their app stores. A companion bill was introduced in the House. On February 3, 2022, the Senate Judiciary Committee approved the Open App Markets Act with an impressive bipartisan vote of 20–2. But the Senate failed to act on it before the end of 2022.[66]

In response to these antitrust actions and congressional pressure, both Apple and Google cut their app store fees. In November 2020, Apple cut its commissions from 30 percent to 15 percent for small developers. A year later, after the state attorneys general had filed their suit against Google's app store practices, after the House Judiciary Committee had passed the legislation that would open the app store business, and after senators had introduced the Open App Markets Act, Google also reduced its fees for many developers to 15 percent. The companies were clearly hoping to ward off further action to restrict their freedom to operate their app stores.[67]

The bills put enforcement authority in the hands of the traditional antitrust agencies, including the FTC. The agencies must still convince a court that company behavior violates the new standards in the reform bills. Consideration of what would be involved in effectively enforcing the bills' provisions reveals that the enforcing agencies need regulatory authority. The oversight required to enforce these restraints on business practices is beyond the capacity of the courts and generalist antitrust agencies.

A mandate that Apple and Google abandon their anti-steering rules, for instance, is not self-enforcing. Any reasonable implementation of that mandate would not force Google and Apple to allow app developers to use their app stores for free. Apple and Google could immediately start charging all app developers, or all apps with a certain number of downloads, not just those with in-app purchases, and a regulator would have to decide whether this was permitted under the new rules. Ongoing oversight of the business practices of all parties would be inevitable to prevent Google and Apple from extracting monopoly profits while still allowing them the ability to charge for the use of its app store and the flexibility to improve the service they offer to consumers and app developers through their control of the operating system and the app markets.

The real concern of the larger app developers is the price they must pay. They naturally think 30 percent of their own rates is too high and would like to pay less or nothing at all. But indirect methods of trying to control this price might very well prove ineffective. This suggests that the remedy is to allow an agency to control prices to app developers for use of the app stores. Price regulation is a tricky and convoluted matter with many opportunities for monopolists to game the system. If 30 percent is too high, what about 15 percent? Is that still too high? Airbnb charges its hosts 3 percent of their rental fees. Credit card companies charge merchants around 3–5 percent as a transaction fee. Are these reliable benchmarks for app store fees? It is hard to find a rational basis for a regulatory choice. In addition, as traditional regulators discovered, it is impossible to set a regulated price without also standardizing the regulated service. These difficulties appear insurmountable in the absence of sustained regulatory oversight, and that explains why reformers are seeking indirect means to accomplish the same result of lower prices for app developers. But at the end of the day some form of direct price regulation might be needed to prevent monopoly abuse, and this can only be administered by a sector agency not by a generalist antitrust enforcer.

The measures to allow non–app store distribution of apps also require the expertise of an industry regulator. Apple objects to any requirement to allow other means of distribution of apps that work with its operating system, claiming only absolute control over which apps are permitted onto its devices would preserve the integrity of its system and the privacy of its users. If users could download apps from non–app store sources, Apple would lose this control. Malware statistics seem to confirm the validity of this concern. According to the 2020 Nokia Threat Assessment Report that records malware threats to communications networks, Android devices were responsible for 26.64 percent of all infected devices, and the iPhone was at 1.72 percent. It attributed this differential to the fact that iPhone apps are available only from the App Store, while Android's open system allows third-party downloads. Nokia's 2021 report similarly concluded that "[a]mong smartphones, Android devices remain the most targeted by malware due to the open environment and availability of third-party app stores. Android devices make up 50.31 percent of all infected devices."[68] Any implementation of a requirement to open app infrastructure to alternative providers would have to accommodate this concern.

The reform bills seek to do this. The Senate app store bill would allow business practices that protect privacy and security, but these bills subject privacy measures to a review that mimics constitutional strict scrutiny. Apple would be required to show its restrictive business practices are applied on a demonstrably consistent basis, are not used as a pretext to exclude, or impose unnecessary or discriminatory terms on business users, and are narrowly tailored and could not be achieved through a less discriminatory and technically possible means. The House Judiciary Committee bill has a similar affirmative defense for companies seeking to protect privacy. It would be available if Apple or Google could show by clear and convincing evidence that a business practice "was narrowly tailored, could not be achieved through a less discriminatory means, was nonpretextual, and was necessary to . . . protect user privacy or other non-public data."[69]

This standard is an unusual way to treat privacy. Privacy is often thought of as a fundamental human right. Mere economic interests are supposed to give way before it. Prioritizing privacy would mean that these other interests can overcome a privacy claim only if the matter is urgent and the infringement on privacy is the least possible intrusion that will accomplish the urgent need.

But the tech reform bills reverse these traditional human rights priorities. Under their standard, a privacy claim can succeed against the mandated procompetition measures only if it can be shown by clear and convincing evidence that it is the narrowest exception necessary to protect user privacy.

To understand the issue that this narrow standard imposes on pro-privacy measures, consider how this standard would apply to Apple's new policy of requiring affirmative opt-in consent before users can be tracked using Apple's technology. Only 5 percent of Apple users voluntarily opt-in to being tracked, a result that might spell economic havoc for app developers and others who rely on targeted ads. This standard for assessing conflicts between competition and privacy built into the bills aiming to protect app developers from abuse by Apple would allow a challenge to the pro-privacy Apple opt-in rule. Such an opt-in rule, it could be argued, is more than is needed to protect user privacy because an opt-out would be less burdensome for the app developers and just as effective in protecting privacy. In effect, the procompetition measure is put in the same position as the First Amendment, requiring privacy measures to pass strict scrutiny. It is worth remembering that this standard allowed US West to successfully challenge the FCC's opt-in privacy rules as an infringement on the company's speech rights because the FCC-required opt-in meant that these rules were not narrowly tailored to achieve their privacy objective. Opt-out rules, the court said, were all that was needed.[70]

A better framework for harmonization is needed to accommodate the conflicting claims of privacy and competition without giving either priority. This accommodative approach recognizes an agency might promote competitive interests to the detriment of privacy interests and vice versa. The balance between opposing interests would likely be case by case, similar to a rule of reason analysis in an antitrust case, rather than in a one-size-fits-all prioritization of one set of interests over the others. As law scholar Erika Douglas says, this accommodative approach "grants equal billing to both areas of law. It automatically prefers neither."[71] The resolution of conflicts in particular cases might be quantitative: How much competitive benefit is gained for how much loss of privacy? The final chapter on the structure and responsibilities of the digital regulator has a further discussion of ways to impose on the agency a more nuanced standard for balancing conflicts between privacy and competition.

Regardless of which standard is the correct one, some balancing must take place to harmonize the needs of the procompetitive measures in these app store bills and the urgent privacy and security interests of app users. It is a task beyond the reach of the courts and the antitrust agencies and requires the expertise and ongoing supervisory role of an industry-specific regulator with a mission to promote both competition and privacy.

Google's Search Monopoly

Google's search monopoly has been the object of several antitrust inquiries in the United States and in Europe over the last decade. In 2013, the FTC dismissed charges against Google relating to favoring its own services in search results. The FTC thought it did not have enough evidence to take legal action against Google based on the specific allegations before it that the company biased its search results to hurt competition. The conduct the FTC commissioners reviewed seemed to them to have substantial procompetitive justifications.

In contrast, in 2017 in the Google shopping case, the European Commission ruled that Google had improperly favored its own shopping service in returning general search results, and it proposed fines for this anticompetitive behavior totaling €2.42 billion. The European Commission found that Google was dominant in the general search market and that its search favoritism was conduct forbidden for a dominant company under the European law banning the abuse of a dominant market position. Google complied with the injunction to treat competing price-comparison-ad services "no less favorably" than its own but appealed the decision and the fine. In November 2021, however, it lost its appeal to the EU's General Court in Luxembourg.

After the 2017 Google shopping case, the Commission was not done with Google. In July 2018, the Commission outlawed various Google practices relating to its Android operating system for mobile phones, and fined Google an additional €4.34 billion. The Commission condemned Google's requirement that phone manufacturers preinstall Google Search and Chrome as a condition for access to the Play Store, its payments to manufacturers to exclusively preinstall the Google Search app on their devices, and its rule barring manufacturers from access to preinstallation of Google apps if they sold any device that runs an incompatible version of Android. All these measures were illegal attempts to maintain its general search monopoly as search migrated onto mobile devices. Google appealed the decision, and in September 2021 it argued before the EU's General Court in Luxembourg that it should be overturned. In September 2022, however, the European General Court upheld the Commission's decision.

In March 2019, the Commission also found that Google abused its dominant position in the online advertising intermediation market through the use of exclusivity clauses in its contracts with business partners and fined Google €1.49 billion. The Commission found that Google is dominant in the online advertising search intermediation market with a market share above 70 percent from 2006 to 2016. Google ceased the illegal conduct when the Commission filed the statement of objections in 2016, but the Commission fined Google €1.49 billion for engaging in the abusive conduct from 2006 to 2016.[72]

In all, the Commission levied €8.3 billion in fines against Google over three years. And yet these repeated fines and mandates to change behavior have yet to alter appreciably the online search market. Google's worldwide market share is stable and above 90 percent. Its share of the European market is a constant 93 percent, well above its US market share of 88 percent, where competition authorities had done nothing.[73] After Google lost its appeal in 2021 in the comparison shopping case, companies aggrieved by the lack of equal treatment in vertical search markets wanted the European Commission to impose additional conduct remedies on Google—four years after the original decision.[74] It seemed clear that traditional antitrust enforcement was not the right tool for promoting competition in this market. The meager results from years of vigorous antitrust action prompted the European Commission to seek additional enforcement tools in its Digital Markets Act, proposed in 2020.

Despite the European experience, US antitrust authorities tried again in late 2020 to reel in Google's conduct in the general search market. In October 2020, the Department of Justice and fifteen state AGs filed a search complaint against Google. The theory of the case is that Google gets almost all the search inquiries, not because it is the best search engine, but because it has locked up all the avenues through which users access search engines, including preferred position as the default browser search engine. The complaint seeks to unwind these exclusionary deals and so give alternative search engines a crack at these preferred positions. The complaint seeks to establish traditional harm to ordinary consumers in the form of higher ad prices: "Every American suffers when Google imposes its monopoly pricing on the sale of targeted advertising." In addition, the complaint alleges a privacy harm, saying that Google's conduct has harmed consumers by "reducing the quality of general search services (including dimensions such as privacy, data protection, and use of consumer data)."

The DOJ complaint was followed quickly by a similar search complaint from thirty-eight state attorneys general filed in December 2020. This complaint repeats the DOJ allegations of anticompetitive agreements and adds that Google continues to impose anticompetitive restrictions on vertical search engines. The consumer harm is that "higher advertising prices are passed along to them."[75]

Google rejects these complaints. In December 2020, Kent Walker, Google's senior vice president of global affairs, said, "People use Google because they choose to, not because they're forced to, or because they can't find alternatives."[76] Excellence, he noted, is not the same as dominance. He added that paying for placement is a standard business practice, and it is easy to switch from Google to search engine alternatives such as Bing or DuckDuckGo. In April 2023, reports surfaced that

Samsung was considering replacing Google with Microsoft's Bing as the default search engine on its devices, perhaps because of Microsoft's integration of ChatGPT with Bing. Shortly thereafter, Google asked the presiding judge to dismiss the case, arguing that its admitted conduct did not violate the antitrust laws and that the advent of ChatGPT in search competitor Bing proved that competition in search was robust. The trial judge rejected these arguments, however, and allowed the case to proceed to trial.[77]

Google's biggest vulnerability in the cases is the payment it makes to Apple for favorable search positions. The DOJ complaint alleged that Google paid Apple between $8 and $12 billion a year for preferred positions on its devices and operating system. If search quality is the only thing that matters, why pay so much for shelf space? The antitrust enforcers, however, will have a hard time showing consumer harm. The price of search to the consumer is zero. The enforcers are clearly grasping at straws with the idea that all consumer products are priced higher because of Google's search monopoly.

Moreover, it might be hard to make a case that Google is blocking an innovative search alternative that is waiting in the wings. It is constantly upgrading and improving its own search technology, and for now Bing is the only other search product that indexes the web. It remains to be seen whether integrating the new AI content-generating software ChatGPT will significantly improve Bing's performance.[78] The upstart search product Neeva uses Bing's underlying search technology and is markedly inferior to Google. A default position on Apple devices would not help jump-start Neeva since it is a pay service that users must affirmatively sign up for.[79]

In addition, it is hard to imagine remedies that might make things better for consumers and competitors. It is certainly feasible to unwind the specific deals Google has constructed to guarantee its good placement for its search engine, but that would still leave its market position untouched and put the burden on search engines to try to match Google's unparalleled store of data that it uses to update and improve its search engine. The search complaint led by Phil Weiser, the attorney general of Colorado, argues that various restrictions on vertical search companies amount to illegal discrimination in pursuit of maintaining a monopoly—mechanisms of harm that artificially limit the ability of specialized vertical providers to acquire customers. It asks that they be enjoined. But the European experience suggests that remedies for search discrimination must be stronger than a simple injunction not to do it.

Bill Baer, a former antitrust enforcer at the FTC, summed up this sense that the antitrust tool might not be fit for purpose in this case, noting that "after-the-fact antitrust enforcement is not always the most timely and efficient way of dealing with markets dominated by one or a few competitors."[80]

So what is to be done about the Google monopoly? Behavioral remedies are certainly needed, but the extent to which such remedies would require ongoing supervision of the industry has not been fully appreciated. The details of the antitrust complaints show that the nature of the abuses resides in very minute business practices that can be fully understood only by people with experience with the industry. It is not reasonable to expect that generalist antitrust enforcers will be able to maintain on-staff experts with this level of knowledge. It is the kind of expertise that resides in agencies devoted to regulating a single industry such as the FCC, the SEC, the Federal Energy Regulatory Commission (FERC), and the banking agencies.

To be effective, legislation aimed at dismantling the Google search monopoly or protecting dependent rivals would have to authorize a specialist agency to monitor the industry and put in place rules that prevent Google as the dominant search engine from discriminating against vertical search rivals, or unfairly locking up priority display positions in the devices and operating systems people use to locate search engines.

The problem of discriminatory treatment might be beyond behavioral remedies. House Judiciary separations legislation calls for a ban on companies providing a platform and providing a service on that platform.[81] This separation requirement might extend to Google's general search and its vertical search services, since the primary way vertical search companies like Yelp reach their customers is through the Google search platform. The result could be that Google might not be able to offer specialized services in areas like shopping, restaurants, and travel.

This separation might control the risk of discrimination, but as we have seen before in the Amazon case, it would require regulatory supervision to ensure that the same prohibited conflict of interest could not emerge through contract. It also has costs to consumers who currently benefit from the integrated results they get through the single Google search site. If all travel searches resulted in referrals to travel intermediaries rather than to airlines, this extra step might be an inconvenience rather than a consumer service. The costs and benefits of requiring search separation cannot be determined in advance by legislators writing enabling statutes. It is exactly the kind of specialized decision that should be delegated to an expert industry agency for determination based on the facts after an appropriate in-depth investigation.

A further idea that might help promote direct competition with Google's currently dominant search engine is data sharing. Reform legislation could allow a regulator to mandate that Google make available its treasure trove of data derived from its billions of search queries and results so that entrepreneurs can train their own search algorithms. The key assumption in this proposed remedy is that the leading position Google has in search results makes its algorithm unbeatable. Scale matters in data analysis, goes the argument. Connections that are invisible with a thousand or a million data points suddenly become clear with a billion cases to analyze. When Google provides search results in response to a query and then observes which result users click on provides the company with an invaluable tool to improve its search algorithm. But it is significant only in the aggregate, and only Google has access to that aggregated data. If it were made available to potential competitors in real time, so goes the argument, then alternative search engines could catch up with Google and provide equally accurate search results. Users would have a variety of search platforms to use, a check against the failure of any one of them to provide good results. Each company would have a strong, competitive reason to improve its results as much as possible to stay ahead of the other peer search firms. Real alternative search engines would now genuinely be just a click away.[82]

This possible remedy is not merely hypothetical. The interoperability requirements of the ACCESS Act passed by the House Judiciary

Committee in June 2021 might mandate data sharing for search, depending on how the FTC implements these requirements. The European Commission's proposed Digital Markets Act requires this kind of data access through its requirement that large gatekeepers "provide to any third-party providers of online search engines, upon their request, with access on fair, reasonable and non-discriminatory terms to ranking, query, click and view data."[83]

Forced data sharing faces all the usual concerns connected to mandating cooperation with competitors. Why would Google continue to invest in high-quality search algorithms if the results of its efforts are immediately made available to its search rivals?[84] Drying up incentives for innovation might be mitigated in this case by noting that it is only the input data that is shared. Google's algorithm itself would remain a proprietary secret. The advantage given to competitors is only to access the results of Google searches so that they might train their own algorithms. If Google marshals its superior capacity for constant upgrading of its algorithm, which it claims (with good reason) that it does today, then it should be able to maintain its lead in search indefinitely.

But Google's investment in the construction of its database cannot simply be disregarded. Search data is useless for training search algorithms without access to the underlying index of the internet upon which it is based, and so this too must be made available to competitors. Google spends billions to index the internet in a comprehensive fashion, a survey far more complete than what Bing does. It must be compensated for the use of its data, rather than making it available for nothing as if the data just dropped from the sky at no cost at all to anyone. Such fair compensation is needed, for one thing, because requiring Google to make the data available for nothing might be a Fifth Amendment taking. For another, Google is a private company that can reallocate its investment to more productive uses (say, the metaverse!) if the rewards from its investment in indexing and search decline precipitously. The result would be an overall decline in search quality.

Data sharing will thus have to be priced, and it will have to be at a price set high enough to compensate Google for its investment and yet low enough to allow competitors to afford access to it. Such a Goldilocks price would have to be set by an expert industry regulator, who would have to solve the perennial difficult-but-solvable regulatory problem of how to set a proper price when there is no market to provide a benchmark on what people are willing to pay for a regulated product or service.[85]

Clearly, devising and implanting a data-sharing regime for search requires ongoing supervision and monitoring of the industry. The House bill calls for the FTC to take on this responsibility in conjunction with a permanent industry technical committee. But a larger problem looms in implementing this proposal. How can it be reconciled with the privacy interests of users? It is one thing for user search history to be known to Google; it is quite a bit more concerning for their search history to be available to any company interested in developing a search engine.

In the case of the related technique of data portability, discussed in the later section on social media, privacy could be preserved through affirmative opt-in. Under data portability, a user wanting to transfer data to another firm would be required to affirmatively ask a company to transfer it. The company wanting the data could not just reach in and take it without this user consent. But privacy safeguard will not work in the case of data sharing for search, where data must be transferred in bulk to be useful, and the process of getting affirmative consent from all users would frustrate the entire project. An opt-out choice might allow greater data sharing but at the expense of greater risk to user privacy.

A standard remedy for mitigating privacy risks in data use is anonymization, which requires the identity of the person to whom the data pertains is not revealed. But that would not work for search, where the point is often to return the results that are of interest to a specific user. Individualized user search history must be part of the data sharing to properly train alternative search engines. Pseudonymization of individual level data might mask the data to remove real identifiers. But the pattern of search history is often enough to uniquely identify individual users, or at least limit users to very narrow segments. To be effective in today's world, search must be personalized, and that cannot be done without effectively revealing key aspects of the identity of the searcher.

This leaves a final possibility of use restrictions to protect user privacy. This is an alternative privacy protection tool that is gaining more and more favor among privacy advocates convinced that the consumer choice model of privacy protection is broken. In this case, the data-sharing measure would restrict the use of the information shared for the purpose of developing search algorithms to that purpose alone and no other. It would not permit users to waive this prohibition. A variant would restrict use in this way unless the search engine received affirmative opt-in consent. This use restriction might be an effective privacy protection. But it would need to be supervised by a regulator since what activities count as developing a search algorithm and what mechanism for consent to use would need to be defined and particular cases adjudicated.

Now a different problem emerges: how to finance the new search engines. This privacy use restriction would prevent the most obvious form of financing a new competitive search algorithm—namely, targeted advertising. A new entrant might want to charge for its search services, the way Neeva does, rather than rely on targeted ads, but it is very hard to compete with free, especially when the free services are from an entrenched incumbent with a dominant market share and a long lead in developing high-quality search tools. The new entrant might make a business through contextual ads that are based only on the subject of the search query and nothing else, similar in concept to the traditional broadcast ads that focused on the likely interest of the audience. These ads raise fewer privacy issues but are not necessarily as lucrative. But Google chose the targeted ad business for a reason; it is far more attractive to advertisers and so likely to be far more profitable than contextual ads. If privacy considerations prevent competitors from using targeted ads as a revenue source, their incentive to enter the market to begin with might be too low, and search competition might never get off the ground.

These difficulties suggest that if data sharing is to be pursued, it should be an option for an implementing agency, rather than a legislative mandate. The agency might decide that data sharing poses insuperable risks to privacy and should not be imposed except as a last resort. The legislation might impose a standard for making this determination and for balancing privacy against competition in any implementation of the policy.

The standard for balancing the privacy interests of users with the competitive interests of new search entrants in the ACCESS Act's interoperability requirements appears to reflect the same prioritization of competition over privacy present in legislation to open the app markets. Interoperability gives way to privacy only when the privacy measure is "narrowly tailored . . . and does not have the purpose or effect of unreasonably denying access or undermining interoperability for competing businesses or potential competing businesses."[86]

As discussed earlier in the app store section of this chapter, and as described later in the chapter on the role of the digital regulator, this prioritization needs to be rethought. A more neutral posture is needed, one that accommodates both privacy and competition but prioritizes neither. No matter what standard is used, the judgment about the right balance between privacy and data sharing would have to be made on a case-by-case basis by an expert industry sector regulator. The details of implementation would overwhelm a general-purpose regulator such as the FTC with responsibility for the entire economy.

THE AD-TECH CONUNDRUM

The ad-tech industry is a complex network of interacting parts. It consists of ad exchanges, ad managers that serve the publishers that provide ad space on their websites, and ad-buying tools that service the advertisers who are seeking to place an ad on a website. Ad exchanges run the enormously complicated and unfathomably fast real-time bidding auctions that produce a sale. The ad exchanges link the ad servers that control website ad inventory—also called ad managers or supply-side platforms—with ad-buying tools, including demand-side platforms for large advertisers that allow advertisers to obtain ad space on websites. The supply-side ad server acts as the publisher's inventory management system and helps the publisher sell its ad inventory. The marketplaces or exchanges match buyers and sellers of display ads. The demand-side ad-buying tools are used by advertisers as their middleman to buy display inventory from exchanges.[87]

This complex ad infrastructure is under serious antitrust investigation and the subject of several antitrust enforcement actions. In December

2020, a group of US state attorneys general led by the Texas attorney general filed an antitrust complaint against Google alleging it had market power in the ad-tech market and had obtained and maintained this market power through various anticompetitive practices. It amended this complaint in March 2021, released an unredacted version of it in October 2021, and amended it still further in November 2021.[88]

The state AG complaint notes that publishers typically use a single ad server to manage all their web display inventory; using multiple ad servers would substantially frustrate a publisher's ability to effectively optimize management of their inventory and maximize revenue. For almost the entire market, Google's supply-side ad manager is that ad server. According to the state AG complaint, Google monopolizes this market with more than a 90 percent market share through its product called Google Ad Manager (GAM), which it acquired in a 2008 merger with DoubleClick.

According to this complaint, Google also owns and operates the largest display ad exchange in the United States, historically called the Google Ad Exchange or "AdX." It charges exchange rates higher than its competitors. The state AG complaint alleges that Google has a conflict of interest in managing both an ad server and an exchange and takes advantage of its position on both sides of the market to steer its ad-server business to the Google exchange, where it charges supra-competitive rates.

On the buyer side of the market, according to the complaint, Google operates the largest middlemen for large advertisers called DV360 and the largest buying tool for small advertisers called Google Ads. Google's exchange gives Google Ads and DV360 information and speed advantages when bidding on behalf of advertisers. Such preferred access helps explain why Google's ad-buying tools win the overwhelming majority of the auctions hosted on Google's dominant ad exchange, AdX.

Network effects operate at the level of ad exchanges, which are more valuable to the extent that they service companies on both sides of the market. Google takes advantage of these network effects using various strategies aiming to funnel traffic to its ad exchange from the services it controls on both sides of the market.[89]

All in all, the state AGs have a formidable case. In January 2021, Google responded that the ad-tech space is crowded, not dominated by a single provider, and its prices for publishers were reasonable.[90] In a blog on January 21, 2022, after the state AGs had updated their complaint twice, Google claimed that some allegations such as collusion with Facebook was mere assertion, lacking any real evidence, and said other charges were based on conduct that Google had ceased years ago and were legal in any case. At the same time, the company filed a motion to dismiss the case.[91]

In September 2022, the US District Court for the Southern District of New York largely rejected this motion to dismiss the case. It ruled, however, that the complaint did not plausibly allege illegal collusion between Facebook and Google, and it refused to consider injunctive relief against Google conduct that ended in 2019. The remainder of the case was allowed to proceed to discovery.[92]

Other antitrust actions against Google's ad-tech dominance are under consideration in the United States and abroad. In July 2022, reports surfaced that the US Department of Justice (DOJ) was considering its own ad-tech antitrust suit against Google and was seeking a divestiture of parts of Google's ad-tech business, while Google was prepared only to segregate the different ad-tech functions into separate divisions of the parent company. On January 24, 2023, DOJ sued Google and explicitly asked for a breakup of the company's ad-tech business.[93]

In June 2021, the European Commission opened an investigation into Google's ad-tech business, focused on whether it had favored its own online display advertising technology services in the ad-tech supply chain. In March 2022, in conjunction with the UK Competition and Market Authority, it opened an additional investigation into an allegedly illegal agreement between Google and Facebook to preserve Google's dominance. In October 2022, reports emerged that the European Commission was contemplating issuing a statement of objections and that it was in discussions with Google over a possible settlement.[94]

In May 2022, the United Kingdom's Competition and Markets Authority launched an investigation of Google ad-tech practices, including whether its operation of its ad exchange made it more difficult for rival ad servers to compete and whether its publisher ad server favored its own ad exchange. This followed an announcement in March 2022 of a joint investigation by CMA and the European Commission of the Google-Facebook agreement that was also raised in the US state AG case against Google.[95]

Ultimately, the courts will have to judge whether the claims of anti-competitive conduct are stronger than the defenses that Google can muster. But the key problem with these cases is not showing anticompetitive conduct; it is devising effective remedies.

The US state AG complaint asks for no specific remedies to end the anticompetitive conduct and restore a competitive market. It took months of investigation to uncover these alleged abuses, and there is no reason to think simply telling Google not to do it anymore will be effective in preventing the company from engaging in other abuses. Unless, that is, there is a serious ongoing effort of supervision that will make sure Google's future conduct does not improperly disadvantage competitors. The resources needed for such ongoing supervision are well beyond the feasible budgets of generalist antitrust regulators and are, in this case, even further from realization because the case is brought by state officials who have little capacity to engage in full-time monitoring of one of the biggest corporations on the planet.

This divestiture remedy proposed by the DOJ would effectively unwind the DoubleClick purchase from 2008 and spin off the ad platform that links publishers and advertisers. The result would be that the ad exchange, the publisher ad server, and the company serving the marketers would have to operate at arm's length. The thought is that this would allow greater ability of competitors to engage with the separated companies, and presumably this would lower prices for advertisers.

A breakup seems to avoid hard-to-enforce behavioral rules. As we have seen before, that's an illusion. An enforcing agency would have to ensure the abusive conduct does not reappear in the form of contractual arrangements between the separated entities. A dominant publisher-side ad server could say, for instance, that it works exclusively with one of the ad exchanges but not the others. Separation doesn't change or cure such dominance, nor the incentives of a dominant company to seek anticompetitive exclusive deals.

The DOJ could accompany its separation order with a nondiscrimination requirement, but then it would have to supervise that, and then agency is back to messy behavioral regulation. These behavioral rules could be effectively enforced only through full-time regulation, not through antitrust enforcers who bring a big case and then, win or lose, go on to other things.[96]

The new legislative measures that might be brought to bear to remedy the loss of competition in ad tech include many of the measures we have examined before. Nondiscrimination would prevent Google from privileging its own services, while separation would attempt to address the same self-preferencing problem through divestiture and line-of-business restrictions on the owner/operator of ad exchanges. At the end of the day, making sure procompetitive measures are effective would require a dedicated industry specialist. This would be even more necessary if price regulation was needed to protect dependent companies in ad tech, publishing, and advertising.

In many ways, the digital ad industry calls out for its own regulatory structure. It is the primary funding mechanism for the vast array of vital products and services available on the internet. It plays an infrastructural role in the internet economy akin to the role played by financial services companies in raising and allocating financial resources for the real economy. The proper functioning of this vital financing mechanism for the internet is as important to the country's overall economic well-being as it is to the safety and soundness of the financial sector.

The industry trade association, the Network Advertising Initiative, tries valiantly to develop and evangelize self-regulatory best practices for the industry, but in its current form it is not structured or authorized to play this role of infrastructure regulator.[97] Its efforts would be far more effective if backed by a real government regulator empowered by Congress to oversee and supervise the industry. One model for such a co-regulatory approach might be the Financial Industry Regulatory Authority (FINRA), the self-regulatory authority for broker-dealers that has rulemaking and enforcement power backed by the SEC.[98]

It is hard to think that the virtually invisible ad-tech world is so important to the country that it deserves its own regulator. But ad tech plays a vital role in today's economy and has its own unique complexities and contingencies. Congress should consider empowering the digital regulator to supervise and oversee this essential industry and in the process find a reasonable balance between the demands of promoting competition and protecting privacy.

A digital regulator would be in a good position to adjudicate the conflicting claims of privacy and antitrust in ad tech. One aspect of the state AG complaint highlights once again the tensions between privacy and competition that we have seen before. The state AG complaint attacked Google's Privacy Sandbox as an anticompetitive "ruse" because it would raise barriers to entry and exclude competition in the exchange and ad buying tool markets.

The Privacy Sandbox is a Google initiative that aims to replace tracking of individuals across websites and substitute cohort advertising that targets ads to users only as part of larger segments of users. On March 3, 2021, Google announced it would be removing third-party cookies from its Chrome browser. Earlier, Apple's Safari browser and Mozilla's Firefox had blocked cookies by default. But because Chrome had two-thirds of both desktop and mobile browser usage, and because it would not give users a choice about using cookies, Google's initiative would effectively end use of third-party cookies. Google also pledged to avoid any other technology for tracking individuals as they browse the web. In its place, Google proposed cohort tracking, whereby companies could use third-party ad services to target ads only to larger groupings instead of individual users. It argued that such a change is needed to respond to increasing privacy concerns about tracking of individuals across websites.[99]

US attorneys general sought to outlaw the Privacy Sandbox as anticompetitive. At a time when public sentiment against online tracking is at a high point, this would be an unfortunate and counterproductive role for antitrust. Antitrust action that seeks to lock the ad industry into yesterday's privacy-intrusive technology in the name of promoting ad-tech competition would only discredit the mission of antitrust. As

Wired's political editor Gilad Edelman said in his insightful 2021 article on a collision course between privacy and antitrust, "Just about everyone agrees that third-party cookies are terrible. It would be weird if Google was prevented from killing them in the name of antitrust law."[100]

Even though seeking to stop the Privacy Sandbox would be an antitrust overreaction, the Privacy Sandbox does pose competition challenges. In implementing it, Google might allow itself to have access to individual-level user web histories through Chrome while denying that opportunity to other ad service providers. This could be addressed by conditioning the implementation of Privacy Shield on nondiscriminatory safeguards and imposing a system of regulatory supervision to enforce them.

The CMA in the United Kingdom has also expressed concern about Google's Privacy Sandbox, and its sensible resolution of its concerns gives an indication of what might be involved in supervising the activities of the ad-tech giant to control anticompetitive conduct. At the behest of ad-tech competitors, CMA began a market investigation of Google's Privacy Sandbox in January 2021. Its concerns included discriminatory implementation. CMA promised to consult with the UK privacy regulator, the Information Commissioner's Office, to address any "legitimate privacy concerns," but it clearly suspected that the privacy issues were pretextual.[101]

In June 2021, however, the CMA obtained from Google certain commitments on how it will proceed in implementing its Privacy Sandbox. These commitments included a pledge to work with the regulator to "ensure that whatever emerges from Privacy Sandbox does not leave it with an unfair advantage." Google apparently accepted the idea that it cannot retain access to individual-level information about a Chrome user's web browsing history, while depriving its advertising rivals of access to this information. It also agreed to share information and consult regularly with CMA before implementation, creating a substantial system of regulatory supervision. With these commitments, CMA seemed prepared to allow Google to move forward with the Privacy Sandbox and remove support for cookies in its Chrome browser.[102] Shortly thereafter,

Google announced it would delay implementation of its plan to scrap cookies until late 2023.[103]

With this approach, CMA would become involved in close regulatory supervision over Google. This is all to the good. Such a supervisory approach could be enhanced in two ways. The first is through a sector agency, with responsibility for the entire online ad industry and a mission to promote and maintain competition there. The CMA simply has too broad a mandate as a general antitrust enforcer to devote the needed resources to monitor Google's ad-tech practices. Second, to make sure the privacy issues are given appropriate weight, this sector regulator should also be given the responsibility to promote and maintain privacy in the digital ad space. Given the tensions and synergies between privacy and competition in this vital digital sector, that regulator should also be given the job of finding regulatory measures that balance these policy objectives.[104]

The Australian Competition and Consumer Commission also expressed concern about Google's dominance in the ad-tech space. But its approach in its September 2021 report on ad tech illustrates even more starkly the conflict between privacy and competition. The thrust of the report was to back measures that make targeted advertising more effective through the promotion of competition among ad-tech suppliers. It recognized, however, that according to a 2020 privacy survey conducted by the Office of the Australian Information Commissioner more than half of Australian consumers do not like targeted ads and would probably look unfavorably upon measures to make them even more intrusive. Nevertheless, the agency sought authority to develop and enforce special rules to promote ad-tech competition, including data access requirements that would require Google to give other ad-tech companies access to the data it collects from search, Maps, and YouTube. It acknowledged that such a data access rule would not adequately protect consumer privacy and would conflict with existing Australian privacy law. It "hopes," however, that "technological developments" might resolve the conflict.[105]

The tension between privacy and competition in ad tech also manifested itself in the controversy over Apple's decision in 2021 to require mobile app developers to get affirmative user consent before using the

Apple identifier for advertisers (IDFA) to track users across the mobile web. The program went into effect as part of an iOS update in June 2021, and shortly thereafter, in July 2021, it had already produced a noticeable decline in online tracking—users gave iOS apps permission to track their behavior just 25 percent of the time. Not surprisingly Facebook, which relies on mobile tracking to deliver information to advertisers about sales resulting from ads, was upset. The advertisers themselves feared a marked decline in the efficiency of their ad efforts.

The results in September 2021 bore out this fear. Facebook, Snapchat, Twitter, and YouTube collectively lost almost $10 billion in ad revenue because of the Apple privacy changes. The losses continued in 2022. Snap Inc., which runs Snapchat, lost $422 million in the second quarter of 2022. Prices for online ads soared, and advertisers began to seek out other outlets for their ads such as streaming video.[106]

Naturally, advertisers and ad-tech companies sought government help against Apple's privacy push. But the avenue they chose for pursuing their grievance against Apple is revealing. In the United States, Facebook threatened to provide information for a government antitrust suit against Apple. In Europe, the industry went to the French competition authority, which considered and then rejected an antitrust complaint from advertising groups brought against Apple. In making this judgment, it received an opinion from the powerful French data protection authority, CNIL, on the privacy implications. In May 2021, the advertising groups were preparing to make a similar complaint against Facebook before the German competition authority.[107]

This use of antitrust enforcement to further the ad business agenda, regardless of the effect on privacy, indicates the extent to which some groups at least understand the depth of the tensions between privacy and competition. Naturally, competition authorities are alert to this attempt to misuse the powerful tools they have at their disposal. But the best way to counteract the potential for misuse by industry advocates is by giving industry regulators additional missions. They must be authorized to promote privacy as well as competition, to seek out policy measures that build on the many synergies between privacy and competition, and to avoid or mitigate to the greatest extent possible any tensions.

Facebook's Mergers

Facebook acquired Instagram in 2012 and WhatsApp in 2014. Both mergers were reviewed and approved by competition authorities in the United States and Europe. But critics, including Senator Elizabeth Warren, antitrust activist Dina Srinivasan, and the FTC, in an antitrust complaint charged that these mergers were an anticompetitive attempt to ward off nascent competition by buying the potential rivals. In the FTC's words, Facebook "resorted to an illegal buy-or-bury scheme to crush competition after a string of failed attempts to innovate."[108]

The FTC's antitrust complaint filed in August 2021 relied heavily on Srinivasan's theory that Facebook won its market share through competition on privacy, and then reaped monopoly profits in the form of consumer privacy invasions. The idea is that initially Facebook promised users better protection for their data than that provided by its early competitors Myspace and Friendster. Once it routed those rivals, it began to exploit user data more fully to please its advertising customers. When a competitive threat emerged, such as Google+, it halted its pace of increasing data usage for advertising purposes but then continued its intense data mining and profiling of its users as soon as the competitive threat waned. Now that it enjoys an undisputed monopoly, it is free to exploit its consumer data with no genuine constraint at all.

An example of privacy abuse related to market power is Facebook's requirement that its users allow it to collect data on their web histories outside their use of their core social media product. By making this a nonnegotiable condition of use, Facebook can combine data from the open web and its affiliated services, Instagram, and WhatsApp to construct ever more detailed profiles of its users' activity. One advantage of this all-but-universal tracking is that Facebook has reliable information about what goods its users might have bought on other websites after viewing an ad on Facebook and can give advertisers accurate information about the effectiveness of their ad campaigns.

But why would anyone agree to this intrusive surveillance unless they had no real alternative? Only a company with significant market power could make and enforce such an obviously anti-consumer condition of use. Srinivasan, the former digital advertising executive turned Facebook critic, makes the point clearly. "Who the heck consents to having a company track them across the internet," she says. "They could only do it because they had monopoly power to do something that clearly goes against consumer interests."[109]

Under this theory, the monopoly harm for consumers is not a monetary price increase, but an intangible "price" increase in terms of lost privacy. Unwinding the mergers, the theory goes, will free Instagram and WhatsApp from Facebook's control. If Facebook used its monopoly position to degrade privacy protections for its users, then it seems logical to expect that restoring competition through the remedy of retroactive divestiture will restore the lost privacy protections.

But this would expect too much from the case. The likely result of the proposed divestitures will be more choice and lower prices for advertisers, but not improved privacy for users. For the same reasons, those hoping for improved content moderation from the divestitures are likely to be disappointed.

An independent WhatsApp will be in the business of instant messaging, competing with free messaging services offered by Apple, Google, and Facebook itself. A spun-off Instagram will be a mobile photo-sharing app, competing primarily with the free services of Snapchat and TikTok. They will face fierce competition in these businesses, only now without access to Facebook's marketing support, user data, and most especially the powerful algorithms that can generate engagement and personalize advertising.

Crucially, these companies will continue to fund their businesses through advertising. As the House Antitrust Committee's report on digital markets noted, online markets are the site of ruthless competition for user data to cater to the insatiable appetite of advertisers for ever more targeted messages.[110] Other revenue models exist, but they all depend on charging the user, which is an enormously risky bet for newly spun-off companies competing with free alternatives. No one should expect a spun-off WhatsApp to revert to the privacy-friendly, advertising-averse start-up it was a decade ago.

The need to please advertisers will inevitably frustrate the widespread expectation that a Facebook breakup will lead to better privacy protections for users. True, there will be a one-time benefit for user privacy as Facebook's integrated database is ripped apart into separate profiles of WhatsApp, Instagram, and Facebook users. But each of these companies will rapidly rebuild their user profiles with new data and continue their efforts to exploit this data to personalize services and advertising.

This will be a boon for advertisers. Many of them, especially small- and medium-sized businesses and news publishers, are heavily dependent on Facebook to reach their customers, and they pay a premium for these advertising services. With Instagram and WhatsApp as two newly independent advertising outlets, they can expect a broader range of choices and some decrease in ad prices.

But if reinvigorated antitrust enforcement does succeed in bringing more competition to digital markets dependent upon advertising, this result might only worsen the competitive race to the bottom for user privacy. The solution to privacy violations in digital industries is not more antitrust efforts, but better privacy law.

More competition for social media will not help with content moderation issues either—and for the same reason. The need to generate user engagement to build ad profiles and personalize service is in tension with the goal of content moderation to limit harmful online conduct such as the spread of hate speech and disinformation. Separate measures to establish content moderation rules would be needed regardless of the state of competition in the marketplace.

The bottom line is that an effective regulatory regime for social media companies will require an agile digital agency empowered to protect privacy, preserve user content moderation rights, and promote competition in social media. Policymakers should not expect antitrust alone to do the job of regulating dominant social media companies to protect the public interest.[111]

Still, social media competition itself might be increased by a breakup, even if privacy is not thereby increased. Senator Warren proposed unwinding these Facebook mergers, and the FTC's amended 2021 antitrust complaint against Facebook asked the court for divestiture.

The prospects for a court-ordered divestiture are not good under existing antitrust law. Facebook has its own plausible version of its history—that it acquired and built up these platforms in ways that would have been impossible but for Facebook's support. In June 2021, a district court rejected the FTC's initial complaint for failure to properly establish Facebook's market power and was clearly skeptical of the narrative that it merged to crush competition. In August and September 2021, the FTC filed amended complaints, and the district court has allowed the case to proceed to discovery.

A key question is whether it is more important to unwind past mergers than to prevent harmful future ones. In January 2021, commentator Casey Newton warned against Meta's efforts to snap up all the biggest studios and talent in virtual reality and augmented reality, particularly its acquisition of Within, makers of the breakout hit subscription fitness app Supernatural.[112]

On July 27, 2022, the FTC fulfilled Newton's prediction by challenging Facebook's acquisition of Within, filing a complaint and request for preliminary injunction in the US District Court for the Northern District of California to halt the transaction. This complaint was a risky attempt to push the envelope of antitrust merger enforcement, alleging that Meta's acquisition is anticompetitive because Meta could have developed a fitness app to compete with Supernatural, which would have provided an additional alternative to users and spurred other developers to work harder to improve their own apps. "Instead of competing on the merits, Meta is trying to buy its way to the top," said FTC Bureau of Competition Deputy Director John Newman.

In the face of Meta's objections that its applications did not compete with those of Within, the FTC narrowed its case to concern only potential competition. On October 7, 2022, it acknowledged that current Facebook apps don't compete with Supernatural but continued to insist that Meta could and would compete with Supernatural if it were prevented from buying it. And this situation would benefit consumers.

A week later, on October 13, 2022, Meta filed a motion to dismiss the case. The company said the allegations of a loss of potential competition were speculative and without evidence. Moreover, it argued that under relevant Supreme Court precedent the FTC had not proved its potential competition case. For instance, to succeed, such a claim must show a failure of competition in the relevant market, in this case the virtual reality (VR) app market, and the FTC had not even tried to do that. On February 1, 2023, the trial judge declined to halt Meta's acquisition of Within while the case proceeded and shortly thereafter the FTC quietly abandoned the case.[113]

It was certainly a long shot for the FTC to seek to block this merger under current merger review standards. The FTC was clearly trying to use its existing antitrust authority to shape the development of the nascent metaverse industry to protect the public interest, and it was right to take on this risky case. But the outcome demonstrates it might not have tools fit for the purpose.

In the face of this uncertainty, it is worth looking at legislative reforms to merger standards that could help unwind bad mergers and give the agencies clear authority to prevent anticompetitive ones from ever happening. In June 2021, the House Judiciary Committee approved H.R. 3826, the Platform Competition and Opportunity Act of 2021, introduced by Representatives Hakeem Jeffries and Ken Buck. This bill would bar large digital companies, including Facebook, from merging with any company unless they can demonstrate that the company to be acquired does not constitute actual, potential, or nascent competition and that the acquisition would not enhance its market position. Under the bill, a merger that provides a digital company with access to additional data may enhance its market position, indicating that antitrust reviews should reject mergers leading to an excess concentration of data in the hands of the merged company. Under this prohibition, competition includes "competition for a user's attention."[114]

This bill might not require retroactive divestiture of Instagram or WhatsApp. It appears to be directed at preventing further similar mergers by substantially revising the current merger review standard under Section 7 of the Clayton Act and so might be relevant to the FTC's attempt to halt Facebook's Within acquisition. This current Section 7 standard forbids a merger when "the effect of such acquisition may be substantially to lessen competition, or to tend to create a monopoly."

Under this standard, antitrust authorities must prove an acquisition would have this harmful effect on competition before they can block or condition it. The House bill would reverse this burden of proof and bar a merger unless the merging party could show it would not harm actual, potential, or nascent competition.

The House bill goes a long way toward improving the merger review process for tech companies and might prevent future mergers that would crush nascent competition. It goes farther than other suggested improvements in merger review that would shift the burden of proof to the merging party to prove that the merger does not substantially impede competition. For instance, Senator Amy Klobuchar introduced a bill in 2021 that shifts the burden of proof to the merging party to show that a proposed merger is legal and revises the merger review standard to forbid mergers that "create an appreciable risk of materially lessening competition" rather than mergers that "substantially lessen competition," where "materially" is defined as "more than a de minimus amount."[115]

One improvement to the House proposed bill might be to expand the statutory merger standard so that it includes an assessment of whether the merger actually increases competition. The model for this recommendation is merger review by the FCC. The FCC reviews mergers when they involve the assignment and transfer of control of certain spectrum licenses and approves them only when it determines they serve the "public interest, convenience, and necessity." The FCC can and does apply traditional analysis relating to the loss of competition in its merger reviews, but it also must make a broader public interest determination. In particular, the FCC considers "whether a transaction will enhance, rather than merely preserve, existing competition, and often takes a more expansive view of potential and future competition in analyzing that issue."[116]

The effect of these changes in merger review standards would be to make it difficult and, in the case of the House bills focused on the larger tech companies, almost impossible for the tech giants to acquire start-ups in the same or neighboring lines of business. They would certainly put a dent in Facebook's plans to acquire companies for their expertise in the metaverse. The theory is that this would diversify innovation away from the incumbents and over time increase the incentives to innovate in the economy. If start-ups do not have to tailor their innovations to what would fit in with the business models of the current tech giants, they would be free to focus on more fundamental changes that might disrupt these business models. Innovation would be increased and incentivized to move in the direction of more fundamental change.

But these changes might also dry up some incentives for innovation. As Jay Ezrielev, the former economic advisor to former FTC chairman Joseph Simons, notes, "Deterring acquisitions of nascent firms would also limit exit options for investments in risky and innovative startups backed by venture capital. Limiting exit options of venture-backed startups may reduce investments in these firms."[117] Many companies start up with a clever new idea in the expectation that they will reap the rewards of their innovative activity through a buyout by an incumbent tech firm. They have neither the resources nor the skills to take the innovation all the way through to successful implementation as a viable marketable product or service. The incumbent firm acquires the innovative idea and commercializes it in a way that is beyond the capabilities of innovative start-ups. Once this exit ramp is eliminated through merger reform, innovators might choose to focus their efforts elsewhere. The net result might not be the dispersion of innovation in different directions, and to different marketplace participants, but an absolute decline in innovative activity.[118]

This concern counsels caution before moving ahead with merger reform that would dry up incentives for innovation. As communications scholars Sanjary Jolly and Victor Pickard have urged, the test for mergers in the digital world should "more closely resemble the FCC's traditional public interest standard, with a presumption against further consolidation."[119] But a more modest step forward toward this goal would be to embrace the revisions of the merger review standard proposed in the Klobuchar bill as the legislative approach for the digital regulator to apply to digital industries. If that proved ineffective in stemming the tide of problematic mergers in digital industries, further reforms similar to those in the House Judiciary bill can be considered. As in other areas such as antidiscrimination and separation measures to promote competition, an incrementalist approach might be the most prudent course of action.

One other issue needs to be addressed as well. The business lobbying group—the Chamber of Commerce—opposed the House digital merger bill on the grounds that it did not allow the enforcing agency to consider countervailing consumer benefits that might result from a merger.[120] The House bill seems to discount consumer benefits entirely, which is unrealistically one-sided. Merger review authorities should be allowed to consider evidence that a merger would directly and materially benefit consumers by strengthening existing competitors and allowing them to provide new and additional services to users. Lower prices and better service are not nothing and should count for something in merger reviews.

Privacy and Content Moderation in Digital Mergers

In addition to adjusting and strengthening the merger review standard under competition law, merger review for digital industries should be expanded beyond competition issues to include consideration of privacy and content moderation. The question of privacy in the context of merger reviews has been heavily discussed in competition policy commentary, content moderation less so. But the issues raised are similar. An examination of some high-profile digital mergers shows how limited antitrust authorities really are in considering other important issues such as privacy or content moderation in merger reviews.

In 2007, legal scholars and advocates started a discussion on the intersection of privacy and competition law and policy in the context of merger reviews. This discussion arose from the merger of Google and DoubleClick, and the possibility that the privacy practices of the merged entity could be cognizable under antitrust merger review.

At the time, privacy scholar Peter Swire offered the now-standard explanation of how merger reviews under competition law could accommodate privacy concerns. Without taking a position on the merits of the Google-DoubleClick merger, he argued that "privacy harms can lead to a reduction in the *quality of a good or service*, which is a standard category of harm that results from market power. Where these sorts of harms exist, it is a normal part of antitrust analysis to assess such harms and seek to minimize them."[121]

Privacy could be taken into account in merger reviews, in other words, as an aspect or parameter of competition. If companies competed on privacy, then the loss of this privacy competition could be considered a harm to consumers resulting from the merger. Former FTC commissioner Maureen Ohlhausen made the same point, saying, "Privacy therefore increasingly represents a non-price dimension of competition."[122]

This privacy issue must be distinguished from the question of continued availability of competitively valuable data after a merger. Different companies often have different datasets that enable them to compete effectively with each other. After the merger between the two, a single company would control the combined dataset, and this control might preclude any other company from effective competition. In effect, the merger might be a merger to a data monopoly where an adequate supply of relevant data is an essential resource needed for any company to compete in the market.

Antitrust authorities could block or condition a proposed merger if it would lead to a data monopoly. But the privacy issue is different. It concerns whether the merger and the combined dataset that would result from the merger threatens consumer privacy interests, not whether it threatens the ability of companies to compete using data.

In the 2007 review of the Google-DoubleClick merger by the FTC, FTC Commissioner Pamela Harbour argued that privacy as such fell within the scope of merger reviews. Google collected vast amounts of consumer data; DoubleClick did as well. The combined datasets could threaten consumer privacy, she felt.

She remarked, "We really do not know what Google/DoubleClick can or will do with its trove of information about consumers' Internet habits. The merger creates a firm with vast knowledge of consumer preferences, subject to very little accountability." She objected to the merger analysis used that relied on traditional antitrust principles because it "does not reflect the values of the consumers whose data will be gathered and analyzed." Traditional merger review contains "no adequate proxy for the consumers whose privacy is at stake." As a result, she preferred an approach that would "make privacy 'cognizable' under the antitrust laws, and thus would have enabled the Commission to reach the privacy issues as part of its antitrust analysis of the transaction."[123]

The FTC majority at the time, however, thought otherwise. It noted that "some have urged the Commission to oppose Google's proposed acquisition of DoubleClick based on the theory that the combination of their respective data sets of consumer information could be exploited in a way that threatens consumers' privacy." But it rejected the idea of blocking the transaction on privacy grounds. It noted that it was not authorized to intervene in transactions "for reasons unrelated to antitrust concerns, such as concerns about environmental quality or impact on employees" and emphasized that "the sole purpose of federal antitrust review of mergers and acquisitions is to identify and remedy transactions that harm competition."[124]

In saying this, the FTC was following binding Supreme Court precedent under which merger review under the antitrust laws is limited to competition issues. In *United States v. Philadelphia National Bank*, the Supreme Court ruled that the effect upon competition is the sole criterion to determine whether a merger violates Section 7 of the Clayton Act. The court held that the fact that the merger would increase employment in a particular city was irrelevant. More generally, the court rejected the idea that merger reviews should consider other "social or economic" effects of a proposed merger, saying that "a merger the effect of which 'may be substantially to lessen competition' is not saved because, on some ultimate reckoning of social or economic debits and credits, it may be deemed beneficial."[125]

In its review of the Google-DoubleClick merger, the FTC did take privacy into account in the only way it was able to under the antitrust laws. It asked: Did the merger represent a loss of desirable privacy competition? The FTC did an assessment of this question. Despite its view that the prevention of harm to competition is the sole aim of merger review, the FTC also "investigated the possibility that this transaction could adversely affect non-price attributes of competition, such as consumer privacy." It concluded that "the evidence does not support a conclusion that it would do so."

The FTC also investigated the related issue of a merger to a data monopoly. It looked at the possibility "that the combination of Google's database of user information and the data respecting users and competitive intermediaries collected by DoubleClick on behalf of its customers would give Google an overwhelming advantage in the ad intermediation market." It concluded that even after the Google-DoubleClick merger, competitors in the ad intermediation market would have access to the data they needed to compete. It said, "Neither the data available to Google, nor the data available to DoubleClick, constitutes an essential input to a successful online advertising product. A number of Google's competitors have at their disposal valuable stores of data not available to Google."[126]

The FTC approved the merger under the existing antitrust standards, taking privacy and data issues into account in the only way it could under these standards. But it did not make the privacy issue itself—that is, harm to consumer privacy interests—directly cognizable in its review.

Another case from the European Commission also illustrates the limitation of accounting for privacy issues under current antitrust review of mergers. In 2014, the European Commission reviewed and approved the proposed Facebook merger with the messaging service WhatsApp. It applied the standards we have just discussed: Would the merger preserve any significant privacy competition already present in the market? Would it give rise to a monopoly of competitively important data? It dismissed the data monopoly question by concluding that after the merger there would continue to be enough data available to advertising competitors. There would be, it found, no merger to a data monopoly.

Things were more complicated on the privacy question. The Commission noted the companies differed dramatically in their data privacy practices. Facebook operated its Messenger service with data gathering and analysis techniques that were highly intrusive and favorable to its advertising interests. In contrast, WhatsApp's privacy practices were much less privacy invasive since WhatsApp did not have a targeted advertising business model.

The only way the Commission could take this difference into account was to ask whether this difference in data practices made a difference to consumers. After an investigation, it concluded privacy was not an important dimension of competition between the messaging services. The main competitive differences were the functionalities offered and the size of the service's communications network. As a result, the Commission concluded there would be no significant underlying privacy competition to be lost by the merger, and it did not block or condition the merger on that basis.[127]

Going forward, any merger review that aims to address privacy under the current legal standards will have to engage in this messy, imprecise assessment of whether consumers make their purchasing decision exclusively or largely on the data practices of the companies they patronize. This assessment depends on evidence indicating whether another company is offering or is likely to offer more protective data practices and further evidence that this privacy dimension is a crucial basis for consumer choice. But this assessment is not likely to show substantial consumer privacy preferences revealed in marketplace behavior. For most consumers, differences in data privacy practices of the companies they patronize are not as important as the quality of the features that are the main business of the competing companies. Privacy is too often nice to have but not a must-have. Privacy competition, therefore, is a thin reed on which to hang the assessment of privacy interests in merger reviews.[128]

Nevertheless, Commissioner Harbour was on to something in her concern about the privacy dimensions of merger reviews. It is clearly relevant to an overall assessment of whether the merger is in the public interest. And yet, privacy per se cannot be taken into account directly under current antitrust merger review law. If policymakers want those conducting merger reviews to consider it, they must explicitly add it to the list of criteria a reviewing agency must consult in merger reviews.

Transaction reviews conducted by some specialized agencies are able to take issues other than competition into account. When the FCC reviews mergers, for instance, it is required to consider values other than competition, including ensuring a "diversity of sources of information" and "whether the transaction will affect the quality of communications services or will result in the provision of new or additional services to consumers."[129]

Just as the FCC reviews mergers for their effect on speech issues pursuant to authorization in its enabling statute, so the new digital regulator should be authorized to review tech mergers for their effects on privacy. This would allow the agency to block or condition mergers because of harmful effects on user privacy interests, even if these mergers might pass traditional antitrust review. Conversely, the agency would be able to approve mergers because of their positive effects on privacy practices, even if they would have been blocked or conditioned under traditional analysis.

Under this privacy review provision, the digital regulator would be fully empowered to condition, for instance, the Google-Fitbit merger on agreement by Google not to combine or link the Fitbit dataset with its existing user datasets. Merger review authorities are fully authorized under current law to impose this condition, but only to preserve or enhance competition. This need to preserve competition in ad personalization appears to be the basis for the European Commission's insistence that Google maintain data silos after its Fitbit acquisition. The Commission says its concern with the merger is that "by increasing the data advantage of Google in the personalisation of the ads it serves via its search engine and displays on other internet pages, it would be more difficult for rivals to match Google's online advertising services."[130] The basis for this merger condition under the new privacy merger review standard would be its necessity to mitigate the extra privacy risks to users from the combined dataset, not simply the need to preserve ad personalization.

For similar reasons, the digital regulator also should be authorized to consider content moderation issues directly in merger reviews. A merger might very well increase or decrease the level of resources devoted to content moderation above or below what could be devoted to that activity by the separate companies. The digital regulator should be able to take this into consideration when reviewing a potential digital merger, in addition to assessing any harmful effects on competition.

Consider, for instance, a possible merger between Facebook and the competing platform Parler. Ignoring for a moment that in some respects their content standards differ substantively, there is an enormous gap between the resources Facebook brings to bear on content moderation and those available to Parler. At one point in its history, Parler housed a large volume of specific threats of violence and death against named individuals and groups. Some examples include statements like "Death to @zuckerberg @realjeffbezos @jackdorsey @pichai," "White people need to ignite their racial identity and rain down suffering and death like a hurricane upon Zionists," and "HANG THAt N***** ASAP." Parler faced a backlog of twenty-six thousand reported posts that remained on the service. It relied entirely on "volunteers" to moderate content and so could not keep pace. In the comment section on one randomly selected post, roughly 10 percent of the comments "explicitly call for the murder of George Soros." Amazon removed Parler from its servers in January 2021, thereby cutting it off completely from the internet, in part because of this evident inability to engage in necessary content moderation to control these security risks to third parties.[131]

In assessing a proposed merger between Facebook and Parler, the digital agency should be authorized to take into account the likely results on the effectiveness of content moderation. This might cut against the competitive interest in preserving the independence of Parler and its capacity to offer an alternative to Facebook. The agency should be able to consider a company's record of violations of its own content moderation rules (twenty-six thousand unanswered complaints would be an obvious example of violation of these rules) and the likely improvement in compliance when assessing whether to approve a proposed merger involving the company.

This authority to conduct merger reviews for effects on privacy and content moderation in addition to competition does not grant the digital regulator unbridled authority to conduct a generalized assessment of the costs and benefits of a proposed merger across all policy spheres. The Supreme Court in the *Philadelphia National Bank* case cited earlier was rightly concerned about unbridled authority for an agency to consider whatever it wanted in merger reviews. Under the new authority granted to the digital agency to review mergers, it would not be authorized to assess the effect of a merger on the environment, worker safety, wage levels, racial discrimination, or a host of other worthy policy objectives.

Such generalized assessment of the effect of business practices or conduct on the common good should be beyond the reach of any regulatory agency. It is essentially legislative authority reserved for Congress. But neither should the agency be allowed to infer that a merger that passes a test for competition will always and everywhere improve matters in the other areas under the agency's jurisdiction—namely, privacy and content moderation. The agency should be authorized to reach a balanced judgment on proposed mergers taking into account competition, privacy, and content moderation.

To do this effectively, it must have exclusive jurisdiction over mergers in the digital industries it regulates. It might be possible for the traditional antitrust agencies to retain their existing authority to review mergers for anticompetitive effects, just as they do in the case of communications company mergers that also have to be approved by the FCC. But since the digital regulator would be fully authorized to enforce specific competition rules for digital industries, it makes little sense to duplicate the competition review through a generalized antitrust agency that lacks expertise in digital industries.

This issue of exclusive jurisdiction over merger reviews for the digital agency is discussed in more detail in the chapter on the nature of the digital regulator. In the transition period, where the FTC functions as the digital regulator, the issue would not arise, since the FTC would continue to have general merger review authority as well as authority to conduct digital merger reviews. After the transition to a separate digital regulator, the need to integrate and harmonize the different considerations of competition, privacy, and content moderation in merger reviews suggests the efficiency of concentrating review in the new digital agency rather than a more cumbersome and bureaucratic process of review by multiple agencies, where agencies might work at cross-purposes.

Data Portability, Interoperability, and Nondiscrimination for Social Media

Divestitures and stronger merger reviews might help to stimulate competition in social media services. In addition, two other interrelated remedies have been proposed to improve the ability of rivals to compete with dominant social media companies: data portability and interoperability. These measures promote competition by seeking to overcome the network effects that make a large social network so much more desirable to users than a small one. These network effects create consumer lock-in that prevents consumers from switching to an alternative social network, even if they find an attractive one.

Data portability would allow users to take their data with them to other social network providers. Horizontal interoperability is a stronger procompetitive requirement that would allow rival platforms to interconnect in the same way that different telephone networks carry each other's traffic. Vertical interoperability would allow app developers access to Facebook data and features to construct apps that compete with the same functions that Facebook itself provides to its users. Many tech reformers favor these measures to the extent that a digital regulatory authority determines they are the best, proportionate tools to enable effective competition in a digital market such as social media.[132]

But these procompetitive measures appear to be beyond the reach of antitrust remedies. In 2020 and 2021, the FTC asked for interoperability measures in its initial and amended complaints against Facebook. The FTC's theory was that Facebook operated a monopoly, and its refusal to interoperate with app developers who were seeking to compete with it in some service or feature was an illegal attempt to maintain this monopoly. The initial district court decision in 2021 rejected this remedy, however. Even though the FTC filed an amended complaint, the court's grounds for rejecting an interoperability remedy seem insuperable. In its green light for the case to proceed to discovery, the court reiterated its rejection of the interoperability remedy. Monopolies, said the court, have no general duty to deal with competitors and ruled that Facebook's refusal to interconnect with competitors was perfectly legal. Antitrust courts, it seems, are unlikely to adopt any of these procompetitive behavioral measures as remedies for Facebook's anticompetitive conduct. Congress must act if they are to be put into place.[133]

H.R. 3849, the ACCESS Act of 2021, would do this. It mandates data portability and interoperability for large platforms, including social media, to be implemented by the FTC after consultations with a technical committee composed of experts and industry representatives.[134] Considering how such measures could be implemented reveals that, once again, a specialist digital regulator would be needed at every step to ensure effective and beneficial application.

Data portability has a basis in competition law as well as privacy law. Implementing it has the potential to improve both areas, enabling consumer choice in social media companies and furthering their privacy interests by giving consumers greater control over their data. But limits on its utility as a competitive measure and threats to the privacy interests of other users means that the task of implementing a data portability measure is best accomplished by a digital regulator with a combined mission to promote both privacy and competition.

It is important to recognize, first, that data portability goes beyond data access, which is the right of data subjects to get a copy of all the data a company has concerning them. Data access has been a privacy right in Europe for many years. Data portability moves beyond it, providing a right of transfer and focusing on moving data from one provider of service to another, not simply on allowing data subjects to view, inspect, and download data that concerns them.

The European Union has incorporated data portability into its 2018 data protection law, the General Data Protection Regulation. The privacy rationale is that privacy has to do with users' control over their data, and so the law should provide them with the right to move their data to another provider and oblige companies to provide this capability of transfer. Data protection authorities have taken some implementation steps. They have, for instance, distinguished different kinds of data about users and set out a view on which data would be subject to the data portability right. They distinguish data that a user has directly provided to a company from data that the company observes about a user through the user's interaction with the service and distinguishes both from data that the company has inferred about the user. The right to portability, they say, applies to data users provide to a social media firm and the data social media companies gathered through observation of their users' interaction, but not to the proprietary inferences that the social media companies make based on provided and observed data.

Data protection authorities have also tried to address the conundrums that arise when social media data implicates other users such as joint photographs, lists of contacts, email chains, and social media interactions. In the first chapter, we saw that digital data is almost always inherently relational, concerning many data subjects at the same time, and this is especially true of data in social media where the entire point of the services is to involve many users in communication with each other.

Data protection authorities in Europe attempted to resolve the issues by allowing data subjects to transfer data that concerns both them and other parties without consent of the other parties, but with a condition. The condition they would impose to protect privacy interests of these other parties is that the company receiving the data cannot use data concerning these other parties for their own purposes. This might be little comfort, however, for these other users, who have just as much right to think that their side of interactions on social media are their data. A Facebook user whose data has been ported to Parler by one of his Facebook friends might want nothing to do with Parler and place little confidence in an agency's assurance that they cannot use it "for their own purposes." Substantially more experience with data portability in practice will be needed to determine whether this rough rule is adequate to protect the privacy interests of all users.[135]

In the United States, efforts to promote data portability are based primarily on its advantages in promoting competition. The analogy is often made to number portability, one of the procompetitive measures contained in the 1996 Telecommunications Act and implemented by the FCC. Number portability requires telecommunications carriers to enable users who switch carriers to continue to use their existing telephone number. Changing carriers would thus not involve the substantial inconvenience of informing family, friends, and business associates of a change in telephone number.

The analogy is also sometimes made to data transfers in the context of open banking measures, where customers can transfer their banking records to a potential financial competitor to make competition among banks and new financial entrants more effective. This analogy is useful, even though it has yet to be shown that open banking measures have stimulated banking competition where it has been implemented. Moreover, these open banking measures create security risks in the form of exposing users to hackers and phishing attempts that can only be mitigated by banking regulator supervision of the financial institutions involved, even the new entrants. Data portability in social media will have to be accompanied by similar regulatory oversight.[136]

The evidence that data portability by itself will promote social media competition is thin. A group of researchers at New York University found that likely Facebook competitors did not think data portability would help them get off the ground. The consensus was that "you cannot replicate Facebook with exported Facebook data."[137] The measure might have little practical utility as a procompetition tool.

As a result, policymakers might not want to make data portability a statutory mandate, as the ACCESS Act does. A statute should authorize a digital regulator to adopt the measure if it determines that it can advance competition and promote privacy in doing so, but that judgment should be left to the regulator, not made in advance by statute.

The limits of data portability as a procompetitive tool suggest the need for interoperability as a stronger way to overcome the network effects barrier to new social media competitors to Facebook. One version of interoperability would be vertical. It would treat Facebook's platform for applications for Facebook users as an open resource to be made available to all comers on fair and non-discriminatory terms and conditions. This vertical interoperability was one of the interoperability mandates that the FTC was seeking in its complaint against Facebook and which the court rejected as beyond the reach of antitrust remedies. The European Digital Markets Act suggests this type of vertical interoperability with its requirement that gatekeepers, including large social media platforms, "allow business users and providers of ancillary services access to and interoperability with the same operating system, hardware or software features that are available or used in the provision by the gatekeeper of any ancillary services."[138]

But open access and unbundling rules for Facebook are not self-enforcing. As we saw in the telecommunications industry, efforts to open networks through these measures need careful regulatory supervision if they are to be effective.

Consider what social media interoperability might mean. It might mean that users on a new entrant social network would be able to communicate with users on Facebook, sign up to receive content from these users, and ask to send them content, all without joining Facebook. For users dissatisfied with Facebook, interoperability like this would mean they could leave Facebook, join the upstart network, and have a reasonable chance of being able to keep in touch with their old group of family, friends, and business associates. This would be interoperability operating at the same level as the social media platform and aiming to generate horizontal competition to it through new entrants or expansion of existing social media companies.[139]

Making such a system work in practice would be extraordinarily difficult. The key question is defining what service is to be interconnected, what features will be shared alike among all providers of social media platforms. Telecommunication regulators had a crucial role in working with telephone companies to define the communications service that must be interconnected. But this task was relatively easy in the stable world of telephone service. Defining a standardized service in the evolving and fast-change social media business will be a moving target requiring constant vigilance and interaction with Facebook and potential entrants.

Social network platforms, for instance, allow users to engage in a range of activities other than simply sending messages. They can post a variety of audio and video content as well as messages in text form. They can link to other online material. They can send direct messages to a single other user or a subset of other users. They can form and join groups of users based on common interest and exclude others. They can play games and custom design their pages, they can make and edit as well as share videos, and they can buy and sell products and services. A core social media service generally provides a platform for a wide range of apps, some of which it provides itself and some of which are provided by third-party programmers. Which of those activities must be made interoperable? As in the communications industry, some authority working closely with the industry must ultimately define a standardized service to make interoperability practical.[140]

Moreover, interoperability comes with well-known disadvantages. Unless managed properly, interoperability standards may reduce differentiation and result in fewer functions and features for users. It might weaken the incentives to compete through innovation. By ruling out the idea that one company might win the entire market for itself, it discourages the vigorous competition to introduce new features and functions often seen in the early stages of digital industries as companies vie to dominate the market. Often innovation requires redesigning the old platform to create a modified one that is incompatible with the old one. Interoperability might prevent that sort of competition between incompatible systems, resulting in lock-in to an old and inferior platform. Implemented in the wrong way interoperability for social media companies might do more harm than good.[141]

In the evolving social media world, upgrades to basic platform service are occurring all the time. TikTok, for instance, developed an astonishingly effective algorithm for determining which short videos its users would prefer.[142] Snapchat initiated the feature of disappearing photos, but Facebook's Instagram replicated the feature and by 2017 had surpassed Snapchat's daily active user count. There was much criticism of Facebook's copying this innovation and some suggestion that Facebook should be banned from imitating its competitors' social media improvements.[143]

In a world of fully interoperable competing social networks, copycat innovation might be unnecessary because an innovative feature developed on one social media platform would be available to all of them. Upgrades can become common property of the underlying platform service, thereby making sure all users of the platforms benefit, not just the users of the innovative platform. Determining when an upgrade moves from being an innovative add-on to becoming a core platform functionality would require a judgment from an industry standards body supervised by a regulator.

The disadvantage of interoperable systems is that they weaken the incentives to innovate in the first place since the rewards for the innovation will be dissipated among the competing social networks. Snapchat spent the resources to develop its clever disappearing photos feature; TikTok invested heavily in its personalized recommendation engine. These innovative firms could be persuaded to donate their improvements to the common pool of standardized features only through a mechanism of compensation. To make the system able to evolve over time and integrate improvements, a regulator would have the additional responsibility of devising and managing a system that would give the innovator a fair and reasonable return on its innovation.

A fully integrated system for creating fifty Facebooks might produce standardized competition but stifle the urge to innovate. As with data portability, the most sensible way forward is not to mandate full social media interoperability, which would require legislators to predict the balance of costs and benefits into the indefinite future, but to authorize the digital regulator to impose the degree and kind of social media interoperability needed to promote competition and where the downside costs are justified by the procompetitive benefits.

A regulator must monitor any vertical interoperability requirement for Facebook for another reason—unconstrained access to Facebook's system poses privacy problems for Facebook users, as the world learned in the Cambridge Analytica case. In that case, Facebook allowed access to the information of friends and friends of friends in the social graph of Facebook users who had chosen to participate in an online game. By doing so, it allowed outside parties to profile Facebook users and feed them political ads based on these profiles. Facebook closed its completely open access system in response to that incident.[144]

Horizontal interoperability such as that required under the European Union's Digital Markets Act also posed privacy problems. A privacy-protective messaging app such as Signals encrypts user message content and metadata, while a competitor like Facebook's WhatsApp encrypts only message content. Signals, understandably, would welcome interoperability with other messaging services only if they adopted Signals's own privacy standards. Should they be forced to interoperate with a less privacy-protective app in the name of promoting competition?[145]

A regulator seeking to enforce an open access rule must decide when a restriction is a legitimate attempt to protect user privacy and security and when it is a pretext for anticompetitive exclusion. The details of such judgments are too complex and context-dependent to be legislated and would be beyond the competence of generalist antitrust enforcers and judges. The best way to ensure balanced decisions when privacy and competition are in tension would be to have them made by an expert regulator with authority to consider both privacy and competition.

Interoperability might also generate difficulties for social media companies seeking to monitor and moderate content. If interconnection means users outside of Facebook can target Facebook users with messages, it is possible that these messages would violate Facebook's content moderation policies. How can Facebook effectively enforce its content moderation principles under a system of interoperability?

It is possible for Facebook to monitor traffic coming in from an interconnecting social media platform such as Parler and apply the same algorithmic, human-review, and complaint processes that are used for content originating on Facebook and take whatever steps would be needed for Facebook-originating content. But often content moderation involves pattern analysis to detect groups of suspicious actors who might be involved in coordinated inauthentic behavior similar to spam. Some of this activity might take place entirely on another network, which Facebook would not be able to monitor. If Facebook cannot monitor content entirely on other networks, then it will miss many of the signals that could indicate a pattern of abusive conduct. Interoperability comes with some loss of efficiency in content moderation.

Other limitations would be needed to protect users and the public. To protect user privacy, social media companies might be barred from sending ads and recommendations to users on other social media platforms. How would targeted ads work in such an interoperable world? Companies with lax information security practices or that pose national security threats should not be allowed to take advantage of any interoperability rights.

None of this is to say that interoperability in social media is too complex and should be abandoned as a procompetition tool in that line of business. But implementation is not automatic or simple. Enforcing and implementing these complex permissions and restrictions in a balanced way so that interoperability does more good than harm would require an industry regulator with authority to write rules and supervise the conduct of the interoperating social media firms.

Similar issues arise with nondiscrimination rules for digital companies. These rules are embodied in a bill that passed out of the House Judiciary Committee in June 2021. They are also contained in the bill that passed the Senate Judiciary Committee in January 2022, with a bipartisan vote of 16–6. A revised version was prepared for Senate floor action.[146] Despite widespread support on both sides of the aisle, this nondiscrimination legislation did not pass either chamber in 2022.

The general thrust of these bills, both called the American Innovation and Choice Online Act, would be to ban dominant digital platforms from favoring their own services and products over those of their competitors. They would establish in law the attractive principle of fair competition that a digital platform may not compete with its own dependent business users through self-preferencing conduct that privileges its own affiliated companies.

The bill applies to all tech companies but presents a special challenge for social media companies in connection with content moderation. Provisions in the bills forbid platforms to discriminate among similarly situated business users, even if the platform itself does not directly compete with their products or services. The House Judiciary Committee nondiscrimination bill banned any platform conduct that "discriminates among similarly situated business users." Section 3(a)(3) of the revised Senate bill says platforms may not "discriminate in the application or enforcement of the terms of service of the covered platform among similarly situated business users in a manner that would materially harm competition." Depending on how they are interpreted and enforced, these provisions could hinder platform content moderation efforts to control hate speech and disinformation.

Suppose Facebook blocks content from the *New York Post* such as the Hunter Biden story it blocked just before the 2020 election that attempted to discredit Joe Biden's bid for the presidency. Or perhaps, as

Twitter did at the time, Facebook blocks the news outlet entirely. How is the *New York Post* supposed to compete effectively with the *New York Times* when it has lesser or no Facebook distribution? So the bill as written gives the *Post* a cause of action against Facebook for discrimination. The *Post* could argue plausibly that it is "similarly situated" to the *Times* with respect to Facebook since they are both news outlets in the same local market that depend on Facebook's distribution for ad revenue and readers. It could further argue that Facebook's application of its terms and conditions discriminates against it in a way that would materially harm competition—it provides full distribution to the *Times* and other local media publications but denies it to the *Post*.

This ban on discrimination against similarly situated business users is simply too broad as written. The motivation might have been to prevent platforms from engaging in anticompetitive practices accomplished through contract rather than through ownership or control. Platforms could give special preferences to independent companies that paid extra for certain platform services, while withholding these services from other similarly situated companies. In the extreme, they could offer exclusive arrangements to one independent company that provides goods or services on their platform and shut out all others. Ruling out discrimination among similarly situated business users would seem to prevent that kind of anticompetitive platform conduct accomplished through contractual arrangements instead of ownership.

If the focus is to prevent anticompetitive practices accomplished through discriminatory contracts with business partners, the sections of the bill banning discrimination could be expanded to forbid discrimination involving "business partners." But not all exclusive arrangements with business partners are anticompetitive, even for monopoly platforms. It is very hard to craft an effective and narrow statutory prohibition against anticompetitive platform arrangements with business partners, and the vague language in these bills certainly didn't do it.

The revised Senate provision has an additional flaw. The Senate provision seems to address only anticompetitive discrimination accomplished through the application or enforcement of terms of service. But a platform could discriminate in other ways. It could, for instance, sign contracts for carriage with some providers of pornography but refuse to carry other providers, while having nothing in its terms of service that explicitly banned pornography.

Moreover, enforcing a provision against anticompetitive discrimination in content moderation would inevitably involve enforcing authorities in second-guessing platform content moderation decisions. A platform could defend itself against any enforcement action charging anticompetitive discrimination in the application of its pornography ban, for instance, by arguing that some content providers were allowed on the platform because they lived up to its content standards against pornography, while others routinely did not. Resolving that issue would put the enforcing agencies right in the middle of deciding whether a platform's actions constituted legitimate enforcement of its content moderation rules and which amounted to anticompetitive discrimination.

The dangers of doing this should be obvious. As Free Press noted at the time, the revised Senate language would allow state or federal enforcers to block social media content moderation efforts, "claiming that what tech companies rightly define as hate speech, incitements to violence, or vaccine disinformation is really just competing political or health information that must stay up."[147]

In response to conservative concerns about discrimination in content moderation, state legislatures have already passed laws that echo the Senate provision's ban on content moderation discrimination. Florida's content moderation law, which was invalidated in 2022 by a federal district court in Florida on First Amendment grounds, would have required social media companies to enforce its terms of service "in a consistent manner among its users on the platform." A Texas content moderation law, which was upheld by an appeals court in 2022, would have barred social media companies from removing or otherwise limiting content based on the user's "viewpoint." These measures are discussed in more detail in chapter 4.

Without a doubt, if the ban on content moderation discrimination in the Senate bill becomes law, the state attorneys general in Florida and Texas, who have an enforcement role under the bill, would waste no time using it to accomplish the content moderation restrictions sought in these state laws.

None of this means that the nondiscrimination bills should be abandoned. They can and should be revised to respond to content moderation concerns and still deal effectively with obvious and long-standing competitive abuses in digital industries. The key improvement in the bills in connection with nondiscrimination rules, as in the case of data portability and interoperability measures, is the establishment of a digital regulator for implementation. Prohibited discrimination cannot be defined once and for all in statute; it must be clarified by a regulatory agency capable of promulgating trade regulations that define the specific conduct that digital companies must avoid. Dealing with privacy and content moderation issues will be a key part of the implementing regulations.

These intersecting issues of promoting competition, preserving privacy, and facilitating effective content moderation need a nuanced legislative approach. As Congress deals with these issues it must accommodate interests other than promoting competition. It must establish a regulatory structure that provides for competition, privacy, and effective content moderation for digital companies and a regulatory agency to keep any conflicts in balance as it enforces and implements these new laws.

Coda

The narrative of the core digital industries reviewed in this chapter has an arc. In each case, an initial competitive phase gave way to industry domination by one or two players. Left to themselves, these markets will concentrate and stay concentrated.

This result affronts a common and attractive vision of the proper functioning of markets as consisting of a myriad of companies competing for consumer business and providing them with genuine alternatives. If policymakers accept the desirability of having many small companies providing service in digital markets, they will have to adopt specific measures to introduce and maintain competition in the face of natural industry forces that will resist attempts to deconcentrate the market. In the meantime, while measures to introduce competition are being tried, policymakers must also put in place safeguards to protect dependent businesses from abuse by the digital companies with market power.

Antitrust authorities are taking steps to accomplish both goals through complaints brought against Facebook, Google, and Apple. An Amazon case might not be far behind. But these cases are unlikely to produce the desired results, in part because of the uncertainties and resource constraints of large monopolization cases but also because of inherent limitations on available remedies under the existing antitrust laws.

For this reason, policymakers in the United States and in Europe have begun a reform effort. The key elements are measures to separate digital platforms from commerce on the platforms they operate, measures to ensure fair and nondiscriminatory treatment of dependent businesses, and measures for data portability and interoperability. These measures would create new standards for the enforcement agencies to use when they bring actions in court against tech companies. To be effective, however, a regulatory agency must be empowered to write and enforce rules specifying which tech industry practices were illegal.

Implementation would also require balancing the procompetitive measures and what they could reasonably hope to accomplish against the damage that might be done to other important social values, especially privacy and good content moderation.

Competition policy, even in the vigorous form advocated in this chapter, cannot automatically provide protection from the non-economic harms in the area of privacy and free speech. Carl Shapiro, a leading antitrust economist and former antitrust official in the US Department of Justice, summed up the limitations of antitrust and the need for policy laws in other areas:

> *Antitrust is not designed or equipped to deal with many of the major social and political problems associated with the tech titans, including threats to consumer privacy and data security, or the spread of hateful speech and fake news. Indeed, it is not even clear that more competition would provide consumers with greater privacy, or better combat information disorder: unregulated, competition might instead trigger a race to the bottom, and many smaller firms might be harder*

to regulate than a few large ones. Addressing these major problems requires sector-specific regulation.[148]

In the next two chapters, we look at what needs to be done to promote privacy and content moderation in digital industries.

Notes

1. Andy Slavitt, "How Facebook Ruined Everything (with Kara Swisher)," *In the Bubble* podcast, November 8, 2021, https://lemonadamedia.com/podcast/how-facebook-ruined-everything-with-kara-swisher.

2. Mark Scott, "Lessons from the Android Antitrust Battle," *Politico Digital Bridge*, September 2, 2021, https://www.politico.eu/newsletter/digital-bridge/politico-digital-bridge-rt-in-germany-washingtons-digital-tax-fight-online-child-safety.

3. Daniel Marans and Kevin Robillard, "How Joe Biden Became a Trust Buster," *Huffington Post*, July 27, 2021, https://www.huffpost.com/entry/how-joe-biden-became-a-trust-buster_n_60ff432de4b073351629b701?31.

4. Lina M. Khan, "Amazon's Antitrust Paradox," *Yale Law Journal* 126, no. 710 (2017): 718, https://www.yalelawjournal.org/note/amazons-antitrust-paradox.

5. Thurmond Arnold, "The Test Is Efficiency and Service—Not Size," in *The Bottlenecks of Business* (Fairless Hills, PA: Beard Books, 1940); Alan Brinkley documents this Second New Deal turn away from economic concentration and toward consumer-focused antitrust enforcement in Alan Brinkley, "The Anti-Monopoly Moment," in *The End of Reform* (New York: Vintage Books, 1995), 106–22.

6. Furman et al., "Unlocking Digital Competition," 2.

7. Michael J. Sandel, *Democracy's Discontent* (Boston: Harvard University Press, 1996), 265.

8. Sandel. *Democracy's Discontent*, 241–47; Khan, "Amazon's Antitrust Paradox," 739–44; Tim Wu, *The Curse of Bigness* (New York: Columbia Global Reports, 2018), 45–68.

9. Wu, *The Curse of Bigness*, 68–72.

10. Sandeep Vaheesan, "Fair Competition Policy Without a Fair Competition Philosophy," *Law and Political Economy*, November 1, 2021, https://lpeproject.org/blog/fair-competition-policy-without-a-fair-competition-philosophy.

11. Quoted in McCraw, *Prophets of Regulation*, 124; Lina Khan, "The New Brandeis Movement: America's Antimonopoly Debate," *Journal of European Competition Law and Practice* 9, no. 3 (March 2018): 131–32, https://doi.org/10.1093/jeclap/lpy020.

12. Khan, "Amazon's Antitrust Paradox," 739–46; Joshua D. Wright, Elyse Dorsey, Jonathan Klick, and Jan M. Rybnicek, "Requiem for a Paradox: The Dubious Rise and Inevitable Fall of Hipster Antitrust," *Arizona State Law Journal* 51, no. 293, https://arizonastatelawjournal.org/wp-content/uploads/2019/05/Wright-et-al.-Final.pdf; Herbert J. Hovenkamp, "Whatever *Did* Happen to the Antitrust Movement?" Faculty Scholarship at Penn Law, 2018, https://scholarship.law.upenn.edu/faculty_scholarship/1964.

13. Verveer, "Platform Accountability and Contemporary Competition Law."

14. Fiona Scott Morton, quoted in Julia Angwin, "The Many Monopoly Cases Against Google," *The Markup*, October 15, 2022, https://themarkup.org/newsletter/hello-world/the-many-monopoly-cases-against-google.

15. FTC v. Facebook, "US District Court for the District of Columbia," June 28, 2021, 33–50, https://storage.courtlistener.com/recap/gov.uscourts.dcd.224921/gov.uscourts.dcd.224921.73.0.pdf.

16. Khan, "Amazon's Antitrust Paradox," 797–802.

17. Quoted in Sandel, *Democracy's Discontent*, 248.

18. This account of the early telephone history derives from Starr, *The Creation of the Media,* 191–230; Leonard Hyman, Edward DiNapoli, and Richard Toole, *The New Telecommunications Industry: Meeting the Competition* (Dumfries, VA: Public Utilities Reports, 1997), 83–163; F. M. Scherer, "Technological Innovation and Monopolization," Faculty Research Working Paper Series, John F. Kennedy School of Government, Harvard University (Oct. 2007), 13–20, https://papers.ssrn.com/sol3/papers.cfm?abstract_id=1019023; and Milton Mueller, *Universal Service: Competition, Interconnection, and Monopoly in the Making of the American Telephone System* (Washington, DC: AEI Press, 1997). Richard R. John discounts the significance of AT&T's interconnection strategy in an alternative view; see his *Network Nation: Inventing American Telecommunications* (Boston: Harvard University Press, 2015). Tim Wu traces early telephone consolidation to the intentional strategy of AT&T executives. See Wu, "Mr. Vail Is a Big Man," in *The Master Switch.*

19. Tim Wu, "Broken Bell," in *The Master Switch*; Joseph D. Kearney and Thomas W. Merrill, "The Great Transformation of Regulated Industries Law," *Columbia La Review* 98, no. 1323 (1998), https://scholarship.law.marquette.edu/facpub/296.

20. Robert Cannon, "Where Internet Service Providers and Telephone Companies Compete: A Guide to the Computer Inquiries, Enhanced Service Providers and Information Service Providers," *CommLaw Conspectus Journal of Communications Law and Technology Policy* 9, no. 1 (2001): https://ssrn.com/abstract=274660.

21. Scherer, "Technological Innovation and Monopolization," 20–24; Verveer, "Platform Accountability," 10–14; Joseph Kearney, "From the Fall of the Bell System to the Telecommunications Act: Regulation of Telecommunications under Judge Greene," *Hastings Law Journal* 50, no. 1395 (1999): 1403–20, https://scholarship.law.marquette.edu/cgi/viewcontent.cgi?article=1503&context=facpub; Khan, "The Separation of Platforms and Commerce," 1049–51.

22. Verizon Communications Inc. v. Law Offices of Curtis V. Trinko, 540 US 398 (2004). The introductory sections provide a good overview of the scheme of the Telecommunications Act of 1996.

23. Keach Hagey, Amol Sharma, Dana Cimilluca, and Thomas Gryta, "Converging Destinies," *Wall Street Journal*, October 21, 2016, https://www.wsj.com/articles/at-t-is-in-advanced-talks-to-acquire-time-warner-1477061850; see also Steven Colbert's funnier version of the reintegration of the telephone system, "Stephen Colbert Explains AT&T," https://blog.techstaffer.com/colbert-report-explaining-atts-history?hs_amp=true.

24. Paul Starr, "The Great Telecom Implosion, The American Prospect," September 8, 2002, https://www.princeton.edu/~starr/articles/articles02/Starr-TelecomImplosion-9-02.htm.

25. Stephen Breyer, "Antitrust, Regulation and the Newly Liberated Marketplace," *California Law Review* 75, nos. 1005 and 1007: https://www.jstor.org/stable/3480665; Alfred E. Kahn, "Deregulatory Schizophrenia," *California Law Review* 75, no. 1059 (1987), https://www.jstor.org/stable/3480667; Kearney and Merrill, "The Great Transformation"; Tim Wu, "Antitrust via Rulemaking: Competition Catalysts," *Colorado Technology Law Journal* 16, no. 33 (2017), https://scholarship.law.columbia.edu/faculty_scholarship/2056.

26. Al Kramer, "A Lesson from the Landmark AT&T Breakup: Both a Sector-specific Regulator and Antitrust Enforcers Were Needed," Public Knowledge, May 2022, https://publicknowledge.org/wp-content/uploads/2022/05/A-Lesson-From-the-Landmark-ATT-Breakup_Both-a-Sector-specific-Regulator-and-Antitrust-Enforcers-Were-Needed_Al-Kramer_Public-Knowledge_May-2022.pdf.

27. Paul Freiberger and Michael Swaine, *Fire in the Valley: The Making of the Personal Computer*, 2nd ed. (New York: McGraw Hill, 2000); Martin Campbell-Kelly, *From Airline Reservations to Sonic the Hedgehog: A History of the Software Industry* (Los Angeles, CA: Semiotexte/Smart Art, 2004); Alfred Chandler, "The Computer Industry: The First Fifty Years," in David Yoffie, ed., *Competing in the Age of Digital Convergence* (Boston: Harvard Business School Press, 1997), 37–122; D. C. Mowery, "The Computer Software Industry," in D. C. Mowery and R. R. Nelson, eds., *The Sources of Industrial Leadership* (New York: Cambridge University Press, 1999); Thomas Cottrell, "Microcomputer Platforms," in Larry Duetsch, ed., *Industry Studies* (New York: M. E. Sharpe, 2002); David Evans, Albert L. Nichols, and Bernard Reddy, "The Rise and Fall of Market Leaders in Personal Computer Software," in David Evans, ed., *Microsoft, Antitrust and the New Economy: Selected Essays* (New York: Springer, 2002), 265–85; Michael Katz and Carl Shapiro, "Antitrust in Software Markets," in Jeffrey Eisenach and Thomas Leonard, eds., *Competition, Innovation and the Microsoft Monopoly: Antitrust in the Digital Marketplace* (Philadelphia, PA: Kluwer Academic Publishers, 1999), 29–80.

28. Scherer, "Technological Innovation and Monopolization"; Verveer, "Platform Accountability," 14–19; United States v. Microsoft Corp., 253 F.3d 34 (D.C. Cir. 2001), June 28, 2001 (Microsoft III), https://www.justice.gov/atr/case-document/opinion-1.

29. Harry First and Andrew I. Gavil, "Re-Framing Windows: The Durable Meaning of the Microsoft Antitrust Litigation," *Utah Law Review* 641 (2006), https://ssrn.com/abstract=950515; Steven Lohr, "5 Lessons from Microsoft's Antitrust Woes, by People Who Lived It," *New York Times*, June 23, 2019, https://www.nytimes.com/2019/06/23/technology/antitrust-tech-microsoft-lessons.html; Richard Blumenthal and Tim Wu, "What the Microsoft Antitrust Case Taught Us," *New York Times*, May 18, 2018, https://www.nytimes.com/2018/05/18/opinion/microsoft-antitrust-case.html.

30. Elizabeth Warren, "Here's How We Can Break Up Big Tech," Medium, March 8, 2019, https://medium.com/@teamwarren/heres-how-we-can-break-up-big-tech-9ad9e0da324c; House of Representatives, Committee on the Judiciary, Subcommittee on Antitrust, Commercial, and Administrative Law, "Investigation of Competition

in Digital Markets, Majority Staff Report and Recommendations," 2020, https://judiciary.house.gov/uploadedfiles/competition_in_digital_markets.pdf; Ending Platform Monopolies Act, H.R. 3825, 117th Cong. (2021); ACCESS Act of 2021, H.R. 3849, 117th Cong. (2021); American Choice and Innovation Online Act, H.R. 3816, 117th Cong. (2021); Platform Competition and Opportunity Act, H.R. 3826, 117th Cong. (2021).

31. Open Markets Act, S. 2710, 117th Cong. (2021).

32. American Innovation and Choice Online Act, S. 2992, 117th Cong. (2021).

33. Morton in "The Many Monopoly Cases Against Google."

34. Fiona Scott Morton, "Letter to Senators Klobuchar and Grassley on the American Innovation and Choice Online Act," July 7, 2022, https://som.yale.edu/sites/default/files/2022-07/AICOA-Final-revised.pdf; Marcy Gordon, "House Approves Antitrust Bill Targeting Big Tech Dominance," Associated Press, September 29, 2022, https://apnews.com/article/2022-midterm-elections-technology-business-lobbying-congress-6e49cfc65668b99c633647898d114a8b; Margaret Harding McGill, "How Democrats' Big Plans for Big Tech Shrunk to Tiny Steps," Axios, October 14, 2022, https://www.axios.com/2022/10/14/democrats-big-tech-regulations-tiny-steps.

35. Josh Sisco, "White House Antitrust Adviser Tim Wu Set to Depart," *Politico*, December 30, 2022, https://www.politico.com/news/2022/12/30/tim-wu-leaving-white-house-00075859.

36. European Commission, Digital Markets Act, October 2022, https://competition-policy.ec.europa.eu/sectors/ict/dma_en; Regulation (EU) 2022/1925 of the European Parliament and of the Council of 14 September 2022 on contestable and fair markets in the digital sector and amending Directives (EU) 2019/1937 and (EU) 2020/1828 (Digital Markets Act), October 12, 2022, https://eur-lex.europa.eu/legal-content/EN/TXT/PDF/?uri=CELEX:32022R1925&from=EN.

37. Jason Furman et al., "Unlocking Digital Competition: Report of the Digital Competition Expert Panel," United Kingdom, Chancellor of the Exchequer, March 13, 2019, https://assets.publishing.service.gov.uk/government/uploads/system/uploads/attachment_data/file/785547/unlocking_digital_competition_furman_review_web.pdf; UK Department for Digital, Culture, Media & Sport and Department for Business, Energy & Industrial Strategy, "A New Pro-Competition Regime"; United Kingdom, Department for Digital, Culture, Media & Sport and Department for Business, Energy & Industrial Strategy, "Response to the CMA's Market Study into Online Platforms and Digital Advertising," November 27, 2020, https://www.gov.uk/government/publications/government-response-to-the-cma-digital-advertising-market-study.

38. UK DCMS and UK BEIS, "Response to the CMS's Market Study"; UK DCMS and BEIS, "A New Pro-Competition Regime"; Secretary of State for Digital, Culture, Media & Sport and the Secretary of State for Business, Energy & Industrial Strategy, "Government Response to the Consultation on a New Pro-Competition Regime for Digital Markets," May 2022, https://assets.publishing.service.gov.uk/government/uploads/system/uploads/attachment_data/file/1073164/E02740688_CP_657_Gov_Resp_Consultation_on_pro-comp_digital_markets_Accessible.pdf; Tom Smith, "The UK's Digital Markets Unit: We're Not Making Any Progress, But We Promise We Will

'In Due Course,'" *Platform Law Blog*, May 10, 2022, https://theplatformlaw.blog/2022/05/10/the-uks-digital-markets-unit-were-not-making-any-progress-but-we-promise-we-will-in-due-course; Molly Killeen, "UK Introduces Bill to Push Forward Digital Competition Reform," EURACTIV, April 25, 2023, https://www.euractiv.com/section/competition/news/uk-introduces-bill-to-push-forward-digital-competition-reform.

39. Dana Mattioli and Brent Kendall, "FTC Prepares Possible Antitrust Suit Against Amazon," *Wall Street Journal*, February 3, 2023, https://www.wsj.com/articles/ftc-prepares-possible-antitrust-suit-against-amazon-11675438256.

40. Office of the Attorney General for the District of Columbia, "AG Racine Files Antitrust Lawsuit Against Amazon to End its Illegal Control of Prices Across Online Retail Market," May 25, 2021, https://oag.dc.gov/release/ag-racine-files-antitrust-lawsuit-against-amazon; Rebecca Klar, "DC Attorney General Pushes to Revive Antitrust Lawsuit Against Amazon," August 25, 2022, https://thehill.com/policy/technology/3615430-dc-attorney-general-pushes-to-revive-antitrust-lawsuit-against-amazon; Karen Weise and David McCabe, "California Files Antitrust Lawsuit Against Amazon," *New York Times*, September 14, 2022, https://www.nytimes.com/2022/09/14/technology/california-files-antitrust-lawsuit-against-amazon.html.

41. European Commission, "Antitrust: Commission sends Statement of Objections to Amazon for the use of non-public independent seller data and opens second investigation into its e-commerce business practices," November 10, 2020, https://ec.europa.eu/commission/presscorner/detail/en/ip_20_2077; Adam Satariano, "Amazon Moves to End a Long-Running Antitrust Case in Europe," *New York Times*, July 14, 2022, https://www.nytimes.com/2022/07/14/business/amazon-europe-antitrust.html.

42. Monica Nickelsburg, "Breaking Up Amazon: Is It Even Possible? Imagining the Tech Giant Under a US Antitrust Crackdown," GeekWire, March 12, 2019, https://www.geekwire.com/2019/breaking-amazon-even-possible-imagining-tech-giant-u-s-antitrust-crackdown.

43. Stephanie Chevalier, "Number of US Amazon Prime Subscribers 2013–2019," Statista, July 7, 2021, https://www.statista.com/statistics/546894/number-of-amazon-prime-paying-members/?_ga=2.211424661.1471702243.1629650940-1168300728.1629650940; "Number of Sellers on Amazon Marketplace," Marketplace Pulse, August 22, 2021, https://www.marketplacepulse.com/amazon/number-of-sellers; Stephanie Chevalier, "Amazon Third-Party Seller Share 2007–2021," Statista, August 11, 2021, https://www.statista.com/statistics/259782/third-party-seller-share-of-amazon-platform.

44. Hal Singer, "Inside Tech's 'Kill Zone': How to Deal with the Threat to Edge Innovation Posed by Multi-Sided Platforms," *ProMarket*, November 21, 2018, https://promarket.org/inside-tech-kill-zone; American Choice and Innovation Online Act, H.R. 3816, 117th Cong. (2021), sections 2(a) and (b).

45. European Commission, "Antitrust: Commission Opens Investigation into Possible Anti-Competitive Conduct of Amazon," press release, July 17, 2019, http://europa.eu/rapid/press-release_IP-19-4291_en.htm; European Commission, "Commission Sends Statement of Objections to Amazon for the Use of Non-Public Independent Seller Data and Opens Second Investigation into Its E-Commerce Business Practices," press

release, November 2020, https://ec.europa.eu/commission/presscorner/detail/en/ip_20_2077; Dana Mattioli, "Amazon Scooped Up Data from Its Own Sellers to Launch Competing Products," *Wall Street Journal*, April 23, 2020, https://www.wsj.com/articles/amazon-scooped-up-data-from-its-own-sellers-to-launch-competing-products-11587650015; Harold Feld, "Mind Your Own Business: Protecting Proprietary Third-Party Information from Digital Platforms," *Public Knowledge*, July 6, 2020, https://www.publicknowledge.org/documents/mind-your-own-business-protecting-proprietary-third-party-information-from-digital-platforms/; Mark MacCarthy, "Reflections on Special Data Rules for Electronic Marketplaces," *Forbes Washington Bytes*, July 21, 2020, https://www.forbes.com/sites/washingtonbytes/2020/07/21/reflections-on-special-data-rules-for-electronic-marketplaces/#74193a233389.

46. Nilay Patel, "Elizabeth Warren Wants to Break Up Apple, Too," The Verge, March 9, 2019, https://www.theverge.com/2019/3/9/18257965/elizabeth-warren-break-up-apple-monopoly-antitrust.

47. Indian Ministry of Commerce and Industry, "Review of Policy on Foreign Direct Investment (FDI) in E-Commerce," December 26, 2018, https://pib.gov.in/newsite/PrintRelease.aspx?relid=186804.

48. United Kingdom, Department for Digital, Culture, Media & Sport and Department for Business, Energy and Industrial Strategy, "A New Pro-Competitive Regime," 35.

49. Stephanie Chevalier, "Biggest Online Retailers in the U.S. 2022, by Market Share," Statista, August 26, 2022, https://www.statista.com/statistics/274255/market-share-of-the-leading-retailers-in-us-e-commerce.

50. Verizon Communications Inc. v. Law Offices of Curtis V. Trinko, 540 US 398 (2004).

51. ACCESS Act of 2021, H.R. 3849, 117th Cong. (2021).

52. Randy Picker, "Forcing Interoperability on Tech Platforms Would Be Difficult to Do," *ProMarket*, March 11, 2021, https://promarket.org/2021/03/11/interoperability-tech-platforms-1996-telecommunications-act.

53. Dimitrios Katsifis, "New Paper on the App Store Shows Why Antitrust Intervention Is Needed," *Platform Law Blog*, September 21, 2020, https://theplatformlaw.blog/2020/09/21/new-paper-on-the-app-store-shows-why-antitrust-intervention-is-needed.

54. Australian Competition and Consumer Commission, "Dominance of Apple and Google's App Stores Impacting Competition and Consumers," April 28, 2021, https://www.accc.gov.au/media-release/dominance-of-apple-and-google's-app-stores-impacting-competition-and-consumers.

55. Competition and Markets Authority, "CMA to Scrutinise Apple and Google Mobile Ecosystems," press release, June 15, 2021, https://www.gov.uk/government/news/cma-to-scrutinise-apple-and-google-mobile-ecosystems; Competition and Markets Authority, "CMA Plans Probe into Music Streaming Business," press release, October 19, 2021, https://www.gov.uk/government/news/cma-plans-probe-into-music-streaming-market; Competition and Markets Authority, "CMA Plans Market Investigation into Mobile Browsers and Cloud Gaming," June 10, 2022, https://www.gov.uk/government/news/cma-plans-market-investigation-into-mobile-browsers-and-cloud-gaming.

56. European Commission, "Commission Opens Investigation into Apple's Use of Apple Pay," June 2020, https://ec.europa.eu/commission/presscorner/detail/en/ip_20_1075; European Commission, "Antitrust: Commission Sends Statement of Objections to Apple over Practices Regarding Apple Pay," May 2, 2022, https://ec.europa.eu/commission/presscorner/detail/en/ip_22_2764; European Commission, "Commission Sends Statement of Objections to Apple Over Treatment of Music Streaming Services on App Store," April 30, 2021, https://ec.europa.eu/commission/presscorner/detail/en/ip_21_2061; Dimitrios Katsifis, "EU Sends Apple Statement of Objections (music streaming services)," *Platform Law Blog*, April 30, 2021, https://theplatformlaw.blog/2021/04/30/eu-sends-apple-statement-of-objections-music-streaming-services; Adam Satariano, "Apple's App Store Draws E.U. Antitrust Charge," *New York Times*, May 17, 2021, https://www.nytimes.com/2021/04/30/technology/apple-antitrust-eu-app-store.html.

57. Jiyoung Sohn, "Google, Apple Hit by First Law Threatening Dominance Over App-Store Payments," *Wall Street Journal*, August 31, 2021, https://www.wsj.com/articles/google-apple-hit-in-south-korea-by-worlds-first-law-ending-their-dominance-over-app-store-payments-11630403335.

58. Filipe Espósito, "Apple Will Let Developers Redirect Users to Sign Up for Services Outside the App Store," *9to5Mac*, September 1, 2021, https://9to5mac.com/2021/09/01/apple-will-let-developers-redirect-users-to-sign-up-for-services-outside-the-app-store.

59. Authority for Consumers and Markets, "ACM Obliges Apple to Adjust Unreasonable Conditions for Its App Store," December 24, 2021, https://www.acm.nl/en/publications/acm-obliges-apple-adjust-unreasonable-conditions-its-app-store; Damien Geradin, "Is Apple a Threat to the Rule of Law?" *Platform Law Blog*, February 7, 2022, https://theplatformlaw.blog/2022/02/07/is-apple-a-threat-to-the-rule-of-law; Simon Van Dorpe, "Apple's Dating-App Payment Conditions Now 'In Line,' Dutch Regulator Says," *Politico*, June 11, 2022, https://www.politico.eu/article/apples-dating-app-payment-conditions-now-in-line-dutch-regulator-says.

60. State of Utah AG and other State AGs v. Google, "Complaint against Google Play Store," filed July 7, 2021, https://ag.nv.gov/uploadedFiles/agnvgov/Content/News/PR/PR_Docs/2021/Utah%20v%20Google.1.Complaint%20(Redacted).pdf; New York State AG, "Attorney General James Files Second Antitrust Lawsuit in Six Months to End Google's Illegal Monopolies," July 7, 2021, https://ag.ny.gov/press-release/2021/attorney-general-james-files-second-antitrust-lawsuit-six-months-end-googles; Wilson White, "A Lawsuit that Ignores Choice on Android and Google Play," *Google Blog*, July 7, 2021, https://blog.google/outreach-initiatives/public-policy/lawsuit-ignores-choice-android-and-google-play.

61. Chance Miller, "Apple Announces App Store Changes: New Communication Rules, Small Developer Assistance Fund, More," *9to5Mac*, August 26, 2021, https://9to5mac.com/2021/08/26/apple-small-business-app-store-changes.

62. Epic Games, Inc. vs. Apple, Inc., United States District Court Northern District of California, Case No. 4:20-cv-05640-YGR, Judgment, September 10, 2021, https://cand.uscourts.gov/wp-content/uploads/cases-of-interest/epic-games-v-apple/Epic-v.-Apple-20-cv-05640-YGR-Dkt-814-Judgment.pdf; Andrew Ross Sorkin, Jason Karaian, Sarah Kessler, Stephen Gandel, Lauren Hirsch, Ephrat Livni, and Anna Schaverien,

"Why Apple Didn't Lose in the Epic Games Ruling, A Judge's Split Decision in the Lawsuit Mostly Went in Favor of Big Tech," *New York Times*, October 8, 2021, https://www.nytimes.com/2021/09/13/business/dealbook/apple-epic-fortnite-lawsuit.html; Tim Higgins, "Judge Rejects Apple's Request to Delay App Store Order," *Wall Street Journal*, November 9, 2021, https://www.wsj.com/articles/judge-looks-dimly-on-apples-request-to-delay-app-store-order-11636506792; Mark MacCarthy, "The Epic-Apple App Case Reveals Monopoly Power and the Need for New Regulatory Oversight," *TechTank*, Brookings Institution, June 2, 2021, https://www.brookings.edu/blog/techtank/2021/06/02/the-epic-apple-app-case-reveals-monopoly-power-and-the-need-for-new-regulatory-oversight/; Sarah Perez, "US Department of Justice Can Join Arguments in Apple-Epic Antitrust Trial, Court Rules," *Techcrunch*, September 19, 2022, https://techcrunch.com/2022/09/19/u-s-department-of-justice-can-join-arguments-in-apple-epic-antitrust-trial-court-rules; Kif Leswing, "Apple Declares 'Resounding Victory' after Decision Reached in Epic Games Appeal," CNBC, April 24, 2023, https://www.cnbc.com/2023/04/24/apple-declares-victory-after-decision-reached-in-epic-games-appeal-.html.

63. Ohio v. American Express Co., 585 US __ (2018), https://www.supremecourt.gov/opinions/17pdf/16-1454_5h26.pdf.

64. Epic v. Apple, 132.

65. Ending Platform Monopolies Act, H.R. 3825, 117th Cong. (2021); American Choice and Innovation Online Act, H.R. 3816, 117th Cong. (2021), sections 2(a) and (b).

66. "Blumenthal, Blackburn, and Klobuchar Introduce Bipartisan Antitrust Legislation to Promote App Store Competition," press release, August 11, 2021, https://www.blumenthal.senate.gov/newsroom/press/release/blumenthal-blackburn-and-klobuchar-introduce-bipartisan-antitrust-legislation-to-promote-app-store-competition; Open Markets Act, S. 2710, 117th Cong. (2021); "Ranking Member Buck, Congressman Johnson Introduce Bipartisan Plan to Rein in App Store Monopolies," press release, August 13, 2021, https://buck.house.gov/media-center/press-releases/ranking-member-buck-congressman-johnson-introduce-bipartisan-plan-rein; Mark MacCarthy, "The Open App Markets Bill Moves Out of the Senate Judiciary Committee," *Lawfare Blog*, March 8, 2022, https://www.lawfareblog.com/open-app-markets-bill-moves-out-senate-judiciary-committee.

67. Kif Leswing, "Apple Will Cut App Store Commissions by Half to 15% for Small App Makers," CNBC, November 18, 2020, https://www.cnbc.com/2020/11/18/apple-will-cut-app-store-fees-by-half-to-15percent-for-small-developers.html; Lauren Feiner, Kif Leswing, and Jennier Elias, "Google Slashes Service Fees in Its App Store After Similar Move by Apple," CNBC, October 21, 2021, https://www.cnbc.com/2021/10/21/google-slashes-service-fees-in-app-store-after-similar-move-by-apple.html.

68. Quoted in Randal C. Picker, "Security Competition and App Stores," *Network Law Review*, August 23, 2021, https://www.networklawreview.org/picker-app-stores/; "Nokia Threat Intelligence Report 2021," https://onestore.nokia.com/asset/210870.

69. Ending Platform Monopolies Act, H.R. 3825, Section 2(c); Open Markets Act, S. 2710, Section 4.

70. Apple, "User Privacy and Data Use," https://developer.apple.com/app-store/user-privacy-and-data-use; Corrine Reichert, "App Tracking Has Only 5% Opt-In Rate Since iOS 14.5 Update, Analyst Says," *C|Net*, May 10, 2021, https://www.cnet.com/tech/services-and-software/app-tracking-has-only-5-opt-in-rate-since-ios-14-5-update-analyst-says; US West, Inc. v. FCC, 182 F.3d 1224 (10th Cir. 1999), https://cite.case.law/f3d/182/1224.

71. Douglas, "The New Antitrust/Data Privacy Law Interface," 683.

72. Federal Trade Commission, "Google Agrees to Change Its Business Practices to Resolve FTC Competition Concerns in the Markets for Devices Like Smart Phones, Games and Tablets, and in Online Search," press release, January 2, 2013, available at https://www.ftc.gov/news-events/press-releases/2013/01/google-agrees-change-its-business-practices-resolve-ftc; European Commission, "Antitrust: Commission Fines Google €2.42 Billion for Abusing Dominance as Search Engine by Giving Illegal Advantage to Own Comparison Shopping Service," press release, June 27, 2017, at http://europa.eu/rapid/press-release_IP-17-1784_en.htm; Sam Schechner, "Google Loses Appeal of $2.8 Billion EU Shopping-Ads Fine," *Wall Street Journal*, November 10, 2021, https://www.wsj.com/articles/google-loses-eu-shopping-ads-case-appeal-11636539480; European Commission, "Antitrust: Commission Fines Google €4.34 Billion for Illegal Practices regarding Android Mobile Devices to Strengthen Dominance of Google's Search Engine," press release, July 18, 2018, available at http://europa.eu/rapid/press-release_IP-18-4581_en.htm; Sam Schechner and Daniel Michaels, "Google Pushes to Overturn EU's $5 Billion Antitrust Decision on Android," *Wall Street Journal*, September 27, 2021, https://www.wsj.com/articles/google-pushes-to-overturn-eus-5-billion-antitrust-decision-on-android-11632735001; Javier Espinoza, "Google Loses Appeal Against Record EU Antitrust Fine," *Financial Times*, September 14, 2022, https://www.ft.com/content/ff540ebb-7dc6-487f-af4a-a6bb502e4ae0; European Commission, "Antitrust: Commission Fines Google €1.49 Billion for Abusive Practices in Online Advertising," press release, March 20, 2019, https://europa.eu/rapid/press-release_IP-19-1770_en.htm.

73. Statcounter, "Search Engine Market Share Worldwide July 2020–July 2020," https://gs.statcounter.com/search-engine-market-share#monthly-202007-202107; Statcounter, "Search Engine Market Share in Europe, July 2020–July 2021," https://gs.statcounter.com/search-engine-market-share/all/europe#monthly-202007-202107; Statcounter, "Search Engine Market Share in the United States, July 2020–July 2021," https://gs.statcounter.com/search-engine-market-share/all/united-states-of-america#monthly-202007-202107.

74. Simon Van Dorpe, "Vestager's Court Win Opens Way for More Google Cases," *Politico*, November 10, 2021, https://www.politico.eu/article/eu-commission-margrethe-vestager-wins-google-shopping-case.

75. United States v. Google, "DOJ Complaint," October 20, 2020, https://www.justice.gov/opa/press-release/file/1328941/download; State of Colorado and other State AGs v. Google, "Complaint," December 17, 2020, https://s3.documentcloud.org/documents/20431671/colorado-v-google.pdf.

76. Makena Kelly, "Google Accused of Search Manipulation in Third Major Antitrust Lawsuit: A Breakup Isn't Out of the Question," The Verge, December 17, 2020, https://www.theverge.com/2020/12/17/22186994/google-search-antitrust-lawsuit-colorado-nebraska-state-ags; Kent Walker, "A Deeply Flawed Lawsuit that Would Do Nothing to Help Consumers," *Google Blog*, October 20, 2020, https://blog.google/outreach-initiatives/public-policy/response-doj.

77. Diane Bartz, "Google Faces Judge's Questions as It Asks Court to Toss U.S. Antitrust Lawsuit," Reuters, April 3, 2023, https://www.reuters.com/legal/google-ask-judge-toss-us-antitrust-lawsuit-over-search-dominance-2023-04-13/; Nico Grant, "Google Devising Radical Search Changes to Beat Back A.I. Rivals," *New York Times*, April 13, 2023, https://www.nytimes.com/2023/04/16/technology/google-search-engine-ai.html; Diane Bartz, "US Judge Denies Google's Motion to Dismiss Advertising Antitrust Case," Reuters, April 28, 2023, https://www.reuters.com/legal/us-judge-denies-googles-motion-dismiss-advertising-antitrust-case-2023-04-28/.

78. Yusuf Mehdi, "Reinventing Search with a New AI-Powered Microsoft Bing and Edge, Your Copilot for the Web," *Microsoft Blog*, February 7, 2023, https://blogs.microsoft.com/blog/2023/02/07/reinventing-search-with-a-new-ai-powered-microsoft-bing-and-edge-your-copilot-for-the-web.

79. Harry McCracken, "Inside Neeva, the Ad-Free, Privacy-First Search Engine from Ex-Googlers," *Washington Post*, June 29, 2021, https://www.fastcompany.com/90650719/neeva-search-engine-google-alternative-privacy-sridhar-ramaswamy-tech; Kara Swisher, "Meet the Man Who Wants You to Give Up Google," *New York Times*, July 29, 2021, https://www.nytimes.com/2021/07/29/opinion/sway-kara-swisher-sridhar-ramaswamy.html.

80. Brent Kendall, "Google, US Government Each Face Challenges in Court Fight," *Wall Street Journal*, October 21, 2021, https://www.wsj.com/articles/google-u-s-government-each-face-challenges-in-court-fight-11603324647?mod=hp_lead_pos1; Bill Baer, "Assessing the DOJ Lawsuit Against Google," *TechTank*, Brookings Institution, https://www.brookings.edu/blog/techtank/2020/10/21/assessing-the-doj-lawsuit-against-google.

81. Ending Platform Monopolies Act, H.R. 3825, 117th Cong. (2021).

82. Viktor Mayer-Schönberger and Thomas Ramge, "A Big Choice for Big Tech: Share Data or Suffer the Consequences," *Foreign Affairs*, September/October 2018, https://www.foreignaffairs.com/articles/world/2018-08-13/big-choice-big-tech.

83. H.R. 3849—ACCESS Act of 2021; OECD, "Data-Driven Innovation: Big Data for Growth and Well-Being," October 6, 2015, available at http://www.oecd.org/sti/data-driven-innovation-9789264229358-en.htm; European Commission, "Proposal for a Regulation on Contestable and Fair Markets in the Digital Sector (Digital Markets Act)," December 15, 2020, 41, https://ec.europa.eu/info/strategy/priorities-2019-2024/europe-fit-digital-age/digital-markets-act-ensuring-fair-and-open-digital-markets_en; Jacques Cremer, Yves-Alexandre de Montjoye, and Heike Schweitzer, "Competition Policy for the Digital Era," European Commission, 2019, 91–108, http://ec.europa.eu/competition/publications/reports/kd0419345enn.pdf.

84. "Deputy Assistant Attorney General Barry Nigro Delivers Remarks at the Capitol Forum and CQ's Fourth Annual Tech, Media & Telecom Competition Conference," December 13, 2017, https://www.justice.gov/opa/speech/deputy-assistant-attorney-general-barry-nigro-delivers-remarks-capitol-forum-and-cqs.

85. Gus Hurwitz, "Digital Duty to Deal, Data Portability, and Interoperability," Global Antitrust Institute, 2020, https://gaidigitalreport.com/2020/10/04/digital-duty-to-deal-data-portability-and-interoperability; Picker, "Forcing Interoperability on Tech Platforms Would Be Difficult to Do."

86. ACCESS Act of 2021, H.R. 3849, Section 4.

87. Keach Hagey and Vivien Ngo, "How Google Edged Out Rivals and Built the World's Dominant Ad Machine: A Visual Guide," *Wall Street Journal*, November 7, 2019, https://www.wsj.com/articles/how-google-edged-out-rivals-and-built-the-worlds-dominant-ad-machine-a-visual-guide-11573142071?mod=article_inline; "How an Ad Is Served with Real-Time Bidding," Internet Advertising Bureau, https://www.youtube.com/watch?v=-Glgi9RRuJs.

88. State Attorneys General v. Google, "Amended Complaint," March 15, 2021, https://www.texasattorneygeneral.gov/sites/default/files/images/admin/2021/Press/Redacted%20Amended%20Complaint%20FILED%20(002).pdf; State Attorneys General v. Google, "Unredacted Amended Complaint," October 22, 2021, 12, https://storage.courtlistener.com/recap/gov.uscourts.nysd.564903/gov.uscourts.nysd.564903.152.0.pdf; Chris Prentice, "US States File Updated Antitrust Complaint Against Alphabet's Google," Reuters, November 15, 2021, https://www.reuters.com/world/us/us-states-file-updated-antitrust-complaint-against-alphabets-google-2021-11-13.

89. State Attorneys General v. Google, "Amended complaint"; Internet Advertising Bureau, "How an Ad Is Served with Real-Time Bidding."

90. Adam Cohen, "AG Paxton's Misleading Attack on Our Ad Tech Business," *Google Blog*, January 17, 2021, https://blog.google/outreach-initiatives/public-policy/ag-paxtons-misleading-attack-on-our-ad-tech-business.

91. Adam Cohen, "AG Paxton's False Claims Still Don't Add Up," *Google Blog*, January 21, 2022, https://blog.google/outreach-initiatives/public-policy/ag-paxtons-false-claims-still-dont-add-up; Google, "In re: Google Digital Advertising Antitrust Case," January 21, 2021, https://cdn.vox-cdn.com/uploads/chorus_asset/file/23184858/Google_MTD_1_21_2022.pdf.

92. United States District Court for the Southern District of New York, "In re: Google Digital Advertising Antitrust Case," Opinion and Order, September 13, 2022, https://storage.courtlistener.com/recap/gov.uscourts.nysd.565005/gov.uscourts.nysd.565005.209.0.pdf.

93. Miles Kruppa, Sam Schechner, and Brent Kendall, "Google Offers Concessions to Fend Off US Antitrust Lawsuit," *Wall Street Journal*, July 8, 2022, https://www.wsj.com/articles/google-offers-concessions-to-fend-off-u-s-antitrust-lawsuit-11657296591?mod=hp_lead_pos2; Miles Kruppa, Sam Schechner, and Dave Michaels, "DOJ Sues Google, Seeking to Break Up Online Advertising Business," *Wall Street Journal*, January 24, 2023, https://www.wsj.com/articles/u-s-sues-google-for-alleged-antitrust-violations-in-its-ad-tech-business-11674582792.

94. European Commission, "Antitrust: Commission opens investigation into possible anticompetitive conduct by Google in the online advertising technology sector," June 22, 2021, https://ec.europa.eu/commission/presscorner/detail/en/ip_21_3143; European Commission, "Antitrust: Commission opens investigation into possible anticompetitive conduct by Google and Meta, in online display advertising," March 11, 2022, https://ec.europa.eu/commission/presscorner/detail/en/ip_22_1703; Foo Yun Chee, "Exclusive: Google Faces EU Antitrust Charges Over Its Adtech Business—Sources," Reuters, October 13, 2022, https://www.reuters.com/technology/exclusive-eu-antitrust-regulators-preparing-charges-against-google-over-adtech-2022-10-13.

95. Competition and Market Authority, "Google Probed Over Potential Abuse of Dominance in Ad Tech," May 26, 2022, https://www.gov.uk/government/news/google-probed-over-potential-abuse-of-dominance-in-ad-tech; Competition and Market Authority, "CMA Investigates Google and Meta Over Ad Tech Concerns," March 11, 2022, https://www.gov.uk/government/news/cma-investigates-google-and-meta-over-ad-tech-concerns.

96. Mark MacCarthy, "The Weak Link in DOJ's Antitrust Case Against Google's Ad Tech Dominance," *Forbes*, January 30, 2023, https://www.forbes.com/sites/washingtonbytes/2023/01/30/the-weak-link-in-dojs-antitrust-case-against-googles-ad-tech-dominance/?sh=75741f981aac.

97. Network Advertising Initiative website, https://www.networkadvertising.org.

98. The Financial Industry Regulatory Authority website, https://www.finra.org/#.

99. David Temkin, "Charting a Course Towards a More Privacy-First Web," *Google Blog*, March 3, 2021, https://blog.google/products/ads-commerce/a-more-privacy-first-web.

100. Gilad Edelman, "Antitrust and Privacy Are on a Collision Course," *Wired*, April 12, 2021, https://www.wired.com/story/antitrust-privacy-on-collision-course.

101. UK Competition and Markets Authority, "CMA to Investigate Google's 'Privacy Sandbox' Browser Changes," January 8, 2021, https://www.gov.uk/government/news/cma-to-investigate-google-s-privacy-sandbox-browser-changes; UK Competition and Marketing Authority, "Notice of Intention to Accept Commitments Offered by Google in Relation to Its Privacy Sandbox Proposals," June 11, 2021, 22, https://assets.publishing.service.gov.uk/media/60c21e54d3bf7f4bcc0652cd/Notice_of_intention_to_accept_binding_commitments_offered_by_Google_publication.pdf.

102. UK CMA, "Notice of Intention to Accept Commitments."

103. Vinay Goell, "An Updated Timeline for Privacy Sandbox Milestones," *Google Blog*, June 24, 2021, https://blog.google/products/chrome/updated-timeline-privacy-sandbox-milestones.

104. Mark MacCarthy, "Controversy over Google's Privacy Sandbox Shows the Need for an Industry Regulator," *TechTank*, Brookings Institution, June 23, 2021, https://www.brookings.edu/blog/techtank/2021/06/23/controversy-over-googles-privacy-sandbox-shows-need-for-an-industry-regulator.

105. Australian Competition and Consumer Commission, "Digital Advertising Services Inquiry—Final Report," September 2021, 4 and. 12, https://www.accc.gov.au/system/files/Digital%20advertising%20services%20inquiry%20-%20final%20report.pdf.

106. Patrick McGee, "Snap, Facebook, Twitter and YouTube Lose Nearly $10bn after iPhone Privacy Changes," *Financial Times*, October 31, 2021, https://www.ft.com/content/4c19e387-ee1a-41d8-8dd2-bc6c302ee58e; Kate Marino, "Higher Prices, Weaker Targeting Push Companies to Rethink Digital Ads," Axios, October 7, 2021, https://www.axios.com/higher-prices-weaker-targeting-push-companies-to-rethink-digital-ads-807bb2c7-2cf9-4da5-9033-812bfc7cafdf.html; Phoebe Liu, "Snap Stock Plunges 25% after Posting $422 Million Q2 Loss," *Forbes*, July 21, 2022, https://www.forbes.com/sites/phoebeliu/2022/07/21/snap-stock-plunges-25-after-posting-422-million-q2-loss/?sh=355f50fb1a13.

107. Kurt Wagner, "Facebook Users Said No to Tracking. Now Advertisers Are Panicking," *Bloomberg*, July 14, 2021, https://www.bloomberg.com/news/articles/2021-07-14/facebook-fb-advertisers-impacted-by-apple-aapl-privacy-ios-14-changes; Jack Nicas and Mike Isaac, "Facebook Takes the Gloves Off in Feud with Apple" ("the social network said it opposed changes that Apple was making to the tracking of apps and would provide information for an antitrust complaint against the iPhone maker"), *New York Times*, April 26, 2021, https://www.nytimes.com/2020/12/16/technology/facebook-takes-the-gloves-off-in-feud-with-apple.html; French Competition Authority, "Targeted Advertising / Apple's Implementation of the ATT Framework" ("the Autorité does not issue urgent interim measures against Apple but continues to investigate into the merits of the case"), March 2021, https://www.autoritedelaconcurrence.fr/en/press-release/targeted-advertising-apples-implementation-att-framework-autorite-does-not-issue; Scott Ikeda, "Apple Facing Another Antitrust Complaint over New App Tracking Transparency," *CPO Magazine*, May 3, 2021, https://www.cpomagazine.com/data-privacy/apple-facing-another-antitrust-complaint-over-new-app-tracking-transparency-framework.

108. Drina Srinivasan, "The Antitrust Case Against Facebook," *Berkeley Business Law Journal* 16, no. 39 (2019), https://papers.ssrn.com/sol3/papers.cfm?abstract_id=3247362; Warren, "Here's How We Can Break Up Big Tech"; Federal Trade Commission, "FTC Alleges Facebook Resorted to Illegal Buy-or-Bury Scheme to Crush Competition After String of Failed Attempts to Innovate," press release, August 19, 2021, https://www.ftc.gov/news-events/press-releases/2021/08/ftc-alleges-facebook-resorted-illegal-buy-or-bury-scheme-crush.

109. Daisuke Wakabayashi, "The Antitrust Case Against Big Tech, Shaped by Tech Industry Exiles," *New York Times*, December 20, 2020, https://www.nytimes.com/2020/12/20/technology/antitrust-case-google-facebook.html.

110. House of Representatives, Committee on the Judiciary, Subcommittee on Antitrust, Commercial, and Administrative Law, "Investigation of Competition in Digital Markets."

111. Mark MacCarthy, "Do Not Expect Too Much from the Facebook Antitrust Complaints," *TechTank*, Brookings Institution, February 3, 2021, https://www.brookings.edu/blog/techtank/2021/02/03/do-not-expect-too-much-from-the-facebook-antitrust-complaints.

112. Stijn Huijts, "Antitrust Is Turning Its Eye to Gaming," *Platform Blog*, September 1, 2022, https://theplatformlaw.blog/2022/09/01/antitrust-is-turning-its-eye-to-gaming;

Casey Newton, "Meta's Real Antitrust Problems Are Only Beginning," The Platformer, January 11, 2022, https://www.platformer.news/p/metas-real-antitrust-problems-are.

113. Federal Trade Commission, "FTC Seeks to Block Virtual Reality Giant Meta's Acquisition of Popular App Creator Within," July 27, 2022, https://www.ftc.gov/news-events/news/press-releases/2022/07/ftc-seeks-block-virtual-reality-giant-metas-acquisition-popular-app-creator-within; Mark MacCarthy, "FTC's Case Against Meta's Acquisition of Within Seeks to Shape the Emerging VR Market," *TechTank*, Brookings Institution, August 4, 2022, https://www.brookings.edu/author/mark-maccarthy/; Dave Michaels, "FTC Pares Back Lawsuit Targeting Meta Platforms' Bid for Virtual-Reality Company," *Wall Street Journal*, October 7, 2022, https://www.wsj.com/articles/ftc-pares-back-lawsuit-targeting-meta-platforms-bid-for-virtual-reality-company-11665176891; FTC v. Meta, "Complaint Counsel's Unopposed Motion to Amend Complaint, United States District Court for the Northern District Of California San Jose Division," October 7, 2022, https://www.ftc.gov/system/files/ftc_gov/pdf/D09411%20-%20COMPLAINT%20COUNSEL_S%20UNOPPOSED%20MOTION%20TOAMEND%20COMPLAINT%20-%20PUBLIC%20%281%29.pdf; Ashley Gold, "Meta Files to Dismiss FTC Suit Over Within Acquisition," Axios, October 13, 2022, https://www.axios.com/2022/10/13/meta-ftc-virtual-reality-within; FTC v. Meta, "Defendant's Motion to Dismiss Amended Complaint," United States District Court for the Northern District of California San Jose Division, October 13, 2022, https://s3.documentcloud.org/documents/23131717/meta.pdf; Diane Bartz, "FTC Withdraws from Adjudication in Fight with Meta over Within Deal," Reuters, February 10, 2023, https://www.reuters.com/markets/deals/ftc-withdraws-fight-with-meta-over-within-deal-adjudication-2023-02-10.

114. Platform Competition and Opportunity Act, H.R. 3826, 117th Cong. (2021).

115. Competition and Antitrust Law Enforcement Reform Act, S. 225, 117th Cong. (2021), https://www.congress.gov/bill/117th-congress/senate-bill/225.

116. Federal Communications Commission, "Applications of Comcast Corp., Gen. Elec. Co., and NBC Universal, Inc. for Consent to Assign Licenses and Transfer Control of Licenses," Memorandum Opinion and Order, 26 FCC Rcd. 4238, ¶23-24 (2011), https://www.fcc.gov/document/applications-comcast-corporation-general-electric-company-and-nbc-1.

117. Jay Ezrielev, "Shifting the Burden in Acquisitions of Nascent and Potential Competitors: Not So Simple," Competition Policy International, November 4, 2020, https://www.competitionpolicyinternational.com/shifting-the-burden-in-acquisitions-of-nascent-and-potential-competitors-not-so-simple.

118. Lauren Feiner, "Start-ups Will Suffer from Antitrust Bills Meant to Target Big Tech, VCs Charge," CNBC, July 24, 2021, https://www.cnbc.com/2021/07/24/vcs-start-ups-will-suffer-from-antitrust-bills-targeting-big-tech.html.

119. Sanjary Jolly and Victor Pickard, "Towards a Media Democracy Agenda: The Lessons of C. Edwin Baker," *Law and Political Economy*, November 29, 2021, https://lpeproject.org/blog/towards-a-media-democracy-agenda-the-lessons-of-c-edwin-baker.

120. Chamber of Commerce of the United States, Letter to House Judiciary Committee Chairman Nadler and Ranking Member Jordan.

121. Peter Swire, "Protecting Consumers: Privacy Matters in Antitrust Analysis," Center for American Progress, October 19, 2007, https://www.americanprogress.org/issues/economy/news/2007/10/19/3564/protecting-consumers-privacy-matters-in-antitrust-analysis.

122. Maureen K. Ohlhausen and Alexander P. Okuliar, "Competition, Consumer Protection, and the Right [Approach] to Privacy," *Antitrust Law Journal* 80, no. 121, 151 (2015).

123. Pamela Jones Harbour, "Dissenting Statement," Google, Inc., FTC File No. 071–0170, Dec. 20, 2007, https://www.ftc.gov/sites/default/files/documents/public_statements/statement-matter-google/doubleclick/071220harbour_0.pdf.

124. "Statement of FTC," Google, Inc., FTC File No. 071–0170, December 20, 2007, 2, https://www.ftc.gov/system/files/documents/public_statements/418081/071220googledc-commstmt.pdf.

125. United States v. Philadelphia Nat'l Bank, 374 U.S. 321 (1963), https://supreme.justia.com/cases/federal/us/374/321.

126. FTC Statement, 12.

127. Commission Decision of Oct. 3, 2014, "Case M.7217 Facebook/WhatsApp," http://ec.europa.eu/competition/mergers/cases/decisions/m7217_20141003_20310_3962132_EN.pdf.

128. Mark MacCarthy, "Privacy as a Parameter of Competition in Merger Reviews," *Federal Communications Law Journal* 72, no. 1 (2020), https://ssrn.com/abstract=3427317; Douglas, "The New Antitrust/Data Privacy Law Interface."

129. Jon Sallet, "FCC Transaction Review: Competition and the Public Interest," FCC, August 12, 2014, https://www.fcc.gov/news-events/blog/2014/08/12/fcc-transaction-review-competition-and-public-interest.

130. European Commission, "Mergers: Commission Opens In-Depth Investigation into the Proposed Acquisition of Fitbit by Google," press release, August 4, 2020, https://ec.europa.eu/commission/presscorner/detail/en/ip_20_1446.

131. David French, "The Right's Message to Silicon Valley: 'Free Speech for Me, But Not for Thee,'" *Time*, January 16, 2021, https://time.com/5930281/right-wing-silicon-valley-free-speech.

132. Furman et al., "Unlocking Digital Competition," 65–71 (on data mobility) and 71–74 (on open standards); Feld, "The Case for the Digital Platform Act," 78–82; Chris Riley, "Interoperability: Questions of Principle and Principal," Medium, April 27, 2018, https://medium.com/@mchrisriley/interoperability-questions-of-principle-and-principal-6eeb8b4ff2a2; Cremer, Montjoye, and Schweitzer, "Competition Policy for the Digital Era," 73–74 and 81–85; Philip Boucher, "What If Social Media Were Open and Connected?" European Parliament Research Service, May 2018, http://www.europarl.europa.eu/RegData/etudes/ATAG/2018/614559/EPRS_ATA(2018)614559_EN.pdf; OECD, "Data Portability, Interoperability and Digital Platform Competition," OECD Competition Committee discussion paper, June 2021, https://www.oecd.org/daf/competition/data-portability-interoperability-and-competition.htm.

133. FTC v. Facebook, "Complaint," December 9, 2020, https://www.ftc.gov/system/files/documents/cases/051_2021.01.21_revised_partially_redacted_complaint.pdf; FTC

v. Facebook, "Memorandum Opinion"; FTC v. Facebook, "Amended Complaint," August 19, 2021, https://www.ftc.gov/system/files/documents/cases/ecf_75-1_ftc_v_facebook_public_redacted_fac.pdf; Mark MacCarthy, "Facebook's FTC Court Win Is a Much-Needed Wake Up Call for Congress," *TechTank*, Brookings Institution, July 7, 2021, https://www.brookings.edu/blog/techtank/2021/07/07/facebooks-ftc-court-win-is-a-much-needed-wake-up-call-for-congress/; "Memorandum Opinion," US District Court for the District of Columbia, January 11, 2022, https://www.govinfo.gov/content/pkg/USCOURTS-dcd-1_20-cv-03590/pdf/USCOURTS-dcd-1_20-cv-03590-1.pdf.

134. ACCESS Act of 2021, H.R. 3849, 117th Cong. (2021).

135. "Guidelines on the Right of Data Portability," Newsroom, Article 29 Data Protection Working Party, April 5, 2019, https://ec.europa.eu/newsroom/article29/item-detail.cfm?item_id=611233.

136. Furman et al., "Unlocking Digital Competition," 69; Open Banking website, https://www.openbanking.org.uk; "The Risks of Open Banking," Trend Micro, September 17, 2019, https://www.trendmicro.com/vinfo/us/security/news/cybercrime-and-digital-threats/the-risks-of-open-banking-are-banks-and-their-customers-ready-for-psd2; "Open Banking Generates Cybersecurity Risks," October 29, 2019, https://www.fintechnews.org/stronger-security-needed-before-open-banking-arrives.

137. Nicholas and Weinberg, "Data Portability and Platform Competition."

138. European Commission, "Proposal for a Regulation," 40.

139. Przemysław Pałka, "The World of Fifty (Interoperable) Facebooks," *Seton Hall Law Review* 51, no. 1193 (2021), https://scholarship.shu.edu/cgi/viewcontent.cgi?article=1788&context=shlr.

140. Riley, "Interoperability."

141. Jay Ezrielev and Genaro Marquez, "Interoperability: The Wrong Prescription for Platform Competition," Competition Policy International, June 15, 2021, https://www.competitionpolicyinternational.com/interoperability-the-wrong-prescription-for-platform-competition; Hurwitz, "Digital Duty to Deal, Data Portability, and Interoperability."

142. "Investigation: How TikTok's Algorithm Figures Out Your Deepest Desires," *Wall Street Journal*, July 21, 2021, https://www.wsj.com/video/series/inside-tiktoks-highly-secretive-algorithm/investigation-how-tiktok-algorithm-figures-out-your-deepest-desires/6C0C2040-FF25-4827-8528-2BD6612E3796; Molly McGlew, "This Is How the TikTok Algorithm Works," *Later Media*, June 23, 2021, https://later.com/blog/tiktok-algorithm.

143. Evan Niu, "At 250 Million Daily Active Users, Instagram Stories Continues to Crush Snapchat," *Motley Fool*, June 20, 2017, https://www.fool.com/investing/2017/06/20/at-250-million-daily-active-users-instagram-storie.aspx; Greg Ip, "The Antitrust Case Against Facebook, Google and Amazon," *Wall Street Journal*, January 16, 2018, https://www.wsj.com/articles/the-antitrust-case-against-facebook-google-amazon-and-apple-1516121561.

144. Nicholas Confessore, "Cambridge Analytica and Facebook: The Scandal and the Fallout So Far," *New York Times*, April 4, 2018, https://www.nytimes.com/2018/04/04/us/politics/cambridge-analytica-scandal-fallout.html.

145. Julia Angwin, "Back into the Trenches of the Crypto Wars: A Conversation with Meredith Whittaker," *The Markup*, January 7, 2023, https://themarkup.org/hello-world/2023/01/07/back-into-the-trenches-of-the-crypto-wars.

146. "S. 2992, Amendment in the Nature of a Substitute," 2022, https://www.klobuchar.senate.gov/public/_cache/files/b/9/b90b9806-cecf-4796-89fb-561e5322531c/B1F51354E81BEFF3EB96956A7A5E1D6A.sil22713.pdf.

147. "Provision in Senate Antitrust Bill Would Undermine the Fight Against Online Hate and Disinformation," Free Press, January 20, 2022, https://www.freepress.net/news/press-releases/provision-senate-antitrust-bill-would-undermine-fight-against-online-hate-and-disinformation.

148. Shapiro, "Protecting Competition in the American Economy," 9.

Chapter 3

Privacy Rules for Digital Industries

"If you have something that you don't want anyone to know, maybe you shouldn't be doing it in the first place."

—Eric Schmidt[1]

"You have zero privacy. Get over it."

—Scott McNealy[2]

Introduction

In addition to the responsibility to promote competition in core digital lines of business explored in the previous chapter, the digital regulator would have a mission to protect user privacy interests in these lines of business. This sectoral way of protecting privacy is not the way the European Union addresses data protection issues. The European General Data Protection Regulation is a comprehensive framework for protecting privacy across all sectors of the economy. The United States seems to be moving in that direction as well. The major national privacy bills that have been before Congress, including the one that has gone the farthest in congressional consideration, the American Data Privacy and Protection Act of 2022 (ADPPA), all have been economy-wide in scope.[3]

A comprehensive national privacy law makes a good deal of sense. For one thing, gaps in sectoral legislation can lead to confusion and inconsistent privacy protection for users. Why should information about a person's heart rate be regulated under medical privacy laws when collected by a nurse in a doctor's office, but not when collected by Fitbit? So there is a strong case for a uniform privacy law.

Yet assigning privacy protection to a digital sector regulator is in line with the traditional sectoral approach to privacy practiced in the United States since the 1970s. Starting with the Fair Credit Reporting Act and the educational privacy measures in the Family Educational Rights and Privacy Act in the 1970s and continuing through the Cable Communications Act and the Video Privacy Protection Act in the 1980s to the Driver's Privacy Protection Act, the financial privacy provisions of the Gramm-Leach-Bliley Act, the medical privacy regulations established under the Health Insurance Portability and Accountability Act, and the Children's Online Privacy Protection Act in the 1990s, the US approach has always been to establish privacy rules one sector at a time.[4]

The data protection rules described in this chapter are intended primarily to protect the privacy interests of people dependent on the digital companies providing essential services in the core digital industries of search, electronic commerce, social media, and mobile apps. Given the ad-tech industry's close ties to these digital businesses, it makes sense to think of these data protection rules as covering ad tech as well.

The approach is therefore a traditional sectoral approach to privacy. Yet it is not important to put too much weight on this distinction between general and sectoral at the level of enacted law. The key is not whether the general obligations written into law apply just to digital companies or to all companies. The key is that these general duties must be implemented, interpreted, and enforced in a way that protects privacy in digital industries, even if they are stated in terms that apply across the economy.

For instance, a legitimate basis for collecting personal data is the need to provide service. But what this general rule allows and forbids depends on economic sector. Financial services companies have to know the details of your financial history, and doctors need to know your medical history in order to provide service. Digital companies do not need either type of data. Even within digital industries, the same general rule should be interpreted differently. Amazon should be allowed to demand a user's home address in order to deliver goods, while Facebook and Google should not. The meaning of the service necessity rule therefore will be different in different industries, even if the statutory language is the same.

The implementation needed to make these measures workable for digital industries can be done most effectively through rulemaking by an agency with sector-specific expertise. A major purpose of this chapter is to make a sustained argument for the irreplaceable role of a digital regulator in protecting the privacy of digital users.

A comprehensive US privacy law will likely assign privacy enforcement to the Federal Trade Commission, an economy-wide regulator. Would this agency have the sectoral expertise to apply this new law to digital companies? Since around 2000, the FTC has gradually been acquiring knowledge and experience in overseeing the digital industry, including applying its unfair and deceptive acts and practices authority to privacy issues. It now has the capacity to implement a comprehensive privacy law in a way that would protect the privacy of digital users and be workable for digital industries. Its 2022 commercial surveillance rulemaking, for instance, is in principle general, but almost all its focus is on the data practices of digital companies.[5]

The FTC's likely role as the digital privacy regulator also dovetails with its likely role in applying and enforcing the new digital competition rules. New content moderation legislation will also lodge enforcement responsibilities with the FTC. If all these digital reforms pass, the FTC will effectively become the nation's digital regulator. It will have to use its expertise to apply the new privacy law to digital industries, and to balance digital privacy protection with the sometimes-conflicting needs of promoting competition and providing for good content moderation.

In effect, the FTC will have to create a digital regulator inside a generalist, economy-wide law enforcement agency. In my view, this is workable only as a transitional stage. In the longer run, the limitations of an agency trying to be both a generalist law-enforcement agency and a sectoral regulator will become apparent, and Congress will spin off the digital regulatory function to a separate agency. The discussion in this chapter is intended to guide policymakers as they think through the measures that are needed to protect the privacy of digital users and also to address the institutional questions that are essential to effective implementation.

The data protection rules discussed in this chapter are intended to apply to the digital companies that control the provision of essential information services. The key lesson of antitrust is that when consumers have no genuine choices for the provision of a service, they are at the mercy of the dominant provider. When the danger is the compilation, sharing, and use of vast databases of user information, very strong protections must take the place of consumer choice. The extensive data protection rules discussed in this chapter are meant to counteract this failure of competition in digital markets.

Still, market failures other than the failure of competition make it crucial to apply privacy rules to all providers of digital services. Information asymmetries, choice fatigue, the inherent relational character of digital data, and information externalities all combine to require data protection rules to protect all digital service users. For this reason, the digital regulator should apply data protection rules to all service providers in search, social media, electronic commerce, and mobile apps.

The digital regulator would protect both privacy and competition to allow the agency to forbear from applying the full range of data protection rules to the digital companies struggling to compete with the dominant providers. Stronger data protection rules should apply to the dominant digital companies because these companies have an enormous advantage over their users in connection with their use of personal data—their users have nowhere else to go if they want to obtain the core digital services that have become essential for life in the twenty-first century. But competitive digital companies do not have this extraordinary advantage over their users, and so less stringent privacy rules might be appropriate for them.

With the attempt to introduce competition into digital markets described in the previous chapter, the number of competitive companies might increase. Enabling legislation should authorize the digital agency to relax the data protection rules for companies striving to compete with established dominant incumbents. An asymmetric or two-tiered structure of data protection rules might thereby emerge with dominant companies facing enhanced privacy duties and their competitors allowed to observe less stringent data protection rules. Regulatory forbearance, discussed in the last chapter as a way to apply stronger procompetition rules to dominant digital companies, should also be provided in the data protection policy sphere.

This chapter lays out the rationale for privacy regulation in digital industries by a dedicated industry regulator and describes an interlocking system of privacy duties for digital companies. It starts with some background on the nature of privacy and data protection, the inability of traditional antitrust law to fully protect privacy interests, and the limitations of conceiving privacy purely in terms of individual control over personal data.

What Is Privacy?

The right to privacy was first implemented in US law as a system of torts, allowing private parties to sue others to recover damages done to them by various forms of privacy abuses. In their seminal 1890 law review article, Samuel Warren and Louis Brandeis developed a common law right to the privacy of thoughts, feelings, and sensations. Privacy was essentially the right to be left alone, and it protected the principle of an "inviolate personality." They thought law had to evolve to recognize this right to respond to the technological innovations of the time—namely, the development of the snap camera and mass print media.

Sixty years of case law allowed William Prosser, dean of the School of Law at UC Berkeley, to reduce this unitary right to privacy to four separate privacy torts each expressing a different kind of harm from privacy invasions. In turn, Edward J. Bloustein attempted to revive the unitary conception by arguing that the right to privacy in all its manifestations embodied an aspect of human dignity. Bloustein treated privacy as a fundamental right that affirms the value of individual autonomy and independence from the intrusions of state and society. The damage of a privacy violation, Bloustein wrote, is an "injury to our individuality, to our dignity as individuals, and the legal remedy represents a social vindication of the human spirit."[6]

This legal structure based on after-the-fact tort actions proved inadequate to deal with the risks created by the development and deployment of the mainframe computer in the 1960s. Privacy torts were essentially aimed at harms caused by the publication of private information in public media. But the new computer technology allowed the collection, storage, and processing of large volumes of personal information. Governments, businesses, schools, and other large institutions could use these new systems to improve their operations but perhaps to the detriment of the individuals whose information was compiled in secret computer databases.

A regulatory paradigm of fair information practices arose to fill this gap. A legal structure based on these fair information practices would create ex-ante rights for the data subject and enduring responsibilities for data collectors and users, a regulatory structure to be enforced by an agency of government rather than through after-the-fact private suits for damages. These new fair information practices, no less than the privacy tort structure that preceded it, affirmed the power of individuals to defend themselves against the intrusions of powerful institutions whose use of information might be damaging to their interests. It was a conceptual update of privacy to account for the development of new technology.

Fair information practices were first developed in a report from the then Department of Health, Education, and Welfare in the early 1970s. They were incorporated into the Federal Privacy Act of 1974, which applied just to the federal government and not to private sector organizations. From there they jumped across the Atlantic to the Organisation for Economic Co-operation and Development, which in 1980 issued its "Guidelines on the Protection of Privacy," which has ever since been the touchstone of privacy law and policy.

Fair information practices contained important measures to ensure that data collection and use protected the data subject's right to control information. It required notice and consent, access and correction, data minimization, and purpose limitation, among other specific requirements. All these measures worked together as a coherent whole to enforce the right of individuals to control the collection and use of information about themselves.[7]

In the United States, elements of these fair information practices were incorporated into law on a sectoral basis, covering the activities of the federal government, educational institutions, credit reporting agencies, financial institutions, health care providers, cable communications, video rental stores, children's online privacy, and telephone communications. In addition, the FTC attempted to assert jurisdiction over other companies not covered by sectoral laws to apply a limited version of the fair information practices through its authority to regulate unfair or deceptive acts or practices.[8]

Key to this regulatory framework was the notion of privacy as the control of personal information. In the 1960s, leading privacy scholar Alan Westin famously defined privacy as "the claim of individuals, groups, or institutions to determine for themselves when, how, and to what extent information about them is communicated to others."[9] The fair information practices seemed like a reasonable instantiation in law and policy of this right of privacy as individual control of personal information.

In Europe, this legal right to privacy as information control was treated as a matter of fundamental human rights. Various international agreements and treaties ratified in the post–World War II period lent support to the idea of privacy as a human right. Article 12 of the Universal Declaration of Human Rights states, "No one shall be subjected to arbitrary interference with his privacy, family, home, or correspondence, nor to attacks upon his honour and reputation. Everyone has the right to the protection of the law against such interference or attacks." Article 17 of the International Covenant on Civil and Political Rights (ICCPR) repeats this provision almost verbatim, and Article 8(1) of the European Convention on Human Rights says, "Everyone has the right to respect for his private and family life, his home, and his correspondence."[10]

European instruments pick up this theme of privacy as a human right. Article 16 of the Treaty on the Functioning of the European Union says, "Everyone has the right to the protection of personal data concerning them." Article 7 of the Charter of Fundamental Rights of the European Union, relating to the respect for private and family life, says,

"Everyone has the right to respect for his or her private and family life, home, and communications."

Article 8 of the Charter moves beyond the traditional notion of privacy to the more contemporary notion of data protection. It recognizes as foundational in the European Union "the right to the protection of personal data concerning him or her." It explicitly cites some of the fair information practices as fundamental rights, saying that personal data "must be processed fairly for specified purposes and on the basis of the consent of the person concerned or some other legitimate basis laid down by law. Everyone has the right of access to data which has been collected concerning him or her, and the right to have it rectified." It even creates a fundamental right to enforcement of these rules by "independent authority."[11]

In 1995, the European Data Protection Directive implemented this fundamental human right to privacy that had been announced in these international human rights treaties and European charters. Article 1(1) of the Directive states its objective is the protection of "the fundamental rights and freedoms of natural persons, and in particular their right to privacy with respect to the processing of personal data." The 2018 General Data Protection Regulation that updated the data protection directive also has the objective of protecting the fundamental right to privacy and data protection.[12]

The heart of the idea of privacy as a human right is its focus on autonomy and dignity of the individual, and individual consent as the primary way to preserve autonomy. The fundamental privacy principle is that other people should be allowed to access, share, and use a person's personal information only when the data subject agrees. Even when data use would benefit or at least not harm the data subject, the right of the data subject to informed choice remains primary. It is simply an affront to the human dignity of individuals, to their status as full human beings, to collect information that concerns them and share it or use it without their freely given voluntary consent.

A different way of thinking about the fundamental purpose of privacy law and policy was possible. In this alternative framework, privacy aims at the prevention of harm to data subjects. Law professor Paul Ohm has warned of the dangers of a panopticon he calls a "database of ruin," a complete accounting of a person's life that would provide an adversary with sufficient information to discredit him or her and significantly degrade his or her life prospects.[13] In this alternative conception of the nature of privacy, privacy law and policy functions as a way to keep that database out of the hands of our worst enemies, to control the risk that such adversaries could harm us in a range of unspecified and unpredictable ways.

Many privacy scholars and thinkers have developed versions of this harm-based conception of privacy—former Seventh Circuit judge Richard Posner, former FTC officials Howard Beales and Timothy Muris, the founder of the influential legal blog *Lawfare* Benjamin Wittes, and privacy scholar Fred Cate. My own work on privacy falls roughly in that category. All versions of this approach share the idea that privacy policy should focus on the prevention of specific, identifiable harm to individuals and classes of individuals. The harm framework derives from the utilitarian tradition that sees utility or happiness as the major guide to public policy and is less indebted to the deontological tradition of human rights.[14]

In this way of conceiving the basis for privacy law and policy, the value at stake is individual welfare. Privacy is a matter of interests, not fundamental rights. In this approach to privacy, it is legitimate for other people or enterprises to access, share, and use information about a data subject, when on balance it does more good than harm, taking into account the interests of the data subjects as well as the interests of other affected parties. Privacy policymakers should focus on whether access, sharing, and use advances or damages the interests of the individuals and institutions involved. The key notion is consequences, not choice. Consent is useful only as a means to the end of protecting interests, not as a value or as a legitimating process. The crucial requirement is an assessment of costs and benefits of data collection, sharing, and use.

One way to flesh out the notion of harm in this framework is through the FTC's notion of unfairness. An act or practice is harmful when it satisfies the FTC's standard of unfairness—that is, when "the act or practice causes or is likely to cause substantial injury to consumers which is not reasonably avoidable by consumers themselves and not outweighed by countervailing benefits to consumers or to competition."[15] The consumer harm is a privacy harm when the substantial injury involved is connected to the collection, sharing, or use of personal information. Former FTC commissioner Maureen Ohlhausen has outlined many of these privacy harms, including deception or subverting consumer choice, financial injury, health or safety injury, unwarranted intrusion, reputational injury.[16]

This test concentrates on aggregated harm to individuals and suggests at least a qualitative cost-benefit test. It allows small individual-level harms to be aggregated into a large quantitative harm. It is probabilistic and allows a substantial risk of harm to count as harmful. And it recognizes that every act or practice has the potential for positive consequences that need to be weighed before a judgment is made that the act or practice is harmful.[17]

There is a third way to conceive the nature of privacy: as an aspect of social structure. In contrast to the traditional approaches that emphasize respectively rights and welfare, these social theories of privacy view privacy law and policy as efforts to reinforce or maintain entrenched and valuable social structures. This social conception of privacy draws attention to an important and sometimes neglected aspect of privacy—namely, its role in constituting and implementing vital institutional purposes, values, and objectives.

A crucial part of this social approach to privacy is the recognition that public policy or law does not create privacy; nor does privacy derive from the need to protect presocial rights or welfare. Privacy is fundamentally a creature of social life, and its requirements can be supported or suppressed by public policy and law. Privacy norms limit the observability of people when they are engaged in specific social practices; these norms exist to allow these social practices to flourish and derive a part of their justification from playing this social role. Privacy norms function to cloak social practices in those cases where observation would have harmful effects on the social practice itself.

This social conception of privacy is in sharp contrast to the individualist conception that rights-based theories and utilitarian theories share. In thinking of privacy as a human right, the idea is that privacy protects individuals from intrusions by society and state. It is a keep-out sign whereby individual autonomy and dignity can be preserved, even against the demands of the welfare of society as a whole. For utilitarians, privacy is a personal preference that varies randomly in society. Some people are willing to share, and others are not; still others will share depending on the purposes. It is a matter of individual taste.

The social conception of privacy brings privacy into the world of everyday life by thinking of it as vindicating social practices; it is not a way to withdraw from society, but rather a social norm that allows people to communicate and interact to perform their needed tasks in society. Rather than serve as an obstacle to the achievement of public purpose or as a random idiosyncratic matter of individual taste, privacy performs essential social functions.

The models for privacy in this framework are the confidentiality rules that govern the collection, sharing, and use of personal information in law, medicine, education, religion, and the exchange of information within families and between intimate friends and lovers. In each case, the rules are widely understood and accepted as entrenched social norms, not as a matter for individual negotiation or calculation of costs and benefits. The rules differ by context and are not the same for each social institution.

Prominent versions of a social theory of privacy have been developed by philosopher Helen Nissenbaum, legal scholar Robert Post, sociologist Robert Merton, and French philosopher and social critic Michel Foucault. My own notion of privacy as a way to prevent harm to social contexts is a version of this theory as well. In this conception, it is natural for there to be sector-specific privacy rights and duties laid out for medicine, education, financial services, and perhaps digital industries, and enforced through sector-specific agencies.[18]

These three frameworks provide the basis for the data protection rules for digital companies outlined in this chapter. Instead of thinking of them as in competition with each other, it is more helpful from a policy perspective to think of them as complementary. They justify and reinforce different dimensions of legal privacy protections that should govern the conduct of digital companies.

What are those privacy requirements? They are outlined in this chapter and summarized here.

The first privacy duty is that digital companies must be able to demonstrate that they have a legal basis for collecting and using personal information. This is a commonplace in European data protection law. The General Data Protection Regulation requires all companies to have a legal basis for data processing and sets out an array of possible legal justifications for data processing.[19]

US privacy legislation for digital companies should mimic this system. It should require digital companies to show that their data practices live up to one of several alternative standards of acceptability. Three of these possible legal bases for data processing—service necessity, legitimate interest, and consent—are described in this chapter in enough detail to serve as an outline for draft legislation.

US privacy legislation should also require digital companies to abide by certain other measures. They should be required to observe revised and updated principles for data minimization and limited secondary use that limit how much data they can collect in order to accomplish a certain institutional goal and restrain the extent to which they can reuse that data for very different purposes.

To prevent them from manipulating users into divulging more information than is needed to provide a service, they should also be subject to "prohibitions on unreasonably deceptive, abusive, and dangerous design" as outlined in the work of privacy scholar Woodrow Hartzog.[20] To prevent them from putting their own interests in data collection and use above the privacy interests of their users, they should also be required to act as information fiduciaries obliged to advance the informational interests of their users in their collection and use of personal information that pertains to them, as suggested in the work of legal scholar Jack Balkin.[21]

In addition, the legislation would provide the enforcing agency with the authority to prohibit certain data uses if needed to protect user privacy interests. It would also regulate how digital companies share data with service providers, independent companies, and affiliates by requiring agents to abide by the same data protection rules that apply to them.

The different frameworks of privacy as individual rights, harm prevention, and social norms align with and justify these legal privacy requirements for digital companies. The notion of privacy as the right to individual control gives rise to consent as a legal basis for data use. The notion of privacy as contextual integrity validates service necessity as a basis for data use. And the utilitarian framework of privacy as the prevention of harm leads to the idea that the legitimate interests of data controllers can justify data collection and use. The harm framework also provides a basis for data minimization, purpose limitation, and use restrictions. The fiduciary duties of care and loyalty and the prohibition of abusive service designs emerge naturally from the theory of privacy as contextual integrity.

Before moving to the discussion of these data protection rules for digital industries, we need to clear out some underbrush by addressing the limits of approaching privacy solely or primarily as a matter of individual control. This opens the way toward relying on the competing conceptions of privacy as harm prevention and privacy as contextual integrity in the construction of a comprehensive system of data protection for digital industries.

The Limitations of Privacy as Individual Control

The individual choice framework for privacy protection seeks to remedy the imbalance in information and power between those who want to collect, share, and use data and those who are being asked to supply data. It aims to do this by requiring data collectors to explain what data they want to collect and what they want to do with it and then asking users to agree, either by affirmatively consenting or by not opting out of the proposed data collection and use.

In this framework, the substance of the right to privacy is thought of as the right of data subjects to control information about themselves. Control by individuals is the only sensible meaning to give to the notion of privacy, in this view, because people have very different privacy preferences. Privacy scholar Alan Westin established, through a series of surveys going back decades, that people vary in their privacy preferences, ranging from high concern about privacy to medium to low or unconcerned. To accommodate these different privacy preferences, privacy law and policy should rely to the greatest extent possible on expressions of individual consent as the touchstone of legitimate data collection and use.[22]

This model of privacy protection has been heavily criticized, even though it remains the basis of European data protection law, is embodied in recent state privacy statutes, and has animated much of the FTC's enforcement of privacy rights.

The first reason for rejecting privacy as individual control and the one most widely accepted is that relying on notice and choice to protect privacy will overwhelm users with too many choices to manage and too little understanding of what they are being asked to agree to. Privacy notices are widely ignored. An old but well-known study from 2008 showed they would also be astonishingly costly to read—the time spent reading internet privacy notices would cost the economy $781 billion per year.[23]

This choice fatigue will lead data subjects to accept whatever default is offered or to agree to just about anything in order to get on with using a service. By burdening the user with the responsibility to make sensible choices, privacy as individual control allows companies to evade their responsibility to engage in privacy protective data practices. For this reason, cutting-edge privacy advocates have called for relying on consent to the least extent possible in national privacy legislation.[24]

A second concern that is less widely accepted but seems especially important in digital industries is the presence of informational externalities. Informational externalities exist when information disclosed by some people reveals information about others. This feature of information has been a commonplace for years. If the police know a perpetrator of a certain crime is left-handed and has to be one of three suspects, and they find out that two of the suspects are right-handed, then they know that the third person is the guilty one, even though the third person has disclosed nothing at all. Another example, from computer scientist Cynthia Dwork, is that if an analyst knows the average height of Lithuanian women and that Terry Gross is two inches shorter than the average Lithuanian woman, then the analyst knows Gross's height, even if Terry Gross has not disclosed that information.

But information externalities are much more common than these curiosities suggest. Any statistical regularity about people creates a potential for an information externality. Social scientists often know that people having a certain array of characteristics are highly likely to have another characteristic that is of interest. The dependent variable of interest can be inferred from the independent variables, even when that fact about a person is highly sensitive, that person never disclosed it, and it cannot be found in public records.

This well-known property is sometimes called inferential disclosure, defined by the OECD as occurring "when information can be inferred with high confidence from statistical properties of the released data. For example, the data may show a high correlation between income and purchase price of a home. As the purchase price of a home is typically public information, a third party might use this information to infer the income of a data subject."[25]

The new technology of big data analytics makes information externalities the norm in digital industries rather than a curiosity. The standard examples are well-known: pregnancy status can be inferred from shopping choices; sexual orientation can be inferred from the characteristics of social network friends; race can be inferred from name, and even more strongly from zip code and name.[26] As machine-learning algorithms improve, they will be able to more accurately ferret out more and more personal traits that are of interest. In the age of big data analytics, it will be increasingly difficult to keep secret any personal characteristic that is important for classifying and making decisions about people.

Ubiquitous information externalities challenge the traditional core privacy principle that individual control over the flow of information is the front line of defense against privacy violations. Fully informed, rational individuals could make the choice not to reveal some feature of their character or conduct, but if others are willing to reveal that information about themselves and contribute it to the huge datasets that form the input for increasingly sophisticated algorithms, data scientists will be able to make increasingly accurate predictions about that hidden feature of an individual's life.

Privacy as individual control faces a third challenge in addition to choice fatigue and information externalities. Information, especially information collected and used in digital industries, typically concerns a plurality of data subjects. Digital data is inherently relational. A purchase on Amazon, the Apple App Store, or Google Play is "about" the buyer, the seller, and the marketplace. The purchaser bought something, the seller sold something, and the marketplace facilitated the transaction. An interaction on Facebook concerns the person posting a message, all the people who received it, and everyone with whom they shared the post. Most images posted on social media depict groups of people, all of whom have an equally legitimate claim to be the subject of the picture. As demonstrated by the right to be forgotten decision in the EU, inquiries for information about a person on search engines concern the person conducting the search but also relate to the person who is the target of the search inquiry.[27]

The inherently relational character of data is an intrinsic feature of record keeping throughout the economy. People are social creatures, and most of what they do is in relation to other people. As a result, the records of their activity will inevitably involve the people with whom they interact. The records maintained by financial institutions concern the account holders, all the people with whom they transact, and the bank itself. The records maintained by telephone companies concern the people who initiated phone calls, the people who received them, and the telephone company that picked up and delivered the call. When people buy or sell a house, get married, accept employment, go on vacation, take a business trip, purchase insurance, enroll in school, seek out and receive medical care, and subscribe to publications or entertainment services, enabling institutions create and maintain records of these activities and these records concern a plurality of data subjects. Most of what people do in the conduct of the everyday business of life is recorded and preserved in systems of records maintained by facilitating institutions. Almost always these records concern more than one individual.

Privacy scholars and commentators have been aware of this phenomenon of the inherently relational character of data for years and have pondered its implications for privacy policy. Privacy advocate and scholar Bob Gellman illustrates the intractability of this problem of multiple parties with an interest in the same piece of information with an example of a woman who learns that her child is sick with a cold. As the woman deals with this medical situation, that piece of information about her child's medical condition flows from the patient to the patient's family, the school, pharmacy, supermarket, pediatrician, drug manufacturer, social media platform, various websites, internet tracking and advertising companies, and internet service providers. Each of these actors has a legitimate interest in the same information about the child's illness. The attempt to cut this Gordian knot of intersecting relationships by assigning ownership and control over this information to the child or the child's mother does an injustice to the complexity of the interests involved and the need to balance these interests to achieve an acceptable outcome.[28]

Author and consultant Larry Downes drew attention to this issue of multiple interests in the same information in 2013, arguing against the idea people own personal information simply because it refers to them. He emphasizes the point that when information is about more than one person, it is impossible to determine how a property right should be allocated: "Would it be shared property, owned equally by everyone referenced? If not, would any one person hold a veto?"[29]

The final challenge to the idea of privacy as individual control arises from the transaction costs of such a system if it were ever completely implemented. Privacy scholar Nissenbaum suggests the cost of getting consent might make it impossible to engage in even the most socially beneficial uses such as medical research that can put an end to dangerous diseases.[30]

Former Seventh Circuit Court judge Richard Posner also thinks privacy as individual ownership and control would impose unmanageable transaction costs. How, he asks, could a magazine exploit the economic value of its subscriber list if it needed permission from each subscriber to sell it? The cost of obtaining consent would exceed the economic value of the list. Posner also insists that the law should not ratify a general right to conceal information about oneself. Others need access to personal information to form an accurate picture of the people with whom they interact. The case for assigning ownership and control of all personal information to the data subject, he says, is "no better than that for permitting fraud in the sale of goods."[31]

Downes makes the same point that data-subject ownership of information would almost always create "transaction costs higher than the value of the transaction." Downes also points out that assigning ownership of information to the data subject would reduce incentives to create valuable business records. Why would any company put resources into creating records, he asks, if they automatically fall under the control of millions of diverse individuals whose pattern of decisions over what to do with the information—including, of course, simply destroying the record—would make the system unmanageable?

Downes further points out the dangers to freedom of expression in allocating to individuals "a property right to any fact that relates to or describes them." How would journalists ever write about people, he wonders, if they had to get individual consent from each person mentioned in the story? Court cases like *Haynes v. Knopf* hold that general privacy rights do not prevent authors from using factual information about people in their writings.[32]

The notion of privacy as unrestricted ownership and control of personal information that pertains to oneself creates practical difficulties in implementing a privacy rule such as data portability, which would allow people to transfer "their" information to third parties.[33] An unrestricted version of data portability based solely on the alleged individual ownership of personal data will not necessarily increase the level of privacy protection if it allows transfers against the will of the other data subjects whose interests are at stake in almost any piece of digital data.

Put together, these difficulties should suggest that thinking of privacy as purely individual control and ownership does not automatically produce outcomes that its advocates might have hoped for or intended. The other conceptions of privacy as harm prevention and as the preservation of contextual integrity need to be brought to bear to fully protect privacy in the digital age.

Legal Bases for Data Use

A new privacy regime for digital companies would include the requirement that they have an adequate basis for collection of and using information. The implication is that if they do not have one of the legal justifications enumerated in the privacy law, then they may not collect the data at all. Moreover, if it can be shown that they no longer have a legal basis for data processing, they must stop processing and delete the data. This contrasts with the current legal regime in the United States where data collection and use are presumed to be legal, and restrictions have to be based on a violation of a specific privacy rule.

The power of a legal basis requirement was seen in the decision of the European Data Protection Board (EDPB) in January 2023 that Meta (formerly Facebook) cannot rely on its contract with users as providing sufficient legal basis for processing user data for personalized ads. If upheld on appeal, this decision might require social media companies and other online businesses to significantly revise their data-focused advertising business model in the name of protecting privacy.[34]

The Italian data protection authority also wielded the power of a legal basis privacy regime when it barred ChatGPT from access to the Italian market and issued a series of requirements that ChatGPT owner Open AI would have to satisfy to regain access.[35]

The first legal basis that should be incorporated into a new digital privacy law is the "service necessity" justification. Digital companies have a legal basis to engage in data practices that they can show are necessary for providing the service their customers want or have requested. The typical example is the need to know a customer's address in order to deliver his or her purchase. If a digital company needs personal information to provide a service, that serves as a legal basis for collecting and using it for that purpose.

The model for this service necessity basis for data collection and use would be Article 6(1)(b) of GDPR, which states that processing has a legal basis when it is "necessary for the performance of a contract to which the data subject is party or in order to take steps at the request of the data subject prior to entering into a contract."[36] As interpreted by the European Data Protection Board, this provision of European law is to be interpreted very narrowly. Processing is not necessary for the performance of a contract, it says, "when a requested service can be provided without the specific processing taking place." The notion of necessity is strict so that data cannot be collected and used if there are fewer data-intrusive ways of providing the service. According to EDPB, improving a service or developing new functions within the existing service do not count as necessary for providing the service, nor does collecting data for fraud prevention or behavioral advertising, which might be needed to finance an online service. Whether personalization counts as needed for providing a service depends on whether such personalization is an integral part of the service.[37]

The US legal regime contains measures similar to service necessity as a legal basis for data processing. For instance, the Gramm-Leach-Bliley Financial Modernization Act of 1999 (GLB) contains exceptions from its notice and choice requirement for information disclosures "necessary to effect, administer, or enforce a transaction requested or authorized by the consumer."[38] The Cable Communications Act of 1984 prohibits cable operators from using their systems to collect "personally identifiable information" concerning any subscriber without prior consent, unless the information is necessary to render services, or detect unauthorized reception.[39]

Privacy legislation for digital companies would provide for service necessity as a legal basis for data processing. A digital company would pass the legal basis test for data processing if it could show that the personal information was essential for the delivery of a service that the customer wanted or requested. The legislation would adopt the very narrow interpretation of service necessity contained in the EDPB guidance. It would require the digital regulatory agency to follow the path laid out in this guidance as it writes specific rules implementing this legislative requirement and makes judgments and enforce them through fines, penalties, and injunctions in specific cases.

Since customers of dominant digital companies do not have significant alternatives, this narrow interpretation of contractual necessity is especially important. If a dominant technology firm could use an expansive interpretation of what is necessary to provide service, it could leverage its customers' restricted alternatives to extract information that it would be unable to acquire in more competitive circumstances.

The EDPB is narrow about what is necessary for the provision of a service because other legal bases are available to justify collecting and using consumer data. Legitimate interest is one such additional legal basis.

Article 6(1)(f) of the General Data Protection Regulation allows companies to collect and use personal information when "necessary for the purposes of the legitimate interests pursued by the controller or by a third party, except where such interests are overridden by the interests or fundamental rights and freedoms of the data subject which require protection of personal data."[40]

GDPR permits companies to use legitimate interest as a basis for data processing in the case of direct marketing purposes or preventing fraud, transmission of personal data within a group of undertakings for internal administrative purposes, including client and employee data; ensuring network and information security, including preventing unauthorized access to electronic communications networks and stopping damage to computer and electronic communication systems; and reporting possible criminal acts or threats to public security to a competent authority.[41]

Companies that rely on legitimate interests must provide notices to the data subjects and allow them an opportunity to object.[42] The company can nevertheless continue to collect and use personal information despite this objection if it can demonstrate that its compelling legitimate interest overrides the interests or the fundamental rights and freedoms of the data subject.

According to guidance on legitimate interest provided by the Article 29 Data Protection Working Party, data companies can have a broad range of legitimate interests, including the interest of the press to publish public interest stories, the interest in carrying out scientific research, or the need to better target advertisements about products or services.

Companies seeking to base their data practices on their legitimate interests must not only assert with some specificity what the legitimate interest is but also show that the data practices are necessary for the purposes of achieving that interest, including a showing that a no less "invasive" amount of data collection would accomplish the purpose.

In addition to specifying the legitimate interest and showing that the data collection is needed to accomplish the purpose, companies must conduct a balancing assessment showing that the purpose is not overridden by the rights and the interests of the data subjects. The construction of the balancing assessments is in the hands of the company, not regulatory agencies, but they are subject to review by data protection authorities and courts.

The balancing test comparing the legitimate interest of the data processor and the rights and interests of the data subjects is qualitative but scaled. "Minor and not very compelling legitimate interests of the controller" could override "even more trivial" rights and interests of the data subject, while "important and compelling legitimate interests" could "justify even significant intrusion into privacy or other significant impact on the interests or rights of the data subjects."[43]

The United Kingdom suggests that companies conduct a "legitimate interests assessment" when they are basing their data practices on that legal justification. Such assessments would consist of a formal consideration of three tests for legitimate interests—namely, the purpose test, which identifies the compelling legitimate interest; the necessity test, which assesses whether the data collection and use is necessary for accomplishing this purpose; and the balancing test, which considers whether the legitimate interest overrides the individual's rights and interests.[44]

In the United States, companies often have an exemption from consent requirements for uses that resemble the legitimate interest purposes under GDPR. For instance, the GLB contains exceptions from the choice requirement allowing financial service companies to disclose personal information to third parties "to perform services for or functions on behalf of the financial institution" or to use a customer's personal information "to protect the confidentiality or security of the financial institution's records pertaining to the consumer, the service or product, or the transaction therein . . . to protect against or prevent actual or potential fraud, unauthorized transactions, claims, or other liability . . . [or] . . .

for required institutional risk control, or for resolving customer disputes or inquiries."[45] But these exceptions do not require a balancing against consumer interests or rights. The company just asserts them.

Privacy law for digital companies should allow them to assert overriding legitimate interests as a basis for collecting and using personal information. In contrast to existing US law, however, these rules would require a balancing test for any claim to base data use on the pursuit of a legitimate interest. Companies would have to show that the pursuit of this interest was not outweighed by the interests or rights of the data subjects or the public.

The standard of legitimate interest for legal data use and its requirement for a balancing test is especially significant for dominant digital companies. Dominant digital companies might be tempted to use a broad, legitimate interests standard with no balancing requirement to justify expansive data collection from captive customers. The privacy law for digital companies would restrain this exercise in market power by not allowing the pursuit of legitimate interests to become a broad basis for expansive data collection.

To ensure that the balancing requirement is met, the legislation should require the digital regulatory agency to establish by rule provisions requiring digital companies to perform legitimate interest assessments, similar to the ones recommended by the UK regulator, if they avail themselves of this basis for data collection and use. In certain cases, the agency could require these interests to be exceptionally compelling. The requirement for a digital company to assert and describe its legitimate interest will provide an opportunity for the agency to challenge an assertion of interest it finds to be inadequately balanced against the rights and interests of data users or the public.

Finally, the third legal basis for data processing is consent. GDPR provides that data processing has a legal basis when "the data subject has given consent to the processing of his or her personal data for one or more specific purposes." The regulation defines consent as "any freely given, specific, informed, and unambiguous indication of the data subject's wishes by which he or she, by a statement or by a clear affirmative action, signifies agreement to the processing of personal data relating to him or her." The key condition of consent is that "consent should not be regarded as freely given if the data subject has no genuine or free choice or is unable to refuse or withdraw consent without detriment."[46]

The Article 29 Data Protection Working Party issued guidelines on consent under GDPR that clarify many of the ambiguities in the text and recitals of the legislation. It makes it clear, for instance, that consent is not the right legal basis for processing information necessary for the provision of a service and notes that take-it-or-leave-it contracts to "agree with the use of personal data additional to what is strictly necessary" are not consistent with free consent.[47]

Under GDPR, data subjects have a separate and additional right to object to processing in certain circumstances. They have a right to object to processing that has been justified based on legitimate interests or the public interest. The company can nevertheless continue to collect and use personal information despite this objection if it can demonstrate "compelling legitimate grounds for the processing which override the interests, rights and freedoms of the data subject or for the establishment, exercise or defense of legal claims." Data subjects also have an absolute right to object to direct marketing, which cannot be overridden by any showing of compelling legitimate grounds. They also have a right to withdraw consent they have previously granted.[48]

The structure of consent in GDPR provides a template for a similar requirement in US law for digital companies. Privacy law should allow these companies to collect and use information if they can demonstrate that their users had freely given consent. Following GDPR, this form of consent would not allow dominant digital companies to offer their customers take-it-or-leave-it deals for data processing that goes beyond what is necessary to provide service.

This requirement is similar to the privacy regime for consent established under the FTC's 2012 privacy guidelines. These guidelines provide that take-it-or-leave-it contracts for data processing beyond what is necessary for service provision might be legitimate in certain competitive markets, since consumers can always go somewhere else. For essential services in noncompetitive markets, however, the FTC bars the use of take-it-or-leave-it contracts.[49]

In a similar way, in its now-repealed 2016 broadband privacy rules, the FCC prohibited take-it-or-leave-it offerings of broadband service contingent on surrendering privacy protections. Broadband providers could condition service offerings on the disclosure and use of information that was necessary for the provision of the service, but not on the use of personal information for the provision of other services. Affirmative consumer consent for these other services was essential. Take-it-or-leave-it customer acceptance, the agency ruled, is not legal customer approval.[50]

The German competition authority, the Federal Cartel Office (FCO), took note of the same anti-consumer tying arrangement in its 2019 case against Facebook. Facebook required its social media customers to accept the collection and merging of off-site data with the profiles developed from their interactions on the social media service. Facebook was dominant in the market for social media, said the agency. Therefore, the agreement of its users, who had with no genuine alternatives to this extra data collection, was not genuine consent under GDPR. This controversial case is currently before the Court of Justice of the European Union, with preliminary indications (as of September 2022) that the German agency's actions would be upheld.[51]

The California Consumer Privacy Act (CCPA) frowns on take-it-or-leave-it contracts beyond that necessary for the provision of the agreed-upon service. The CCPA provides users with important privacy rights, including the ability to opt out of the sale of personal information. But it allows a company to offer customers a financial incentive or price or service difference to encourage them to agree to the sale of their personal information, provided the difference is reasonably related to the value of the data collected.[52]

Such financial incentives to induce users to agree to data collection beyond what is necessary to provide service seem to be consistent with freely given consent under GDPR, the FCO's Facebook order, and the regulatory approach of the FTC and the FCC. New privacy legislation should provide that one way for digital companies to demonstrate that they have a legitimate basis for collecting and using information would be to show that their users have provided freely given consent.

But to ensure that consent is freely given, the legislation should set out limits on the financial incentives digital companies could offer in exchange for data processing. The digital regulatory agency should not allow companies to make especially attractive or popular features of a service available only to people who surrender their privacy rights. The agency should also review incentive offers to ensure that the quality or price of the service to people who permitted data collection or use are not so much more desirable that no real choice is being offered.

The standard set out for these limits on financial incentives to encourage user consent in the CCPA is that the increase in price or service quality difference must be reasonably related to the extra value provided "to the business by the consumer's data." But this is likely to be unworkable in practice. Proposition 24, which revised the CCPA, has the additional standard that financial incentives may not be "unjust, unreasonable, coercive, or usurious in nature."[53] This is similar to the FCC's standard in its broadband decision. It barred financial incentives that are unjust, unreasonable, unreasonably discriminatory, predatory, or coercive. This should be the standard in legislation establishing the digital privacy rules. The legislation should authorize a regulatory agency to develop and enforce limits on financial incentives, including the authority to ban financial incentives entirely if experience proves that they are too likely to be abused and too difficult to regulate.

Obtaining genuine consent establishes only that a company has a legal basis for data collection, sharing, and use. It does not mean that a digital company has no other data protection duties in connection with their users. Obtaining consent does not mean that any data practice at all is legitimate, the way it does in the older notice and consent model of privacy regulation. In addition, digital companies must satisfy separate requirements designed to protect their users.

Data Minimization and Purpose Limitation

Under the legislation providing for data protection rules for digital companies, consent would be a valid legal basis for data collection and use, but it is not sufficient to protect privacy interests. Digital data collectors have not discharged all their responsibilities to data users and to the public when they obtain individual consent for personal data collection and use. The enabling legislation imposes additional data protection duties on digital companies. This movement from individual control as sufficient for privacy protection to the imposition of data protection duties is consistent with the growing realization that privacy must be provided as a public good if it is to be provided at all.[54]

The enabling legislation for a digital regulator should impose separate data minimization and purpose limitation duties on digital companies. These requirements take some of the burden off individuals to protect their own privacy and layers responsibility on digital companies to protect their users from privacy harms.

Data minimization is a traditional privacy principle that calls for enterprises and others to limit their collection of information to the minimum amount needed to accomplish a clearly specified and narrowly defined specific purpose. The European GDPR, for instance, provides that personal data shall be "adequate, relevant and limited to what is necessary in relation to the purposes for which they are processed."[55] The intent is to make sure companies do not collect too much information and that they do not just collect personal information on the off chance it might be useful in the future. This principle also suggests that as soon as the purpose for which the data have been collected has been accomplished, the data should be discarded or anonymized.

This strong interpretation of the principle might have been appropriate in an era of small datasets, expensive memory, and limited computing power. With the increasing capacity of big data analytics to derive new insights from old data, however, this principle should not be interpreted to mean that institutions should collect the minimum amount of information and throw it away as soon as possible. The routine practice of unrestricted data minimization would sacrifice considerable social benefit.

The interpretation of the data minimization principle must change with changes in technology. Previously, enterprises and other institutions could not use data to perform the astonishing range of activities made possible by new machine learning and artificial intelligence techniques, including high-level cognitive functions that rival or surpass human efforts. Now companies can do these things, provided they retain and analyze truly staggering amounts of information. It is now sensible to retain this information for foreseeable additional uses rather than routinely discarding it.

Digital industries are key sites where the collection of information beyond a bare minimum can have extraordinary benefits. Companies record the details of interactions with online services in ways that vastly increase the value of these services. What users click on when they interact with a social media company or an online marketplace helps the platform provider understand more about their interests and preferences. How long they linger over particular pages or videos is even more revealing of their tastes and can help companies provide more useful features of their services. Imposing a duty to restrict data collection to just the information absolutely needed to provide a minimal version of a digital service would block many of the conveniences digital users have come to take for granted.

This need to collect information beyond the strict minimum does not mean all constraints on data collection and retention should be abandoned. Companies should be required to conduct prior risk-based assessment of the extent of data collection and retention to assess foreseeable privacy harms, and limit data collection when the assessment shows excess risks from this data collection and retention.

An example illustrates the point. Before the introduction of credit cards using a chip, a common way to make a counterfeit card was to hack into a merchant database in the hopes of finding enough information to make counterfeit cards. If the database contained the access codes that had been read from the cards' magnetic stripes, then the thieves could make counterfeit cards. But any fake card without an appropriate access code embedded in its magnetic stripe would not work at the point of sale. This led to a very simple security rule: don't store the access codes. There was no business reason for it to be retained, and there was substantial risk in doing so.

This example suggests that a prior review of data collection and retention practices by merchants would have led them to ignore or delete the access code information that created an unnecessary risk of harm. Data controllers in digital industries should be required to assess the likely harm in retaining the data compared to the likely gains and throw away information or de-identify it when the risks of harm are too great.

The traditional privacy principle of purpose limitation calls for enterprises to seek approval from data subjects when they want to use information collected for one purpose for a purpose that is inconsistent with, unrelated to, or even just different from the original purpose. The European Union's GDPR, for instance, says that personal data shall be "collected for specified, explicit and legitimate purposes and not further processed in a manner that is incompatible with those purposes." When companies are considering secondary use of data originally collected for one limited purpose, they need to ask themselves whether this further use is "incompatible" with the original purpose, a legal standard that has been extensively interpreted by data protection authorities. In making this determination of "incompatibility," these authorities say, data controllers must consider the context in which the personal data have been collected, including the relationship between data subjects and the controller, as well as the possible consequences of the further processing for the data subjects.[56]

One way to try to avoid a need to seek approval for secondary use would be to describe completely the purposes for which an enterprise might want to collect data. But this is exactly what cannot be done in an era of big data analytics. Often information gathered for one purpose is found to be useful for additional purposes. Health information gathered for the purpose of treatment has enormous value for medical research. Information used to assess student learning progress can also be used to examine the effectiveness of new educational tools and programs.

As one commentator put it, "Since analytics are designed to extract hidden or unpredictable inferences and correlations from datasets, it becomes difficult to define *ex ante* the purposes of data processing . . . a notice that explains all the possible uses of data is hard to be given to data subjects at the time of the initial data collection."[57] A privacy principle restricting all secondary uses without further notice and consent would create unnecessary procedural barriers to beneficial uses made possible by new data analysis techniques.

Rebecca Slaughter, commissioner at the FTC, rightly notes, "We should be extremely skeptical about secondary uses of data—that is, uses beyond the purpose for which the data was collected." The vast array of secondary uses in the online world expose consumers to harm and so it is only right to be skeptical about them. But restrictions on secondary use must be based on something other than consumer choice if they are going to be effective in preventing the data abuse which is rightly the commissioner's major concern.[58]

The risks of excessive caution in preventing secondary use to protect privacy are illustrated in the story of the Seattle flu study in the early days of the COVID-19 outbreak in the United States. As part of a research project on the flu, researchers at the University of Seattle had collected and analyzed data from nasal swabs of local residents. In early 2020, as COVID-19 began to spread in the United States, they asked public health officials for permission to retest the samples for coronavirus, but they were initially told that such repurposing of the test information was not possible under the consents that the data subjects had given. They had agreed to flu testing, not coronavirus testing. After weeks of waiting for official approval, the researchers went ahead and tested the data they had already collected without agreement from health officials or data subjects. These tests provided the first evidence of community spread of COVID-19 in the United States, but the discovery of this crucial evidence had been delayed by weeks as health officials sought to protect data subjects from privacy invasions.[59]

Digital industries also need to use data beyond the initial purposes for which it was collected in order to provide their users with important conveniences and benefits.

While the risks of excess caution in data collection and use are real, the need to use information for worthwhile secondary purposes does not mean that any further use of information is automatically legitimate. A contemporary interpretation of the purpose limitation principle would treat secondary uses of personal information as legitimate when they do not pose a significant risk of harm to the data subject or when they are consistent with the context of information collection and use.

Good privacy by design practice suggests a risk analysis of secondary uses beyond what had been contemplated at the time of data collection to assess likely harms and benefits. When there is a significant risk of injury to data subjects, an appropriate level of control might be needed—prohibition, opt-in, or opt-out choice, depending on the severity of the risk. This risk-based interpretation of the purpose limitation principle is more appropriate to meet the challenges of privacy protection in an age of big data. It should be incorporated into the legislation authorizing the digital regulator to implement and enforce data protection rules for digital companies.[60]

Ban on Abusive System Design

Privacy legislation for digital companies should also prohibit what privacy scholar Woodrow Hartzog calls "unreasonably deceptive, abusive, and dangerous design."[61] His focus on prohibiting certain kinds of designs avoids relying on "formalistic notions of 'choice' and 'control' over meaningful privacy protections in a way that wrongfully transfers the risk of loss from data controllers to data subjects." As a result, even though Hartzog presents design regulation as a privacy regime for all companies, not just dominant digital companies, it is especially attractive when consumer choice is further limited by the presence of a dominant company in digital industries. Users who become aware of deceptive, abusive, and dangerous designs practiced by a dominant digital company do not have the ready exit that they would have if there were easily available alternatives for them to turn to.

Hartzog builds his proposal to limit website and app designs on insights from product liability law and consumer protection law. He argues for a new prohibition on deceptive design in technology products and services, including bans on designs that "facilitate" scams, designs that convey false or misleading representations about the product or service, and designs that omit material information that is needed to "keep the overall representations made via technology to consumers from being misleading."

Hartzog has outlined increasingly stringent steps to control the harmful effects of these designs. Education of users, funding of research on privacy-protective designs (including bounties for researchers who uncover dangerous designs), and encouragement of voluntary industry standards for protective design can all be viewed as soft means of discouraging harmful website designs.

Moderate enforcement efforts include mandatory disclosure and transparency and treating elements of design interfaces as implicit promises, where failure to live up to the implied promise might be viewed as illegal deception. It might also impose mandatory processes such as threat modeling, privacy impact assessments, or risk assessments similar to what the FTC already recommends as part of its privacy guidelines. Moderate enforcement measures might also include safe harbors from legal liability for companies that implement good privacy designs.

Robust enforcement measures include liability for defective designs that are the means of producing harms, where the harm involved might be the FTC's notion of consumer harm that cannot be avoided by individual action and has no countervailing benefits. Companies could also be liable for designs that induce people to violate a duty of confidentiality such as revenge porn sites. Robust enforcement would also include certification and authorization regimes that require companies to get approval of their designs before using them. This is how the FDA regulates medical devices. Agencies could say, for instance, that all defaults should be privacy friendly.

Hartzog would also ban any abusive design that does not necessarily lie but "unreasonably frustrates our ability to make autonomous decisions and puts us at greater risk of harm or makes us regret our decisions." He borrows from the statutory prohibition of abusive acts or practices from consumer financial protection law to argue that Congress should set "standards to prohibit design that unreasonably exploits our cognitive limitations, biases, and predictable errors to undermine autonomous decision making."

Hartzog uses the concepts of structure defects and information defects from product liability law to call for a ban on dangerous technology designs whose harmful effects cannot be mitigated by reasonable warnings. He draws on the consumer protection notion of unfair acts or practices to call for a ban on technology designs that impose a substantial risk of consumer harm that has no countervailing benefits and cannot be controlled by any reasonable individual action. He uses this notion of a dangerous design to suggest limits on technological designs that suddenly eliminate barriers that previously kept information secret ("obscurity lurches"), designs that facilitate unexpected and hidden surveillance, and insecure designs that subject people to data breaches.

The need for a legal regime to counter abusive designs is urgent. There is substantial evidence that companies design websites and apps deceptively using "dark patterns" to encourage information sharing that might not be in the best interests of consumers or reflect their true preferences. Jamie Luguri and Lior Strahilevitz recently found that "dark patterns are strikingly effective in getting consumers to do what they would not do when confronted with more neutral user interfaces. . . . Relatively mild dark patterns more than doubled the percentage of consumers who signed up for a dubious identity theft protection service . . . and aggressive dark patterns nearly quadrupled the percentage of consumers signing up." Legislation focused on constraining these abuses has been introduced into the Senate by Senator Mark Warner.[62]

New privacy legislation for digital companies would ban these design practices and empower the agency to write guidance and implementing regulations and to enforce them through fines, penalties, and injunctions in specific cases. Writing these rules and making these assessments will be a challenge. Consumer protection agencies have regulated deceptive statements and omissions for decades, but it is not readily clear how to determine when a manner of presenting information on a website is deceptive and when it is a legitimate nudge. A particular design might exploit a person's cognitive weaknesses to interfere with autonomous decision making or it might be simply making a persuasive appeal based on a person's freely chosen preferences and interests. The distinction between manipulation and persuasion has always been difficult to make.[63]

These challenges in assessing when design is deceptive, abusive, or dangerous should not prevent policymakers from banning these harmful practices. The European Union's proposed regulation on artificial intelligence would ban artificial intelligence (AI) systems that cause or are likely to cause "physical or psychological" harm through the use of "subliminal techniques" or by exploiting vulnerabilities of a "specific group of persons due to their age, physical or mental disability." This ban on manipulative or exploitative AI systems addresses the same problem of dark patterns that Hartzog is aiming at, where companies seek to trick users into making decisions against their own best interests—such as divulging more personal information than is needed to get an online service. This will clearly require specialized agencies to make very specific fact-dependent judgments in particular cases, as well as developing rules for particular industries that define abusive practices.[64]

Making these difficult determinations in particular cases is the kind of thing the FTC and the CFPB (and its predecessor banking regulators) have been doing for generations. Assigning authority to an agency to supervise deceptive, abusive, and dangerous technology designs constitutes a modest extension of existing authority to protect consumers.

But the difficulty of making these decisions also suggests that the responsible agency should have specialized knowledge of the industry it is regulating, not just expertise in consumer protection or privacy as a policy field. Policy expertise in general consumer protection or privacy law might not be sufficient in determining which practices in their particular industry application constitute harmful design practices. Once again, we see the attractiveness of a sector-specific agency to regulate the practices of digital companies.

Fiduciary Duties of Care and Loyalty

Jack Balkin has proposed the notion of an information fiduciary to deal with the vulnerability and dependence of end-users with respect to online service providers' power to collect and use vast amounts of personal information.[65] He notes that the general notion of a fiduciary is one who has special obligations of loyalty and trustworthiness toward another person." Traditional fiduciaries have a "duty of care" that requires them to act so that they do not "harm the interests of the principal, beneficiary, or client." They also have a "duty of loyalty," which requires them to "keep their clients' interests in mind and act in their clients' interests." Under their "duties of confidentiality," traditional fiduciaries may "not say anything that harms their clients or creates a conflict of interest."

Balkin argues that the law should consider online service providers as information fiduciaries with duties of care, loyalty, and confidentiality to their users. These duties would counteract the "information asymmetries" that would otherwise expose users to exploitation and abuse. Balkin says these duties of information fiduciaries are "not identical to those of older kinds of fiduciaries but have similarities to them." They might be "considerably narrower" and "more limited." This is because online service companies use personal information to make money through targeted advertising. If their fiduciary duties are "too broad," they might not be able to "make any money at all" from user data.

Moreover, the fiduciary duties of digital platforms should be limited, because they "do not hold themselves out as taking care of end-users in general." They should not be subject to a general duty of warning their users if they are about to do something harmful, such as looking up an old college roommate who is a "dangerous person." Unlike a traditional fiduciary, the duty of digital platforms "to protect us is quite limited."

He does suggest some general responsibilities for online service providers acting as information fiduciaries. One fiduciary duty is that "online service providers may not act like con men." Another duty is to avoid actions their users "would reasonably consider unexpected or abusive for them to do." Information fiduciaries may not use personal information "in unexpected ways to the disadvantage of people who use their services or in ways that violate some other important social norm," including to use information "to embarrass or manipulate end-users." Balkin says that digital fiduciaries "should have an obligation to facilitate end-users' control over their information and to explain the consequences of privacy settings."

Balkin is clear there is no one-size-fits-all set of fiduciary duties, saying the "scope of the fiduciary duty, however, is not the same for every entity. It depends on the nature of the relationship, the reasonableness of trust, and the importance of preventing self-dealing by the entity and harm to the end-user, client, or beneficiary."

Balkin does not think the law should treat every company as an information fiduciary. These special duties of care and loyalty should apply when user relationships with online service companies "involve significant vulnerability, because online service providers have considerable expertise and knowledge and end-users usually do not." He also thinks they should apply when "we find ourselves in a position of relative dependence with respect to these companies. They provide many kinds of services that we need." The covered companies also are "experts in providing certain kinds of services in exchange for our personal information" who hold valuable data that "might be used to our disadvantage."

These criteria apply to the digital companies that are the focus of our concern. Balkin is pointing to the same circumstances of vulnerability and dependence with respect to the use of personal information that exist when a company has significant market power over their customers and can use that market power to extract information. His notion seems especially apt for the circumstances of digital companies.

Legislation implementing an information fiduciary approach has been introduced in the US Senate.[66] It calls for a duty of care defined as a requirement that an online service provider shall "reasonably secure individual identifying data from unauthorized access" and shall "promptly inform an end user of any breach" involving "sensitive data of that end user." The legislation would ban uses of data when the use is "detrimental" to the user and involves either "physical or financial harm" or would be unexpectedly "offensive." It provides that an online service provider may not disclose or sell or share user data "except as consistent with the duties of care and loyalty" in the bill and must ensure by contract and regular audits that other users of customer data live under the same duties of care and loyalty.

The duty of care in the proposed legislation is the same as is required in many state data security and breach notification statutes and does not seem to expand the FTC's current authority under Section 5 to require all companies to establish and maintain reasonable information security measures. Similarly, the duty to avoid data uses to the "detriment" of customers or that causes them physical or financial harm seems to be encompassed under the FTC's current unfairness authority. Only the ban on uses that would be both unexpected and offensive is a genuinely new duty.

The ADPPA, which was reported from the House Energy and Commerce Committee with an impressive bipartisan vote of 53–2 on July 20, 2022, contains a number of "duties of loyalty."[67] Some of these duplicate other privacy duties we have discussed such as data minimization, design limitations, and restrictions on tying service to waiving privacy rights. Other loyalty duties include restrictions on the use of sensitive information such as social security numbers. While good privacy measures, none of these duties appear to add anything new to digital privacy responsibilities other than being described as a "duty of loyalty."

Lina Khan (when she was a law professor before her appointment as FTC chair) and legal scholar David Pozen have criticized Balkin's information fiduciary proposal on similar grounds. They argue that the substantive duties that an information fiduciary law would impose "turn out not to require fiduciary law or theory at all." They "would simply mirror or marginally refine longstanding consumer protection guarantees and anti-fraud doctrines."

For instance, in connection with the duty to avoid acting like a con man, they note that "deception is already prohibited by a suite of state and federal consumer protection statutes." As for manipulation and abuse, they may already be "proscribed by state tort law or by state and federal consumer protection statutes, which prohibit 'unfair' as well as 'deceptive' practices."

In addition, they say, the fiduciary model replicates the individualistic bias of much privacy law and policy by focusing on the "special relationship of trust and dependency with each of its users" and on what a fiduciary "owes any given individual who signs up for its service." They prefer a model of privacy that treats data protection as a "public good."[68]

These criticisms are not fatal to the fiduciary approach. Requiring digital technology companies to act as if they were information fiduciaries with limited duties of care, loyalty, and confidentiality is far from individualistic. Instead, it has affinities with social theories of privacy, especially Helen Nissenbaum's view of privacy as contextual integrity.[69] In effect, it says that major tech companies like Google and Facebook are already enmeshed in a thick network of implicit social duties and obligations in virtue of the relationships they create among their users and between their users and the company operating the information platform. The legal proposal is that new legislation should protect these preexisting social norms by assigning to digital companies appropriate legal duties and authorizing a regulatory agency to specify them in some detail through rulemaking and then implement and enforce them.

A major advantage of the fiduciary approach is that it goes beyond individual consent as a legal basis for data processing. The new privacy law for digital companies would provide that a digital company would be independently subject to fiduciary obligations, even if it justifies its acquisition and use of personal information on the basis of consent. Moving to an affirmative obligation to avoid harm rather than solely an obligation to give consumers choice seems especially appropriate when setting up data protection duties for digital technology companies, whose market position makes it difficult to design an effective choice architecture.

Despite the Khan and Pozen criticism that the fiduciary approach is irredeemably individualistic, the intrinsic momentum of the approach is to move to a social conception of privacy, where privacy is needed to protect and preserve relationships that form the context of our social lives.[70] In this way, the information fiduciary approach moves beyond the individualistic biases of much privacy thinking and treats privacy to some degree as a public good.

It is true that the specific duties Balkin discusses as part of fiduciary obligations for information companies and those duties contained in the proposed legislative implementation of these fiduciary obligations in the Data Care Act or the American Data Privacy and Protection Act are not novel; they largely duplicate existing responsibilities. But that calls for the approach to be refined not abandoned. In privacy legislation, fiduciary duties could function as a residual category, providing the digital regulator with authority to impose additional duties beyond those specified under data minimization, purpose limitation, and the other statutory data protection duties.

In this way, privacy legislation for digital companies should require them to live up to separate duties of care, loyalty, and confidentiality toward their users. It would authorize a regulatory agency to define these duties through rulemaking and decisions in specific cases and to enforce these decisions through fines, penalties, and injunctions. Rather than laying out these duties as specific requirements, the law would specify them only as very general requirements for care, loyalty, and confidentiality and leave the details to agency rulemaking and decisions in specific cases.

Hartzog and Neil Richards defend the idea that duties of loyalty should be implemented in a two-tiered structure of statutory mandates and subsidiary rules established by agency rulemaking.[71] They follow Balkin in thinking of a duty of loyalty as "an enforceable obligation on companies to act in the best interests of their human customers." In contrast, a duty of care "requires that fiduciaries take care not to cause harm to those they owe fiduciary duties to—most often the vulnerable parties that the law is stepping in to protect like wards, shareholders, and professional clients." These general duties to avoid harming users (care) and to promote their best interests (loyalty) might be incorporated into legislated rules such as requiring companies "to act at all times in the best interests of users regarding their data" or "prohibiting them from taking any actions with respect to processing data or designing user interfaces that conflict with the best interests of their users." They suggest that the legislation then could assign a regulator with sufficient rulemaking authority to write and implement future subsidiary rules.

Such open-ended flexibility is needed to allow the agency to take into account the changing and industry-specific context of application. The statute should not be too specific if it is to allow the agency to respond to the rapidly shifting dynamics of digital industries. This need for flexibility in determining the specific obligations implied by fiduciary duties makes it all the more important for the implementing agency to have industry-specific knowledge and expertise.

Restrictions on Data Use

As many commentators have noted, GDPR provides procedural, not substantive protections. Its goal is not to limit any specific use of information but to ensure that all uses are subject to certain fair procedures to ensure the protection of the rights and freedoms of data subjects. Most existing and proposed privacy statutes in the United States similarly permit any data use at all provided certain procedures are followed. For instance, the most prominent comprehensive state privacy law, the California Consumer Privacy Act, which is the model for other state privacy statutes, only provides for the due process protection of an opt-out from selling personal information.[72]

But a few privacy statutes in the United States ban certain uses of information, rather than requiring companies to obtain consent or demonstrating legitimate interest or providing other procedural protections. For instance, the Student Online Personal Information Protection Act (SOPIPA) prevents internet and cloud-based sites, applications, and services designed for K–12 educational purposes from selling, using, or distributing student data for targeted marketing purposes. Federal health privacy law generally prohibits the sale of health information and its use for underwriting purposes. The Genetic Information Nondiscrimination Act prohibits US health insurance companies and employers from making decisions based on information derived from genetic tests. The Gramm-Leach-Bliley Act regulating financial information bans the sharing of account numbers for marketing purposes. The extensive confidentiality rules and witness privileges also limit the extent to which information can be used in certain contexts.[73]

The earliest privacy statute in the United States, the Fair Credit Reporting Act, imposes procedural protections to ensure that the use of consumer credit reports protects consumers, but it does so in the context of confining the use of consumer reports to certain statutorily prescribed permissible purposes.[74] They can be used for credit underwriting, for instance, but not for marketing. This restriction to permissible purposes was part of a policy balance that allowed credit bureaus to compile vast quantities of information about people, so long as they used that information solely for certain purposes that were determined to be important enough to justify data collection of that scale and magnitude.

Federal law also bans the use of information about a person's membership in a protected class to make decisions in the contexts of employment, insurance, housing, and lending. Title VII of the Civil Rights Act of 1964 makes it unlawful for employers and employment agencies to discriminate against an applicant or employee because of such individual's "race, color, religion, sex, or national origin." The Equal Credit

Opportunity Act makes it unlawful for any creditor to discriminate against any applicant for credit based on "race, color, religion, national origin, sex or marital status, or age." Title VIII of the Civil Rights Act of 1968, the Fair Housing Act, prohibits discrimination in the sale, rental, or financing of housing "because of race, color, religion, sex, familial status, or national origin." The act also protects people with disabilities and families with children. The Age Discrimination in Employment Act of 1967 (ADEA) makes it unlawful for an employer to refuse to hire or to discharge or to otherwise discriminate against any individual because of the individual's age. Section 1557 of the Affordable Care Act of 2010 prohibits discrimination in health care and health insurance based on race, color, national origin, age, disability, or sex.[75]

Enforcement of these laws is given to specific agencies such as the economy-wide Equal Employment Opportunity Commission and sector-specific agencies regulating housing and financial services. Of course, these laws apply to digital companies. Insofar as they are providing advertising services to housing and rental companies, for instance, they are covered by the fair housing laws enforced by the Department of Housing and Urban Development (HUD). In fact, HUD has sued Facebook for violation of these laws in connection with the use of its ethnic affinities marketing classifications for housing advertisements.[76]

Recently proposed privacy and algorithmic fairness legislation would impose more general duties to avoid discrimination in the use of data and data analytics. For instance, Senator Kirsten Gillibrand has introduced legislation making it unlawful for any data aggregator or service provider to commit any unlawful, unfair, deceptive, abusive, or discriminatory acts or practices in connection with the collection, processing, or sharing of personal data. The proposed bill also establishes an economy-wide data protection agency with authority to define these prohibited acts and enforce rules against them. It also creates a new office of civil rights within this new data protection agency. Senator Ron Wyden has introduced the Algorithmic Accountability Act, which requires companies to assess their automatic decision systems for risks to "privacy and security of personal information" and risks of "inaccurate, unfair, biased, or discriminatory decisions" and to address the results of their assessments. The

FTC would enforce this requirement. The European Union's proposed regulation of artificial intelligence also requires prior assessments of advanced analytic systems for discrimination and other harms.[77]

This movement to restrict or ban discriminatory information uses is part of what legal scholar Frank Pasquale calls the "second wave of algorithmic accountability" where policymakers, developers, and users ask whether the advantages of new software and data use really outweigh their social costs. There might be additional uses of data beyond their use for discriminatory purposes that should be banned, rather than be subjected to the procedural limits in traditional privacy law. Some cities and states have proposed limits on the use of facial recognition technology for both commercial and governmental purposes. Illinois has a strong opt-in law that requires companies to get affirmative consent before using biometric information including facial information. These restrictions and prohibitions on the use of personal information for biometric or facial recognition would apply to digital companies as well as any other company seeking to use data for this purpose.[78]

It would not be prudent to establish additional sweeping bans of data uses in legislation. Congress certainly has the authority to prohibit specific data uses for the digital companies, but it has neither the expertise nor the time to develop such expertise to compile and evaluate the evidence needed to justify a complete ban on specific data uses.

Nevertheless, it is possible and maybe likely that core digital companies will seek to engage in dangerous uses of personal information that cannot be controlled by reasonable warnings or other regulations and that are beyond the power of market forces to discourage. For this reason, the new privacy law should reserve to the regulatory agency the discretion to ban such dangerous uses, contingent on a finding after a rulemaking proceeding with notice and public comment that the use creates a substantial risk of harm that cannot be reasonably avoided by consumers and has no countervailing benefits to the public, which is the standard the FTC uses now to define an unfair act or practice.[79]

This need to make fact-heavy context-dependent judgments about the dangers of specific industry data practices suggests once again that that the digital regulator should be an expert in the business practices of these core lines of business, not an economy-wide regulator with a policy focus on privacy.

Expert and Balanced Enforcement

Comprehensive privacy legislation could provide the FTC with additional authority and resources to act as a federal privacy regulator. Alternatively, it could create a new regulatory agency dedicated solely to privacy enforcement, similar to the data protection authorities in Europe that enforce the GDPR. It seems most likely that Congress will assign the enforcement to the FTC, an economy-wide agency but one that has broad authority over antitrust and consumer protection. The leading national privacy bill, the ADPPA, which passed the House Energy and Commerce Committee in July 2022 with an impressive bipartisan vote of 53–2, assigned enforcement responsibility to the FTC.[80]

This is the right way to go. Privacy enforcement through the FTC is generally consistent with the ideal proposed in this book for a digital agency with multiple missions including privacy, competition, and content moderation. As discussed in the last chapter, the FTC already has substantial antitrust authority which would be enlarged and focused by new competition reform laws aimed at anticompetitive digital practices. Adding privacy duties to that would enable it to balance privacy and competition issues.

The agency already polices privacy violations through its authority to prohibit unfair and deceptive acts and practices. It has brought dozens of cases against digital companies for privacy violations, including strong action against two of the leading digital companies, Facebook and Google. In August 2022, it opened a rulemaking to consider establishing privacy trade rules against unfair or deceptive online data practices that are prevalent in the market.[81] It appears focused on abuses in the core digital industries that are the focus of this book. Expanding and clarifying its privacy authority in a new privacy law would build on the substantial expertise that the FTC already possesses in privacy and especially in digital privacy issues.

As a transition, this enforcement and implementation mechanism would work. Even though the FTC is an economy-wide regulator, it has developed the specialized knowledge of the digital industry to administer a privacy law in ways that would work to protect the privacy of digital users. No new dedicated privacy agency would have that body of expertise from the beginning. FTC enforcement has the enormous advantage of housing privacy and competition issues in the same agency, allowing a single administrative determination of the proper balancing between these sometimes competing and sometimes complementary policy spheres. But long term, it would not be viable.

Privacy enforcement for digital industries must eventually migrate from an economy-wide agency like the FTC to a digital agency with specialized knowledge and expertise in digital industries. This is because the FTC's digital responsibilities would eventually outgrow its institutional role as an economy-wide antitrust and consumer protection agency.

A specialist regulator with authority over digital companies would be best positioned to make the difficult decisions in interpreting, applying, and enforcing the new privacy duties. The privacy duties envisioned in the new privacy law could be formulated in a general fashion to be applicable in principle to all companies. Indeed, the privacy provisions we outlined in the last several sections were all constructed to be universally applicable. But interpretation and enforcement for the digital context would require a specialist regulator with detailed knowledge of the technology industry.

Other sector regulators handle privacy issues as part of their duties to supervise the industry under their jurisdiction. The FCC was able to develop and enforce privacy rules for broadband because it had decades of experience enforcing privacy rules for telephone and cable companies, as well as a deep understanding of their business. Financial regulators have broad and deep understanding of the business of banking and can bring that experience to bear in understanding how to develop privacy guidance and enforcement priorities for the industry. The Department of Health and Human Services understands the different roles and actors in the health care industry and as a result is able to craft nuanced and flexible privacy rules that meet the needs of physicians, hospitals, insurance companies, and payment systems while protecting the confidentiality of health information.

The new privacy regulator for the tech industry will need sector-specific expertise to make effective privacy decisions. Some examples drawn from the previous discussion in this chapter highlight the need for specialist industry experience:

- When is personal information necessary to provide a digital company's service? It depends, among other things, on exactly what the service is, which group of users it is seeking to serve, what interests and expectations these users bring to the marketplace, and what alternatives are technically and economically feasible.
- What is the dividing line between a data practice that is necessary for satisfying a company's legitimate interest and a data practice that is useful or helpful in achieving a legitimate goal but not strictly necessary? When is that company interest so important that it outweighs the rights and interests of users?
- When is a design for an app store or an electronic marketplace abusive? It depends, among other things, on what user expectations are, what practices they have grown accustomed to, what other providers in the same market do, and what alternative design strategies are available that could accomplish the same purposes.
- What exactly do the duties of care and loyalty amount to for a particular digital line of business? It depends on the business context, the expectations of users in this context, and the practices and norms that have grown up in the context. What users expect from an online store differs from what they expect from an off-line store.
- What financial incentives for data sharing beyond what is necessary to provide the service still allow meaningful consent? If the test is based on the value of the data to the data subject or the company, as it is in the California privacy law, only intimate knowledge of industry practices and economics can determine that.[82]
- What industry uses are so dangerous that reasonable warnings or other regulations cannot protect users of the public from

> significant risks of harm? Only detailed knowledge of the specific line of business in the digital industry can provide an answer to this question.

A generalist privacy regulator will simply not know how to address these context-specific questions. Inevitably it would be too strict or too lax. Or still worse, it would be unable to enforce the statute at all for lack of resources or expertise. It does not seem possible for a single omnibus privacy agency to engage in the detailed enforcement of enhanced privacy rules for digital companies if they are also responsible for enforcing privacy rules for the entire economy.

Of course, the FTC's current expertise in digital matters gives it an enormous advantage over a new agency in assessing these issues. But over time, the more and more detailed demands for detailed digital industry expertise will overwhelm an agency that also has to deal with the entire rest of the economy.

The need to balance other policy objectives with privacy concerns also speaks in favor of a sectoral regulator. Privacy regulation for dominant technology companies can reinforce procompetitive regulation, because, as public interest advocate Harold Feld has noted, "their gigantic stockpiles of accumulated personal information constitute an impossible burden to successful competition."[83] As outlined in the previous chapter on promoting competition in digital industries, significant procompetitive issues arise from the omnipresent collection, sharing, and use of personal data in digital lines of business, and must be addressed through regulatory tools involving data portability, data sharing, and perhaps even mandated data access for rivals. However, procompetitive regulation to provide needed resources for industry players and start-ups to compete with incumbent technology companies might very well create privacy risks.

Procompetition bills in the US House of Representatives recognize that privacy issues will need to be addressed at the same time as procompetitive measures. The mandate for data portability and interoperability, for example, requires platforms to establish privacy and security standards governing access to data for competing businesses, and it requires competing businesses to comply with these standards. It requires that user data cannot be transferred to competing businesses without the "affirmative express consent" of the user and has an extended definition of the notion of affirmative consent. Additionally, it requires the FTC to develop technical standards for data portability and interoperability that "protect data security and privacy."[84]

By assigning enforcement responsibilities to the FTC, the legislation takes a positive step by housing privacy and competition issues within the same regulatory structure. This allows a single regulator to make the trade-offs that might be needed to balance the policy goals of promoting competition and protecting privacy in particular cases.

Some proposed procompetitive bills also attempt to set a standard for reconciling privacy and competition when they are in tension. A standard or list of considerations for balancing the privacy interests of users with the competitive interests of existing digital rivals and new entrants has to be established in legislation. Unfortunately, some pro-competition measures get this standard wrong by imposing a one-sided, quasi-constitutional preference for promoting competition over protecting privacy. For instance, the House bill that imposes interoperability rules on digital companies also mandates a priority of competition over privacy, requiring the enforcing agency to limit interoperability in favor of privacy only when the privacy measure is "narrowly tailored . . . and does not have the purpose or effect of unreasonably denying access or undermining interoperability for competing businesses or potential competing businesses."[85]

A list of considerations for balancing privacy and competition in a particular case might include a qualitative risk assessment that instructs the agency to examine the extent of the privacy risks and the gains to competition from a particular measure. This assessment might be qualitative but scaled. Minor and not very compelling gains for competitors might override even more trivial advances of privacy interests of the data subject, while important or compelling advances in promoting competition might justify even a significant impact on user privacy interests. In addition, when there is cultural or societal recognition of the legitimacy and importance of the privacy interests involved that should weigh more heavily in the balancing test against the promotion of competition, other factors to consider include the nature of personal data, the way the information is being processed, the reasonable expectations of the data subjects, and the status of the companies involved and the data subjects.[86]

One reason to assign the promotion of competition in digital industries to an agency also responsible for protecting privacy is to prevent an independent agency focused solely on competition to give little consideration to privacy issues. At the same time, the digital regulator must not allow digital companies to use privacy as a cover for anticompetitive conduct. The agency must carefully devise, and supervise company compliance with, data protection measures to ensure that digital companies are not using privacy rules as a shield to create or maintain barriers to entry. A pure privacy regulator unconcerned with the competitive impact of industry practices might be inclined to ignore or tolerate anticompetitive practices dressed up as privacy measures. Once again, a combined regulatory structure provides the best protection against pursuing a single objective at the expense of overall policy coherence.

The way forward is through a two-step process in which privacy enforcement is initially lodged with the FTC. When the limitations of having privacy for digital industries enforced by a generalist regulator are made evident, Congress could then transfer these privacy enforcement and implementation duties, as well as the digital competition responsibilities, to a sectoral regulator able to implement privacy duties with the nuance and flexibility needed to meet the privacy needs of digital users and to balance these policy choices to also provide for competition and good content moderation in digital industries.

First Amendment Issues

In the United States, privacy is secondary to free speech. Free speech has constitutional protection under the First Amendment. The Fourth Amendment protects people from unreasonable searches and seizures by the government but offers no such protection against commercial use of personal information. As a result, privacy statutes are subject to challenge as potentially violating the First Amendment.

Strict First Amendment scrutiny requires the statute to serve a compelling government interest and use the least restrictive means of achieving that interest. Intermediate scrutiny requires the less demanding standard of serving a substantial government interest with means narrowly tailored to that purpose. Commercial speech—that is, speech such as advertising that proposes an economic transaction or that concerns only the firm and its intended audience—receives a form of intermediate scrutiny. Both are forms of heightened scrutiny above the rational basis test courts use for economic regulation to ensure that it is rationally related to a legitimate need.[87]

Courts have regularly rejected free speech challenges to privacy statutes under the standard of intermediate scrutiny. In 2001, for instance, it upheld the Fair Credit Reporting Act in the face of a First Amendment challenge. The FCRA prevents credit reporting agencies from using information in credit reports for marketing purposes but allows use for eligibility decisions. Trans Union challenged on First Amendment grounds. The Court of Appeals for the District of Columbia ruled that the information in credit reports is private commercial information of no public interest, and so the FCRA restrictions should be reviewed under intermediate scrutiny. It found that the statute passed that test. It had no trouble finding that the government interest in FCRA rules of protecting the privacy of consumer credit information was substantial. It rejected the "less burdensome alternative" of allowing consumer reporting agencies to sell credit information as long as they notify consumers and give them the ability to opt out, since, under intermediate scrutiny, the FCRA does not have to embody the least burdensome alternative. Finally, it ruled that the FCRA could appropriately single out credit reporting agencies for marketing restrictions, and no other companies, because they have unique access to a broad range of continually updated, detailed information about millions of consumers' personal credit histories.[88]

Privacy rules in telecommunications have also been challenged. In US West, the Court of Appeals for the Tenth Circuit, reviewed the FCC's privacy rule for telecommunications firms under intermediate scrutiny, and found them wanting. The FCC's rules required carriers to get opt-in consent to use customer information for marketing purposes.

The court found, however, that an opt-out choice would be just as effective in protecting privacy, and so the rules were not narrowly tailored. The FCC then revised its privacy rules to require opt-in for third-party data sharing, but only opt-out for affiliate sharing, and the Court of Appeals for the District of Columbia upheld these revised privacy rules.

In 2016, the FCC adopted new privacy rules for broadband privacy. These rules would have required broadband providers to get opt-in consent for all marketing activities, except those related to offering communications services. In particular, they would have been required to get opt-in consent to base marketing activities on information they had about subscriber web visits. The industry filed a First Amendment challenge, but Congress repealed the rules in 2017 before the court could rule on it.[89]

The 2011 *Sorrell v. IMF* case suggested, however, that privacy statutes might be more vulnerable to constitutional challenge than previously thought. A Vermont statute required opt-in approval from doctors to allow pharmacies to share their prescription information with analytics firms that provided marketing services to pharmaceutical companies. It did not require this approval for other uses of prescription information such as health research. The Supreme Court struck down the law. It ruled that the process of gathering and analyzing data in preparation for speech such as marketing is protected by the First Amendment. But the Vermont statute forbids or allows information sharing based on the content of the speech and who is speaking. It disfavors marketing and companies engaged in marketing while favoring other uses of data such as research.[90]

The dire consequences that some predicted would flow from *Sorrell* have not materialized in the decade since the Court took action. It did not usher in a new regime of strict scrutiny for any speaker- or content-based speech regulation of commercial speech. For instance, Maine passed a broadband privacy law similar to the repealed federal regulation in 2019 and in 2020 the US District Court for the District of Maine used intermediate scrutiny to deny an industry motion for final judgment on the claim that the Maine law was a facially unconstitutional violation of the First Amendment.[91] Moreover, no First Amendment challenge has emerged to the 2018 California privacy law or to the other comprehensive state privacy laws. General privacy law seems well positioned to withstand constitutional scrutiny.

Still, it would be prudent to craft carefully the federal law giving the digital regulator authority to enforce data protection rules to anticipate a First Amendment challenge. Any constraints on the use of information will have to be narrowly defined and justified by the special risks to privacy posed by these uses. Since the statute would not impose use restrictions, but only provide authority to the digital regulator to adopt them, the law likely would not be subject to a facial challenge. But any exercise of the authority granted to the agency to restrict or ban data uses would face a higher burden of showing under intermediate scrutiny that it was narrowly tailored to achieve a substantial government interest.

Coda

The focus on harms resulting from data collection and use has encouraged reformers to look beyond privacy into other areas of law and policy. Policymakers are beginning to go beyond privacy law to address harms that go well beyond the failure to observe good procedures in the collection and use of personal information. The primary area where this has occurred is in discussions of algorithmic fairness and the need for broad risk assessments before deploying advanced analytic techniques. Senator Gillibrand's data aggregator bill, Senator Wyden's algorithmic accountability bill, and the European Union's artificial intelligence regulation all put heavy emphasis on prior and ongoing assessments as a way to understand and mitigate the harms that might result from the use of algorithms in high-risk cases.

One of the harms associated with algorithms is information disorder in social media and other digital industries. Algorithmic techniques for amplifying and personalizing comments and posts disseminate misinformation, disinformation, and hate speech widely on social media platforms. In line with our visual image of a Venn diagram of three intersecting policy circles, the measures needed to protect against information disorder overlap with and also go beyond the measures needed to promote competition and privacy. It is to this vitally urgent topic of how to mitigate information disorder in social media that we turn in the next chapter.

Notes

1. "Google CEO on Privacy (video): 'If You Have Something You Don't Want Anyone to Know, Maybe You Shouldn't Be Doing It,'" *Huffington Post*, March 18, 2010, https://www.huffpost.com/entry/google-ceo-on-privacy-if_n_383105.

2. Polly Sprenger, "Sun on Privacy: 'Get Over It,'" *Wired*, January 26, 1999, https://www.wired.com/1999/01/sun-on-privacy-get-over-it.

3. American Data Privacy and Protection Act, H.R. 8152, 117th Cong. (2022), https://www.congress.gov/bill/117th-congress/house-bill/8152.

4. Fair Credit Reporting Act, 15 U.S.C. § 1681; Family Educational Rights and Privacy Act, 20 U.S.C. § 1232g; Cable Communications Policy Act, 47 U.S.C. § 551; Video Privacy Protection Act, 18 U.S.C § 2710; Driver's Privacy Protection Act, 18 U.S.C. § 2721; Health Insurance Portability and Accountability Act, 42 U.S.C. § 1320d; Gramm-Leach-Bliley Financial Modernization Act of 1999, 15 U.S.C. § 6801–09, 20, Title V; Health Insurance Portability and Accountability Act, 15 U.S.C. Chapter 91, 45 CFR Parts 160 and 164.

5. FTC, "Trade Regulation Rule on Commercial Surveillance and Data Security."

6. Samuel D. Warren and Louis D. Brandeis, "The Right to Privacy," *Harvard Law Review* 4, no. 5 (Dec. 15, 1890): 193–220, https://www.cs.cornell.edu/~shmat/courses/cs5436/warren-brandeis.pdf; William L. Prosser, "Privacy," *California Law Review* 48, no. 3 (Aug. 1960): 383–423, https://www.jstor.org/stable/3478805; see the short history of the evolution of privacy law in Ohm, "Broken Promises of Privacy," 1731–39; Edward J. Bloustein, "Privacy as an Aspect of Human Dignity," reprinted in Edward J. Bloustein, *Individual and Group Privacy* (Piscataway, NJ: Transaction Books, 1978), 1–47.

7. See Robert Gellman, "Fair Information Practices: A Basic History," Version 2.20, January 26, 2021, http://bobgellman.com/rg-docs/rg-FIPShistory.pdf; "Privacy," OECD 1980, http://www.oecd.org/document/18/0,2340,en_2649_34255_1815186_1_1_1_1,00.html.

8. Fred Cate, "Failure of Fair Information Practice Principles," in Jane K. Winn (ed.), *Consumer Protection in the Age of the Information Economy* (New York: Routledge, 2006), 369–75, https://papers.ssrn.com/sol3/papers.cfm?abstract_id=1156972.

9. Alan Westin, *Privacy and Freedom* (New York: Atheneum, 1967), 7.

10. "Universal Declaration of Human Rights, Article 12," United Nations, http://www.un.org/en/documents/udhr; "International Covenant on Civil and Political Rights, Article, 17," United Nations, http://www.ohchr.org/Documents/ProfessionalInterest/ccpr.pdf; "European Convention on Human Rights, Article 8(1)," http://www.echr.coe.int/Documents/Convention_ENG.pdf.

11. "Treaty on the Functioning of the European Union, Article 16," http://eur-lex.europa.eu/legal-content/EN/TXT/PDF/?uri=CELEX:12012E/TXT&from=EN; "Charter of Fundamental Rights of the European Union, Articles 7 and 8," http://eur-lex.europa.eu/LexUriServ/LexUriServ.do?uri=OJ:C:2010:083:0389:0403:en:PDF.

12. "Directive 95/46/EC of the European Parliament and of the Council of 24 October 1995 on the protection of individuals with regard to the processing of personal data and on the free movement of such data," *Official Journal of the European Communities* no. L281 (1995): 31, http://eur-lex.europa.eu/legal-content/EN/TXT/PDF/?uri=CELEX:31995L0046&from=en; "General Data Protection Regulation," *Official Journal of the European Communities* no. L119 (2016): 37, http://eur-lex.europa.eu/legal-content/EN/TXT/PDF/?uri=OJ:L:2016:119:FULL&from=EN.

13. Ohm, "Broken Promises of Privacy," 1748.

14. Richard Posner, "The Right of Privacy," *Georgia Law Review* 12, no. 393 (1978): 393–404, http://digitalcommons.law.uga.edu/cgi/viewcontent.cgi?article=1021&context=lectures_pre_arch_lectures_sibley; Howard Beales III and Timothy J. Muris, "Choice or Consequences: Protecting Privacy in Commercial Information," *University of Chicago Law Review* 75, no. 109 (2008), https://chicagounbound.uchicago.edu/uclrev/vol75/iss1/6; MacCarthy, "New Directions in Privacy," 425–512; Benjamin Wittes, "Databuse: Digital Privacy and the Mosaic," Brookings Institution, April 1, 2011, http://www.brookings.edu/~/media/Files/rc/papers/2011/0401_databuse_wittes/0401_databuse_wittes.pdf; Cate, "Failure of Fair Information Practice Principles," 369–75.

15. Federal Trade Commission Act, 15 U.S.C. 45(n) (2006).

16. See Maureen Ohlhausen, "Painting the Privacy Landscape: Informational Injury in FTC Privacy and Data Security Cases," Federal Trade Commission, September 19, 2017, https://www.ftc.gov/system/files/documents/public_statements/1255113/privacy_speech_mkohlhausen.pdf.

17. MacCarthy, "New Directions in Privacy."

18. Helen Nissenbaum, *Privacy in Context* (Palo Alto, CA: Stanford University Press, 2009), chapters 7–9; Helen Nissenbaum, "Privacy as Contextual Integrity," *Washington Law Review* 79, no. 119 (2004), https://crypto.stanford.edu/portia/papers/RevnissenbaumDTP31.pdf; Robert C. Post, "The Social Foundations of Privacy: Community and Self in the Common Law Tort," *California Law Review* 77, no. 5 (1989), http://digitalcommons.law.yale.edu/cgi/viewcontent.cgi?article=1210&context=fss_papers; Robert Merton, *Social Theory and Social Structure* (New York: Free Press, 1968), 395–433; Michel Foucault, *Discipline and Punish: The Birth of the Prison*, trans. Alan Sheridan (New York: Vintage Books, 1977), excerpt on Panopticism available at http://foucault.info/documents/disciplineAndPunish/foucault.disciplineAndPunish.panOpticism.html; Mark MacCarthy, "Privacy Policy and Contextual Harm," *Journal of Law and Policy* 13, no. 400 (2017), https://papers.ssrn.com/sol3/papers.cfm?abstract_id=3093253.

19. "EU Charter of Fundamental Rights, Article 8," *Official Journal of the European Communities* no. 303/17, https://fra.europa.eu/en/eu-charter/article/8-protection-personal-data; GDPR, "Art.6 GDPR Lawfulness of Processing," (1), https://gdpr-info.eu/art-6-gdpr.

20. Hartzog, *Privacy's Blueprint.*

21. Jack M. Balkin, "Lecture, Information Fiduciaries and the First Amendment," (2016), https://lawreview.law.ucdavis.edu/issues/49/4/Lecture/49-4_Balkin.pdf.

22. Ponnurangam Kumaraguru and Lorrie Faith Cranor, "Privacy Indexes: A Survey of Westin's Studies," Institute for Software Research International, Technical Report, CMU-ISRI-5–138) (2005), http://www.cs.cmu.edu/~ponguru/CMU-ISRI-05-138.pdf.

23. Aleecia McDonald and Lorrie Faith Cranor, "The Cost of Reading Privacy Policies," (2008), http://lorrie.cranor.org/pubs/readingPolicyCost-authorDraft.pdf.

24. Hartzog, *Privacy's Blueprint*, 21–56; Kerry, Morris, Chin, and Turner Lee, "Bridging the Gaps"; Rebecca Slaughter, "Disputing the Dogmas of Surveillance Advertising," National Advertising Division Keynote 2021, October 1, 2021, https://www.ftc.gov/system/files/documents/public_statements/1597050/commissioner_slaughter_national_advertising_division_10-1-2021_keynote_address.pdf.

25. See MacCarthy, "New Directions in Privacy." See OECD Glossary of Statistical terms, available at https://stats.oecd.org/glossary/detail.asp?ID=6932; Cynthia Dwork, "Differential Privacy," 33rd International Colloquium on Automata, Languages and Programming, part II (ICALP 2006), 1–12, https://www.microsoft.com/en-us/research/publication/differential-privacy.

26. Charles Duhigg, "How Companies Learn Your Secrets," *New York Times*, February 16, 2012, available at http://www.nytimes.com/2012/02/19/magazine/shopping-habits.html; Carter Jernigan and Behram F. T. Mistree, "Gaydar: Facebook Friends Expose Sexual Orientation," *First Monday* 14, no. 10 (October 5, 2009), http://firstmonday.org/article/view/2611/2302; "Using Publicly Available Information to Proxy for Unidentified Race and Ethnicity: A Methodology and Assessment," CFPB, Summer 2014, https://files.consumerfinance.gov/f/201409_cfpb_report_proxy-methodology.pdf.

27. Mark MacCarthy, "Privacy Is Not a Property Right in Personal Information," *Forbes Washington Bytes*, November 2, 2018, https://www.forbes.com/sites/washingtonbytes/2018/11/02/privacy-is-not-a-property-right-in-personal-information/#199d3236280f.

28. Robert Gellman, "Health Information Privacy Beyond HIPAA: A 2018 Environmental Scan of Major Trends and Challenges, A Report for the National Committee on Vital and Health Statistics (NCVHS) and Its Privacy, Security, and Confidentiality Subcommittee," US Department of Health and Human Services, December 13, 2017, 9–12, https://ncvhs.hhs.gov/wp-content/uploads/2018/05/NCVHS-Beyond-HIPAA_Report-Final-02-08-18.pdf.

29. Larry Downes, "A Rational Response to the Privacy 'Crisis,'" The Cato Institute, *Policy Analysis* no. 716 (January 7, 2013): 21, http://dx.doi.org/10.2139/ssrn.2200208.

30. Helen Nissenbaum, "Stop Thinking About Consent: It Isn't Possible and It Isn't Right," *Harvard Business Review* (September 24, 2018), https://hbr.org/2018/09/stop-thinking-about-consent-it-isnt-possible-and-it-isnt-right.

31. Posner, "The Right of Privacy," 393–404.

32. Downes, "A Rational Response to the Privacy 'Crisis.'"

33. GDPR, "Art. 20 GDPR Right to Data Portability," https://gdpr-info.eu/art-20-gdpr.

34. Mark MacCarthy, "The European Data Protection Board Goes After Tech's Personalized Ad Business Model," *TechTank*, Brookings Institution, February 1, 2023, https://www.brookings.edu/blog/techtank/2023/02/01/the-european-data-protection-board-goes-after-techs-personalized-ad-business-model.

35. Livvy Doherty and Sharon Braithwaite, "Italy Blocks ChatGPT over Privacy Concerns," CNN, March 31, 2023, https://www.cnn.com/2023/03/31/tech/chatgpt-blocked-italy/index.html; Chris Wood, "Italy Lays Out Requirements for ChatGPT's Return," *Martech*, April 13, 2023, https://martech.org/italy-lays-out-requirements-for-chatgpts-return.

36. GDPR, "Art. 6 GDPR Lawfulness of Processing," (b).

37. European Data Protection Board, "Guidelines 2/2019 on the Processing of Personal Data under Article 6(1)(b) GDPR in the Context of the Provision of Online Services to Data Subjects," version 2.0, October 8, 2019, par. 17, 23, 30, 25, 32, and 57, https://edpb.europa.eu/sites/edpb/files/files/file1/edpb_guidelines-art_6-1-b-adopted_after_public_consultation_en.pdf.

38. Gramm-Leach-Bliley Financial Modernization Act of 1999, 15 U.S.C. § 6802(e), https://www.law.cornell.edu/uscode/text/15/6802.

39. Cable Communications Policy Act, 47 U.S.C. § 551(b), https://www.law.cornell.edu/uscode/text/47/551.

40. GDPR, "Art. 6 GDPR Lawfulness of Processing," (f).

41. GDPR, "Recital 47–50," https://gdpr-info.eu/recitals/no-47.

42. GDPR, "Article 13 GDPR Information to Be Provided Where Personal Data Are Collected from the Data Subject," (1)(d), https://gdpr-info.eu/art-13-gdpr, and "Article 21 GDPR Right to Object," https://gdpr-info.eu/art-21-gdpr.

43. Article 29 Data Protection Working Party, 844/14/EN, WP217, Opinion 06/2014 on the notion of legitimate interests of the data controller under Article 7 of Directive 95/46/EC, adopted on April 9, 2014, https://www.huntonprivacyblog.com/wp-content/uploads/sites/28/2014/04/wp217_en.pdf.

44. "How Do We Apply Legitimate Interest in Practice?" Information Commissioner's Office, https://ico.org.uk/for-organisations/guide-to-data-protection/guide-to-the-general-data-protection-regulation-gdpr/legitimate-interests/how-do-we-apply-legitimate-interests-in-practice.

45. Gramm-Leach-Bliley Financial Modernization Act of 1999, 15 U.S.C. § 6802(b)(2), (e)(3), https://www.law.cornell.edu/uscode/text/15/6802.

46. GDPR, "Art. 6 GDPR Lawfulness of Processing," (1)(a); GDPR, "Art. 4 GDPR Definitions," (11), https://gdpr-info.eu/art-4-gdpr; GDPR, "Art. 7 GDPR Conditions for Consent," (4), https://gdpr-info.eu/art-7-gdpr; and GDPR, "Recital 43 Freely Given Consent," https://gdpr-info.eu/recitals/no-43.

47. European Commission, Article 29 Data Protection Working Party, "Guidelines on Consent under Regulation 2016/679," English WP259 rev. 01, April 10, 2018, 8, https://ec.europa.eu/newsroom/article29/item-detail.cfm?item_id=623051.

48. GDPR, "Art. 21 GDPR Right to Object," https://gdpr-info.eu/art-21-gdpr; and "Art. 7 GDPR Conditions for Consent," (3).

49. FTC, "Protecting Consumer Privacy in an Era of Rapid Change," March 2012, 51–52, https://www.ftc.gov/sites/default/files/documents/reports/federal-trade-commission-report-protecting-consumer-privacy-era-rapid-change-recommendations/120326privacyreport.pdf.

50. FCC, "Protecting the Privacy of Customers of Broadband and Other Telecommunications Services, Report and Order," *FCC Record* 31, no. 13911 (Oct. 26, 2016): paragraphs 12, 30, 36, 295, and 296, https://www.fcc.gov/document/fcc-releases-rules-protect-broadband-consumer-privacy.

51. "Bundeskartellamt Prohibits Facebook from Combining User Data from Different Sources," Bundeskartellamt press release, February 7, 2019, https://www.bundeskartellamt.de/SharedDocs/Publikation/EN/Pressemitteilungen/2019/07_02_2019_Facebook.html; MacCarthy, "Enhanced Privacy Duties for Dominant Technology Companies"; Matthias Inverardi, "German Court Turns to Top European Judges for Help on Facebook Data Case," Reuters, March 24, 2021, https://www.reuters.com/business/legal/german-court-turns-top-european-judges-help-facebook-data-case-2021-03-24; Foo Yun Chee, "Meta's Privacy Obligations May Be Added to German Antitrust Probe, Court Adviser Says," Reuters, September 20, 2022, https://www.reuters.com/technology/german-antitrust-watchdog-may-assess-metas-privacy-obligations-court-adviser-2022-09-20.

52. California Consumer Privacy Act of 2018, Civil Code § 1798.100–198, https://leginfo.legislature.ca.gov/faces/codes_displayText.xhtml?division=3.&part=4.&lawCode=CIV&title=1.81.5; "Chapter 20. California Consumer Privacy Act Regulations," Office of California Attorney General, August 14, 2020, https://oag.ca.gov/sites/all/files/agweb/pdfs/privacy/oal-sub-final-text-of-regs.pdf; "Non Discrimination and Financial Incentives in the CCPA," Nixon Peabody, Feb. 9, 2021, https://www.nixonpeabody.com/en/ideas/blog/data-privacy/2021/02/09/non-discrimination-and-financial-incentives-in-the-ccpa.

53. "Text of Proposed Laws," Office of California Attorney General, https://vig.cdn.sos.ca.gov/2020/general/pdf/topl-prop24.pdf.

54. Joshua A. T. Fairfield and Christoph Engel, "Privacy as a Public Good," *Duke Law Journal* 65 (2015): 385, http://scholarship.law.duke.edu/dlj/vol65/iss3/1.

55. "Regulation of the European Parliament and of the Council of the European Union on the protection of natural persons with regard to the processing of personal data and on the free movement of such data, and repealing Directive 95/46/EC (General Data Protection Regulation)," *Official Journal of the European Union*, April 27, 2016, Article 5(1)(c), available at http://eur-lex.europa.eu/legal-content/EN/TXT/PDF/?uri=CELEX:32016R0679&from=EN.

56. GDPR, "Art. 5 GDPR Principles Relating to Processing of Personal Data," (1)(b), https://gdpr-info.eu/art-5-gdpr; "Art. 6 GDPR Lawfulness of Processing," (4), https://gdpr-info.eu/art-6-gdpr; Article 29 Data Protection Working Party.

57. Alessandro Mantelero and Giuseppe Vaciago, "Data Protection in a Big Data Society: Ideas for a Future Regulation," *Digital Investigation* 15 (2015): 104–9, post-print version available at http://dx.doi.org/10.1016/j.diin.2015.09.006.

58. Slaughter, "Disputing the Dogmas of Surveillance Advertising."

59. Sheri Fink and Mike Baker, "'It's Just Everywhere Already': How Delays in Testing Set Back the U.S. Coronavirus Response," *New York Times*, March 3, 2020, https://www.nytimes.com/2020/03/10/us/coronavirus-testing-delays.html.

60. This discussion is based on Mark MacCarthy, "In Defense of Big Data Analytics," in *The Cambridge Handbook of Consumer Privacy*, edited by Evan Selinger, Jules Polonetsky, and Omar Tene (New York: Cambridge University Press, 2018), http://dx.doi.org/10.2139/ssrn.3154779.

61. Hartzog, *Privacy's Blueprint*, 120–57.

62. "Deceived by Design," Norwegian Consumer Councils, June 27, 2018, https://fil.forbrukerradet.no/wp-content/uploads/2018/06/2018-06-27-deceived-by-design-final.pdf; Jamie Luguri and Lior Strahilevitz, "Shining a Light on Dark Patterns," *Journal of Legal Analysis* 13, no. 43 (2021), http://dx.doi.org/10.2139/ssrn.3431205; Daniel Solove, "Dark Patterns Reading List and Resources," April 18, 2021, https://teachprivacy.com/dark-patterns-reading-list-and-resources; Deceptive Experiences to Online Users Reduction Act, S. 1084, 116th Cong. (2019), https://www.congress.gov/bill/116th-congress/senate-bill/1084/text.

63. Daniel Susser, Beate Roessler, and Helen Nissenbaum, "Online Manipulation: Hidden Influences in a Digital World," *Georgetown Law Technology Review* 4, no. 1 (2019).

64. Mark MacCarthy and Kenneth Propp, "Machines Learn that Brussels Writes the Rules: The EU's New AI Regulation," *TechTank*, Brookings Institution, May 4, 2021, https://www.brookings.edu/blog/techtank/2021/05/04/machines-learn-that-brussels-writes-the-rules-the-eus-new-ai-regulation.

65. Balkin, "Lecture, Information Fiduciaries and the First Amendment."

66. Data Care Act, S. 3744, 115th Cong. (2018), https://www.congress.gov/bill/115th-congress/senate-bill/3744.

67. American Data Privacy and Protection Act, H.R. 8152, 117th Cong. (2022).

68. Lina Khan and David E Pozen, "A Skeptical View of Information Fiduciaries," *Harvard Law Review* 133, no. 497 (2019): 500, https://ssrn.com/abstract=3341661.

69. Nissenbaum, *Privacy in Context*.

70. Mark MacCarthy, "Privacy Policy and Contextual Harm," *A Journal of Law and Policy for the Information Society* 13, no. 400 (2017), https://papers.ssrn.com/sol3/papers.cfm?abstract_id=3093253.

71. Woodrow Hartzog and Neil M. Richards, "The Surprising Virtues of Data Loyalty," *Emory Law Journal* 71, no. 985 (2022), https://scholarlycommons.law.emory.edu/elj/vol71/iss5/4.

72. Gabriela Zanfir-Fortuna, "Why Data Protection Law Is Uniquely Equipped to Let Us Fight a Pandemic with Personal Data," Future of Privacy Forum, Apr. 7, 2020, https://fpf.org/2020/04/07/why-data-protection-law-is-uniquely-equipped-to-let-us-fight-a-pandemic-with-personal-data; California Civil Code § 1798.100–198.

73. Student Online Personal Information Protection Act, California Business and Professional Code § 22584(a)–(b)(4) (2016); Health Insurance Portability and Accountability Act, 45 C.F.R. § 164.502(a)(5); Genetic Information Nondiscrimination Act of 2008, *Public Law*, no. 110–233, 122 Stat. 881 (2008); Gramm-Leach-Bliley Financial Modernization Act, 15 U.S.C. § 1602(d); MacCarthy, "Privacy Policy and Contextual Harm."

74. Gramm-Leach-Bliley Financial Modernization Act of 1999, 15 U.S.C. § 1681(b) (2015).

75. 42 US Code § 2000e-2—Unlawful Employment Practices, http://www.law.cornell.edu/uscode/text/42/2000e-2; 15 US Code § 1691—Scope of Prohibition, http://www.law.cornell.edu/uscode/text/15/1691; 42 US Code 3604—Discrimination in the Sale or Rental of Housing and Other Prohibited Practices, http://www.law.cornell.edu/uscode/text/42/3604; 29 US Code § 623—Prohibition of Age Discrimination, https://www.law.cornell.edu/uscode/text/29/623; 42 US Code § 18116—Nondiscrimination, https://www.law.cornell.edu/uscode/text/42/18116.

76. HUD v. Facebook, "Charge of Discrimination," March 28, 2019, https://www.hud.gov/sites/dfiles/Main/documents/HUD_v_Facebook.pdf.

77. Office of Senator Kirsten Gillibrand, "Gillibrand Introduces New and Improved Consumer Watchdog Agency to Give Americans Control over Their Data," press release, June 17, 2021, https://www.gillibrand.senate.gov/news/press/release/gillibrand-introduces-new-and-improved-consumer-watchdog-agency-to-give-americans-control-over-their-data; Data Protection Act, S. 2134, 117th Cong. (2021), https://www.congress.gov/bill/117th-congress/senate-bill/2134/text; Algorithmic Accountability Act, S. 1108, 116th Cong. (2019), https://www.congress.gov/bill/116th-congress/senate-bill/1108; Mark MacCarthy, "An Examination of the Algorithmic Accountability Act of 2019," Transatlantic Working Group on Content Moderation and Free Expression, October 24, 2019, https://ssrn.com/abstract=3615731; MacCarthy and Propp, "Machines Learn that Brussels Writes the Rules."

78. Frank Pasquale, "The Second Wave of Algorithmic Accountability," *Law and Political Economy*, November 25, 2019, https://lpeproject.org/blog/the-second-wave-of-algorithmic-accountability; Mark MacCarthy, "Mandating Fairness and Accuracy Assessments for Law Enforcement Facial Recognition Systems," *TechTank*, Brookings Institution, May 26, 2021, https://www.brookings.edu/blog/techtank/2021/05/26/mandating-fairness-and-accuracy-assessments-for-law-enforcement-facial-recognition-systems; Mark MacCarthy, "Who Thought It Was a Good Idea to Have Facial Recognition Software?" Brookings Institution, August 20, 2020, https://www.brookings.edu/research/who-thought-it-was-a-good-idea-to-have-facial-recognition-software.

79. Federal Trade Commission Act, 15 U.S.C. § 45(n) (2006).

80. Christine Bannan and Raj Gambhir, "Does Data Privacy Need Its Own Agency? Comparing FTC and DPA Enforcement of a Future Federal Privacy Law," New America Foundation, Open Technology Institute, June 9, 2021, https://lpeproject.org/blog/the-second-wave-of-algorithmic-accountability; American Data Privacy and Protection Act, H.R. 8152, 117th Cong. (2022).

81. FTC, "Trade Regulation Rule on Commercial Surveillance and Data Security."

82. *See* California Civil Code § 1798.100–198.

83. Public Knowledge Report, 116.

84. ACCESS Act of 2021, H.R. 3849, 117th Cong. (2021), Section 4.

85. ACCESS Act of 2021, H.R. 3849, 117th Cong. (2021), Section 4.

86. Article 29 Data Protection Working Party.

87. Daniel Solove, "Free Speech, Anonymity and Accountability," in *The Future of Reputation* (New Haven, CT: Yale University Press, 2007), chapter 6, 125–36, https://papers.ssrn.com/sol3/papers.cfm?abstract_id=2899125.

88. Trans Union Corp. v. FTC, 245 F.3d 809, (DC Cir. 2001), https://www.casemine.com/judgement/us/5914b947add7b0493478a3f8.

89. US West, Inc. v. FCC, 182 F.3d 1224 (10th Cir. 1998), https://law.justia.com/cases/federal/appellate-courts/F3/182/1224/627512; National Cable & Telecommunications Association v. F.C.C., 555 F.3d 996 (DC Cir. 2009), https://www.cadc.uscourts.gov/internet/opinions.nsf/C6ED6CF3564BECAA852578000074E4D9/$file/07-1312-1164901.pdf; FTC, "Protecting the Privacy of Customers of Broadband and Other Telecommunications Services"; Lawrence Tribe, "The Federal Communications Commission's Proposed Broadband Privacy Rules Would Violate The First Amendment," CTIA, May 2016, http://www.ctia.org/docs/default-source/default-document-library/ctia-ncta-ust-file-tribe-paper.pdf; "Joint Resolution," *Public Law*, no. 115–22, 131 Stat. 88 (2017), https://www.congress.gov/115/plaws/publ22/PLAW-115publ22.pdf.

90. Sorrell v. IMS Health Inc. 564 US _ (2011), http://www.supremecourt.gov/opinions/10pdf/10-779.pdf.

91. ACA Connects—America's Communications Association et al. v. Frey et al., Order on Cross Motions for Judgment on the Pleadings, July 7, 2020, https://www.govinfo.gov/content/pkg/USCOURTS-med-1_20-cv-00055/pdf/USCOURTS-med-1_20-cv-00055-0.pdf.

CHAPTER 4

Content Moderation Rules for Social Media Companies

"If you imagined some force or agency in the world that was leading us towards doom and destruction, towards the dark, and then you imagined what kind of tools and technologies it would use, you'd come up with something like social media."

—JOHN LANCASTER[1]

"Like it or not, social media now plays a foundational role in public and private life alike; it can't be un-invented or simply set aside."

—P. W. SINGER AND EMERSON T. BROOKING[2]

INTRODUCTION

The rampant disinformation and hate speech on social media platforms cry out for the kind of regulation that seeks to control externalities in other areas of life such as environmental pollution. But government regulation of the content distributed by media firms has a bad reputation in the United States, and for good reason. Still, the dangers of private domination of the public's information space are real. Social media reformers need to pay attention to the dangers of government *and* private sector censorship in crafting measures that can respond to the rampant information disorder on social media platforms.

This disorder breaks down into three parts. The first is the amount of purely illegal material that circulates online. The second is the widespread availability of harmful material that is aimed at causing psychological or other damage to identifiable individuals, including children. The last is the social problem created from large-scale amplification of misinformation, disinformation, and hate speech.

Other works and ongoing news reports amply document the extent to which social media platforms distribute and amplify far too much harmful and illegal material. The present task in this chapter is different. It is to sort through the range of possible solutions to these problems. The major policy dilemma is to find measures that reduce the harmful material in a way that preserves the role of platforms as a space for robust discussion and action on the political, social, economic, and cultural issues of our time.

Other countries, far less concerned about government overreach of content regulation, are taking vigorous steps to control these problems. The European Union, Ireland, the United Kingdom, Australia, and Canada have given their government agencies extensive powers to control harmful and illegal online speech. China has always provided its government agencies with substantial responsibilities to work with and compel, if necessary, media firms to promote political stability and public safety, and from the beginning of the internet it has sought to maintain an online environment that achieves these social and political goals.[3]

In the United States, current First Amendment jurisprudence sharply limits what the government can do. A series of court cases in hate speech illustrate the constitutional difficulty of government control over the speech of social media users.[4]

Perhaps the most revealing case is *R.A.V. v. City of St. Paul*, in which the Supreme Court unanimously struck down a local bias-motivated criminal ordinance that prohibits the display of any symbol that "arouses anger, alarm, or resentment in others on the basis of race, color, creed, religion, or gender." Three white teenagers had been convicted under the ordinance for burning a KKK cross on a black family's lawn. The court ruled that this ordinance discriminated against protected speech based solely on the viewpoint expressed. It noted that under the ordinance, for example, one could hold up a sign declaring all anti-Semites are bastards but not that all Jews are bastards. Government, the court said, has no authority "to license one side of a debate to fight freestyle, while requiring the other to follow the Marquis of Queensbury Rules."[5]

Racist speech clearly and transparently causes psychological harm; causing such harm is the undisguised intent of the speaker. It seeks to marginalize and diminish people because of their race, which is by law in the United States a protected class status. But words, gestures, films, images, signs, blog posts, tweets, and so on aimed to marginalize and diminish people because of their race, gender, or sexual orientation are, according to current First Amendment jurisprudence laid out in *R.A.V.* and other cases, expressions of a point of view—namely, the idea that such people should be marginalized and diminished below the level of other citizens. Racism, in short, is a protected point of view in the United States, whether it is expressed on a lawn sign, on someone's front yard, or in a post on social media.

Other harmful material also enjoys constitutional protection. Misinformation about COVID-19 makes it extraordinarily difficult to take effective public health measures. False claims that an election was stolen lead people to commit violent acts. Deliberate disinformation campaigns aim to sow discord and confusion that makes political governance more difficult. Amplified material on social media platforms lowers self-esteem and creates depression in children. But all this material is protected. Any attempt to outlaw it or put it under special burdens would fail First Amendment scrutiny. This includes measures that target social media companies and make it illegal for them to distribute messages from their users that constitute hate speech, misinformation, disinformation, psychologically harmful information, and so on. Social media companies can regulate such material on their own and perhaps should be encouraged to do so in various ways explored in this chapter, but they cannot be forced to do it without violating their users' speech rights.

Perhaps this line of cases should be revisited and stronger protections against rising racism and disinformation in the United States should be permitted. But there are absolutely no signs that Congress is interested in passing such a law or that the Supreme Court would countenance it if Congress did pass one. In view of that reality, it would be fruitless for Congress to contemplate a measure requiring social media companies to ban speech that is currently legal, even if it is harmful.

It might not be possible under the US system of free expression for the government to do as much as these other countries to control online speech harms. But that does not mean the problems are nonexistent or that the government should do nothing. This chapter focuses on remedies to online information disorder that seem politically feasible, constitutionally defensible, and likely to do some good.

To craft effective remedies, it is essential to understand the unique position social media companies have in the current media environment. They carry the speech of others the way common carriers do, and they edit the material on their system the way broadcasters and newspapers do. They embody elements of both types of traditional media companies. But it would be a mistake to assimilate them to these earlier media forms.

Because of their unique status, social media companies should not enjoy the full freedoms from government regulation accorded to newspapers. Policymakers can and should impose on them obligations that are not the full common carrier obligations of old-fashioned telephone companies. Like broadcasters, social media companies are in an intermediate state between newspapers and common carriers. Unlike broadcasters, they hold themselves out to members of the public as a way for them to distribute content to an indefinitely large number of other members of the public. They therefore owe obligations to their users that might in some ways be similar to the obligations of broadcasters and yet in other ways be similar to the obligations of common carriers. These duties might be called the public interest obligations of social media companies in imitation of the public interest responsibilities of broadcasters.

The key obligation they owe to the public is transparency to their own users. User transparency is so closely connected to due process that they often go together. Companies must inform the public what their content rules are and must put in place due process policies and procedures that constrain the way they enforce these rules, including complaint and redress procedures. A key requirement in due process is recourse to an independent nongovernmental dispute resolution system not controlled by the social media company itself.

An implication of this due process obligation is that if members of the public follow the social media company's rules, they will be allowed to access the service and use its facilities to distribute content to other users. Members of the public can be excluded from a social media service but only upon showing that they are not following the content criteria the social media company has developed for its community. This gives members of the public a kind of carriage right, a right of access; the social media company "must carry" members of the public who follow their rules.

These due process rights do not themselves directly address the information disorder on social media platforms. The first essential step in dealing with the issues of harmful content online is a different kind of transparency: transparency reports and access to social media data for researchers. Companies should be required to publish regular reports on their content moderation systems. The largest social media firms should conduct and publish risk assessments evaluating the extent of harmful and illegal material on their systems, revealing how their content moderation and operational algorithms contribute to the prevalence of this material, and outlining the steps they are taking to mitigate these risks. They should provide access to regulators and vetted researchers to assess how well their content moderation systems work and the extent to which their algorithmic amplification systems are making these problems worse. As part of their transparency obligations, social media companies should have extensive duties to disclose information about political ads, including, most important of all, sponsorship identification.

Many proposals seek to avoid the free speech problems with social media content moderation by mandating certain types of algorithmic regulation. But at this point not enough is known about how algorithmic systems contribute to online harms or what measures would be effective in reducing these algorithmic harms. Algorithmic regulation is premature. The wisest course of action is to gather information about how these systems work through mandated access to internal social media algorithms and data. With better understanding of how they work, industry and government might together be able to craft effective and constitutionally viable remedies.

Reform of Section 230 of the Communications Decency Act is often presented as a way to address legal but harmful material online. But this is a mistake. Section 230 limits the liability of social media companies for *illegal* material on their systems. Repeal of Section 230 would not expose them to liability for the legal hate speech and disinformation that constitutes the vast bulk of the harmful material online. Still, reform of Section 230 would help reduce the illegal material on social media. In 2023, the Supreme Court considered cases seeking to deprive social media companies of some of the Section 230 protections for algorithmic amplification but ultimately made no change in how Section 230 is applied. Congressional reform would be preferable, and the notice liability system described in this chapter would go a long way to re-establishing appropriate legal liability for illegal material on social media sites.

Other attractive and plausible reform proposals are considered in this chapter, but they all face insuperable implementation issues. One is the imposition of political fairness duties, similar to the balance obligations for broadcasters. Because of their outsized impact on public discourse, dominant social media companies might plausibly be subjected to such an obligation for political pluralism. In 2021, Texas and Florida passed social media legislation that imposed such fairness obligations, as well as extensive transparency rules.

Unfortunately, it is not at all clear how to apply this ideal of political pluralism to social media companies. Far-reaching mandates for political pluralism and additional obligations for fairness to political candidates should be left for further study and assessment.

The First Amendment challenges to a system of regulation for social media are substantial but not insuperable. Supreme Court decisions in broadcasting and cable allow limitations on their free speech rights. These cases provide a rationale for the courts to uphold social media regulation for transparency, due process, access to data, and perhaps even political pluralism. Consumer protection law also provides a constitutional basis for transparency measures. Court rulings on the Texas and Florida social media laws seem to vindicate some transparency regulation while striking down broader fairness rules. Ultimately the Supreme Court will need to decide these First Amendment issues. While there is a good case that some carefully designed measures for political pluralism and must-carry rights for political candidates would withstand First Amendment scrutiny, the most likely judicial outcome from review of the state social media laws is that transparency measures will be upheld while the further measures for carriage and no censorship will be severely restricted.

Congress should be crystal clear about its objective in regulating the content moderation and algorithmic practices of social media companies. The touchstone of the entire regulatory edifice constructed to deal with information disorder on social media is the injunction of Article 19 of the Universal Declaration of Human Rights to allow users "to seek, receive and impart ideas and information" and the ideal of US communications law of the widest possible distribution of information from "diverse and antagonistic sources of information."[6] These principles should be enshrined in the authorizing statute as the key objectives to guide the activities of the digital regulator in all its regulatory actions in connection with content moderation on social media.

User Transparency

In response to the information disorder on social media platforms, governments around the world are imposing transparency requirements in the hopes they will improve content moderation practices. But a surprising number of academics, observers, and policymakers say "meh." One participant in a Georgetown University tech policy symposium in 2022 said transparency is a "timid" solution. Another participant shared that disclosure rules imply that whatever the companies do is fine as long as they are transparent about it. Haven't policymakers learned anything from the failures of privacy notice and consent rules? Transparency initiatives, the critics say, just distract from the hard work of developing and implementing more effective methods of control.

The main point of this chapter is that transparency is a necessary first step in creating a regulatory structure for social media companies. Of course, to produce useful disclosures requires an active regulator.

Disclosure requirements alone are not self-enforcing. A dedicated regulatory agency must define and implement them through rulemaking and must have full enforcement powers, including the ability to fine and issue injunctions. That will help ensure that disclosure actually happens as mandated by law.

While transparency itself is not a panacea to stem the tide of disinformation and hate speech, it is the *sine qua non* of social media regulation. Without transparency, no other regulatory measures will be effective. Whatever else governments might need to do to control social media misbehavior in content moderation, they have to mandate openness, which requires implementing specific rules governing these disclosures.[7]

Social media laws pending or in place in Australia, Canada, the European Union, Germany, Ireland, the United Kingdom, and the United States outline user transparency and due process requirements. The measures outlined below are drawn from these models.[8]

To ensure the fair operation of content moderation programs, legislation should require social media companies to disclose the following:

- content rules—the types of content and activity not permitted on the service
- enforcement procedures—criteria for demotion, delay, or deletion of content and suspension or termination of service
- notification process—how to notify the service of illegal or violative content
- explanations—reasons for content moderation action
- complaint process—for redress when content is removed or not removed after notice
- misuse policy—for unfounded notifications or complaints
- misuse warnings—prior to suspension or termination of accounts

Transparency and due process procedures for social media content moderation have been recognized in the civil liberties standard for online content called the Manila Principles, the Santa Clara Principles for content moderation, and the application of international human rights principles to social media companies.[9]

These social media requirements are in line with the due process tradition in US administrative law that typically provides individuals meaningful opportunities to understand and challenge adverse decisions by government agencies. In 2014, law professors Danielle Citron and Frank Pasquale urged that these due process principles should be extended to cover the operation of automated decision systems such as algorithmic evaluation of credit worthiness.[10] Social media content moderation decisions are sufficiently like the decisions of administrative agencies and automated evaluation of personal characteristics for consequential decision making so that they should adhere to a similar set of procedural safeguards.

Due process requirements include creating and maintaining an easy-to-use accessible system that allows users to file a complaint and track its status, regarding content that might violate the social media policy or constitute illegal material or activity or appealing a decision to remove or not to remove content posted by a user. The social media company should have a process in place to respond expeditiously to these complaints about illegal content or violative activity, including a process for a user to reply to allegations of illegality or violation of company policy. When the company makes a decision, it should also have in place a process for notifying the affected parties and providing them with an explanation for the basis of the decision as well as a process for appealing it. To ensure accountability, the social media company must employ an external independent private dispute resolution service to which users can appeal after having exhausted the internal appeal mechanism available to them. The company must agree to be bound by the decisions of the external dispute mechanism.

In the United States, several bills have been introduced that require user transparency. One is the Platform Accountability and Transparency Act of 2021, introduced by US Senator Brian Schatz on March 17, 2021. The bill requires social media companies to publish an acceptable use policy that outlines what content is out of bounds on the system, what the company does to enforce the policy, and how users can notify the company of material violating its policy. The companies must also establish a complaint system and process complaints within fourteen days. It must explain any action to remove content to the user and provide an opportunity to appeal, and it must inform both the person complaining about content and the person whose content is at issue what decision the company has made concerning removal. The measures are enforced by the FTC, and violations are treated as unfair and deceptive acts or practices. The agency has rulemaking authority to implement the provisions of the act. The FTC, however, has no authority to "review any action or decision by a [social media company] related to the application of the acceptable use policy of the provider."[11]

To some degree, such new social media transparency rules would require social media companies to do what they are already doing voluntarily. Most major platforms publish their community standards for the public to see and evaluate.[12] Some platforms, in addition, publish their enforcement guidelines, which allows the public to see how these general rules are interpreted and applied in particular cases.[13] The major improvements over the current system would be to mandate additional due process protections and to install a supervisory regulator that could oversee the adequacy of the disclosures geared to provide users and the public with enough information to file complaints and to seek redress if not satisfied with social media company decisions.

These due process and transparency regulations call for social media platforms to reveal what they are doing in content moderation and provide adequate redress mechanisms for users. But they would not mandate any particular content moderation standards. Platforms would remain free to moderate content according to whatever criteria they feel is appropriate; their obligation under the legislation would be to tell the user, the regulatory agency, and the public what their policies are and how they would enforce them, and to provide an adequate opportunity for appeal and redress. The diversity of content moderation practices in the current social media world would persist under the new content moderation law.

Approaches in other countries add to the requirements of due process and transparency a requirement to avoid distributing harmful material online. Ireland, for instance, enumerates categories of "harmful online content." It includes material that is a criminal offense to disseminate under Irish law, such as child sexual abuse material, content containing or comprising incitement to violence or hatred, and public provocation to commit a terrorist offense. It also refers to cyberbullying material, which the law describes as material "likely to have the effect of intimidating, threatening, humiliating, or persecuting a person to which it pertains and which a reasonable person would conclude was the intention of its dissemination." The category of harmful material also includes material promoting self-harm and suicide and material promoting eating disorders. The notion excludes defamatory statements and material that violates consumer protection law, privacy, or copyright law, since these offenses are covered under other laws enforced by different agencies.

Ireland's proposed law adopted the strategy of enumeration rather than definition of harmful material, given the difficulties of arriving at a suitable, broad, and principle-based description of the meaning of this phrase. Ireland's new law would provide authority for its regulatory agency, the Media Commission, to develop regulations covering new categories of harmful online material beyond those enumerated in statute. But approval from the Irish government and legislature would be needed before a proposed extension to new categories of harm becomes binding. The Irish law would also provide authority for the Media Commission to issue online safety codes, including measures to be taken by designated online services in relation to harmful online content and user complaints and issues handling.[14]

Australia also regulates the way companies deal with harmful material online by using enforceable industry codes. Its online safety bill adopted in 2021 enumerates the sections of internet industry covered. This list includes social media service, electronic service, designated internet service, internet search engine, an app distribution service, a hosting service, an internet carriage service, or providing equipment for use by end-users in connection with a social media service, a relevant electronic service, a designated internet service, or an internet carriage service.

The Australian law encourages each section of the online industry to create an association or representative body to develop an industry code.

These industry codes should set out procedures for dealing with restricted or prohibited material on their systems, including complaint procedures. It authorizes a regulatory body, the eSafety Commissioner, to request an industry association to develop a code and to register an industry code that has been developed through public and industry consultations. The commissioner is also authorized to develop a binding industry standard for a section of the online industry if the industry association does not develop a code or the commission finds the industry's code to be deficient. The commissioner may require industry participants to comply with registered industry codes or with the industry standard it has developed, and fine participants who violate it.[15]

The transparency requirements proposed for and adopted in the United States, however, do not create such a regulatory structure. They allow social media companies to define for themselves the categories of material they will moderate and set out their own enforcement measures. In these laws and proposals, the enforcing agency is not empowered to mandate specific content choices. The transparency and due process mandates require only that social media companies develop and enforce their own freely chosen content standards in a fair and open manner.

However, this freedom of choice for the platforms would create obligations once it is exercised. A new social media content moderation law would allow digital social media platforms to make their own chosen promises to the public concerning their content moderation practices. But it might also make it clear that they are not free to make promises to their users that they do not keep. The supervising regulatory agency would be authorized to enforce these promises. Later sections of this chapter describe an independent dispute resolution mechanism for individual complaints against social media content decisions and a regulatory audit of these dispute resolution results. This structure would allow a regulator to determine whether the social media company is acting at variance from its announced content policies. The agency would not be authorized to second-guess the individual content decisions of a social media company, but it would be empowered to order social media companies to remedy systematic departures from their own announced policies.[16]

Transparency Reporting

Additional transparency measures beyond those needed for facilitating an effective due process regime are needed to provide public accountability. Existing and proposed social media content moderation legislation requires social media companies to provide the public and regulators with regular reports and disclosures concerning the operation of the content moderation program and its associated algorithms. The purposes of these mandated reports and disclosures are to put public pressure on companies to do an effective and fair job of moderating the content on their system and to highlight areas for improvement.

These required reports should disclose the following:

- number of government orders on illegal content and action taken
- number of notices by type of illegal content and action taken
- number of content moderation actions by type and basis of measure
- number of complaints of improper content moderation, including reversals
- number of out-of-court disputes
- number of suspensions
- number of unfounded notifications
- number of unfounded complaints
- purpose and accuracy of content moderation algorithms

The requirements build on the reports that social media companies are providing voluntarily or that are required under existing law. For instance, many online platforms provide voluntary reports in connection with their enforcement of their community standards. These voluntary reports outline much of the same information that would be required by the new social media law, including overall volume of content reported and removed, as well as information on appeals.[17]

In October 2018, several digital social media platforms, including Google, Facebook, and Twitter, signed a voluntary agreement with the

European Commission on disinformation, which committed the platforms to disclosures of political ads and issue ads, identifying automated bots, prioritizing authentic information, and not discouraging good faith research into disinformation.[18] Microsoft joined in May 2019, while TikTok became a signatory in June 2020.

The commission presented a Guidance to strengthen this Code of Practice on disinformation in May 2021. The agreement also requires the platforms to file regular reports with the commission on their compliance with this voluntary code, which are then reviewed and published on the commission website. In May 2022, the companies signed a strengthened code of practice on disinformation, requiring additional disclosures. The disclosures under this voluntary arrangement are likely to be upgraded and made mandatory under the commission's new Digital Services Act.[19]

The European Digital Services Act requires social media companies to file annual public reports on content moderation programs that contain the number of government orders on illegal content and action taken, number of notices by type of illegal content and action taken, number of self-initiative content moderation actions by type and basis of measure, and the number of complaints of improper content moderation measures, including reversals.[20]

In Germany, the Network Enforcement Act (NetzDG) requires social media companies with two million or more registered users in Germany that receive more than one hundred complaints per year about online content to submit semi-annual reports about how the company handles complaints. These reports must include information on the actions taken by the platform to remove illegal content, descriptions of how to submit complaints and criteria for handling those complaints, a tally of those complaints and how they were handled, personnel and training metrics for moderators, whether the platform consulted outside organizations when making takedown decisions, and other information about removal statistics and timing.

The social networks have complied to some degree with this requirement to file public reports. The German Office of Justice reviews these public reports and is authorized to issue fines for failure to report enforcement activity adequately and completely. In July 2019, this office fined Facebook for underreporting the number of complaints under NetzDG.[21]

A new social media law in the United States would build on these voluntary and legal requirements. Such new disclosure requirements would compel companies to disclose more than they do now and would remove discretion from the companies in determining what and how they report. The reports would be fully public and as a result should not contain confidential business information and personal information of users.

The law should also require social media companies to publish systemic risk assessments that catalog the ways in which their amplification systems contribute to the spread of harmful material online. The risk assessments must also outline the measures the companies are taking to counteract the reach this material has on their systems. Such assessment studies are required in legislation proposed by Senator Ron Wyden and also contained in the European Commission's final Digital Services Act and in its proposed AI regulation of high-risk algorithms.[22] These assessments should examine threats to public policy objectives such as the distribution of illegal content, violations of rights to freedom of expression and information, consumer protection, privacy, and nondiscrimination, or adverse impacts on public health, public safety, or political governance.

To ensure that these requirements for public disclosures are timely, relevant, and up to date, US social media legislation should authorize the digital regulator to specify the form and manner of the disclosures, reports, and assessments required under the legislation. The agency should also be authorized to require more or different types of information as needed to ensure full transparency and accountability and to update these requirements as necessary to keep up with changing business models and threats.

This includes reports and internal audits of platform content moderation activity, the risks created through social media company activities, the role of algorithms in distributing harmful speech, assessments of what the companies do about hate speech, disinformation, material harmful to teens, and other problematic content. Transparency reporting could also include a company's own assessment of whether its activities are politically discriminatory, a favorite topic of political conservatives. For instance, a 2021 internal Twitter assessment found greater algorithmic amplification of tweets by conservative political leaders and media outlets.[23]

A regulator is absolutely key in implementing the requirements for transparency reports. An agency must specify what risks need to be assessed and what statistics need to be provided to assess these risks. It cannot be left up to the companies to determine the content of these reports, and the details cannot be specified in legislation. How to measure prevalence of harmful material on social media is not an immediately obvious thing. Is it views of hate speech, for instance, as a percentage of all views of content? Or is it hateful posts as a percentage of all posts? Or both?

The metrics that must be contained in these reports have to be worked out by the regulator in conjunction with the industry and with researchers who will use this public information to assess platform success in content moderation. There might be a place here, although not a determinative one, for a social media self-regulatory group, similar to FINRA, the broker-dealer industry organization, to define common reporting standards. Almost certainly the important and relevant statistics will change over time, and so there must be regulatory procedures to review and update reporting statistics.

In the United States several bills have been introduced that require transparency reports. One is the Platform Accountability and Transparency Act of 2021, introduced by Senator Schatz on March 17, 2021. Under the bill, social media companies must publish biannual reports on the operation of their content moderation system. It requires the disclosure of the number of users, the number of instances of flagging illegal material or material that violated the company's content policies, how often the company acted against this material and what type of action was taken, the number of appeals of content moderation action, and the number of restorations. Unfortunately, the bill does not provide the FTC with authority to implement this statute by rulemaking.[24]

Section 3608 of the bill—the "Nudging Users to Drive Good Experiences on Social Media Act" or the "Social Media NUDGE

Act"—mandates social media companies publish public transparency reports every six months. It specifies in some detail what the reports must contain. For instance, it requires the larger social media companies to calculate "the total number of views for each piece of publicly visible content posted during the month and sample randomly from the content." It would also require information about content posted and viewed that was reported by users, flagged by an automated system, removed, restored, labeled, edited, or otherwise moderated. This focus on the details of reports is a welcome addition to other approaches that remain at a higher level of generality. But it also fails to provide the FTC with rulemaking authority to further specify the contents of public reports.[25]

In December 2021, a bipartisan group of US senators unveiled the Platform Accountability and Transparency Act (PATA) that would remedy this lack of rulemaking authority in other proposals. It would require social media companies to provide information and reports to the public concerning the impact of their systems on "consumers, institutions, and society." The FTC is authorized to establish rules concerning these reports, including their "form and frequency." It is also authorized to take steps to protect user privacy and business confidentiality.[26]

Mandated public reports are likely to improve content moderation, just as accounting reporting requirements encourage good corporate financial conduct. When companies know they will have to issue these detailed assessments, they are more likely to take steps to mitigate problems in order to reduce the reputational risks that would come with a bad report card.

Access to Social Media Data for Researchers

An additional dimension of transparency is the disclosure of internal company data about the operation of a social media company's systems for content moderation, advertising, and algorithmic amplification. The companies are free to disclose as much of this information as they want to the public, consistent with their privacy obligations. But social media transparency legislation should require them to make it available to the regulator and to researchers vetted and approved by the regulator.

Some existing and proposed social media laws would provide for access to data for researchers. A draft bill circulated in October 2021 by Nathaniel Persily, professor of law at Stanford Law School and director of the Stanford Cyber Policy Center, required access to social media data for researchers. Persily tried to work with Facebook in its Social Science One initiative that fell apart because of restrictions Facebook placed on data access by researchers. The apparent reason for the failure was the need to protect user privacy and a disagreement on the best way to do that. Persily's draft bill mandates disclosures to vetted researchers with a regulator making decisions on who can access data and what privacy restrictions are needed to preserve user privacy and business confidentiality.[27]

The proposed Social Media DATA Act of 2021, introduced by US Representative Lori Trahan on May 31, 2021, moves in the direction of more access to internal data for researchers. It would require social media companies to maintain advertisement libraries and make them available to academic researchers and the FTC. Each library must include, among other things, a digital copy of the advertisement content, a description of the target audience, and the number of views generated from the advertisement.[28]

In addition to mandating public reports, PATA would require social media companies to share a broad array of platform data with qualified independent researchers. The researchers would have to be university affiliated and approved by the National Science Foundation. The data to be made available would include input data, the algorithm or model used to process the data, and the output data. The FTC is given rulemaking authority to determine what data needs to be provided to researchers.[29]

Article 40 of Europe's Digital Services Act, which was adopted in 2022, provides regulators with access to information they need "to monitor and assess compliance" with the regulation. It also provides access to data for "vetted researchers" affiliated with a research organization, which may include civil society organizations. The data to be made available would be that which is needed for the purpose of "conducting research that contributes to the detection, identification and understanding of systemic risks in the Union . . . and to the assessment of the adequacy, efficiency and impacts of the risk mitigation measures." Regulators determine the dimensions of access and adjudicate disputes between the companies and researchers.[30]

Based on these examples, a new social media law in the United States should mandate disclosures of system operation data to regulators and vetted researchers and could include the following data and algorithms:

- average monthly users
- operational algorithms—technical detail on how content is ordered, prioritized, and recommended
- content moderation algorithms—technical detail on automated enforcement methods
- user data relevant to assessing operational and content moderation algorithms
- user data relevant to audits for systemic risk
- advertising data
- content of the advertising messages, including identification as an ad
- sponsorship—who is the beneficiary of the candidate ad
- audience—both total and targeted audience size
- main targeting criteria—meaningful information on the basis for receiving the ad

The legislation should authorize a regulator to require independent audits of the operation of content moderation programs and to work with vetted researchers to investigate the sources of the spread of harmful material online, including the contribution of algorithmic amplification to the distribution of this material. These independent audits would validate or supplement the internal systemic risk assessment undertaken by the companies themselves. The proprietary technical details of content moderation operational algorithms should be available only to regulators and vetted researchers. User data should be anonymized or pseudonymized unless personally identifying information is necessary to conduct the assessments. The agency should be required to publish these independent audit reports, redacted of confidential and personally identifiable information, to promote public accountability.

Legislation should also authorize the regulator to obtain books and records of the regulated social media companies as a routine matter as part of its general responsibility to supervise the company's business activity. The regulator should not have to rely on whistleblowers to access internal research and reports concerning the effect of the company's activity on the public and vulnerable users, as occurred in the revelations of a former Facebook employee to the media and congressional committees in October 2021.[31]

Access to data for researchers is a very powerful transparency tool, perhaps the most important one of all. It requires social media companies to provide qualified researchers with access to all the internal company data the researchers need to conduct independent evaluations. These outside evaluations would not be under company control and would assess company performance on content moderation and the prevalence of harmful material. Data transparency would also allow vetted researchers to validate internal company studies, such as Twitter's assessment of political bias mentioned earlier. The regulator in conjunction with research agencies such as the National Science Foundation or the National Institutes of Health would have to vet the researchers and the research projects. Researchers and civil society groups working with an industry self-regulatory organization can help define access parameters, but, ultimately, they will have to be approved by a government agency.

But key to implementation is the presence of an active and alert regulator. The regulator must at a minimum assure that companies do not seek to frustrate the goals of access transparency by not providing timely or accurate data. But even assuming company goodwill to comply with the rules, there are lots of controversies in this area that only a regulator can resolve.

One is whether access should be provided on-premises, through application programming interfaces, or a combination of both. Resolving this might require the regulator to make a balancing judgment on compliance burden versus data utility. Another issue is whether the data has to be provided to researchers in a form that technologically protects privacy, and if so, which form. Is it differential privacy or K-anonymity or some other technique? Alternatively, perhaps some research demands access to identifiable data, and privacy can only be assured by contract such that a researcher involved in a serious privacy violation would be banned from further access to social data and might face financial penalties as well.

Proprietary algorithms need to be protected from public disclosure and yet researchers need access to algorithmic input data, output data, and the algorithm itself in order to assess the systematic effects of social media policies and practices on information disorder. Confidentiality conditions must be specified and enforced by the regulator.

Another controversial issue is whether access should be limited to researchers with an academic or research institute affiliation. What about civil society groups, advocacy groups, and journalists? This could be specified in advance by legislation, but only a regulator can decide whether a particular institutional affiliation counts as one of the approved affiliations. In addition to vetting researcher qualifications and affiliations, the regulatory agency must develop techniques to avoid or mitigate the risks of partisan hatchet jobs or industrial espionage disguised as research. Resolution of each of these issues will require the combined efforts of all the stakeholders and ultimately a regulatory decision to reach closure.

No one should pretend implementation of these transparency measures will be easy, but without an authoritative regulatory to get to closure on these questions and to enforce decisions once made, the entire transparency project is at risk of being an empty exercise.

Regulation of Social Media Algorithms

The problems of disinformation and misinformation are real, but not new. In 1919, the public intellectual and journalist Walter Lippman warned about the dangers of propaganda obscuring an accurate picture of the world, saying, "The cardinal fact always is the loss of contact with objective information. Public as well as private reason depends upon it. Not what somebody says, not what somebody wishes were true, but what is so beyond all our opining, constitutes the touchstone of our sanity. And a society which lives at second-hand will commit incredible follies and countenance inconceivable brutalities if that contact is intermittent and untrustworthy."[32]

In 2018, a high-level group of the European Commission recommended moving forward with strong measures to counter this century's version of propaganda—disinformation on social media. It defined "disinformation" as "all forms of false, inaccurate, or misleading information designed, presented, and promoted to intentionally cause public harm or for profit." The hallmarks of disinformation are false context, imposter content, manipulated content, and fabricated content. In contrast, misinformation is "misleading or inaccurate information shared by people who do not recognize it as such." The group urged regulators and companies to work together to address these issues. This report helped spur the movement toward disclosure in the Code of Practice on Disinformation in Europe and its codification in the Digital Services Act.[33]

Understanding the disinformation and misinformation problem, much less creating effective solutions, has not progressed much since 2018. Even estimating the prevalence of disinformation on social media platforms is hampered by the lack of access to information. Ethan Zuckerman, a researcher at the University of Massachusetts at Amherst, points out that measures of the prevalence of false information available on a platform are useless unless researchers also know how much material is available on the platform and how it is distributed. But social media companies affirmatively prevent outsiders from accessing this information. A regulatory requirement to disgorge this data to qualified researchers would begin to give regulators and policymakers the knowledge they need to begin to understand the scope of the problem and to craft effective remedies.[34]

It is not as though no research is being done. The problem is that much of it remains locked up inside the social media companies themselves. In the fall of 2021, Frances Haugen, the Facebook employee turned whistleblower, released ten thousand pages of internal documents, many revealing research initiatives undertaken by Facebook. A lot has been made of how these research results show how much Facebook knew without taking remedial action. However, the more important implication of the release of this treasure trove of internal research is how much

Facebook knew that no one else did. Mandated disclosures would include release of the internal studies Facebook itself commissioned, perhaps only to regulators and vetted researchers. More important, it would include requirements for the internal data itself to be released so that independent researchers can devise and carry out research initiatives of their own that can help the public understand how the social media systems work and can inform efforts to create effective regulatory solutions.[35]

How much good transparency measures and risk assessments would do to remedy the information disorder on social media is open to debate, but they are needed to inform any additional steps that might be required.

Nevertheless, in the absence of real data, commentators and analysts have moved beyond transparency requirements to recommend more sweeping measures to mitigate the harmful effects of the misinformation and disinformation on social media platforms. In 2020, the Forum on Information and Democracy, a group of international experts co-chaired by the Nobel Peace Prize–winning journalist Maria Ressa and former member of the European Parliament Marietje Schaake released a series of recommendations. Also in 2020, the Roosevelt Institute advocated for substantial technical measures to counteract information disorder. In 2021, the Aspen Institute convened a different group of experts and business and political leaders, chaired by journalist Katie Couric, that addressed the same issues and recommended specific technical and operational responses to the disinformation challenges.

Measures recommended by these groups include due priority for credible news sources, tagging posts as misinformation that authoritative sources discount, removing or downgrading false and misleading information that threatens public safety or health, circuit breakers to reduce the velocity of posts until they can be checked, and in general limiting the use of algorithms to spread material on social media.[36]

The problem is that no one knows whether these measures would be effective. On its face, tagging seems to be an attractive strategy. Labeling material as harmful or deceptive or false or identifying the nature of its source seems likely to reduce the spread of the material that is tagged. But internal Facebook studies suggest it is not very effective, and some data suggests that in the case of misinformation from former president Donald Trump labels actually amplified the misinformation.[37]

Critics blame algorithms for many of the ills on social media, and policymakers around the world seek to hold social media companies responsible for the online harms it algorithmically amplifies. But would getting rid of algorithmic amplification do any good? Facebook attempted to assess the effect of removing algorithmic amplification and feeding users information solely based on reverse chronological order. But the study found that user engagement dropped, and users seemed less satisfied with what they found in their feed—they hid (blocked from everyone but the user and his audience) 50 percent more posts. The experiment found no decrease in harmful content. Facebook itself claims that neutral feeds exacerbate the harmful content problem. This might be more self-serving assertion than empirically grounded research, but still what we do know suggests that algorithm-free feeds would be limited as a way to deal with harmful content online.[38]

A 2021 Twitter study showed that tweets from political leaders see algorithmic amplification when compared to political content on the reverse chronological timeline. But it is not clear that this measures anything significant since users with an algorithmic feed who click on political content from political leaders will inevitably see more such content. It is hard to measure algorithmic effects except relative to two different algorithms. Moreover, the study still has no assessment of how users reacted to the amplified content. It is also not generalizable to other social media services such as YouTube and TikTok that have no chronological feed at all that can serve as a baseline.[39]

Less to address harmful content and more as a matter of consumer choice, policymakers might consider mandating social media companies to offer an amplification-free news feed. Facebook and Twitter offer these options, but they are hard to find and revert to the default algorithmic feed when the user logs on again. TikTok and Instagram have no algorithm-free feed. In 2021, bipartisan legislation was introduced in the House and Senate to provide users with a way to opt out of algorithmically ordered feeds. The bills lodge enforcement with the FTC but do not provide the agency with rulemaking to define ex-ante acceptable ways to provide unamplified content feeds. Separately, different legislation aims to remove Section 230 immunity when a company amplifies certain material such as terrorist material.[40]

In February 2022, Senator Amy Klobuchar introduced Senate Bill 3608, the "Nudging Users to Drive Good Experiences on Social Media Act" or the "Social Media NUDGE Act." It would require the National Science Foundation and the National Academies of Sciences, Engineering, and Medicine to conduct an initial study, and biennial ongoing studies, to identify "content-agnostic interventions" that the larger social media companies could implement "to reduce the harms of algorithmic amplification and social media addiction." After receiving their report on the initial study, due a year after the enactment of the law, the FTC would be required to begin a rulemaking proceeding to determine which of the recommended social media interventions should be made mandatory.

The bill lists examples of possible content-neutral interventions that "do not rely on the substance" of the material posted, including "screen time alerts and grayscale phone settings," requirements for users to "read or review" social media content before sharing it, and prompts (that are not further defined in the bill) to "help users identify manipulative and microtargeted advertisements." The bill also refers approvingly to "reasonable limits on account creation and content sharing" that seem to concern circuit breaker techniques to limit content amplification.

The NUDGE bill takes an evidence-based approach. It requires the government's science agencies that rely on the academic community for expertise to take the lead in generating the recommendations for algorithmic interventions. To prevent the agency from improvising on its own, it explicitly prevents the agency from mandating any intervention that has not been addressed in the reports from the national academies.

Without access to internal social media company data, however, the researchers working with the national science agencies will be shooting in the dark. They should be allowed broad, mandated access to internal social media data, including internal studies and confidential data about the operation of content moderation and recommendation algorithms. Only with this information will they be able to determine empirically which interventions are likely to be effective.

The bill is prudent to require the science agencies to conduct ongoing studies of interventions. But the FTC must be required to update its mandated interventions considering these ongoing studies. The first set of mandated interventions will be almost certainly only moderately effective at best. Much will be learned from follow-on assessments after the first round of interventions have been put into practice. The FTC should have an obligation to update the rules based on the new evidence it receives from the science agencies.[41]

The United States is not alone in seeking to regulate algorithms. China recognizes that algorithmic amplification might be related to certain social harms and is taking steps to address the issue. In its privacy law, the Personal Information Privacy Act, it has provided for consumer choice to turn off algorithmic amplification. But beyond that, the government seems to realize that the issue is not susceptible to a quick fix and wants to take three years of work with the tech companies to develop an appropriate system of algorithmic regulation.[42]

In many ways the rush to blame algorithmic amplification for the hate speech and misinformation online and to ban or limit amplification might be a way to avoid having to face an inconvenient truth. It might be that amplification on social media companies does not inculcate false beliefs or pernicious ideologies in people who were not persuaded before exposure to this material on social media. Social media amplification might instead enable certain groups to voice collectively sentiments of hate or disbelief in authoritative sources of information that they have always harbored but had no way to express easily in public before.

Some research suggests that this is not just a possibility. In connection with their 2019 study of radicalization on YouTube, Penn State researchers Kevin Munger and Joseph Phillips embrace this idea. "We believe that the novel and disturbing fact of people consuming white nationalist video media was not caused by the supply of this media 'radicalizing' an otherwise moderate audience," they write. "Rather, the audience already existed, but they were constrained" by limited supply.[43]

A 2021 study of the rise of Hindu nationalism in India suggests that it is not Facebook's algorithms that are moving people away from the ideal of a secular and religiously pluralistic state, but rather the deliberate maneuverings of political leaders. These leaders use the affordances of social media platforms to reach and inspire an audience to strive to create a governance structure in which people of the Hindu community have a privileged position. As this view becomes more popular, it spreads organically on social media without the help of recommendation engines artificially pushing it to the top of people's news feed. To suppose that adjusting Facebook's algorithms could reverse this political trend is fanciful thinking.[44]

The truth of the matter is that no one at this point really knows how social media algorithms affect political beliefs and actions. One systematic review of the literature found that "[e]xperimental evidence concerning media effects on radicalization is limited, inconclusive, and of low quality." Even though counter-radicalization strategies focus on the internet and social media as key sources of risk for radicalization, the study found that "whether Internet-related risk factors do indeed have greater impacts than other forms of media remain another unknown." It called for more systematic investigations, as "the relationship between media and radicalization has not been systematically investigated."[45]

Just showing that people who click on content of type X will receive more content of type X does not show that recommendation systems cause radicalization. That's what all recommendation systems do. But that result does not establish whether people have prior interests in topic X or whether exposure on social media causes the user interest. In addition, such a study would not have insight into user reaction to exposure to content of type X.[46]

Skeptics of an algorithmic fix to the ills of social media focus on this difficulty of disentangling cause and effect in the social media world. "Is social media creating new types of people?" asked BuzzFeed's senior technology reporter Joseph Bernstein in a 2021 *Harper's* article. "Or simply revealing long-obscured types of people to a segment of the public unaccustomed to seeing them?"[47]

Other skeptics point to a genuine weakness in an algorithmic fix to the problems of disinformation, misinformation, and hate speech online. "It's a technocratic solution to a problem that's as much about politics as technology," says *New York Times* columnist Ben Smith. He adds, "The new social media-fueled right-wing populists lie a lot and stretch the truth more. But as American reporters quizzing Donald Trump's fans on camera discovered, his audience was often in on the joke."[48]

In 2022, the Knight First Amendment Institute and the International Communication Association both held major conferences that provided disinformation researchers and scholars a chance to raise doubts about the assumptions of the field and propose new directions.[49]

This new thinking challenges many of the presuppositions of disinformation initiatives undertaken thus far by governments and social media companies. As participants explored at these conferences, too often these efforts treat citizens as ignorant or irrational, or even as foreign enemies. They seem to be built on the assumption that disinformation began in 2016 with social media companies, although it has long been a feature of political life, persisting through changes in media technology and business models. The new thinking emphasizes the limitations of content regulation, fact-checking, and media literacy efforts as remedies for our current political crises. Critically, the new thinking reminds us that the key work of political governance should not be technocratic efforts to police discourse for accuracy, but rather constructing attractive and achievable political visions of collective life.

This new direction was a welcome breath of fresh air. Policymakers, social media companies, and activists have focused too much on technocratic algorithmic adjustments as our salvation from political trauma.

There is also risk in this new direction. Its emphasis on the limits of disinformation measures could potentially lead social media companies to abandon or reduce their efforts to purge lies and disinformation from their platforms. It could likewise lead policymakers to stop encouraging social media companies to keep their systems as free as possible from falsehoods and propaganda. Throwing out the baby with the bathwater would be a mistake. Blatantly false political or public health narratives may not be the major cause of our political challenges, and better information may not restore the "good old days" of moderation and political cooperation. But a steady flow of accurate information is an absolute necessity for any effective system of political governance.

It doesn't follow from the fact that cause and effect are hard to discern in social media, that algorithms and targeted advertising have no effect and contribute nothing to the problems of hate speech and disinformation. Bernstein, for instance, seems to think that because advertising and propaganda don't always work to sell products or indoctrinate populations into certain political beliefs, they have no effect at all and are just part of a giant scam perpetrated on businesses and the public by the advertising industry. If media environments meant nothing, then public opinion would be the same in China and the United States, which is obviously not the case. (Some things are the same, however; Taylor Swift is as popular in China as she is in the United States!)

Facebook's own research demonstrates the effectiveness of manipulations on social media. The company's controversial 2013 emotional contagion study showed that the emotional valence of the news to which users are exposed on social media affects the emotional valence of subsequent user posts.[50] MIT researcher Zuckerman, who insists we don't know the extent of the algorithmic amplification problems, is under no illusions about the effectiveness of social media manipulations. In 2019, he wrote, "Research conducted by Facebook in 2013 demonstrated that it may indeed be possible for the platform to affect election turnout. When Facebook users were shown that up to six of their friends had voted, they were 0.39 percent more likely to vote than users who had seen no one vote."

These effects on mood and election turnout might sound small, but they would be enough to swing a close election if Facebook decided to selectively mobilize some voters but not others. Conservatives are not imagining things when they worry about the electoral power of social media. As Zuckerman notes, election results might be influenced if social media companies "suppressed information that was damaging to one candidate or disproportionately promoted positive news about another."[51]

Moreover, it is not as though we know nothing about how to address hate speech and misinformation on social media platforms. Solid, empirical work by careful scholars like Leticia Bode at Georgetown's Communication, Culture & Technology program shows that some interventions do work to correct misinformation if they are carefully crafted and skillfully applied.[52]

The problem is not that algorithms have no effect and we are imagining a problem that doesn't exist. Nor is the problem that nothing works to counteract the effect of misinformation and hate speech online, or that we know nothing about effective interventions. The problem is that we do not know enough to mandate algorithmic solutions or require specific technical or operational interventions.

Until a lot more is known about the extent and causes of the problem and the effectiveness of remedies, advocates and policymakers should not be giving amateur advice to social media companies about what technical measures to use to control harmful information. Still less should they be seeking to mandate specific techniques in legislation. The matter is one for experimentation and evidence not intuitions about what is most likely to work. This needs to be done in conjunction with regulatory oversight so that the social media companies have a real incentive to find the techniques that actually work rather than engaging in public relations exercises to create the appearance of effectiveness. Transparency and access to data are vital tools in seeking effective remedies.

Congress need not be completely passive in the face of the difficulties of regulating algorithms. The requirements for risk assessments and access to data should keep the focus on how information disorder arises on social media and what can be done about it. Congress should require both the social media companies themselves and the enforcing regulatory agency to assess the effect of social media company technologies and business practices on various social problems including cyberbullying, psychological harm to children, hate speech, and health and political disinformation that might have a material impact on public health or the effective operation and integrity of elections and the extent to which the operation of content moderation systems and algorithmic amplification serves the goal of political pluralism. Congress should also authorize the agency to access company information needed to carry out these investigations and to authorize and vet independent researchers to access company information for these purposes.

Kids' Online Safety

In September 2021, the Facebook whistleblower Frances Haugen released a trove of internal Facebook documents. These documents showed, among other things, that Facebook knew Instagram was toxic for teen girls. One slide summarizing internal company research stated, "Thirty-two percent of teen girls said that when they felt bad about their bodies, Instagram made them feel worse."[53]

These revelations turbocharged policymakers at the state level to enact laws aimed at protecting kids online. A year after her revelations, California adopted the California Age-Appropriate Design Code Act, a kids' online safety law modeled on the Age-Appropriate Design Code adopted in the United Kingdom in 2020. The new California law requires online websites that are "likely to be accessed" by children under eighteen to prioritize child safety and to take a variety of measures to identify and mitigate systemic risks to their mental health and well-being.[54]

The Kids Online Safety Act (KOSA), a federal bill sponsored by Senators Richard Blumenthal and Marsha Blackburn, took a similar risk-based system design approach to protecting kids from online harms. KOSA narrowly missed inclusion in the comprehensive budget bill that passed Congress at the end of 2022. A revised version with more than thirty bipartisan co-sponsors was reintroduced into the Senate in May 2023.[55]

As KOSA neared passage in 2022, a group of free speech and civil rights groups argued against it. They thought the bill established a burdensome and vague "duty of care" to prevent harms to minors. It would require broad content filtering to limit minors' access to certain online content. Moreover, online services would face substantial pressure to over-moderate, including from state attorneys general seeking to make political points about what kind of information is appropriate for young people. Finally, the bill would cut off a vital avenue of access to information for vulnerable youth.[56]

These UK, California, and federal measures seem focused on allowing kids to enjoy social media and other online experiences but with design constraints to make sure they do so in a safe manner. The UK code, for instance, explicitly says it aims at kids' safety online "not by seeking to protect children from the digital world, but by protecting them within it."

Utah, however, has taken a different direction in reacting to online dangers. It recently adopted a parental consent law that requires social media companies to obtain parental consent before allowing children eighteen or under to access their services. A companion Utah law would ban addictive social media features and designs for minors. These laws seem aimed at restricting kids' access to online material, as if the legislatures had made an implicit cost-benefit assessment that the risks of online harms justified measures to make it harder for children to avail themselves of online tools.[57]

In the United States, the existing federal online child protection law is a privacy law, the Children's Online Privacy Protection Act, passed in 1998 in the wake of the first national scare about online harms to children. It requires websites that are directed toward children under thirteen years of age and websites that have actual knowledge that they are collecting personal information online from a child under thirteen years of age to obtain verifiable parental consent before collecting personal data from this age group.[58]

COPPA was not the only legislation passed in the early internet era aimed at protecting kids. Policymakers' initial concern in these early days was pornography, and they passed the Communications Decency Act in 1996. But in *Reno v. ACLU*, a landmark First Amendment decision, the Supreme Court struck down the indecency portions of the statute, holding that they were not narrowly tailored since other effective means were available to block indecent material from children and that the age verification defenses proposed were not workable in practice.[59]

Unsurprisingly then, industry and civil liberties groups raised free speech concerns in connection with the contemporary measures to protect kids online. After the California law passed the legislature, the industry trade association NetChoice filed a First Amendment challenge, arguing that the law was overly broad in applying to virtually all websites. According to NetChoice, the requirement that online companies conduct an assessment of the risks of various online harms to children and create a plan to mitigate these risks before launching a new product or service "will pressure businesses to identify distant or unlikely harms—and to self-censor accordingly." It said the law's age verification requirement is "unrealistic" and will result in "self-censorship." It also said the ban on using children's information in ways that are materially detrimental is plagued by "undefined" terms, "amorphous" concepts, and "generalities," thus leading companies to "self-censor."

NetChoice has not yet brought a case against the Utah bill, but in its letter to Utah governor Spencer J. Cox urging him to veto the bill, it argued that the bill was unconstitutional. The trade group said the bill violates the First Amendment by banning anonymous speech and by infringing on adults' lawful access to constitutional speech. Moreover, it endangers children by requiring them to share their sensitive personally identifiable information, thereby creating new risks of abuse.[60]

Despite these First Amendment concerns, which will be resolved in court in due course, states in 2023 appeared to be rushing to pass laws to protect children, with red states moving toward the parental consent model and blue states looking to design restrictions to make it safe for children to be online. This put pressure on Congress to act by moving toward either a design approach or a parental consent model. In spring 2023, in addition to the revised KOSA bill, Congress was considering the Protecting Kids on Social Media Act, a bipartisan bill that would ban children under thirteen from having an account at a social media firm and would require parental consent for kids thirteen to seventeen.[61]

My own preference is for a version of the design restrictions approach. It creates a framework for managing online risks to children. The danger of stifling kids' exploration of the online world can be managed, and it avoids the overly restrictive steps of banning children's access or requiring parental control. Regardless of which approach is taken, however, nothing can be expected to change unless the congressional legislation empowers a strong regulatory agency to implement and enforce the new requirements. Much of the vagueness in KOSA, for instance, could be remedied by detailed guidelines imposed by regulation. KOSA and the Protecting Kids on Social Media Act put the FTC in charge of enforcement, but both would be stronger if they authorized the agency to promulgate regulations under the Administrative Procedure Act to carry out and clarify the provisions.

A new national law to protect kids no matter what state they live in would be a good thing and might very well be politically feasible. As we have seen time and again, however, such a new kids' online safety bill must create or designate a fully empowered regulator to implement and enforce the laws. Such a mission could appropriately be added to the duties of a digital regulator with a mission to control information disorder on social media, while protecting and preserving free speech.

A Dispute Resolution Program for Social Media Companies

A mandated transparency and due process regime for social media companies is an attractive way to begin to address the vast amount of legal but harmful hate speech, misinformation, and disinformation on social media platforms. This would require disclosure of content standards and enforcement methods, informing users and the public so that companies would be on record about their commitment to take action against this harmful material.

It would also be attractive to require social media companies to act consistently with their own announced rules. This consistency requirement would create a kind of carriage right, an assurance that users will be afforded full access to the platform's communication services if they stay within the company's boundaries of acceptable discourse. This consistency requirement would satisfy many public policy goals, most prominently consumer protection from unfair and deceptive practices.

But this idea faces an apparently insurmountable problem. How could a government agency enforce consistency without analyzing content decisions—and thereby increasing the very real and present danger of partisan abuse of regulatory authority? Suppose a social media company and a user disagreed about whether a post should be taken down under the social media company's rules prohibiting hate speech. A government agency as the adjudicator of this dispute would have to compare the posted material to the company's hate speech standard and decide whether it really was hate speech. This need for agency judgment creates the danger of partisan abuse. Agency leaders in a conservative administration might be tempted to treat harsh speech from progressives as hate speech and seek its removal. Conversely, agency heads in a progressive administration might condemn right-wing speech as falling under the hate speech prohibition.

A nongovernmental dispute resolution agency supervised by a government agency might provide a way out of this enforcement dilemma. FINRA, the self-regulatory organization established to oversee broker-dealers, provides a model. The best defense against the danger of partisan abuse of regulatory authority would be to arrange a dispute resolution structure that provides independent accountability against arbitrary social media action and at the same time insulates the independent review of social media content decisions from regulatory action by a government agency.

To provide necessary accountability without government review of content decisions, the legislation setting up a digital regulator should mandate that—in addition to their internal dispute resolution procedures—the social media companies must establish and maintain external nongovernmental dispute resolution procedures. This would allow users to appeal content moderation decisions to an independent body empowered to second-guess company decisions. An independent reviewing body is a vital element in accountability. If companies can pick their own review boards, the way Facebook has done in setting up its own review board, this independence is not genuine. Over the long term, the company could effectively control the outcomes of these supposedly independent reviews.

To avoid this lack of real independence, Congress should require social media companies to join an industry self-regulatory organization that would provide affordable and efficient arbitration and mediation services to social media companies to satisfy this obligation for independent review. Any such self-regulatory organization would have to be approved by and under the supervision of the digital regulator. All acceptable dispute resolution agencies would have to have a board consisting of an equal number of representatives of the social media industry and representatives of the public and would have to be funded through membership fees. The legislation would not require all covered social media companies to join the same dispute resolution agency, but they would have to join one and it would have to be approved by the supervising digital regulator.

A nongovernmental dispute resolution agency would have the necessary insulation from government to provide user redress through arbitration and mediation services, without the specter of government partisanship. The digital regulator should be authorized to supervise the operations of the dispute resolution agency, but only to ensure procedural regularity and to guard against inefficiency, neglect, or corruption or systematic bias. A dispute resolution agency that always or disproportionately favored the social media company, for instance, could be disapproved by the digital regulator. The digital regulator itself should be explicitly forbidden to take any action to second-guess the judgment of the dispute resolution agency. Senators Brian Schatz and John Thune provide a model for this in their bipartisan legislation, which would establish a transparency regime for social media companies supervised by the FTC. The bill would not allow the FTC "to review any action or decision by a provider of an interactive computer service related to the application of the acceptable use policy of the provider." It would be an easy matter to extend this prohibition on second-guessing to cover the decisions of the dispute resolution agency.

Many details of such a dispute resolution system would need to be resolved before this proposal is ready for legislative consideration. The dispute resolution system established and operated by FINRA for regulated broker-dealers might provide a model that would help to flesh out these crucial details.

The major lesson from the FINRA example is that establishing a self-regulatory structure for social media would be neither simple nor cheap, but it could be done. Based on the FINRA model, an acceptable digital dispute resolution service would enable social media users to bring complaints to the service for resolution. Users would be required to pay a small initial filing fee, refundable if the award is favorable to their complaint. Administrative fees and arbitration fees would be paid by the dispute resolution service. The company and the users involved in a dispute would have to agree on a three-person arbitration panel chosen from a list selected by the service.

Arbitrators could not be employed by the social media industry or provide professional services to the industry. However, they could have held such positions in the past and be eligible to serve as arbitrators after a certain period. Arbitration panels should have no more than one person formerly associated with the industry and would be required to have one from both civil society and academia. Each dispute resolution agency would maintain a list of arbitrators who are experts in various fields associated with content moderation, specifically for hate speech and disinformation.

The decision of the panel would be final and binding. It would not be appealable to the dispute resolution service itself, to the digital regulator, or to the courts. The arbitration panel would be empowered to order the social media company to take down or to reinstate content, to end demotion and delay measures or to impose them, to order accounts suspended or restored, and so on. In short, it would act as an appeals court authorized to reverse any of the content moderation enforcement actions taken by the social media company itself. It would not be authorized to impose fines or penalties on the social media company or the user.

Much more would need to be done to build out the details of this dispute resolution mechanism. However, the model of FINRA and these suggestions toward adapting that model to the case of social media oversight show that such a program could be operated successfully on a large scale, without direct government control, and could be funded through industry fees with no burden on the taxpayers.

A key protection is that this system is insulated from the digital regulator itself. In other systems, notably Australia, users can appeal directly to a regulator if not satisfied with a social media company's resolution of their complaint, and the regulator can order removal of the content regardless of the social media company's initial judgment. This would not work in the US system where all parties are alert to the dangers of partisan abuse of such regulatory authority. As mentioned, the PACT provides a good model for this insulation.[62]

An industry dispute resolution agency would use the standards in place at the social media company as its touchstone for resolving disputes. It would not apply US law. It would not appeal to international human rights instruments or interpretations of these instruments. At the outset, its only function, in the words of the philosophers Jean-Jacques Rousseau and Immanuel Kant, would be to require the social media companies to obey the laws they have made for themselves.[63]

But the self-regulatory organization developed to administer the dispute resolution system could develop its own code for the entire industry, a code that each social media company would use. The voluntary code developed by National Association of Broadcasters (NAB) provides one example of such an industry code.[64]

Many might be suspicious of an industry content code as creating pressure toward uniformity, but it would be a mistake to prohibit what might be a natural evolution of the industry. An approved dispute resolution agency should be permitted to (but need not) promulgate its own content standards for social media companies to follow. The larger social media platforms have extensive content rules and enforcement procedures of their own and might want to extend these practices to other social media companies through adoption by a dispute resolution agency. It might be that as the industry evolves, the need for uniform standards grows, and the codes and procedures worked out in practice by one or more of the larger companies might serve as a model for the entire industry. Smaller social media companies might benefit from standardized content rules and enforcement procedures. A dispute resolution agency should be permitted to provide services to all companies that share the same content standards and enforcement procedures. In time this might come to include all or predominantly all social media companies, thereby imposing a kind of uniformity on the industry.

The digital regulator should not be empowered to discourage or prohibit this development. Indeed, it might make sense for the agency to encourage it. This kind of uniformity might be an effective way for the industry to respond to the wave of hate speech, misinformation, and disinformation that have inundated social media platforms. A united front of social media companies might be just what is needed to bring this problem under control. There is no need to prevent this solution by legislative or regulatory prohibitions.[65]

Notice Liability

Section 230 of the Communications Decency Act of 1996 provides legal immunity for platforms when they act as the publishers of material posted by their users, including when the platforms edit or fail to edit this material. It is a paradoxical provision of law whose oddity can be brought out by phrasing it as what it is: an instruction to the courts not to treat social media companies as publishers of the material posted by their users insofar as they are acting as publishers of this material.[66]

Progressives and conservatives in Congress both want to reform the law and put in place a new system that provides for greater accountability when social media companies fail to take action against illegal material on their system. They have reached this judgment because Section 230 provides such broad protection for social media companies that users who have been clearly and, in some cases, deliberately harmed by social media posts have no recourse to the courts to obtain redress for their evident and often substantial injuries.

As we shall see in the discussion that follows, reform of Section 230 would do very little to combat hate speech and misinformation on social media because such material is legal. Nevertheless, reform is warranted to provide recourse for injured parties. The reforms described and endorsed in this section would allow these injured parties to have their day in court. As such, they have almost nothing to do with the responsibilities and powers of the digital regulator.

Section 230 reform intersects with content moderation issues in at least one respect. Reformers often face the charge that if Section 230 is eliminated or reformed, then social media companies will not be able to moderate any content on their systems at all. David French, a noted lawyer and conservative political commentator, asks Section 230 reformers, "So you want nudity on Facebook?" The argument is that without Section 230, social media companies will be liable for the illegal content on their systems if they take any steps at all to moderate content. If they act as a common carrier, however, they can escape legal liability. The result would be that social media platforms become unusable cesspools of hate speech, disinformation, and pornography. So, French concludes, people who want to reform Section 230 must really be in favor of nudity on Facebook.[67]

However, without Section 230 protections, social media companies could take the other choice of censoring everything. They learned long ago that content moderation is required for them to have a business. Instead of turning themselves into passive common carriers, which would be the effective end of their business, they could instead adopt a policy of screening all content for violation of law and taking down all the material that posed even the slightest risk of legal liability. This would reduce the content on social media to the blandest, safest material, a return to the monoculture of broadcast television.

Thus, reform of Section 230 seems to create the risk of one of two undesirable outcomes. This section outlines why that widespread analysis is wrong and how a system of notice liability can hold social media firms accountable for the illegal material on their system without forcing them to become common carriers unable to keep harmful but legal speech off their systems and without requiring them to become draconian censors presiding over increasingly bland platforms.

How likely is political agreement on Section 230 reform? Some conservative advocates for reform of the statute want to constrain platform editorial discretion to create a more favorable climate for their political perspectives. But they also want to exempt from Section 230 immunity certain especially harmful illegal activity, such as sex trafficking and child sexual abuse material. Progressives pushing for reform, meanwhile, want platforms to be less hostile toward speech from marginalized groups struggling for social, economic, and racial justice, but they also want platforms to take action against hate speech and white supremacy.

It is not clear whether both sides in Congress will be able to arrive at a unified reform. At one point in time, the Supreme Court appeared poised to address the issue. In a 2020 statement concurring with dissent from the Supreme Court's denial of a petition of a writ of certiorari involving a Section 230 claim, Justice Clarence Thomas argued that judges have extended Section 230 far beyond what Congress intended. He proposed a reinterpretation of Section 230 that would "par[e] back the sweeping immunity courts have read into §230." It seemed as if the Supreme Court under Justice Thomas's leadership could have acted to "pare back" Section 230 immunity in some way.[68]

In the fall of 2022, the Supreme Court agreed to review two cases involving Section 230. The key one, *Gonzalez v. Google*, concerned a claim that YouTube recommended terrorist recruitment videos to its users and thereby aided and abetted the commission of terrorist acts. The case raised the question of whether Section 230 immunizes social media companies when they make targeted recommendations or whether it limits their liability only when they engage in traditional editorial functions such as deciding whether to display or delete material. In June 2021, the US Court of Appeals for the Ninth Circuit held that the district court in *Gonzalez* properly ruled that Section 230 bars these claims.[69]

The fact that the Supreme Court agreed to hear the case suggested it intended to make a change, but a change in the immunity of social media recommendations is not a minor adjustment. Recommended material constitutes a substantial portion of what appears on social media sites. In some cases, all or almost all the content is recommended. TikTok, for instance, is nothing but recommended content.

Perhaps for that reason, the oral argument in the spring of 2023 created a consensus among commentators that the court is unlikely to make major changes in Section 230. The justices appeared suspicious of the extent of immunity Google claimed under Section 230, but they also seemed wary of exempting amplification from Section 230 for fear that this would amount to a wholesale repeal. On May 18, 2023, as expected, the Supreme Court ruled that Twitter had not aided and abetted the commission of terrorist acts and consequently the Court "declined to address the application of §230."[70]

In any case, it would be better to have Congress establish a new liability regime rather than allow the Supreme Court to establish the new regime disguised as interpretation of a twenty-five-year-old statutory text. The Court's decision in *Gonzalez* shows it has no intention of reforming Section 230 through novel interpretation of the statute, and so it is up to Congress to put in place a new regime.

In the spring of 2023, a lively debate broke out on the application of Section 230 to the generative AI programs typified by ChatGPT. A minority argued that ChatGPT already enjoys Section 230 immunity—they are indistinguishable from search engines that are already covered under Section 230. The predominant view, typified by Duke University scholar Matt Perault and the congressional authors of Section 230, is that ChatGPT helps to create the content it returns in response to questions and so is not covered by Section 230, which covers only content that is entirely provided by users of systems.

Despite this consensus, Perault and others (including the *Washington Post*) think ChatGPT should be provided with some limited immunity. Developers cannot reasonably anticipate all the output that could be generated by users of their system, and so potential liability would inhibit the growth of the new technology.[71]

It is likely that this new issue of the application of Section 230 to ChatGPT and other forms of content generating AI will be folded into congressional consideration of Section 230. In this process, Congress must consider whether these new technologies will be included in any reform proposal or whether they be liable if and to the extent that other systems would be without reference to Section 230.

What is the best way forward? Sometimes it pays to examine a road not taken. In this case, the notice liability regime, rejected by the courts in 1997 as an interpretation of Section 230, might be worth reconsidering. It would require social media companies to take down content promptly after notification that it was illegal or face whatever liability exists under current law for having it up on their system. This notice liability system would be a major improvement over the current system and might be something the warring partisan factions in Congress can agree on.

This is different from an alternative approach to Section 230 reform, increasingly popular in Congress, that involves piecemeal carve-outs that focus on particularly egregious online harms and illegality. Congress did its first carve-out from Section 230 in 2018 by passing the Allow States and Victims to Fight Online Sex Trafficking Act (FOSTA), creating liability for online companies that facilitate or promote sex trafficking. The bill passed the Senate on an overwhelming bipartisan vote of 97–2. In a similar vein, the proposed Earn It Act sponsored in 2020 by Republican Senator Lindsey Graham, with bipartisan co-sponsorship, including Democratic Senator Richard Blumenthal, would withdraw Section 230 protection for violations of child sexual abuse laws.

Some bills target algorithmic amplification of content rather than the mere presence of content on a social media platform. Democratic Representatives Anna Eshoo and Tom Malinowski introduced the Protecting Americans from Dangerous Algorithms Act in October 2020 to withdraw Section 230 immunity for the amplification of content connected to civil rights violations or involving acts of international terrorism. One year later, in October 2021, in response to the revelations of Facebook whistleblower Frances Haugen about Facebook studies showing that Instagram use contributed to mental health issues for pre-teens, Representative Eshoo and colleagues on the House Energy and Commerce Committee built upon that earlier bill and introduced the Justice Against Malicious Algorithms Act. This bill eliminates Section 230 immunity if an online platform knowingly or recklessly uses an algorithm to recommend content to a user based on that personal information and if that recommendation materially contributes to physical or severe emotional injury.

The Safeguarding Against Fraud, Exploitation, Threats, Extremism and Consumer Harms (Safe Tech) Act introduced by Democratic senators Mark R. Warner, Mazie Hirono, and Amy Klobuchar in February 2021 would make sure Section 230 does not apply to ads or other paid content, does not bar injunctive relief, does not impair enforcement of civil rights laws, does not interfere with laws that address stalking and cyber-stalking or harassment and intimidation on the basis of protected classes, does not bar wrongful death suits, and does not bar suits under the Alien Tort Claims Act.

The explanation of the Safe Tech Act released along with the text notes a crucial element of most Section 230 reform proposals. Typical piecemeal reforms "do not guarantee that platforms will be held liable in all, or even most, cases. . . . Rather, these reforms ensure that victims have an opportunity to raise claims without Section 230 serving as a categorical bar to their efforts to seek legal redress for harms they suffer—even when directly enabled by a platform's actions or design." FOSTA is an exception; it created a new offense of promoting or facilitating prostitution.[72]

Sometimes these measures target particular Section 230 court decisions. Representative Eshoo's proposal to remove immunity for algorithmic amplification in connection with suits involving terrorism strikes at the decision in *Force v. Facebook, Inc.*, where the US Court of Appeals for the Second Circuit granted immunity to Facebook for recommending that terrorists should read each other's posts and meet each other.

The Safe Tech Act responds, among other things, to the *Herrick v. Grindr* case, in which the US Court of Appeals for the Second Circuit issued a summary order upholding a district court decision immunizing the dating app from a product defect claim alleging that it did not have an effective system to prevent harassment and threats to physical safety.[73]

This piecemeal approach is a mistake. By picking and choosing among the possible sources of litigation against social media companies, this carve-out approach inevitably increases the burden of legal analysis on social media companies to determine whether they have immunity in particular cases. Moreover, as law professors Danielle Citron and Mary Anne Franks note, piecemeal reform is "inevitably underinclusive." It creates an open-ended drive for Congress to update Section 230 exceptions whenever a new egregious harm presents itself. The House Energy and Commerce Committee bills illustrates this dynamic. In October 2020, the proposed bill targeted algorithmic amplification of terrorist material; in October 2021, in response to the new problem of mental health problems consequent on personalized recommendations to pre-teens, the updated bill targeted this new harm.[74] The piecemeal approach also increases the difficulty of finding bipartisan agreement on which immunities to remove and which to leave in place in a particular measure.

In June 2020, the US Department of Justice, reflecting the views of many political conservatives, focused its Section 230 reform proposal on modifications of Section 230(c)(2)'s requirement that platforms act in "good faith" when they remove content. But this proposal is based on a misunderstanding of how Section 230 works in practice. As legal scholar Eric Goldman—the best and most knowledgeable defender of Section 230—has noted, the platforms rarely use Section 230(c)(2) to escape liability for their content removal decisions. This is because Section 230(c)(2)'s requirement to show good faith imposes a high litigation burden, including the expensive and time-consuming burden of discovery. The major advantage for platforms from Section 230's grant of immunity is not that platforms will necessarily win cases after lengthy court proceedings, but that they can short-circuit the case before it can proceed. As a result, in practice, platforms get their immunity without extended court processes by invoking Section 230(c)(1)—which courts have interpreted broadly to immunize any action where a platform acts as a publisher, including content removal or filtering, and which does not require any showing of good faith for such removals.[75]

But this idea to grant Section 230 immunity only if companies are acting in good faith when they remove material illustrates the second major branch of reform efforts. This approach conditions Section 230 immunity on some attractive or desirable behavior. In 2019, conservative Senator Josh Hawley embraced this path to Section 230 reform. Responding to complaints of bias against conservatives on social media platforms, he introduced legislation to condition Section 230 immunity on a regulatory finding of a platform's political neutrality.

In 2017, legal scholars Citron and Wittes also embraced the conditional approach to Section 230 reform. They want to make Section 230 immunity contingent on a court's determination of reasonable content moderation practices. In 2021, Facebook endorsed a version of this idea of granting Section 230 immunity only when a company has in place reasonable content moderation practices. "Instead of being granted immunity," Facebook CEO Mark Zuckerberg told Congress, "platforms should be required to demonstrate that they have systems in place for identifying unlawful content and removing it."

These requirements for good behavior need not be tied to Section 230. If these practices are good policy ideas, Congress could mandate them directly and put a regulator in charge of interpreting and enforcing these rules. There is no need for a complicated detour through assignment of liability to enforce these requirements when direct enforcement by a digital regulator will be quicker and more certain. Conditioning

Section 230 immunity on satisfying these obligations is an ineffective and indirect compliance mechanism.[76]

Section 230 reform is not the right vehicle for addressing many issues that might need to be resolved in crafting a regulatory framework for social media companies. Reform of Section 230 cannot deal with social media controls on legal but harmful information on platforms including hate speech and disinformation, which are protected by the First Amendment. It is also the wrong mechanism for imposing transparency and accountability for content moderation practices for violations of a platform's own content rules involving legal speech.

Section 230 reform is really about the extent to which platforms are liable for illegal speech and activity on their systems—not about these very different regulatory issues. Progressives and conservatives largely agree there is too much illegal and harmful material on social media platforms and a reform of the current liability system could go a long way to eliminating much of it. But piecemeal reform and conditioning immunity on satisfying other unrelated conditions are poor ways to accomplish what needs to be a more fundamental reform.

The past has something to teach today's policymakers in Congress about the way forward. Back in 1997, the US Court of Appeals for the Fourth Circuit in the case of *Zeran v. America Online* had a chance to allow a notice and takedown system to develop under Section 230. The idea the court reviewed was that Section 230 immunity would not apply if a service provider got adequate notice about illegal material on its system and failed to act. But the court rejected this idea as inconsistent with the purpose of Section 230 to provide an incentive for self-regulatory content moderation. The judges also thought notice liability would lead to excessive content removal. Faced with a blizzard of notices and in the absence of any liability for removals, the court wrote, platforms would have a "natural incentive simply to remove messages upon notification."[77]

This is now settled Section 230 law. But it was a mistake then—and it is bad policy for today's online world. A notice and takedown system would be far more effective in policing illegal content than immunizing companies for their failure to act, which is what Section 230 does. And the risks to free speech can be managed.

The United States has had more than twenty years of experience with the notice and takedown regime established in the 1998 Digital Millennium Copyright Act (DMCA), which provides a safe harbor from copyright infringement for platforms that act to remove infringing material upon notification. While neither content owners nor platforms are completely satisfied, this law has provided a workable system that protects both copyright interests and free speech. It requires strict conditions on adequate notices such as identifying the specific work infringed, a statement of good faith, and a statement under pain of perjury that the complainant is authorized to act for the copyright owner. The DMCA also requires the platform to provide an opportunity for the alleged infringer to file a counter-notice, and if the alleged infringer does so, the platform must restore the removed material unless the complaining party goes to court within ten days alleging copyright infringement.[78]

Regulators in the European Union reproduced the DMCA's model of notice liability in its 2000 Electronic Commerce Directive, which provided immunity to online service providers only if they acted expeditiously to remove illegal material once they obtained actual knowledge of its illegality. This provided the legal basis for member countries to establish general notice and takedown schemes, even though few did so.

Europe's new Digital Services Act (DSA), among other things, would establish a pan-European notification and takedown regime. Under the proposed new system, receipt of adequate notice concerning illegal material would require platforms to act expeditiously to remove the material in order to maintain immunity. In addition, the act would require complaints to contain an explanation of alleged illegality, identifying information, and a statement confirming good faith. Platforms must also establish redress mechanisms for users whose content is removed, including internal complaint-handling mechanisms, out-of-court dispute settlement, and judicial redress.

As with other Section 230 reforms, these new rules under the DSA do not determine that the platform is liable for damages if it does not remove the material upon complaint. The new DSA rules do not create any new causes of action. They say only that if the platform fails to act, it loses immunity from whatever liability already exists under other laws for leaving such material in place. As Recital 17 of the DSA says, the new rules "should not be understood to provide a positive basis for establishing when a provider can be held liable, which is for the applicable rules of Union or national law to determine."[79]

Social media companies know how to operate a notice and takedown system in areas outside of the DMCA's regime for copyright enforcement. In late 2021, Twitter voluntarily adopted a notice-and-takedown system in the United States for protecting user privacy, announcing it would take down nonconsensual posts of intimate photos. Under this system, when Twitter is notified by individuals depicted or by an authorized representative that they did not consent to having their private image or video shared, the company will remove it. The user who posted the content will also receive a notification about the request, as well as an opportunity to dispute any takedown. Although new to the United States in 2021, Twitter has enforced this policy in countries with strict privacy laws, such as Australia, New Zealand, the United Kingdom, and countries in the European Union.[80]

Congress should move ahead to establish a platform notice and takedown regime modeled on the systems in the DMCA and the DSA. Such a system would not require platforms to review material before it is posted. It would build on the complaint systems the larger social media companies already have in place and would rely on these complaints to alert platforms that someone has posted potentially illegal and harmful material.

Under the current regime, the dating service Grindr was able to have a legal complaint dismissed, even though it ignored repeated notices that its system was being used to harass the plaintiff and expose him to potential physical harm. Under a notice liability regime, Grindr would continue to enjoy immunity from liability until the victim of the impersonation and harassment notified the company, and it would remain immune from liability if it acted expeditiously to block the harmful activity. If it failed to act, it would have to face a court proceeding, and it might succeed in defending itself against the charge that a defect in its management of its system was responsible for the harassment. All the notice liability system would provide for would be the possibility that the court case would be allowed to go forward if the dating site ignored complaints of illegal activity.

A different kind of suit might also be allowed under notice liability. In October 2021, an animal rights group sued YouTube for failing to remove thousands of hours of animal abuse videos, accusing it of breach of contract. The suit claims that the platform failed to live up to its agreement with users by allowing animal abuse videos to be uploaded and by failing to act when alerted about the content. Under the current system, YouTube could claim immunity under Section 230 and seek to have the suit dismissed, but such a defense would not be available under a notice liability system. Under notice liability, the case would be allowed to proceed to determine whether failure to remove so many hours of videos that violate its terms of service, after repeated notices, amounts to a breach of contract.[81]

It is commonly said that liability for illegal material will cause risk-averse social media companies to take down too much content. To avoid this result, some reformers repeal immunity from liability only for material that a social media company has amplified. If a company doesn't amplify material, but just distributes it without any ranking or recommendation, then it retains its legal immunity.

If over-removals are a problem for Section 230 reform, proposals that allow liability just for amplification of illegal material do not solve this problem. Legal scholar Daphne Keller properly notes that "since the algorithms behind features like newsfeeds or recommendations rank every item, this would effectively expose platforms to liability under any law for anything users post." As a result, she argues, a rational platform "would presumably respond by either eliminating amplification features entirely or excluding broad categories of content." She views this result as intolerable for free speech.

The Facebook whistleblower, Haugen, agreed with Keller's assessment, saying, "If we reformed 230 to make Facebook responsible for the consequences of their intentional ranking decisions, I think they would get rid of engagement-based ranking." In contrast to Keller, Haugen welcomes the change, thinking it would prevent online harms. Roddy Lindsay, a former Facebook engineer, also agreed, saying, "There is no

A.I. system that could identify every possible instance of illegal content. Faced with potential liability for every amplified post, these companies would most likely be forced to scrap algorithmic feeds altogether." He, too, welcomed the change. Presumably the enemies of surveillance capitalism would also look to this change in Section 230 to do the work of banishing that business model.[82]

These arguments vastly overstate the likely effect of making social media companies liable for amplifying illegal content, since most harmful posts are not illegal. None of the proposals for algorithmic liability create new liability by inventing a new cause of action. Litigants would have to find a cause of action under some existing law. Almost all the harmful material online, including hate speech, disinformation, and misinformation, is constitutionally protected. Even if social media companies are liable for the material they amplify, the underlying speech laws are so forgiving that the actual legal risk is modest and easily controllable.

In any case, these arguments simply do not work against a notice liability regime. Liability under this regime occurs only after companies receive a properly constituted notice. If a social media company amplifies some content and then receives a notice explaining its illegality, it would face no liability whatsoever if it promptly removes the content or ceases to amplify it.

The risk is not that it faces uncontrolled liability that will force it to change its business model. The risk is that it will treat each notice as a command to remove material regardless of the merits of the complaint. The result might be that more material is removed than illegal material.

To control the risks of excessive removals, the new system should include all the protections in the DMCA law upon which it is modeled. These measures would include provisions for counter-notice and reinstatement in the absence of beginning court proceedings, requirements for detailed and specific complaints citing relevant statutes, and requirements for good faith and perjury penalties. Others could be considered, including liability for wrongful removal, which might allow recourse to courts when perfectly legal material is removed in error, and fee shifting for frivolous lawsuits. The law also could require platforms to act against repeat offenders and groups that abuse the complaint process and to develop a trusted reviewer program that privileges the complaints of verified users. In addition, the new requirements could be limited to the largest platforms, which create the greatest risks of illegal conduct, and which have resources to manage notification liability. As Keller points out, these measures would mitigate the First Amendment concern that a notice liability system would result in unconstitutional over-removal of legal material.[83]

No system that imposes notice liability can avoid creating some incentive for excess removals, but the current system errs in the opposite direction of allowing too much illegal and harmful material. Measures against abuse like ones just described have rendered the operation of the DMCA tolerable over the last decades and should mitigate the risks of extending it to broader liability.

An additional concern about the use of Section 230 immunity has arisen in connection with the application of federal statutes. Section 230 was clearly not intended to provide immunity from the application of the Fair Housing Act, the Americans with Disabilities Act, or Title II of the Civil Rights Act. And yet courts have dismissed cases under the statutes citing a conflict with Section 230.

One case seems especially troublesome. A court case from May 2021 found that companies housing consumer reports on online computers—that is, every company in the consumer reporting business—is exempt from the Fair Credit Reporting Act. In October 2021, CFPB director Rohit Chopra and FTC chair Khan issued a statement arguing that this decision created a competitive imbalance between traditional consumer reporting agencies and newer online companies performing the same function. But this misses the real import of the decision. Every company in the consumer reporting business is an online company, and so under the decision, they are all exempt from the law. The decision effectively repeals the FCRA, or at least means that the law cannot be applied to any company. In November 2022, the Fourth Circuit Court of Appeals overruled the district court, finding that Section 230 does not preempt the Fair Credit Reporting Act, and that Section 230 does not extend to public data aggregation. But the new standard it developed is controversial, and it is unclear how it would be applied to future cases.[84]

To remedy this conflict between Section 230 and federal law, the Platform Accountability and Transparency Act leaves Section 230 in place in general but provides that it does not apply to the enforcement of federal civil statutes or regulations.[85] The notice liability system should be implemented in a way that ensures it would not interfere with the enforcement of federal civil statutes or regulations.

It is worth noting how little a notice liability system would do for the larger issues confronting social media. Proponents of reform often say that reform would encourage social media companies to reduce the amount of disinformation and hate speech on their systems and to stop algorithmic amplification, personalization, or recommendation of this harmful material. But notice liability just allows a possible court case to proceed if the social media company does not take down the harmful material or cease to amplify it. It does not make it illegal to distribute or amplify the offending material. Distributing hate speech, misinformation about COVID-19 or the results of an election, or white nationalist material is not against the law.

Some Section 230 litigation raised novel legal questions such as whether recommending social media users join a terrorist group or follow a known terrorist leader constitutes a legal offense. This issue was at the heart of the *Force v. Facebook, Inc.* and also the *Gonzalez* case that went up to the Supreme Court. But in *Force* the court never reached this novel legal question and instead decided the case over the irrelevant question of whether amplification of content counted as publishing under Section 230. Having decided that amplification was publishing, the court dismissed the case without reaching the key legal issue. Similar novel legal issues arise concerning claims against social media companies under product liability law. Urging people to attend a demonstration that later turns violent is almost certainly not actionable, but amplifying material that directly aids in the commission of a crime, such as the Capitol Hill riots on January 6, 2021, might very well be activity for which social media companies could be held liable.

The extent to which distributing or amplifying content on social media is illegal could have been sorted out by the courts over the last twenty-five years. Section 230 stopped this natural evolution of the law.

A notice liability would allow the law to address these issues as social media companies press their sense that, even without Section 230 immunity, they are not liable for the harmful consequences of the material their users post, even if they extend the reach of these posts through algorithmic amplification.

Progressives and conservatives should be able to agree that a notice and takedown system is a reasonable Section 230 reform. Both sides want to cut down on the illegal and harmful material that appears far too often on platforms under the current system. They disagree about whether platforms are taking down too much legal conservative content. But this issue and others such as the need for political neutrality and reasonable access to platform services for all political perspectives are outside the scope of Section 230 reform and can be pursued through other vehicles. The same is true for mandates for fairness, accountability, and transparency in content moderation.

If policymakers want to collaborate in reducing illegal and harmful online content, they will face a choice between piecemeal Section 230 reform such as the Earn It Act or the Safe Tech Act, conditioning Section 230 immunity on certain good behavior or more fundamental reform such as a notice and choice regime. Piecemeal reform poses many problems: It does not solve the underlying issues, raises the specter of partisan gridlock on any specific measure, and opens the door to an endless series of exceptions. Conditioning immunity on good behavior is a needless detour, since the good behavior could be mandated directly.

The better course of action for the warring partisan factions would be to press ahead with a comprehensive reform of the current Section 230 regime and establish a new notice liability system modeled after the DMCA and the updated European system.

Political Pluralism

Political pluralism is a fundamental principle of US communications law, expressed by the Supreme Court in its 1945 *Associated Press* ruling as "the widest possible dissemination of information from diverse and antagonistic sources." It is at the heart of the 1969 *Red Lion* case in which the Supreme Court, in upholding the broadcasting fairness doctrine, established the "paramount" right of the public "to receive suitable access to social, political, esthetic, moral, and other ideas and experiences." It is also recognized in Article 19 of the ICCPR, which treats as a fundamental human right the "freedom to seek, receive, and impart information and ideas of all kinds" regardless of medium.[86]

The lodestar of political pluralism is a fair representation of the views of the community in the media systems that serve the public. This is not quite the same as a right for representatives of particular political perspectives to speak as much as they want or can afford. As free speech theorist Alexander Meiklejohn put it, "What is essential is not that everyone shall speak, but that everything worth saying shall be said."[87] The regulatory philosophy of legal scholar Owen Fiss also embodies this vision of political pluralism in its emphasis on the need to restrict private company control over the range of ideas and experiences available to the public in order to make sure the rights of the public to receive information are protected from private censorship.[88]

It seemed at first that the internet and then social media would automatically satisfy the ideal of political pluralism by giving people an uncensored mechanism for expressing their views. But the rise of dominant social media platforms engaged in extensive content moderation makes it clear that the dangers of monoculture have not been relegated to the past. The new online gatekeepers have the power to be just as repressive as the old ones in traditional media.

Conservatives and progressives both see the major social platforms as biased against their political perspectives, even though these complaints have not been substantiated by any serious research. What research there is tends to support the idea that conservative ideas dominate on social media less because of conscious bias by social media firms and more because the conservative style of anger, outrage, and grievance tends to attract an audience in a medium that values engagement above all else.

These complaints of political bias, however, raise fundamental issues. To what extent should social media companies promote political pluralism? Should they be required in some fashion to provide their users with a diversity of political views? Should they be able to moderate content based on political viewpoint? Should they be allowed to propagate their own views to the exclusion of others? Should they allow their system to be dominated by the strongest political perspective of the moment?

In today's politically polarized landscape, there is a realistic danger that dominant social media companies on their own or subject to political pressure might suppress or favor one side of the nation's fierce political debate, and users of these services would have nowhere else to turn.

For liberals who dismiss such concerns as a conservative fantasy, it might be worth reflecting what the world would look like to them if Rupert Murdoch controlled Facebook or Twitter and installed an algorithmic amplification system that mirrored the editorial policy of Fox News. The rise of Elon Musk to the control of Twitter in late 2022 displayed this danger as a realistic possibility, not a fanciful speculation.

Policymakers should be aware of the dangers of private censorship by the social media companies that increasingly dominate the nation's political discussion. Now is the time to engage on this question of political pluralism because an unusual confluence of political left and political right creates a once-in-a-lifetime opportunity to devise a regulatory system that might respond to this danger of private social media censorship.

While the time is right to start this conversation on political pluralism, now is not the time to mandate it for social media companies. As we shall see in this section, requirements for political pluralism suffer from conceptual difficulties, potentially irresolvable value conflicts, and perhaps insuperable implementation difficulties. Congress should establish a congressional advisory commission to conduct further research and assessment of the ideal of political pluralism and how it might be implemented in practice by social media platforms. The advisory commission should work together with the digital regulator to explore these issues and report back to Congress with their findings and legislative recommendations.

One way forward comes from political scientist Francis Fukuyama and his colleagues. They have developed an alternative to mandated political pluralism. Their "middleware" approach would install an "editorial layer" between dominant social media companies and their users. This would outsource "content curation," including political filtering, to other organizations, which would allow consumers to tailor their feeds to their own political and other preferences. Dominant social platforms would be required to open their systems to third parties who would receive the platform's entire feed and filter it according to their own criteria, which could include political preferences, and then make that curated feed available to their own users.[89]

This middleware approach has the advantages of keeping the government away from diversity mandates. But it seems far-fetched. It is not at all clear that it is technically feasible, and there is no discernible way to generate revenue to pay for the moderation costs involved. Facebook already spends billions and employs thousands of monitors and immensely sophisticated moderation algorithms. Each one of the middleware providers would have to duplicate that infrastructure, which seems economically implausible.

Moreover, privacy issues interfere with the needed interoperability in the same way they would for interoperability mandates designed to foster full competition to dominant platforms. Does the middleware provider have access to all the material posted by a user's friends and followers? If yes, that intrudes on the privacy of these other users who might want nothing to do with that middleware provider. If no, how can the middleware provider effectively filter the newsfeed?[90]

More important, this middleware idea is not a way to foster genuine interchange among citizens about issues of public importance. It is more a recipe for us to retreat to our corners, creating filter bubbles of like-minded people and excluding the rest of society.

Segregating ourselves so we do not have to listen to people who differ from us is not a remedy for the information externalities that make hate speech and misinformation so dangerous, even to people who are not exposed to it. People cannot remain indifferent to what other people in society believe because what other people believe affects them. If enough people reject vaccines and other public health measures, we are all at risk of the next pandemic. If enough people become racists or intolerant of the LGBTQ community, significant parts of our community are not safe in their own society. And how are we going to agree on what to teach our children if there is no uniform public platform where we can exchange ideas?

Another approach to political pluralism is through common carriage. In April 2021, Justice Thomas turbo-charged the debate over social media with a defense of common carrier status for social media companies. His key point was that First Amendment review by the courts might very well uphold a state or federal statute that treated social media platforms as common carriers or places of public accommodation and restricted their ability to remove content on their systems based on political point of view.[91]

The idea is not new and is popular across the political spectrum. Years ago, First Amendment lawyer Jeff Rosen recommended carriage of all lawful content for social media companies, treating their attempts to moderate content as if they were government attempts to suppress speech. Much of the push to impose international human rights law on social media companies is an attempt to have them live up to the same constraints of necessity and proportionality that governments live under, and to suppress no speech that the government itself could not suppress.[92]

Some on the progressive left have also endorsed the idea of treating social media as common carriers. In a 2021 post on the *Law and Political Economy* blog, law professors Genevieve Lakier and Nelson Tebbe argued that users have a constitutional right to carriage on social media that is needed to counteract "the threats to freedom of speech that result from private control of the mass public sphere." Lakier also posted a series of favorable tweets on the Thomas opinion.[93]

More recently, European courts have upheld requirements for social media companies to carry lawful speech. The 2020 decision by the Italian Court of Appeals in Rome implicitly adopted this position by ruling that Facebook could not remove the neofascist political party CasaPound from its platform, even if it violated Facebook's terms of service against the incitement of hate and violence, since under Italian law CasaPound was a legal political party with rights of free speech and association. In a 2019 German case a court ordered Facebook to reinstate the far-right neo-Nazi party the Third Way, suggesting social media companies cannot deplatform legal political parties, even if their messaging violates social media rules.

Poland is attempting to make this approach explicit. The right-wing ruling Law and Justice party has proposed a law that would fine tech companies for regulating any speech that isn't strictly illegal. It was inspired in part by the deplatforming of President Trump. Common carrier constraints on the power of social media companies are part of a larger international conservative push to use government power to counteract the ability of private institutions to impose their own speech rules to the detriment of conservative positions on issues such as gender identity and racial diversity.[94]

Despite its widespread appeal across the political spectrum, common carrier status for social media companies is not the right way to go. In a response to Lakier and Tebbe on the *Law and Political Economy* blog, renowned First Amendment scholar Robert Post is right to note that treating social media companies as common carriers means they would be "compelled to broadcast intolerable and oppressive forms of speech." It might thereby "invalidate even the minimal content moderation policies that these social media platforms currently deploy" and exacerbate the problem of "atrocious communication in the digital public sphere."

Post also notes that Congress cannot remedy this problem through content regulation of social media companies because "the atrocious communication in the digital public sphere" is protected speech, harmful perhaps, but legal. In the US system, Post notes, policymakers largely rely on the private sector, not the government, to set the boundaries of acceptable speech. If social media companies cannot do this because they are treated as common carriers, then nothing is to stop them from becoming cesspools of pornography, hate speech, white supremacist propaganda, and disinformation campaigns, all of which are constitutionally protected under current First Amendment jurisprudence. A common carrier rule to distribute all legal speech would be such a narrow limit for social media companies that it would prevent them from keeping social media discourse free of the racist, discriminatory, and misogynistic attacks and abuse that make online political discussion impossible.[95]

Republican Senator Bill Hagerty has put forward a version of the common carrier idea that remedies these difficulties. He introduced a bill in April 2021 that would treat the larger online platforms as "common carrier technology companies" with obligations not to give any undue or unreasonable preference, prejudice, advantage, or disadvantage to "any particular person, class of persons, political or religious group or affiliation, or locality." This would rule out any discrimination based on, among other things, political perspective. It would be enforced by private rights of action and cases brought by state attorneys general and other state officials.

But Senator Hagerty's bill would also provide freedom for social media companies to engage in substantial content moderation. It does this through a provision that would provide online companies with immunity from liability for "any action voluntarily taken in good faith to restrict access to or availability of material that the provider or user considers to be obscene, lewd, lascivious, filthy, excessively violent, harassing, promoting self-harm, or unlawful, whether or not such material is constitutionally protected."

While phrased as a Section 230 reform, the effect of this provision is to provide an exemption from the bill's common carrier nondiscriminatory carriage requirements for enforcement of certain approved content standards. None of these allowable bases in the bill for content moderation would countenance political preferencing. This approach appears to allow social media companies to engage in a wide variety of content moderation activities, provided these actions do not amount to political discrimination.[96]

Senator Hawley has a similar approach that assigns a role to the FTC to enforce a requirement of social media political neutrality. In 2019, he introduced legislation that would restrict "politically biased" content moderation. Content moderation would be biased if it is done in a manner "designed to negatively affect a political party, political candidate, or political viewpoint" or that "disproportionately restricts or promotes access to, or the availability of, information from a political party, political candidate, or political viewpoint."

Senator Hawley's bill could easily be transformed into a freestanding requirement to avoid politically biased content moderation to be enforced by the digital regulator. This approach, too, would allow social media companies substantial leeway to moderate content as they see fit, just not in a politically partisan way.[97]

A Texas law signed by Texas governor Greg Abbott on September 1, 2021, a few months after Justice Thomas's opinion on common carriage, embodied this viewpoint neutral approach. It denied social media companies the ability to operate its content moderation program to "block, ban, remove, deplatform, demonetize, de-boost, restrict, deny equal access or visibility to, or otherwise discriminate against expression" based on political viewpoint. The Fifth Circuit Court of Appeals upheld his viewpoint neutrality mandate, and the case is likely on its way to the Supreme Court.[98]

A third way of adopting a policy of political pluralism is through an affirmative mandate for fairness. Political discrimination might not be intended by the platform, and it might not operate through the content moderation system. It might arise instead because the criteria used to amplify or downplay material coincides with a particular political perspective or through the manipulation of social media technologies by powerful political interests.

Some people, including Haugen, the Facebook whistleblower, claim that algorithm amplification discriminates against the political center. It encourages extremism of both the left and the right by responding to the emotions of anger and hate that are more prevalent in extreme partisans.[99]

But other evidence suggests that social media companies favor right-wing views. Twitter's internal study, mentioned earlier, suggested that amplification favors conservative views. Law professor Mary Ann Franks also finds that social media companies tend to disproportionately amplify right-wing views, not left-wing views or both extremes equally. The basis for this imbalance seems to be the tendency of right-wing commentators and news outlets to employ more polarizing and inflammatory language than left-wing outlets. Social media algorithms pick up on this more inflammatory content and amplify it because the systems have learned that it creates more engagement than less inflammatory content. This tendency to promote inflammatory content is in itself politically neutral, but in combination with the propensity of right-wing commentators to be more inflammatory, it produces a result that is not politically neutral or proportionate.[100]

This suggests that political pluralism should be implemented through an outcome-oriented approach, where there is an affirmative obligation for fairness and balance. A social media regulator might enforce a mandate for political pluralism the same way financial regulators enforce the requirement for fair lending. Assessments and audits of financial lending decisions can detect patterns of unjustified discriminatory lending, and the financial agencies can issue orders to require financial institutions to adjust their lending criteria to come into compliance with fair lending rules. Agencies never have to assess a specific individual lending decision.

In the same way, the digital regulator could be authorized to review external assessments and audits to detect patterns of unjustified partisanship in the distribution of political material on social media sites. The digital agency can do this without assessing any specific bit of content. It could rely instead on its own audits or on studies, audits, and assessments from independent researchers.

A model for this political fairness obligation can be found in the now-repealed Fairness Doctrine, which required broadcasters to devote some of their airtime to discussing controversial matters of public importance and to air contrasting views regarding those matters. Broadcasters had discretion to cover issues and provide contrasting views through a wide range of programming, including news segments, public affairs shows, or editorials.[101]

Even today broadcasters in the United Kingdom live under duties to practice "due impartiality and due accuracy" and to avoid "undue prominence of views and opinions." These broadcaster responsibilities in the United Kingdom are designed to further the goal of political pluralism and to prevent one-sided presentation of information and news.[102]

Despite its appeal and its implementation for other media, political pluralism for social media faces such serious obstacles that it is not ready for prime time. Conservative commentator David French raised one of the major concerns with any form of mandated political pluralism. He notes conservative sites and posts do very well on Facebook, and then he asks, "Will a Kamala Harris administration decide that disproportionate conservative success violates political neutrality?" Do you trust the government, he asks, "to control Facebook's political content?"[103]

Partisanship in applying a rule of political pluralism is one issue, but it might be dealt with by constraints on the implementing agency, including a ban on second-guessing particular content moderation decisions.

Another problem is assessing the political viewpoint of material on social media platforms, surely a thorny and controversial matter. In one study, law professor Yochai Benkler and his colleagues constructed a five-point measure of political leanings from right to center-right to center to center-left to left. They then identified users during the 2016 presidential campaign who retweeted Donald Trump as being on the political right and users who retweeted Hillary Clinton as being on the left. They would then classify a website as politically on the left when it drew attention in ratios of at least 4:1 from Clinton supporters and on the right when it drew support in a 4:1 ratio from Trump supporters. Center sites were retweeted more or less equally by supporters of each candidate. Center-left sites drew Clinton supporters in a ratio of 3:2, and center-right sites drew Trump supporters in a ratio of 3:2. Such a method will obviously not be useful for all assessments of political perspective, but it would be a usable option for some purposes.[104]

There will need to be other methods and measurement techniques, and it will take substantial research to develop and refine suitable tools for assessing political perspective, but at this point they are simply not precise enough to operate as part of a regulatory mandate. What is left, right, and center, in general? On what issues? All of them? What if political perspective on one issue does not line up with political perspective on others? Defining categories of political belief for research purposes is one thing. It is entirely different to craft such measures to enforce a statutory mandate for fairness.

Moreover, it is not clear how to measure political bias. Clearly, content rules that reject conservative or liberal or progressive perspectives are biased on their face, but the major social media companies have politically neutral rules. If there is bias, it has to result from biased enforcement priorities or from the operation of content moderation or recommendation algorithms.

A disparate impact assessment might detect inadvertent or system political bias in the same way that disparate impact assessments can detect unintentional discrimination in employment, housing, insurance, and lending.[105] But a disparate effect on one point of view might not prove bias, since people with that perspective might have violated content rules more often. As with discrimination based on protected class characteristics, methodologies must be developed to allow companies to refute allegations of bias by showing the rules were applied in a way that served legitimate content moderation or business purposes, even if they had a measurable disparate impact on certain points of view.

The Texas social media law adopted in September 2021 would demand that social media companies not deny material "equal access or visibility" based on its political viewpoint. Even if that notion of equality were clear, which it is not, it seems to be the wrong target.[106] The basic idea is not equal visibility but proportionate representation. Proportional to what, though? The distribution of views in the real-world community? Or the online community itself? And wouldn't that change over time, quickly and dramatically? How would a social media company take action to increase fairness? Would users get political perspectives they don't like inserted into their feeds? Would this increase their awareness and appreciation of other perspectives or just annoy them?

In addition, the key notions involved political pluralism on social media—salience and prevalence of political perspective—are poorly understood at this point. What is salience on social media? The number of appearances of a perspective as a percentage of all political content, or the number of times a typical user was exposed to a post with a particular perspective? How do you develop a baseline for fairness or neutrality?

Raising these questions reveals that there is not yet a clear understanding of what an acceptably diverse political conversation on social media would look like and the techniques needed to achieve it. Social media is not broadcasting. So it is not possible simply to measure fairness by what is put on the air. Key notions of social media prevalence—salience and visibility—have no accepted operational meaning at this point. Until they do, it is pointless to legislate a pluralist mandate.

Moreover, a demand for political pluralism in social media raises fundamental value issues that might not be amenable to resolution by further research. The intent of a pluralist mandate is not to eliminate content moderation of harmful speech but to allow it so long as it is done in a viewpoint neutral way. Under a pluralist mandate, for instance, the intent is that social media companies continue to ban hate speech, but they would not be permitted to ban hate speech by conservatives and permit it by progressives.

However, this intent dissolves in the face of the ambiguity of the idea of a political viewpoint. In any reasonable conception of legitimate political perspective, hate speech, racist expression, misogynistic treatment of women, and hounding those with whom you disagree until they withdraw from the conversation are not legitimate political perspectives. But that is not how the Supreme Court treats them. As we have seen, under current First Amendment jurisprudence, racism, for instance, is a viewpoint against which the law may not discriminate. Combing a duty to provide a fair representation of all political perspectives with this expansive view of what counts as a political perspective might severely limit the ability of social media companies to regulate speech on their own systems. Facebook's current ban on white supremacist and white nationalist groups, for instance, might not withstand this kind of scrutiny. A duty to promote political pluralism might require the transmission and even amplification of racist speech.

Each way out of this problem poses insuperable difficulties. One way out of this dilemma would be to allow the social media companies reasonable discretion to define the limits of acceptable political discourse on their systems and to adjust these limits in light of changing political developments. But this discretion to define edges of legitimate political discourse would restore exactly the unconstrained power to control political debate that motivated the duty for political pluralism to begin with. It would enable social media companies to exclude certain political perspectives tolerated under US law in a way that is unchecked by any external accountability mechanism.

Another way out is for the industry's self-regulatory organization (SRO) to review social media judgments about the separation of acceptable political discourse from unacceptable hate speech using a reasonableness test. The SRO could intervene only when the definitions of political boundaries would be so extremely broad or narrow that no reasonable person could accept it. As in the SRO determination of compliance with company content standards, the digital regulator would have no role in reviewing social media determinations of the contours of acceptable political discourse. But turning a decision of this magnitude over to an industry self-regulatory group seems no more legitimate than allowing the individual companies themselves to make the decision.

The problem is that viewpoint neutrality must allow platforms to moderate legal but truly harmful material, but it cannot allow them to define the borderline between harmful and legitimate material. To avoid this problem, the law would have to specify, positively, which viewpoints would receive the benefit of platform neutrality or, negatively, which viewpoints would not receive this legal protection.

The Texas law attempts to do this negatively by excluding from its mandate for viewpoint neutrality material that is "the subject of a referral or request from an organization with the purpose of preventing the sexual exploitation of children and protecting survivors of sexual abuse from ongoing harassment" and expression that "directly incites criminal activity or consists of specific threats of violence targeted against a person or group because of their race, color, disability, religion, national origin or ancestry, age, sex, or status as a peace officer or judge." Senator Hagerty's bill has a similar list of exclusions.

In this way, the legislature would limit the range of viewpoints that would receive special legal protection of viewpoint neutrality on social media. However, the fast-moving and ever-changing nature of political debate and discussion in the United States makes it unrealistic for the legislature to determine once and for protected viewpoints. This implies a flexible and rapid regulatory process to update any legislative list.

The danger of partisanship in designating this list is obvious. Moreover, the legitimacy of allowing regulators to set the limits of protected viewpoints is also questionable. Both dangers could be reduced through court review, in which both the initial legislative list and the regulatory updates would be subject to timely and expeditious judicial appraisal.

Such a system of extensive regulatory oversight and flexible, rapid judicial review might be workable.

This is a radical departure from our current system, however, which gives no special treatment to certain legal viewpoints in comparison with others. As we shall see in the next section, such a drastic departure from tradition might prompt rejection by the courts on First Amendment grounds—that is, on the grounds that it violates constitutional guarantees of free speech for social media users or platforms or both. But it is questionable purely on policy grounds of whether this would be a system that could fairly promote the reasoned and balanced discussion that effective political governance requires.

The attractiveness of the ideal of political pluralism should not blind policymakers to the very real challenges of imposing such a duty on social media companies. As a way forward, Congress should establish a congressional advisory commission to conduct further research on how political pluralism might be implemented in practice by social media platforms. The advisory commission should work together with the digital regulator to explore these issues and report back to Congress with its findings and legislative recommendations.[107] Think tanks, academic institutions, and public policy centers might help to further develop the idea and seek a way forward. The difficulties and obstacles described here might have practical solutions that a commission could articulate and develop. For now, however, the idea is not ready for prime time and should not be on the congressional agenda.

Social Media Duties to Political Candidates

As part of their public interest responsibilities, social media companies could be required to provide fair treatment of political candidates. Social media rules mimicking the rules already in place for the broadcast industry to provide candidates with reasonable access, no censorship, and equal time are enormously attractive in principle and would go a long way to ensuring that powerful social media companies cannot unduly influence the choice of the nation's political leaders. However, like the related ideal of political pluralism, these ideas are not well-developed enough for congressional action and need to be more fully developed and thought through. Congress should, however, consider moving forward with an analogue of the sponsorship identification rules for political ads for candidates for federal office. This disclosure mandate would bring some additional transparency to the opaque world of social media political ads.

Considering the great deplatforming of then–president Trump in January 2021, it might seem obvious that the time has arrived for legal constraints on the ability of social media companies to treat political candidates as they see fit. The Florida social media law adopted in 2021 responded to this concern by providing political candidates with access rights to social media platforms.[108]

Many progressives and liberals are blinded by their fear that former president Trump might become the Republican nominee for president in 2024 and might even win. Some seem to think Trump should stay banned from social media, even if he were to become the Republican presidential candidate. They would urge social media companies to use their discretion to keep Trump off their platforms.

To their credit, when Facebook reinstated Donald Trump in January 2023, free speech groups praised the decision. The ACLU said, "Like it or not, President Trump is one of the country's leading political figures and the public has a strong interest in hearing his speech." The Knight First Amendment Institute agreed, saying, "Like it or not, Trump is a political leader and a political candidate." But both groups thought the decision was entirely up to the platforms. The Knight First Amendment Institute did not like "the idea of Meta or any other big social media company deciding which political candidates we hear from and which ones we don't." It did not support the reinstatement decision because it thought Trump had a legal right to be on Facebook. It said explicitly that Trump had no such right: "It's a private platform. Meta can make whatever decisions it wants to about whether Trump is on or off." The best that could be done, according to the ACLU, was "to press the tech giants to be fair and impartial stewards of our political discourse."[109]

But this defense of unfettered platform discretion might be short-sighted. In a system where political leaders are chosen by open elections, it is simply unacceptable to have the candidate supported by a majority or a near-majority of people to be shut out of the political discussion on the larger social media platforms through the potentially partisan choices of a few social media leaders. One could say exclusion from social media is not a big deal, that the rejected presidential candidate could use newspapers or broadcast stations, or even mimeograph machines to reach his or her audience. But this relegation of one candidate to yesterday's technology is not a handicap that should be tolerated in a country that selects its leaders by public elections.

To give the problem a historical context, imagine that the three radio networks in the 1930s refused to provide access to their networks to President Franklin D. Roosevelt for his famous fireside chats, saying that he could always put an op-ed in a newspaper if he wanted to reach the American people. To make today's problem real for those on the left side of the political spectrum, imagine that Musk or Murdoch, as head of Twitter or Facebook, decides to ban from his platforms the next Democratic presidential candidate—say, Senator Bernie Sanders, Senator Elizabeth Warren, or Representative Alexandria Ocasio-Cortez.

Other legal systems are beginning to address the responsibilities of social media companies to political parties and candidates in the context of elections. In 2019 a German court ordered Facebook to reinstate the account of the neo-Nazi party the Third Path during the European Parliament elections. Facebook had deleted a specific post as a likely criminal violation of Germany's hate speech law and then banned the party from its platform for violation of its own rules against hate speech. The German Federal Constitutional Court refused to reinstate the post but issued a temporary injunction ordering Facebook to restore the political party's account so that it could participate in the ongoing elections to the European Parliament. The German court gave heavier weight to the freedom of political expression in the context of an election, since it found that Facebook was the party's main channel of communication with voters.[110]

The visionary policymakers who established the US regulatory regime for broadcasting understood the danger of private interests using the most powerful new communications technology of its time to manipulate the outcome of elections. To prevent censorship and favoritism by broadcasters and to put the interests of the electorate in free and fair elections ahead of the interests of the broadcasters, they devised an intricate policy web that requires reasonable and equal access to broadcasting stations for political candidates. And they explicitly banned broadcasters from censoring candidate communications with their audience.

Section 312(a)(7) of the Communications Act of 1934 requires broadcasters to provide "reasonable access" to their airwaves for political communications by "a legally qualified candidate for federal elective office on behalf of his candidacy." In addition, Section 315 of the Communications Act says that if a broadcaster allows one "legally qualified for any public office" to use his station, then "he shall afford equal opportunities to all other such candidates for that office" to use his station.

The no-censorship provision is stated explicitly as part of Section 315's equal time rule: broadcasters "shall have no power of censorship over the material broadcast under the provisions of this section (the equal time rule)." The no-censorship rule is an integral part of this policy regime. It prevents broadcasters from evading the intent of the access and equal time rules by censoring the ads of one candidate, while allowing their preferred candidates free rein.[111]

To provide adequate disclosure of a candidate's use of broadcasting services for campaigning, the law also requires an on-air announcement on candidate ads disclosing the "true identity" of the person sponsoring the political ad. In addition, for television ads, the sponsor shall be identified in the ad "with letters equal to or greater than four percent of the vertical picture height that air for not less than four seconds." The broadcast station or network must likewise maintain a list of these sponsoring groups and make it available for public inspection.[112]

This broadcast model provides an outline of a workable set of ideas for a regulatory regime for social media needed to preserve the integrity of the democratic electoral process in the digital age.

An element of that structure must be transparency. In 2019, Senator Klobuchar, joined by Senators Warner and Graham, reintroduced the Honest Ads Act that would require the larger social media companies to maintain a public file of all political ads, recording the content of the advertisement, a description of the targeted audience, the number of views generated, the dates and times of publication, the rates charged, and the contact information of the purchaser. The bill also calls for the identity of the ad sponsor to be disclosed in a clear and conspicuous manner in the ad itself.[113]

Many platforms voluntarily provide public archives of political advertisements. Twitter stopped carrying political ads in November 2019, but it archived the ads it did carry before that. Google, including YouTube, continues to accept political ads and publishes a political ad transparency report. Facebook also carries political ads and discloses political ad sponsors, authenticates political ad sponsors, and provides an archive of political ads for research.[114] But these archives are woefully incomplete and do not allow timely and effective research.[115]

This law should be part of the structure of social media regulation. It would need to be updated to take into account the differences between broadcast disclosures and those appropriate for the social media environment. The law should also clarify the duty of social media companies to pierce the veil of the nominal sponsor and to "fully and fairly disclose the true identity of the sponsor" of candidate ads.[116]

A new social media regulatory regime could also provide candidates for federal office with mandatory access to the organic messaging services of the larger social media companies and to any advertising services they offer, with no restrictions on any ad-targeting criteria. Moreover, the rules could include a no-censorship provision that bars social media firms from censoring the political ads of candidates for federal office.

In addition, a digital equal time rule for social media could require the larger social media companies to develop and maintain the capacity to enable political candidates to target each other's audiences. When social media companies allow one candidate to reach a targeted audience with their message, they would have to provide other candidates for the same office with the option to reach the same audience with their own message. This would address the concern that online targeted political ads create enormous opportunities for undetected abuse. These secretly targeted ads might be racially or socially inflammatory or materially false, and only their intended audience is likely to see them.

The digital regulatory agency could be empowered to write implementing regulations and proactively enforce them, just as the FCC oversees the broadcast candidate rules.[117]

Many would look upon these ideas that go beyond sponsorship identification as wrong-headed. These proposals would accept ad targeting as a norm for political campaigns, whereas many commentators want to ban targeted ads as part of an intrusive surveillance society. Some social media companies such as Twitter have just stopped accepting political ads, while continuing to allow candidates to deliver their messages to their own organic audience. But this discretion to block political candidate access to advertising services is fraught with peril for the integrity of democratic elections. For generations candidates have used political advertising to reach their likely voters. Today, targeted social media campaigns are the most effective way to get out their voters. If policy allows political ads at all, political candidates should be allowed to use the most effective advertising methods available and that includes targeting to any and all groups chosen by the candidate.

Other criticisms focus on the nonpublic nature of targeted ads. Targeted campaign ads seem especially problematic because they are aimed at individuals or small groups and are outside normal public awareness. But that is why a digital equal time rule would be needed to give the groups with the greatest incentive to correct the record the technical capacity to reach the original audience with the correction.

These proposed regulations for access and no censorship would privilege federal political candidates over ordinary citizens by exempting them from social media content rules at a time when some of the biggest violators of the rules of civility on social media are political candidates themselves. This inequality seems unfair, and many citizens would resent it. Moreover, the extent of the harm that could be caused by inflammatory rhetoric from political candidates is much greater than the harm due to ordinary user misbehavior. Why prevent social media companies from disciplining those with the greatest potential for public harm?

Moreover, the details of how to structure candidate access to social media platforms and a digital equal time rule are not at all clear. Does no censorship really mean candidates could target ads to those likely to vote for their opponents giving the wrong times and places for voting? Reply mechanisms might not prevent such last-minute attempts to corrupt the election process.

These difficulties appear insuperable at the current time, even though the need for some mechanism to rein in the unbridled discretion of social media firms to discriminate against candidates is undeniable. Congress should explore these access and no-censorship ideas through the same mechanism suggested for political pluralism—namely, a congressional advisory commission assisted by the digital regulator to survey the issues and issue a report with legislative recommendations.

Any such measures, even political ad sponsorship identification rules, face the challenge of passing First Amendment review. The Supreme Court is poised to take up these large questions through its consideration of state social media laws. For these First Amendment challenges, we turn to the next section.

First Amendment Issues

Regulation of social media content moderation is the free speech issue of our time. The preceding sections have argued that transparency measures in all their aspects—disclosures to users, public reports, access to data for researchers—would enhance the power of users to understand and control the conditions under which they are able to speak their mind on social media platforms. They would enhance the speech rights of social media users. Special rules for political candidates would also ensure the ability of social media users to receive uncensored candidate messages, providing them with more complete information to guide their voting decisions. Algorithmic regulation and political pluralism, however attractive in principle as methods to further user speech rights, suffer from implementation difficulties that make them not ready for prime time.

Regardless of whether these measures would increase user speech rights, they might also unacceptably abridge the speech rights of social media companies. Are these measures consistent with the First Amendment's prohibition on government censorship? Courts are beginning to address this question in the context of two state social media laws that impose, in different ways, elements of transparency, candidate access, nondiscrimination, and algorithmic regulation.

The Florida and Texas social media laws passed in 2021 were widely seen by both their proponents and their detractors as attempts by conservative forces to discipline social media companies for deplatforming President Trump and refusing to distribute the *New York Post*'s Hunter Biden story that criticized then–presidential candidate Joe Biden on the eve of the November 2020 election. More generally, the bills responded to conservative complaints of unfair treatment on social media platforms.

Both bills called for restrictions on the ability of platforms to engage in unfettered content moderation—the Texas law banned viewpoint discrimination, and the Florida law required platforms to carry political candidates and journalistic enterprises without censorship. Both bills imposed various transparency measures such as mandated disclosure of content standards and explanations of content moderation actions.[118]

Not surprisingly, the tech industry filed First Amendment challenges. District courts in Texas and Florida rejected both laws in their entirety as violations of platforms' free speech rights and stayed implementation pending further court review. On May 23, 2022, the US Court of Appeals for the Eleventh Circuit released a ruling on the Florida social media law in connection with an appeal of the lower court stay that blocked enforcement of large parts of the Florida law, including its must-carry and no-censorship provisions. In September, Florida asked the Supreme Court to review the decision, and in October the tech industry asked for Supreme Court review of the parts of the Florida law that the Eleventh Circuit had upheld.[119]

Surprisingly, however, on May 11, 2022, the US Court of Appeals for the Fifth Circuit lifted the stay on the Texas bill, while it considered the case. The industry filed an emergency appeal to reinstate the stay, which the Supreme Court granted on May 31, in a 5–4 ruling that did not detail its reasoning.[120]

Justice Samuel Alito, joined by Justices Thomas and Neil Gorsuch, dissented from this decision. The dissent telegraphed the Court's intention to take up the social media laws, saying the application for a stay "concerns issues of great importance that will plainly merit this Court's review." They would have allowed the Texas law to go into effect pending the Fifth Circuit's decision. Alito's dissent raised the constitutional issues in a very clear form. The Texas social media law and the social media business model, he said, are novel and existing precedents are mixed. Social media companies think the law's nondiscrimination requirements impermissibly interfere with their editorial discretion and they claim a First Amendment right not to disseminate speech generated by others. It is true that the Supreme Court has upheld the right of organizations to refuse to host the speech of others in cases involving a parade organizer and a newspaper, but it has rejected such claims in other cases involving shopping centers and cable operators.[121] "It is not at all obvious," the dissent concludes, "how our existing precedents, which predate the age of the internet, should apply to large social media companies."

Then on September 16, 2022, the US Court of Appeals for the Fifth Circuit made its decision on the Texas law. It upheld the constitutionality of the Texas law, finding that it "does not chill speech; instead, it chills censorship." It clearly took the side of user speech rights over platform rights, saying, "Today we reject the idea that corporations have a freewheeling First Amendment right to censor what people say." The court agreed to stay the ruling while the industry asked the Supreme Court to review the case, which the industry did on October 24, 2022. Rather than granting or denying review, on January 23, 2023, the Supreme Court instead opted to seek the views of the Biden administration. The court is still likely to grant review, since the lower courts are in conflict; a decision will not be forthcoming until 2024. In the meantime, the state laws will not be enforced.[122]

In what follows, I discuss the Eleventh Circuit decision on the Florida bill and then the Fifth Circuit decision on the Texas bill. The section concludes with some remarks on considerations relevant to the likely Supreme Court review of these bills.

The 2021 Florida law banned deplatforming candidates running for election in Florida and exempted them from platform content moderation rules. It had an access right and a no-censorship rule for journalistic enterprises, including newspapers and broadcast stations. It required social media companies to apply its standards "in a consistent manner among its users on the platform." It allowed users to eliminate algorithmic personalization of content in favor of sequential or chronological posts and contained what are by now standard features of content moderation bills—namely, public disclosure of content rules, requirements for notices for content moderation actions, appeals processes, transparency reports, and the like.[123]

Florida's defense against First Amendment challenge is that these measures treat platforms as common carriers, and the state can legitimately treat platforms as common carriers without triggering any First Amendment review at all. This is because common carriers are not engaged in protected speech but act merely as distributors of the speech of others.

The Eleventh Circuit rejected this reasoning and ruled that a platform's content moderation and organizing activity constitutes speech for purposes of First Amendment review. Even though they distribute the speech of others, they still have their own speech rights. "Neither law nor logic," the court writes, "recognizes government authority to strip an entity of its First Amendment rights merely by labeling it a common carrier." The court is clearly right that merely uttering the magic words "common carrier" does not and should not absolve legislators from doing the hard work of formulating precise purposes for social media regulation and ensuring that its requirements are appropriately restricted to fulfilling those purposes.

The Eleventh Circuit rejects the law's "must carry" measures for candidates and journalistic enterprises under heightened scrutiny. It finds "no legitimate—let alone substantial—governmental interest in leveling the expressive playing field" through these provisions. It recognizes that the provisions would ensure "that political candidates and journalistic enterprises are able to communicate with the public." But carriage on social media, the court ruled, is not needed for them to reach the public, since these entities could use "other more permissive platforms, their own websites, email, TV, radio, etc." to reach their audiences.

University of Minnesota Law School scholar Alan Rozenshtein points out that this opinion embraces "a highly restrictive view of what counts as a legitimate government interest" that reflects a "stingy view of what users can legitimately expect from their digital town squares." He correctly says that this "cramped" view, while consistent with some earlier Supreme Court rulings, is not compelled by these precedents.

Rozenshtein also points out that rejecting the poorly drafted "must carry" provision for journalistic enterprises did not require the court to hold that the entire question of the extent to which "social media giants have unfettered control over the digital public square" is devoid of "legitimate public and governmental issues."[124]

The Eleventh Circuit Court's ruling also is hasty in its reasoning. It completely ignores the political broadcasting rules that require TV and radio stations to carry the uncensored campaign ads of qualified candidates for federal office, even though candidates have alternative outlets. And it barely mentions the actual finding of the *Turner Broadcasting* case, which required cable carriage of local broadcast signals even though these stations were technically able to reach the public using the frequencies assigned to them by the FCC.[125]

The Eleventh Circuit broke new ground in its assessment of Florida's transparency requirements. It determined that proper First Amendment review of social media laws does not mean strict or even intermediate scrutiny. The court reviewed the Florida bill's disclosure requirements under a less demanding standard set out in *Zauderer v. Office of Disciplinary Counsel.* Under *Zauderer*, disclosure requirements must be "reasonably related to the State's interest in preventing deception of consumers" and must not be "unduly burdensome" or "chill speech."[126]

The Eleventh Circuit thought the disclosure provisions of the Florida bill required only the disclosure of "purely factual and uncontroversial information" about platform conduct toward its users and the "terms under which" its services will be made available. The less stringent *Zauderer* level of review is appropriate, the court said, because these measures "impose a disclosure requirement rather than an affirmative limitation on speech." The court acknowledged that this standard is usually applied "in the context of advertising" but thought it broad enough to cover social media disclosure requirements that "provide users with helpful information that prevents them from being misled about platforms' policies."

Under this standard of review, the Eleventh Circuit approved the provisions in the Florida law, requiring platforms to publish their content standards, inform users about changes to these standards, provide users with view counts of their posts, and inform candidates about free advertising. The court ruled these measures are not unduly burdensome and are reasonably related to the legitimate purpose of ensuring that users who are involved in commercial transactions with platforms are "fully informed about the terms of that transaction and aren't misled about platforms' content-moderation policies."

In its reaction to the Eleventh Circuit's ruling, the Knight First Amendment Institute properly took a victory lap. The court embraced its nuanced approach that allowed for transparency and disclosure measures that respect platform speech rights, and even accepted the *Zauderer* standard the institute had recommended to assess disclosure measures.[127]

The Eleventh Circuit Court rejected a poorly drafted requirement for notices and explanations of content moderation actions. But a more carefully drafted measure with implementation by a regulatory agency would almost certainly pass the test of being reasonably related to consumer protection without being unduly burdensome.

The Eleventh Circuit applied a heightened standard of review for the Florida bill's requirements that platforms allow users to opt out of content curation to receive "sequential or chronological posts and content" and that platforms must apply their content moderation authority "in a consistent manner among its users on the platform." The court reasoned that these provisions are not disclosures of "purely factual and noncontroversial information," but rather "affirmative limitation[s] on speech." The court found, for instance, that the consumer opt-out provision would prevent platforms "from expressing messages" through its recommendation and content moderation algorithms.

The court found no government interest in these measures and rejected them. But this finding is oddly at variance with the court's ruling in connection with platform disclosures, since these measures seek to achieve the same consumer protection purpose the court embraced for disclosure requirements. The consistency requirement, for instance, works together with the standards disclosure requirement, seeking to prevent platforms from announcing standards that it does not apply at all or that it applies arbitrarily.

The court's rejection of an opt-out from algorithmic content curation is disturbing. It is true that regulating algorithmic amplification instead of mere passive distribution of social media material is not an end run around the First Amendment. Many people seem to think it would be constitutional to ban social media companies from amplifying harmful but legal speech or to mandate that they downgrade such speech. This is because, it is said, freedom of speech does not include freedom of reach.[128] But a government mandate to downgrade harmful but legal user speech online would likely fail a First Amendment test just as much as a mandate to ban it. As legal scholar Keller has pointed out, a line of Supreme Court cases establishes that government burdens on protected user speech are just as problematic as government bans.[129]

The opt-out provision in the Florida bill is different. It allows consumers to avoid platform algorithms they find distracting, confusing, abusive, annoying, or overly limiting. This consumer protection measure is an idea whose time has come around the world, contained, for instance, in Article 38 of the European Union's final Digital Services Act and in Article 17 of China's Internet Information Service Algorithmic Recommendation Management Provisions. It would be an irony indeed if, in the name of freedom for social media companies to "express messages" through their algorithms, US social media users had less control over their social media feeds than consumers in Europe and China.[130]

The Eleventh Circuit's consumer protection approach to content moderation is a huge win for social media users. As legal scholar Goldman has pointed out, transparency would be unconstitutional as applied to other media. Newspapers do not have to disclose their editorial standards to anyone, and they can change them without notice. Parade operators don't have to disclose their criteria for deciding which groups participate in their events. Broadcasters and cable operators, which enjoy fewer speech rights than newspapers, don't have to disclose standards for carrying programs or channels. If legislatures required these entities to publish their standards, the courts would likely overturn them as chilling the entities' speech by limiting their unfettered freedom to print, arrange parades, or choose programming as they see fit. Indeed, in 2019, the US Court of Appeals for the Fourth Circuit rejected a Maryland law that required, among other things, websites to display the identity of the purchaser of a political campaign ad as "chilling the speech" of the websites.[131]

So, it is welcome news that the Eleventh Circuit recognized the consumer interest in social media disclosure. But it is not the first time courts have accepted a consumer protection rationale for restraining the First Amendment rights of communication companies.

The US Court of Appeals for the District of Columbia Circuit relied on a consumer protection rationale in upholding the FCC's 2016 net neutrality rules. It rejected a First Amendment challenge on the grounds that broadband providers held themselves out as providers of neutral, indiscriminate access to websites, not purveyors of curated websites filtered by editorial criteria such as being family friendly. The court ruled that broadband providers were not required to adopt such a neutral posture, but once they made promises of neutrality to their users, they were bound by these promises. "The First Amendment," said the court in explaining this "if you say it, do it" theory, "does not give an [internet service provider] the right to present itself as affording a neutral, indiscriminate pathway but then conduct itself otherwise."[132]

The DC Circuit's invocation of consumer protection law in the case of broadband companies easily extends to social media firms. To the extent that social media companies represent themselves in certain ways, to the extent they promise their users certain things, they necessarily limit their First Amendment right to do something different from what they have promised. As in all cases of consumer deception, social media companies do not have a free speech right to tell consumers they will do something and then not do it.

I turn now to the 2021 Texas social media law. The Texas law bars social media companies with more than fifty million monthly active users from removing or otherwise limiting content based on the user's "viewpoint." Despite this ban on viewpoint discrimination, the law allows social media platforms to take action against child sexual abuse material and material that "directly incites criminal activity or consists of specific threats of violence targeted against a person or group because of their race, color, disability, religion, national origin or ancestry, age, sex, or status as a peace officer or judge." The law also imposes standard disclosure measures, including requirements to publish "acceptable use policies," set up an "easily accessible" complaint system, produce a "biannual transparency report," and "publicly disclose accurate information regarding its content management, data management, and business practices."[133]

The Fifth Circuit says that the nondiscrimination requirement does not affect platform speech rights because the platforms do not affirmatively select content to host the way that newspapers approve and edit the stories that appear in their publications or the way that broadcasters select programming on their stations or cable operators choose cable channels to distribute or law schools choose recruiters to appear at their job fairs or parade organizers select participants in their events. Rather, social media companies allow all comers to post whatever they want and then winnow out the ones that violate their terms of service after the fact. That might be "expressive conduct" of a kind, the court says, but it does not rise to the level of speech protected by the First Amendment.

As a result, the Fifth Circuit concludes, there are no First Amendment barriers to the decision by Texas to treat social media companies like common carriers and to impose viewpoint neutrality rules on them. The court recounts the history of common carrier regulation, which, the court says, shows that state and federal legislatures have imposed nondiscrimination requirements on companies without First Amendment objection for well over a century and a half. He notes that the First Amendment interposed no objection to treating telegraph companies as common carriers, even though they would have liked, for business reasons, to give preferences to some users over others.

The Fifth Circuit misses the mark here, as it later inadvertently admits in noting that a social media company "conveys or intends to convey" a message "through its (after the fact) censorship." In taking a content moderation action against a post, a social media company is saying something—namely, that it disapproves of the message contained in the post. This after-the-fact editorial selection expresses an opinion and deserves First Amendment protection as much as the affirmative, before-the-fact approvals typical of traditional media. Perhaps after weighing other interests against this speech right, the courts could approve treating social media as common carriers in the way that the law treats telegraph and telephone companies. But that is a far cry from saying that First Amendment considerations do not apply at all, since no speech is involved at all. As the Eleventh Circuit said about the Florida social media law, legislatures cannot avoid First Amendment review of a law affecting speech simply by labeling the speaker a common carrier.

But if First Amendment review is warranted, the Fifth Circuit continues, it should be intermediate scrutiny since viewpoint neutrality rules are themselves content neutral. This is because the ban on social media viewpoint censorship "in no way depends on what message a Platform conveys or intends to convey through its censorship." The bar on social media censorship "applies equally regardless of the censored user's viewpoint." The court rejects the industry's argument that the exceptions allowing content moderation in some cases make the viewpoint neutrality rule content based because, the court says, these exceptions are "unlawful" speech, unprotected by the First Amendment.

The Fifth Circuit says the viewpoint neutrality rules pass intermediate scrutiny. The interest involved is "the widespread dissemination of information from a multiplicity of sources," and the court, echoing the Supreme Court's decision in the *Turner* case, finds this interest is "a governmental purpose of the highest order."

The Fifth Circuit says the viewpoint neutrality rule satisfies the requirement for being no more extensive than necessary to accomplish this substantial government purpose. The alternative of having the state create its own social media platform is not feasible because of the "network effects" that render competition impossible in social media markets.

Rozenshtein chides the Fifth Circuit for its perfunctory analysis of whether the law is no more burdensome than necessary to accomplish its purposes. He notes, "There's no easy switch that platforms can flip to comply with the Texas law, which will require them to spend vast technological and organizational resources." He thinks a greater assessment of the compliance costs of the law is called for to show that the neutrality mandate is no more restrictive of speech than necessary.[134]

This misstates the necessity prong of First Amendment scrutiny. The necessity test is a cost-effectiveness analysis, saying the cost in terms of lost speech should not be greater than needed to accomplish the government's purpose. For example, an objection to an opt-in privacy law based on lack of necessity cannot merely state that the opt-in makes it harder for a company to advertise, which is a form of speech; to succeed, it must also show that a more advertiser-friendly alternative such as opt-out choice would accomplish the same level of privacy protection as opt-in choice. In connection with the viewpoint neutrality rule, the only alternative under consideration was for the government to start its own social media network and to this the court gave a perfectly adequate response that it was not a feasible alternative considering the economic characteristics of the industry.

The dissent in the Fifth Circuit case correctly describes the neutrality provision as a "broad-based prohibition against engaging in this editorial discretion whenever 'viewpoint' is at issue." Then it simply asserts that it is "hardly narrow tailoring that 'does not burden substantially more speech than necessary' to further a legitimate interest." If the legitimate goal is to ensure the widespread availability of different political points of view on social media, however, how else could legislators achieve that goal other than by banning viewpoint discrimination?

It might be possible to argue that the breadth of the intrusion into social media speech needed to provide for viewpoint diversity means that this goal is not a legitimate one. But the dissent did not argue that and in any case, it would collapse the two-pronged heightened scrutiny standard into a freestanding cost-benefit policy review of the legislative measure that seems out of place in a constitutional review.

The real First Amendment difficulty with the nondiscrimination mandate is vagueness. It might be clear what the Texas legislature thought it was achieving in using the word "viewpoint" to describe the nondiscrimination rule. It hoped to allow social media companies to engage in content moderation of harmful content such as hate speech, but to bar them from doing so based on the political perspective of the user or the user's post. Hate speech from progressives and conservatives would have to be treated alike. But the word "viewpoint" is undefined in the statute, and so a possible interpretation of the nondiscrimination rule is that it forbids content moderation of hate speech itself. Indeed, considering the Supreme Court's ruling in *R.A.V.* and its progeny—that racism is a protected point of view—that is a reasonable interpretation. But it also seems likely that this is not what the Texas legislature had in mind.

The industry itself makes this point in arguing that the law might prevent them from acting against "pro-Nazi speech, terrorist propaganda, [and] Holocaust denial[s]." The Fifth Circuit rejects this complaint as speculation about "hypothetical" or "imaginary" cases, thereby neatly demonstrating the vagueness involved in the word "viewpoint." Surely "pro-Nazi speech" is a viewpoint, even if a horrible one. Moreover, these cases are not fiction. They are exactly what social media firms face thousands of times every day, and the instructions from the law leave them entirely in the dark as to whether they are required to allow these expressions as "viewpoints" protected by the Texas law or whether they are permitted to remove them as violations of their terms of service as long as they do so impartially.

Perhaps the charge of void for vagueness could be refuted if Texas had provided some guidance to an enforcing or regulatory agency on how to interpret the idea of viewpoint. It might even be avoided if there were a mandated process for an enforcing agency to further define the term through rulemaking. But none of that is present in the Texas law. It presents the undefined term "viewpoint" as if its meaning were well understood in context when in fact reasonable people of common intelligence would be at a loss until the courts began to interpret the phrase in particular enforcement cases.

In connection with the Texas law's disclosure and operational requirements, the Fifth Circuit adopted the same *Zauderer* analysis that the Florida court used. Under *Zauderer*, legislatures may require commercial enterprises to disclose "purely factual and uncontroversial information" about their services recognizing that "unjustified or unduly burdensome disclosure requirements might offend the First Amendment by chilling protected commercial speech." Under this standard the court assessed the Texas law's requirements to post an acceptable use policy, to issue biannual reports, and to have a notice and complaint process. It finds that under the *Zauderer* standard they do not impose, as written, an undue burden on social media companies. Particular cases might impose an excess burden, such as the application of notice and explanation requirements to the billions of take downs of comments on YouTube. But those cases can be handled at the implementation stage, the court said, and are not a basis for invalidating the requirement as such.

These Court of Appeals decisions are significantly at variance with the earlier district court reviews. The initial certainty of some observers that the courts would strike down these laws as blatantly unconstitutional was borne out by the district court actions. These lower courts rejected both laws in their entirety by embracing the idea of an unabridgeable constitutional right for media companies against any form of social media regulation, even transparency.[135]

In their complete rejection of the state social media bills, the district courts relied upon the 1974 Supreme Court case *Miami Herald v. Tornillo*. In it the Court rejected a right of access to newspapers for political candidates, saying that such a right of access intruded upon the editorial function of newspapers. The Court recognized that the monopolized media market in the 1970s placed "in a few hands the power to inform the American people and shape public opinion." But it ruled that the right of editors to publish or not publish what they want was absolute, that no intrusion into this discretion for any reason was justified. A responsible press providing opportunities for replies from its readers might be a desirable goal, it said, but not one that could be legislated.[136]

The decisions by the courts of appeals in these two cases rejected the blanket application of *Miami Herald* to social media companies. This alone would call for review of these decisions by the Supreme Court. In addition, the court of appeals decisions are inconsistent with each other. The Eleventh Circuit said that existing precedents did not allow any social media regulation beyond transparency. The Fifth Circuit agreed about transparency but insisted that existing precedents allowed substantial additional regulation in the form of a viewpoint neutrality requirement.

What might the Supreme Court do when it takes up these cases? In a concurring statement in a 2020 case, Justice Thomas suggested he might uphold a social media common carrier law against First Amendment challenge. As precedent, he cited the *Turner Broadcasting* case that required cable operators to carry broadcast signals. He quoted a key passage in that decision that "it stands to reason that if Congress may demand that telephone companies operate as common carriers, it can ask the same of cable operators." He said this passage might apply also to "digital platforms."[137]

In taking this step, Justice Thomas moved well beyond the traditional pro-business conservative position. Parts of the conservative movement are now culturally hostility to business. The open warfare between Florida governor Ron DeSantis and Disney that culminated in a Disney lawsuit claiming the governor was engaged in a "relentless campaign to weaponize government power" against the company is an example of this new conservative dislike of business prerogatives.[138]

The new cultural gap between a new generation of conservatives and business leaders perceived as political enemies is affecting how conservative judges interpret the First Amendment. There is a visceral animus against the tech industry in the Fifth Circuit's opinion on the Texas social media law that reflects this new conservative perspective. It was authored by US Circuit Judge Andrew Oldham, a Federalist Society conservative in good standing. As Rozenshtein says, the anti-business conservativism on display in Judge Oldham's opinion is not "your grandma's conservativism."

Rozenshtein is certainly right to warn against the two flavors of First Amendment absolutism, the one holding that social media companies have no First Amendment rights and the other holding that governments can do nothing that infringes on the editorial discretion of social media companies. There is every reason to believe that the Supreme Court will not adopt either of those two extremes when it takes up the state media cases.

More interesting, Rozenshtein notes a convergence with progressive critics of big business in this Fifth Circuit opinion. Oldham's analysis of common carrier regulation could have been written, he says, by a "neo-Brandeisian." In fact, Judge Oldham quoted and relied on progressive law scholar Lakier's research on common carrier law as a non–First Amendment way to protect user speech rights. It is hard to know what to make of this convergence, but it might be, in part, a shrewd attempt to woo support from the Supreme Court's remaining liberals.[139]

Progressive scholars like Lakier and Tebbe have been taking the lead in challenging the libertarian interpretation of the First Amendment. They are not alone. Legal scholar and former Biden administration official Wu has explored how the First Amendment has moved from an enabler of social progress to a way for businesses to evade regulation. The libertarian interpretation of the First Amendment, he says, threatens to become an obsolete roadblock standing in the way of social progress. But he holds out hope that "doctrinal evolution may involve the First Amendment accommodating robust efforts to fight the new tools of speech control." While he is not, on policy grounds in favor of a "fairness doctrine for social media," he adds that "it seems implausible that the First Amendment cannot allow Congress to cultivate more bipartisanship or nonpartisanship online."[140]

Lakier, Tebbe, and Wu are following in this tradition on the left of stepping outside the libertarian policy paradigm that gives private companies the unfettered right to decide what is said on the media platforms they operate. They are exploring new ways to use state power to constrain the power of digital companies over speech and to enhance user speech rights.[141]

This emerging bipartisan coalition of First Amendment reform forces recalls the 1980s fight to codify the Fairness Doctrine that pitted a coalition of left and right led by consumer advocate Ralph Nader and conservative activist Phyllis Schlafly against broadcasters and pro-business deregulators. The coalition persuaded Congress to pass legislation codifying the Fairness Doctrine after the FCC had removed it from its requirements for broadcasters. Then-president Ronald Reagan's antigovernment instincts prevailed over his conservative instincts. He vetoed the bill and consigned broadcast fairness to the dustbin of history.[142]

Considerations of market power and centrality in today's media world and the larger ideological shifts in both left and right approaches to state power might well occupy the minds of the Supreme Court justices when they take up the Texas and Florida social media laws. My own sense is that these considerations cannot justify the unconstitutionally vague viewpoint neutrality rule in the Texas law. But they might be enough to allow the candidate-access and no-censorship provisions of the Florida law.

In addition, the Supreme Court is likely to look favorably on the use of the relaxed *Zauderer* standard for evaluation of these measures, given the importance of social media platforms in the lives of ordinary citizens and the lack of alternatives created by the economic dominance of the larger social media platforms.

Coda

Any movement away from the libertarian tradition that prioritizes the speech rights of media companies sparks a great fear in the hearts of many believers in the value of limited government. This great fear is this: What would my political opponents do with a regulatory power over speech? Would they use it to silence my point of view? Conservative free speech advocate David French is explicit about this. "One of the best ways to evaluate the merits of legislation," he says, "is to ask yourself whether the bill would still seem wise if the power you give the government were to end up in the hands of your political opponents." The libertarian First Amendment tradition seems to be an effective barrier against the partisan use of the power of government censorship.[143]

But the libertarian tradition does more that constrain partisan exploitation of government power. This dread of partisanship has paralyzed thinkers for generations, preventing them from exploring ways in which state power could be used to constrain the power of private companies. Partly as a result, the opposite form of oppression is already upon the country in the form of social media domination of political discourse. To deal with that, a digital regulator must have the power to promote due process, transparency, data access, sponsorship identification. These measures all provide for public accountability and would disclose valuable information that could drive further regulation. Steps need to be taken to prevent the digital regulator from abusing these powers including insulating the regulator from prescribing social media content standards or second-guessing content decisions of social media companies. But confining the state to a passive role is a recipe for the continuing encroachment on user speech freedoms by private companies.

The libertarian First Amendment tradition is not necessarily a permanent feature of US law and policy, and reformers from the left and the right should reject it. Existing precedents from the broadcast and cable industry and consumer protection law suggest a way forward to allow significant elements of a regulatory structure for social media companies constraining their content moderation and algorithmic operations. A path is open for the Supreme Court to uphold these measures as ways to balance the power of social media companies with the rights of citizens to fair process in social media content moderation and to the widest possible dissemination of ideas from diverse and antagonistic sources. Policymakers should move ahead with these measures in the reasonable expectation that they will survive any First Amendment challenge.

Notes

1. John Lancaster, *Reality and Other Stories* (New York: W. W. Norton, 2021), 75.

2. P. W. Singer and Emerson T. Brooking, *Likewar: The Weaponization of Social Media* (New York: HarperCollins, 2018), 265.

3. Margaret Roberts, *Censored* (NJ: Princeton University Press, 2018).

4. Terminiello v. Chicago, 337 US 1 (1949), https://supreme.justia.com/cases/federal/us/337/1/#tab-opinion-1939623; Brandenburg v. Ohio, 395 US 444 (1969), https://supreme.justia.com/cases/federal/us/395/444; National Socialist Party v. Skokie, 432 US 43 (1977), https://supreme.justia.com/cases/federal/us/432/43; Snyder v. Phelps, 562 US 443 (2011), https://supreme.justia.com/cases/federal/us/562/443; Matal v. Tam, 582 US __ (2017), https://supreme.justia.com/cases/federal/us/582/15-1293.

5. R.A.V. v. City of St. Paul, 505 US 377 (1992), https://supreme.justia.com/cases/federal/us/505/377.

6. "Universal Declaration of Human Rights," December 10, 1948, https://www.un.org/en/about-us/universal-declaration-of-human-rights; "Associated Press v. United States, 326 US 1 (1945)."

7. Mark MacCarthy, "Transparency Is Essential for Effective Social Media Regulation," *TechTank*, Brookings Institution, November 1, 2022, https://www.brookings.edu/blog/techtank/2022/11/01/transparency-is-essential-for-effective-social-media-regulation.

8. "Online Safety Bill 2021," Parliament of Australia, https://www.aph.gov.au/Parliamentary_Business/Bills_LEGislation/Bills_Search_Results/Result?bId=r6680; "eSafety Commissioner, Legislative Functions," Australian Government, https://www.esafety.gov.au/about-us/who-we-are/our-legislative-functions; "Safety by Design," https://www.esafety.gov.au/about-us/safety-by-design; "The Government's Proposed Approach to Address Harmful Content Online," Government of Canada, Department of Canadian Heritage, July 29, 2021, https://www.canada.ca/en/canadian-heritage/campaigns/harmful-online-content.html; "Regulation (EU) 2022/2065 of the European Parliament and of the Council of 19 October 2022 on a Single Market for Digital Services and Amending

Directive 2000/31/EC (Digital Services Act) (Text with EEA relevance)," https://eur-lex.europa.eu/legal-content/EN/TXT/?toc=OJ%3AL%3A2022%3A277%3ATOC&uri=uriserv%3AOJ.L_.2022.277.01.0001.01.ENG; "Network Enforcement Act of 2017 (NetzDG)," English Translation, German Law Archive, https://germanlawarchive.iuscomp.org/?p=1245; "Culture, Arts, Gaeltacht, Sport and Media, Online Safety and Media Regulation Bill," Republic of Ireland, Department of Tourism, updated June 2, 2021, https://www.gov.ie/en/publication/d8e4c-online-safety-and-media-regulation-bill/#; "BAI Publishes Submission on Regulation of Harmful Online Content / Implementation of New Audiovisual Media Services Directive," Republic of Ireland, Broadcasting Authority of Ireland, June 24, 2021, https://www.bai.ie/en/bai-publishes-submission-on-regulation-of-harmful-online-content-implementation-of-new-audiovisual-media-services-directive; UK Department for Digital, Culture, Media & Sport, "Online Safety Bill"; "Transparency in the Regulation of Online Safety Research Report for Ofcom," PA Consulting Group, May 2021, https://www.ofcom.org.uk/__data/assets/pdf_file/0020/220448/transparency-in-online-safety.pdf; UK Competition and Markets Authority, "The Digital Regulation Cooperation Forum"; PACT Act, S. 4066, 116th Cong. (2020), https://www.congress.gov/bill/116th-congress/senate-bill/4066; "California, AB 587, Social Media Companies: Terms of Service," September 14, 2022, https://leginfo.legislature.ca.gov/faces/billTextClient.xhtml?bill_id=202120220AB587; MacCarthy, "Transparency Requirements for Digital Social Media Platforms."

9. "Electronic Frontier Foundation and Others 'Background Paper on the Manila Principles on Intermediary Liability,'" ManilaPrinciples, May 30, 2015, https://www.eff.org/files/2015/07/08/manila_principles_background_paper.pdf#page=49; "The Santa Clara Principles on Transparency and Accountability in Content Moderation," May 7, 2018, https://santaclaraprinciples.org; "Report of the Special Rapporteur on the Promotion and Protection of the Right to Freedom of Opinion and Expression," UN Human Rights Council, Document A/HRC/38/35, April 6, 2018, https://documents.un.org/prod/ods.nsf/xpSearchResultsM.xsp.

10. Danielle Keats Citron and Frank A. Pasquale, "The Scored Society: Due Process for Automated Predictions," *Washington Law Review* 89, no. 1 (2014), http://digital.law.washington.edu/dspace-law/bitstream/handle/1773.1/1318/89WLR0001.pdf?sequence=1.

11. PACT Act, S. 797, 117th Cong. (2021), https://www.congress.gov/117/bills/s797/BILLS-117s797is.pdf.

12. Facebook's community standards are available here at https://www.facebook.com/communitystandards; Google's community guidelines are available at https://about.google/intl/en_us/community-guidelines; Twitter's rules and policies are available at https://help.twitter.com/en/rules-and-policies/twitter-rules; and Reddit discloses its content policy at https://www.redditinc.com/policies/content-policy-1.

13. See Mark Zuckerberg's post from April 24, 2018, at https://www.facebook.com/zuck/posts/10104874769784071; "Facebook Releases Content Moderation Guidelines—Rules Long Kept Secret," *The Guardian*, April 24, 2018, https://www.theguardian.com/technology/2018/apr/24/facebook-releases-content-moderation-guidelines-secret-rules;

Facebook's interpretative guidelines are now incorporated directly into the community standards, available at https://www.facebook.com/communitystandards/introduction.

14. Irish Online Safety Bill, Sections 139A-C, and Chapter 3, is available at https://www.irishstatutebook.ie/eli/2022/act/41/enacted/en/html.

15. "Industry Codes," Australia Online Safety Act, Division 7, available at https://www.esafety.gov.au/industry/codes.

16. Mark MacCarthy, "A Consumer Protection Approach to Platform Content Moderation," in B. Petkova and T. Ojanen (eds), *Fundamental Rights Protection Online: The Future Regulation of Intermediaries* (Northampton, MA: Edward Elgar), 2019, https://ssrn.com/abstract=3408459; Mark MacCarthy, "Some Reservations About a Consistency Requirement for Social Media Content Moderation Decisions," *Forbes*, July 29, 2020, https://www.forbes.com/sites/washingtonbytes/2020/07/29/some-reservations-about-a-consistency-requirement-for-social-media-content-moderation-decisions/?sh=3c5eec2b76d7.

17. Facebook's latest community standards enforcement report is available at https://transparency.facebook.com/community-standards-enforcement; Google's latest "Community Guidelines Enforcement Report for YouTube" is available at https://transparencyreport.google.com/youtube-policy/removals?hl=en_GB.

18. European Commission, "Code of Practice on Disinformation," September 26, 2018, https://ec.europa.eu/digital-single-market/en/news/code-practice-disinformation; European Commission, "Commission Presents Guidance to Strengthen the Code of Practice on Disinformation," May 26, 2021, https://ec.europa.eu/commission/presscorner/detail/en/ip_21_2585.

19. European Commission, Code of Practice on Disinformation"; European Commission, "Commission Presents Guidance"; European Commission, "Fourth Intermediate Results of the EU Code of Practice Against Disinformation," May 17, 2019, https://ec.europa.eu/digital-single-market/en/news/fourth-intermediate-results-eu-code-practice-against-disinformation; European Commission, "The 2022 Code of Practice on Disinformation," June 16, 2022, https://digital-strategy.ec.europa.eu/en/policies/code-practice-disinformation.

20. Regulation (EU) 2022/2065 of the European Parliament.

21. The reporting requirements are in Section 2(1) and Section 2(2) of NetzDG. See https://germanlawarchive.iuscomp.org/?p=1245; public reports for Facebook are available at https://fbnewsroomus.files.wordpress.com/2018/07/facebook_netzdg_july_2018_english-1.pdf; Instagram, https://instagram-press.com/wp-content/uploads/2019/07/instagram_netzdg_July_2019_english.pdf; Twitter, https://transparency.twitter.com/en/countries/de.html; Google's "Network Enforcement Law" is available at https://transparencyreport.google.com/netzdg/overview?hl=en_GB; Thomas Escritt, "Germany Fines Facebook for Under-Reporting Complaints," *Reuters*, July 2, 2019, https://www.reuters.com/article/us-facebook-germany-fine/germany-fines-facebook-for-under-reporting-complaints-idUSKCN1TX1IC.

22. Algorithmic Accountability Act, S. 1108, 116th Cong. (2019); Regulation (EU) 2022/2065 of the European Parliament; European Commission, "Proposal for a Regulation of the European Parliament and of the Council Laying Down Harmonised Rules

on Artificial Intelligence (Artificial Intelligence Act) and Amending Certain Union Legislative Acts," April 21, 2021, https://eur-lex.europa.eu/legal-content/EN/TXT/?qid=1623335154975&uri=CELEX%3A52021PC0206.

23. Rumman Chowdhury and Luca Belli, "Examining Algorithmic Amplification of Political Content on Twitter," *Twitter Blog*, October 21, 2021, https://blog.twitter.com/en_us/topics/company/2021/rml-politicalcontent.

24. PACT Act, S. 797, 117th Cong. (2021).

25. Social Media NUDGE Act, S. 3608, 117th Cong. (2022), https://www.congress.gov/bill/117th-congress/senate-bill/3608.

26. PACT Act, S. 797, 117th Cong. (2021).

27. Nathaniel Persily, "Facebook Hides Data Showing It Harms Users. Outside Scholars Need Access," *Washington Post*, October 5, 2021, https://www.washingtonpost.com/outlook/2021/10/05/facebook-research-data-haugen-congress-regulation; Nathaniel Persily, "Platform Accountability and Transparency Act," October 5, 2021, https://www.dropbox.com/s/5my9r1t9ifebfz1/Persily%20proposed%20legislation%2010%205%2021.docx?dl=0.

28. Social Media DATA Act, H.R. 3451, 117th Cong. (2021), https://www.congress.gov/bill/117th-congress/house-bill/3451.

29. PACT Act, S. 797, 117th Cong. (2021).

30. Regulation (EU) 2022/2065 of the European Parliament.

31. Casey Newton, "The Facebook Whistleblower Testifies: What Frances Haugen Gets Right—and Wrong," *Platformer*, October 5, 2021, https://www.platformer.news/p/the-facebook-whistleblower-testifies.

32. Walter Lippman, "The Basic Problem of Democracy," *The Atlantic*, November 1919, https://www.theatlantic.com/magazine/archive/1919/11/the-basic-problem-of-democracy/569095.

33. European Commission, "A Multi-Dimensional Approach to Disinformation," Report of the Independent High Level Group on Fake News and Online Disinformation, March 11, 2018, https://op.europa.eu/en/publication-detail/-/publication/6ef4df8b-4cea-11e8-be1d-01aa75ed71a1/language-en.

34. Ethan Zuckerman, "Facebook Has a Misinformation Problem and Is Blocking Access to Data About How Much There Is and Who Is Affected," *The Conversation*, November 2, 2021, https://theconversation.com/facebook-has-a-misinformation-problem-and-is-blocking-access-to-data-about-how-much-there-is-and-who-is-affected-164838.

35. "The Facebook Files."

36. "250 Recommendations on How to Stop 'Infodemics,'" Forum on Information & Democracy, Nov 12, 2020, https://informationdemocracy.org/2020/11/12/250-recommendations-on-how-to-stop-infodemics; Anya Schiffin, "Beyond Transparency: Regulating Online Political Advertising," Roosevelt Institute, September 29, 2020, https://rooseveltinstitute.org/publications/beyond-transparency-regulating-online-political-advertising; Commission on Information Disorder, November 15, 2021, https://www.aspeninstitute.org/programs/commission-on-information-disorder.

37. Kayla Gogarty, "Facebook Keeps Touting Its Labels, but Data Suggests Labels Actually Amplified Trump's Misinformation," *MediaMatters*, June 2, 2021, https://www.mediamatters.org/facebook/facebook-keeps-touting-its-labels-data-suggests-labels-actually-amplified-trumps.

38. Alex Kantrowitz, "Facebook Removed the News Feed Algorithm in an Experiment. Then It Gave Up," *Big Technology*, October 25, 2021, https://bigtechnology.substack.com/p/facebook-removed-the-news-feed-algorithm; Will Oremus, "Why Facebook Won't Let You Control Your Own News Feed," *Washington Post*, November 13, 2021, https://www.washingtonpost.com/technology/2021/11/13/facebook-news-feed-algorithm-how-to-turn-it-off.

39. Rumman Chowdhury and Luca Belli, "Examining algorithmic amplification," *Twitter Blog*, October 21, 2021, https://blog.twitter.com/en_us/topics/company/2021/rml-politicalcontent.

40. Protecting Americans from Dangerous Algorithms Act, H.R. 8636, 116th Cong. (2020), https://www.congress.gov/bill/116th-congress/house-bill/8636/text; "E&C Leaders Announce Legislation to Reform Section 230," House Energy and Commerce Committee press release, October 14, 2021, https://democrats-energycommerce.house.gov/newsroom/press-releases/ec-leaders-announce-legislation-to-reform-section-230; Ashley Gold, "Exclusive: New Bipartisan Bill Takes Aim at Algorithms," Axios, November 9, 2021, https://www.axios.com/algorithm-bill-house-bipartisan-5293581e-430f-4ea1-8477-bd9adb63519c.html.

41. S. 3608—Social Media NUDGE Act; Mark MacCarthy, "Senator Klobuchar 'Nudges' Social Media Companies to Improve Content Moderation," *TechTank*, Brookings Institution, February 23, 2022, https://www.brookings.edu/blog/techtank/2022/02/23/senator-klobuchar-nudges-social-media-companies-to-improve-content-moderation.

42. Stephanie Yang, "China Leaps Ahead in Effort to Rein in Algorithms," *Wall Street Journal*, October 5, 2021, https://www.wsj.com/articles/china-leaps-ahead-in-effort-to-rein-in-algorithms-11633408289?mod=tech_lead_pos4.

43. Paris Martineau, "Maybe It's Not YouTube's Algorithm that Radicalizes People," *Wired*, October 23, 2019, https://www.wsj.com/articles/china-leaps-ahead-in-effort-to-rein-in-algorithms-11633408289?mod=tech_lead_pos4.

44. Vinay Sitapati, "Facebook and India's Paradox of Inclusion," *Foreign Affairs*, November 24, 2021, https://www.foreignaffairs.com/articles/india/2021-11-24/facebook-and-indias-paradox-inclusion.

45. Michael Wolfowicz, Badi Hasisi, and David Weisburd, "What Are the Effects of Different Elements of Media on Radicalization Outcomes? A Systematic Review," Campbell Collaboration, June 8, 2022, https://arxiv.org/abs/2208.01534.

46. Mihaela Curmei, Andreas Haupt, Dylan Hadfield-Menell, and Benjamin Recht, "Toward Psychologically-Grounded Dynamic Preference Models," *ArXive*, August 6, 2022, https://arxiv.org/abs/2208.01534.

47. Joseph Bernstein, "Bad News," *Harper's*, September 2021, https://harpers.org/archive/2021/09/bad-news-selling-the-story-of-disinformation.

48. Ben Smith, "Inside the 'Misinformation' Wars," *New York Times*, November 28, 2021, https://www.nytimes.com/2021/11/28/business/media-misinformation-disinformation.html.

49. "Lies, Free Speech and the Law," Knight First Amendment Institute at Columbia University, April 8, 2022, https://knightcolumbia.org/events/symposium-lies-free-speech-and-the-law; "What Comes After Disinformation Studies?" Center for Information, Technology and the Public Life, May 25, 2022, https://citap.unc.edu/ica-preconference-2022; Mark MacCarthy, "Purging the Web of Lies Will Not, of Itself, Repair our Politics," Center for International Governance Innovation, October 26, 2022, https://www.cigionline.org/articles/purging-the-web-of-lies-will-not-of-itself-repair-our-politics.

50. Adam D. I. Kramer, Jamie E. Guillory, and Jeffrey T. Hancock, "Experimental Evidence of Massive-Scale Emotional Contagion Through Social Networks," *Proceedings of the National Academy of Sciences* 111, no. 24 (2014): 8788–90, available at http://www.pnas.org/content/111/24/8788.full.html.

51. Ethan Zuckerman, "Building a More Honest Internet," *Columbia Journalism Review* (Fall 2019), https://www.cjr.org/special_report/building-honest-internet-public-interest.php.

52. See, for instance, Leticia Bode and Emily K. Vraga, "In Related News, That Was Wrong: The Correction of Misinformation Through Related Stories Functionality in Social Media," *Journal of Communication* 65, no. 4 (August 2015): 619–38, https://doi.org/10.1111/jcom.12166.

53. Georgia Wells, Jeff Horwitz, and Deepa Seetharaman, "Facebook Knows Instagram Is Toxic for Teen Girls, Company Documents Show," *Wall Street Journal*, September 14, 2021, https://www.wsj.com/articles/facebook-knows-instagram-is-toxic-for-teen-girls-company-documents-show-11631620739?mod=article_inline.

54. AB-2273, The California Age-Appropriate Design Code Act, September 15, 2022, https://leginfo.legislature.ca.gov/faces/billTextClient.xhtml?bill_id=202120220AB2273; "Age Appropriate Design: A Code of Practice for Online Services," United Kingdom, Information Commissioners Office, October 17, 2022, https://ico.org.uk/media/for-organisations/guide-to-data-protection/ico-codes-of-practice/age-appropriate-design-a-code-of-practice-for-online-services-2-1.pdf.

55. Kids Online Safety Act, S. 3663, 117th Cong. (2022), https://www.congress.gov/bill/117th-congress/senate-bill/3663/text; Dan Frechtling, "Will the U.S. Update Laws for Children's Digital Privacy?" *Forbes*, March 7, 2023, https://www.forbes.com/sites/forbestechcouncil/2023/03/07/will-the-us-update-laws-for-childrens-digital-privacy/?sh=3a3bf3bd3f17; Office of Senator Marsha Blackburn, "Blackburn, Blumenthal Introduce Bipartisan Kids Online Safety Act," press release, May 2, 2023, https://www.blackburn.senate.gov/2023/5/blackburn-blumenthal-introduce-bipartisan-kids-online-safety-act.

56. "Coalition Letter Opposing Kids Online Safety Act," Center for Democracy and Technology, November 28, 2022, https://cdt.org/wp-content/uploads/2022/11/Coalition-letter-opposing-Kids-Online-Safety-Act-28-Nov-PM.pdf.

57. Utah State Legislature, S.B. 152, Social Media Regulation Amendments, signed by Utah Governor Spencer Cox, March 23, 2023, https://le.utah.gov/~2023/bills/static

/SB0152.html; Utah State Legislature, H.B. 311 Social Media Usage Amendments, signed by Utah Governor Spencer Cox, March 23, 2023, https://le.utah.gov/~2023/bills/static/HB0311.html.

58. FTC, Children's Online Privacy Protection Rule, 16 CFR Part 312, https://www.ftc.gov/legal-library/browse/rules/childrens-online-privacy-protection-rule-coppa.

59. Reno v. ACLU, 521 U.S. 844 (1997), https://supreme.justia.com/cases/federal/us/521/844/.

60. NetChoice v. Rob Bonta, Attorney General of the State of California, Petition for Declaratory and Injunctive Relief, https://netchoice.org/wp-content/uploads/2022/12/NetChoice-v-Bonta_-Official-AB-2273-Complaint-final.pdf; NetChoice, Request for Veto: H.B. 311 (Social Media Usage) and S.B. 152 (Social Media Regulation), March 2, 2023, https://aboutblaw.com/7dA.

61. Gopal Ratnam, "States Act to Curtail Kids Online, Raising Pressure on Congress," *Roll Call*, April 11, 2023, https://rollcall.com/2023/04/11/states-act-to-curtail-kids-online-raising-pressure-on-congress/; Rebecca Shabad and Liz Brown-Kaiser, "Children Under 13 Would Be Banned from Social Media under Bipartisan Senate Bill," NBC News, April 26, 2023, https://www.nbcnews.com/news/amp/rcna81598.

62. Online Safety Bill, Parliament of Australia; The Platform Accountability and Transparency Act of 2021.

63. In Jean-Jacques Rousseau's *Of the Social Contract* (1762), he says, "Obedience to a law one prescribes to oneself is freedom."

64. A.L.A. Schechter Poultry Corp. v. United States, 295 US 495 (1935), https://supreme.justia.com/cases/federal/us/295/495.

65. MacCarthy, "A Dispute Resolution Program."

66. Communications Decency Act of 1996, 47 U.S.C. § 230, Cornell School of Law's Legal Information Institute, https://www.law.cornell.edu/uscode/text/47/230.

67. David French, "The Growing Threat to Free Speech Online," *Time*, January 24, 2020, https://time.com/5770755/threat-free-speech-online; Jason Thacker, "A Conversation with David French on Social Media, Free Speech, and Cultural Division," *WeeklyTech* podcast, March 10, 2021, https://jasonthacker.com/2021/03/10/a-conversation-with-david-french-on-social-media-free-speech-and-cultural-division.

68. Concurring Statement of Justice Clarence Thomas in Malwarebytes Inc. v. Enigma Software, No. 19–1284, October 13, 2020, https://www.supremecourt.gov/orders/courtorders/101320zor_8m58.pdf.

69. Amy Howe, "Court Agrees to Hear Nine New Cases, Including Challenge to Tech Companies' Immunity Under Section 230," *SCOTUSblog*, October 3, 2022, https://www.scotusblog.com/2022/10/court-agrees-to-hear-nine-new-cases-including-challenge-to-tech-companies-immunity-under-section-230; Gonzalez v. Google LLC, 2 F.4th 871 (9th Cir. 2021), https://casetext.com/case/gonzalez-v-google-llc.

70. Mark MacCarthy, "Congress Should Reform Section 230 in Light of the Oral Argument in Gonzalez," *Lawfare Blog*, March 22, 2023, https://www.lawfareblog.com/congress-should-reform-section-230-light-oral-argument-gonzalez; Twitter, Inc. v. Taamneh, ___ US ___ (2023), https://www.supremecourt.gov/opinions/22pdf/21-1496_d18f.

pdf; Gonzalez v. Google, 598 US ____ (2023), https://www.supremecourt.gov/opinions/22pdf/21-1333_6j7a.pdf.

71. Michael Masnick, "Yes, Section 230 Should Protect ChatGPT and Other Generative AI Tools," *TechDirt*, March 17, 2023, https://www.techdirt.com/2023/03/17/yes-section-230-should-protect-chatgpt-and-others-generative-ai-tools/; Matt Perault, "Section 230 Won't Protect ChatGPT," *Lawfare Blog*, February 23, 2023, https://www.lawfareblog.com/section-230-wont-protect-chatgpt; Cristiano Lima, "AI Chatbots Won't Enjoy Tech's Legal Shield, Section 230 Authors Say," *Washington Post*, March 17, 2023, https://www.washingtonpost.com/politics/2023/03/17/ai-chatbots-wont-enjoy-techs-legal-shield-section-230-authors-say/; Editorial Board, "Who's Responsible When ChatGPT Goes Off the Rails? Congress Should Say," *Washington Post*, March 19, 2023, https://www.washingtonpost.com/opinions/2023/03/19/section-230-chatgpt-internet-regulation/.

72. Communications Act of 1934 amendment, Public Law 115–164, April 11, 2018, https://www.congress.gov/115/plaws/publ164/PLAW-115publ164.pdf; EARN IT Act of 2020, S. 3398, 116th Cong. (2020), https://www.congress.gov/bill/116th-congress/senate-bill/3398/text; Protecting Americans from Dangerous Algorithms Act, H.R. 8636, 116th Cong. (2020); "E&C Leaders Announce Legislation to Reform Section 230," House Energy and Commerce Committee; SAFE TECH Act, S. 299, 117th Cong. (2021), https://www.congress.gov/bill/117th-congress/senate-bill/299/titles?r=4&s=1; "Warner, Hirono, Klobuchar Announce the SAFE TECH Act to Reform Section 230," Office of Senator Mark Warner press release, February 5, 2021, https://www.warner.senate.gov/public/index.cfm/2021/2/warner-hirono-klobuchar-announce-the-safe-tech-act-to-reform-section-230.

73. Force v. Facebook Inc., No. 18-397 (2d Cir. 2019), https://law.justia.com/cases/federal/appellate-courts/ca2/18-397/18-397-2019-07-31.html; Herrick v. Grindr LLC, United States Court of Appeals for the Second Circuit, Summary Order, March 27, 2019, http://www.cagoldberglaw.com/wp-content/uploads/2018/09/Second-Circuit-Decision.pdf.

74. Danielle Keats Citron and Mary Anne Franks, "The Internet as a Speech Machine and Other Myths Confounding Section 230 Reform," *University of Chicago Legal Forum* 2020, Article 3, https://chicagounbound.uchicago.edu/uclf/vol2020/iss1/3.

75. US Department of Justice, Section 230—Nurturing Innovation or Fostering Unaccountability? June 2020, https://www.justice.gov/file/1286331/download; Eric Goldman, "Why Section 230 Is Better Than the First Amendment," *Notre Dame Law Review* 95, no. 33 (2019), https://ssrn.com/abstract=3351323.

76. Ending Support for Internet Censorship Act, S. 1914, 116th Cong. (2019), https://www.congress.gov/bill/116th-congress/senate-bill/1914; Danielle Keats Citron and Benjamin Wittes, "The Internet Will Not Break: Denying Bad Samaritans § 230 Immunity," *Fordham Law Review* 86, no. 401 (2017), https://ir.lawnet.fordham.edu/flr/vol86/iss2/3; Testimony of Mark Zuckerberg, Hearing Before the United States House of Representatives, Committee on Energy and Commerce, Subcommittees on Consumer Protection & Commerce and Communications & Technology, March 25, 2021, https://

energycommerce.house.gov/sites/democrats.energycommerce.house.gov/files/documents/Witness%20Testimony_Zuckerberg_CAT_CPC_2021.03.25.pdf.

77. Zeran v. America Online Inc., 129 F.3d 327 (4th Cir. 1997), https://www.eff.org/files/zeran-v-aol.pdf.

78. Digital Millennium Copyright Act, 17 U.S.C. § 512, Cornell School of Law.

79. "Directive 2000/31/EC of the European Parliament and of the Council of 8 June 2000 on Certain Legal Aspects of Information Society Services, in Particular Electronic Commerce, in the Internal Market ('Directive on Electronic Commerce')," *Official Journal of the European Communities*, https://eur-lex.europa.eu/legal-content/EN/TXT/PDF/?uri=CELEX:32000L0031&from=EN; Regulation (EU) 2022/2065 of the European Parliament.

80. Allison Prang and Deepa Seetharaman, "Twitter Bans Sharing of Private People's Photos, Videos Without Consent," *Wall Street Journal*, November 30, 2021, https://www.wsj.com/articles/twitter-bans-sharing-of-private-peoples-photos-videos-without-consent-11638290037.

81. Daisuke Wakabayashi, "YouTube Sued over Animal Abuse Videos, Accused of Not Enforcing Ban," *New York Times*, October 19, 2021, https://www.nytimes.com/2021/10/19/technology/youtube-sued-animal-abuse.html.

82. Lindsay, "I Designed Algorithms at Facebook."

83. Daphne Keller, "Amplification and Its Discontents," Knight First Amendment Institute at Columbia University, June 8, 2021, https://knightcolumbia.org/content/amplification-and-its-discontents.

84. Chicago Lawyers' Committee for Civil Rights Under Law v. Craigslist Inc., 2008 WL 681168 (7th Cir. March 14, 2008), https://caselaw.findlaw.com/us-7th-circuit/1046308.html; National Association of the Deaf v. Harvard University, 2019 WL 1409302 (D. Mass. March 28, 2019), https://casetext.com/case/na-of-deaf-v-harvard-univ; Noah v. AOL Time Warner Inc., 261 F. Supp. 2d 532 (E. D. Va. 2003), https://law.justia.com/cases/federal/district-courts/FSupp2/261/532/2515648; Henderson v. The Source for Public Data, 2021 WL 2003550 (E.D. Va. May 19, 2021), https://digitalcommons.law.scu.edu/cgi/viewcontent.cgi?article=3467&context=historica; Statement of CFPB Director Rohit Chopra and FTC Chair Lina M. Khan on Amicus Brief filed in Henderson v. The Source for Public Data, L.P., October 14, 2021, https://www.ftc.gov/system/files/documents/public_statements/1597534/joint_statement_on_henderson_amicus.pdf; Tyrone Henderson, Sr. v. The Source for Public Data, L.P., No. 21–1678 (4th Cir. 2022), https://law.justia.com/cases/federal/appellate-courts/ca4/21-1678/21-1678-2022-11-03.htm.

85. PACT Act, S. 4066, 117th Cong. (2021).

86. Associated Press v. United States, 326 US 1 (1945); Red Lion Broadcasting Co. Inc. v. FCC, 395 US 367 (1969); International Covenant on Civil and Political Right, Adopted December 16, 1966, https://www.ohchr.org/en/professionalinterest/pages/ccpr.aspx.

87. Alexander Meiklejohn, *Free Speech and Its Relation to Self-Government* (New York: Harper & Brothers, 1948), https://search.library.wisc.edu/digital/ACOJRL3HHCHP678U.

88. Owen Fiss, "Free Speech and Social Structure," *Tel Aviv University Studies in Law* 8, no. 249 (1988), https://www.law.yale.edu/sites/default/files/documents/faculty/papers/freespeech_socialstructure.pdf.

89. Fukuyama et al., "Report of the Working Group on Platform Scale."

90. Keller, "The Future of Platform Power," 168–72.

91. Concurring Statement of Justice Clarence Thomas, Biden v. Knight First Amendment Institute, no. 20–197, April 5, 2021, https://www.supremecourt.gov/opinions/20pdf/20-197_5ie6.pdf.

92. Jeffrey Rosen, "The Deciders: The Future of Privacy and Free Speech in the Age of Facebook and Google," *Fordham Law Review* 80, no. 1525 (2012), https://ir.lawnet.fordham.edu/flr/vol80/iss4/1; "Report of the Special Rapporteur," UNHRC.

93. Lakier and Tebbe, "After the 'Great Deplatforming.'"

94. Facebook v. CasaPound, Case Analysis, Global Freedom of Expression, Columbia University, April 2020, https://globalfreedomofexpression.columbia.edu/cases/casapound-v-facebook; Matthias C. Kettemann and Anna Sophia Tiedeke, "Back Up: Can Users Sue Platforms to Reinstate Deleted Content?" *Internet Policy Review* 9, no. 2 (June 3, 2020), https://doi.org/10.14763/2020.2.1484; "Polish Government to Pass Law that Will Allow It More Control over the Internet Content and Legitimize Blocking Access to Certain Websites," *National Law Review* (February 12, 2021), https://www.natlawreview.com/article/polish-government-to-pass-law-will-allow-it-more-control-over-internet-content-and; Elisabeth Zerofsky, "How the American Right Fell in Love With Hungary," *New York Times Magazine*, October 19, 2021, https://www.nytimes.com/2021/10/19/magazine/viktor-orban-rod-dreher.html.

95. Robert Post, "Exit, Voice and the First Amendment Treatment of Social Media," *Law and Political Economy*, April 6, 2021, https://lpeproject.org/blog/exit-voice-and-the-first-amendment-treatment-of-social-media/.

96. 21st Century FREE Speech Act, S. 1384, 117th Cong. (2021), https://www.congress.gov/bill/117th-congress/senate-bill/1384.

97. Ending Support for Internet Censorship Act, S. 1914, 116th Cong. (2019).

98. Texas H.B. 20, Codified in Relevant Part at Texas Business & Communication Code §§ 120.001–003, 120.051–053; 120.101–104, 120.151; Texas Civil Practice & Rem. Code §§ 143A.001–008, https://capitol.texas.gov/tlodocs/872/billtext/pdf/HB00020F.pdf#navpanes=0; NetChoice LLC v. Paxton, No. 21–51178 (5th Cir. 2022), September 16, 2022, https://www.ca5.uscourts.gov/opinions/pub/21/21-51178-CV1.pdf.

99. Nadine Batchelor-Hunt, "Facebook Is 'Making Hate Worse' as Algorithms 'Prioritise Extreme Content,' Says Whistleblower," Yahoo News, October 25, 2021, https://news.yahoo.com/facebook-algorithms-making-hate-worse-173228077.html.

100. Mary Ann Franks, "Testimony Hearing Before the US Senate Committee on Homeland Security & Governmental Affairs on Social Media Platforms and the Amplification of Domestic Extremism & Other Harmful Content," October 26, 2021, https://www.hsgac.senate.gov/imo/media/doc/Testimony-Franks-2021-10-28.pdf.

101. Victor Pickard, "The Fairness Doctrine Won't Solve Our Problems—But It Can Foster Needed Debate," *Washington Post*, February 4, 2021, https://www.washingtonpost

.com/outlook/2021/02/04/fairness-doctrine-wont-solve-our-problems-it-can-foster-needed-debate.

102. "Due Impartiality and Due Accuracy and Undue Prominence of Views and Opinions, Guidance," Ofcom, March 22, 2017, https://www.ofcom.org.uk/__data/assets/pdf_file/0033/99177/broadcast-code-guidance-section-5-march-2017.pdf; "Various news items on protests in Hong Kong were not duly impartial on a matter of major political controversy and a major matter relating to current public policy," Ofcom, May 26, 2020, https://www.ofcom.org.uk/__data/assets/pdf_file/0031/195781/The-World-Today-and-China-24,-CGTN.pdf.

103. David French, "Josh Hawley's Internet Censorship Bill Is an Unwise, Unconstitutional Mess," *National Review*, June 20, 2019, https://www.nationalreview.com/2019/06/josh-hawley-internet-censorship-bill-unconstitutional.

104. Yochai Benkler, Robert Faris, and Hal Roberts, *Network Propaganda* (NY: Oxford University Press, 2018), 47.

105. Mark MacCarthy, "Standards of Fairness for Disparate Impact Assessment of Big Data Algorithms," *Cumberland Law Review* 48 no. 102 (2017), https://papers.ssrn.com/sol3/papers.cfm?abstract_id=3154788.

106. Texas H.B. 20.

107. "Congressional Commissions: Overview and Considerations for Congress," Congressional Research Service, January 22, 2021, https://sgp.fas.org/crs/misc/R40076.pdf.

108. Florida S.B. 7072: Social Media Platforms (2021), https://www.flsenate.gov/Session/Bill/2021/7072/BillText/er/PDF.

109. Institute's Jameel Jaffer Talks to "TMZ Live" about Meta's Decision to Reinstate Trump, Knight First Amendment Institute, January 27, 2023, https://knightcolumbia.org/blog/institutes-jameel-jaffer-talks-to-tmz-live-about-metas-decision-to-reinstate-trump; "ACLU Comment on Meta's Decision to Reinstate Trump on Facebook," press release, January 25, 2023, https://www.aclu.org/press-releases/aclu-comment-on-metas-decision-to-reinstate-trump-on-facebook.

110. Der Dritte Weg v. Facebook Ireland Ltd., Global Freedom of Expression, Columbia University, May 2012, https://globalfreedomofexpression.columbia.edu/cases/der-dritte-weg-v-facebook-ireland-ltd; "The Fight Against Disinformation and the Right to Freedom of Expression," study requested by the LIBE Committee, 31, https://www.europarl.europa.eu/RegData/etudes/STUD/2021/695445/IPOL_STU(2021)695445_EN.pdf.

111. Communications Act of 1934, 47 U.S.C. § 312, https://www.law.cornell.edu/uscode/text/47/312; 47 US Code § 315, https://www.law.cornell.edu/uscode/text/47/315.

112. Communications Act of 1934, 47 C.F.R. § 73.1212, https://www.law.cornell.edu/cfr/text/47/73.1212.

113. Honest Ads Act, S. 1356, 116th Cong. (2019), https://www.congress.gov/bill/116th-congress/senate-bill/1356.

114. Twitter's political ad transparency center is available at https://ads.twitter.com/transparency; Google's latest transparency report on political advertising on Google, including YouTube, is available at https://transparencyreport.google.com/political-ads/

home?hl=en_GB; Facebook's political ad archive is available at https://about.facebook.com/actions/preparing-for-elections-on-facebook.

115. Paddy Leerssen, Jef Ausloos, Brahim Zarouali, Natali Helberger, and Claes H. de Vreese, "Platform Ad Archives: Promises and Pitfalls," *Internet Policy Review* 8, no. 4 (2019), https://doi.org/10.14763/2019.4.1421.

116. Complaint of Campaign Legal Center, Common Cause, and Sunlight Foundation Against ABC Owned Television Stations, owner and operator of WLS-TV, Chicago, IL for Violations of the Communications Act of 1934, § 317 and FCC Rule 47 CFR § 73.1212, November 12, 2014, https://campaignlegal.org/sites/default/files/WLS_Complaint_Final.pdf.

117. Mark MacCarthy, "Social Media Companies Shouldn't Censor Campaign Ads from Legitimate Political Candidates," *CIO*, October 24, 2019, https://www.cio.com/article/3448280/social-media-companies-shouldnt-censor-campaign-ads-from-legitimate-political-candidates.html; Mark MacCarthy, "An 'Equal Time' Rule for Social Media," *Forbes*, January 21, 2020, https://www.forbes.com/sites/washingtonbytes/2020/01/21/an-equal-time-rule-for-social-media/?sh=762a63c5338a.

118. Texas H.B. 20; Texas Civil Practice & Rem. Code; Florida S.B. 7072: Social Media Platforms.

119. NetChoice LLC v. Moody, No. 21-12355 (11th Cir. 2022), May 23, 2022, https://media.ca11.uscourts.gov/opinions/pub/files/202112355.pdf.

120. NetChoice LLC v. Moody, 4:21cv220-RH-MAF (N.D. Fla. June 30, 2021), https://storage.courtlistener.com/recap/gov.uscourts.flnd.371253/gov.uscourts.flnd.371253.113.0_1.pdf; NetChoice LLC v. Paxton, 1:21-CV-840-RP (W.D. Texas, December 1, 2021), https://cdn.vox-cdn.com/uploads/chorus_asset/file/23057162/order.pdf; Andrew Zhang, "Texas Law Prohibiting Social Media Companies from Banning Users over Their Viewpoints Reinstated by Appeals Court," *Texas Tribune*, May 11, 2022, https://www.texastribune.org/2022/05/11/texas-social-media-law-reinstated; NetChoice LLC v. Paxton, on Application to Vacate Stay, May 31, 2022, 596 US __ (2022), https://s3.documentcloud.org/documents/22046720/21a720-order.pdf.

121. Hurley v. Irish American Gay, Lesbian and Bisexual Group of Boston Inc., 515 US. 557 (1995), https://supreme.justia.com/cases/federal/us/515/557; Miami Herald Publishing Co. v. Tornillo, 418 US 241 (1974), https://supreme.justia.com/cases/federal/us/418/241; PruneYard Shopping Center v. Robins, 447 US 74 (1980), https://supreme.justia.com/cases/federal/us/447/74; Turner Broadcasting System Inc. v. FCC, 512 US 622 (1994), https://supreme.justia.com/cases/federal/us/512/622.

122. NetChoice LLC v. Paxton, No. 21-51178 (5th Cir. 2022), September 16, 2022, https://www.ca5.uscourts.gov/opinions/pub/21/21-51178-CV1.pdf; Rebecca Klar, "Tech Groups Ask Supreme Court to Hear Case on Florida Social Media Law," *The Hill*, October 24, 2022, https://thehill.com/policy/technology/3702115-tech-groups-ask-supreme-court-to-hear-case-on-florida-social-media-law; Amy Howe, "Justices Request Federal Government's Views on Texas and Florida Social-Media Laws," *SCOTUSblog*, January 23, 2023, https://www.scotusblog.com/2023/01/justices-request-federal-governments-views-on-texas-and-florida-social-media-laws.

123. Florida S.B. 7072: Social Media Platforms.

124. Alan Z. Rozenshtein, "First Amendment Absolutism and Florida's Social Media Law," *Lawfare Blog*, June 1, 2022, https://www.lawfareblog.com/first-amendment-absolutism-and-floridas-social-media-law.

125. FCC, "Statutes and Rules on Candidate Appearances & Advertising," https://www.fcc.gov/media/policy/statutes-and-rules-candidate-appearances-advertising; Turner Broadcasting System Inc. v. FCC, 520 US 180 (1997), https://supreme.justia.com/cases/federal/us/520/180/#tab-opinion-1960089.

126. Zauderer v. Office of Disc. Counsel, 471 US 626 (1985), https://supreme.justia.com/cases/federal/us/471/626.

127. "Knight Institute Comments on Federal Court's Decision Keeping Florida's Social Media Law Blocked," Knight First Amendment Institute, May 23, 2022, https://knightcolumbia.org/content/knight-institute-comments-on-federal-courts-decision-keeping-floridas-social-media-law-blocked.

128. Renee Diresta, "Free Speech Is Not the Same as Free Reach," *Wired*, August 3, 2018, https://www.wired.com/story/free-speech-is-not-the-same-as-free-reach.

129. United States v. Playboy Entertainment Group Inc., 529 US 803 (2000), https://supreme.justia.com/cases/federal/us/529/803; Keller, "Amplification and Its Discontents."

130. Regulation (EU) 2022/2065 of the European Parliament; "Internet Information Service Algorithmic Recommendation Management Provisions," DigiChina, January 10, 2022, https://digichina.stanford.edu/work/translation-internet-information-service-algorithmic-recommendation-management-provisions-effective-march-1-2022.

131. Eric Goldman, "The Constitutionality of Mandating Editorial Transparency," *Hastings Law Journal* 73, no. 1203 (2022), https://ssrn.com/abstract=4005647; The Washington Post v. McManus, No. 19–1132 (4th Cir. 2019), https://law.justia.com/cases/federal/appellate-courts/ca4/19-1132/19-1132-2019-12-06.html.

132. United States Telecom Assoc. v. FCC, 855 F.3d 381 (2017), May 1, 2017, https://www.cadc.uscourts.gov/internet/opinions.nsf/06F8BFD079A89E13852581130053C3F8/$file/15-1063-1673357.pdf.

133. Texas H.B. 20; Texas Civil Practice & Rem. Code §§ 143A.001–008.

134. Alan Z. Rozenshtein, "The Fifth Circuit's Social Media Decision: A Dangerous Example of First Amendment Absolutism," *Lawfare Blog*, September 20, 2022, https://www.lawfareblog.com/fifth-circuits-social-media-decision-dangerous-example-first-amendment-absolutism.

135. NetChoice LLC v. Moody, 4:21cv220-RH-MAF (N.D. Fla. June 30, 2021), https://storage.courtlistener.com/recap/gov.uscourts.flnd.371253/gov.uscourts.flnd.371253.113.0_1.pdf; NetChoice LLC v. Paxton, 1:21-CV-840-RP (W.D. Texas, December 1, 2021), https://cdn.vox-cdn.com/uploads/chorus_asset/file/23057162/order.pdf.

136. Miami Herald Pub. Co. v. Tornillo, 418 US 241 (1974), https://supreme.justia.com/cases/federal/us/418/241.

137. Concurring Statement of Justice Clarence Thomas, Biden v. Knight First Amendment Institute; Turner Broadcasting System Inc. v. FCC, 512 US 622 (1994), https://supreme.justia.com/cases/federal/us/512/622.

138. Kevin Breuninger, "Disney Sues Florida Gov. Ron DeSantis, Alleges Political Effort to Hurt Its Business," CNBC, April 26, 2023, https://www.cnbc.com/2023/04/26/disney-sues-florida-gov-ron-desantis-alleges-political-effort-to-hurt-its-business.html.

139. Rozenshtein, "First Amendment Absolutism"; Genevieve Lakier, "The Non-First Amendment Law of Freedom of Speech," *Harvard Law Review* 134, no. 2299, https://harvardlawreview.org/2021/05/the-non-first-amendment-law-of-freedom-of-speech.

140. Wu, "Is the First Amendment Obsolete?"; Tim Wu, "The Right to Evade Regulation: How Corporations Hijacked the First Amendment," *New Republic*, June 3, 2013, http://www.newrepublic.com/article/113294/how-corporations-hijacked-first-amendment-evade-regulation.

141. Lakier and Tebbe, "After the 'Great Deplatforming'"; Genevieve Lakier and Katy Glenn Bass, "New Research Project Focuses on Lies and the Law," Knight First Amendment Institute at Columbia University, September 21, 2021, https://knightcolumbia.org/blog/new-research-project-focuses-on-lies-and-the-law.

142. Pickard, "The Fairness Doctrine."

143. French, "Josh Hawley's Internet Censorship Bill Is an Unwise, Unconstitutional Mess."

Chapter 5
The Digital Regulator

"The single overarching idea that tied the competing philosophies together was the conviction shared by a majority of New Dealers that economic regulation by expert commissions would bring just results."
—Thomas K. McCraw[1]

"Our different purposes also are at war with each other. Where one can't crush the other out, they compromise; and the result is again different from what any one distinctly proposed beforehand."
—William James[2]

Introduction

The premise underlying this book is that new laws are needed specifically applicable to digital companies for promoting competition, protecting privacy, and combining free expression with effective content moderation. In the past several chapters we have outlined what some of these new digital measures might look like and made suggestions for policymakers to consider as they develop new legislation mandating new digital rules.

In some ways, however, the details of the new digital requirements are less important than developing an adequate institutional structure to administer and enforce them. The effectiveness of the new regulatory regime might depend less on getting the initial policy details right and more on the nature and powers of the institution that implements the new rules for digital industries. As we have seen in example after example, the new digital legislation itself cannot determine anything but the central questions of policy. Many of the implementation details and the way in which the new policies will work in practice for each differing line of business depend on the institutional structure developed to administer and enforce the new rules.

Around the world, in the United Kingdom, the European Union, Australia, Ireland, Canada, and now in the United States, proposed governance regimes for digital companies have moved away from sole or primary reliance on self or industry regulation and toward regulation by a government agency or agencies. The key question in this chapter is what form such a regime should take.

Regulatory proposals in other countries can provide some guidance. International steps toward regulation of social media companies have generated diverse approaches to institutional implementation. The United Kingdom has proposed an online safety bill to impose certain content moderation and risk assessment obligations of social media companies. It would expand the authority of its current media regulator, the Office of Communications (Ofcom), to include responsibility for online safety. Ireland is looking to expand the role of the Broadcasting Authority of Ireland (BAI) to include a new Online Safety Commissioner and would rename the expanded agency the Media Commission. Other jurisdictions opt for a separate agency with sector-specific responsibilities for online safety. In 2015, Australia created a brand-new agency, the eSafety Commissioner, to supervise online content, and expanded its powers in 2021. Canada is seeking to expand the role of its media regulator, the Canadian Radio-television and Telecommunications Commission (CRTC), to supervise online broadcasting firms such as Netflix and YouTube, but not to deal with online harms. Instead, it has proposed creating a new Digital Safety Commission separate from its existing media regulator CRTC to deal with online harms.[3]

The European Commission has adopted a complex institutional approach in connection with regulating online harms in its finalized Digital Services Act (DSA). The European Commission would enforce the

DSA's obligations for the larger online platforms. Each member country would designate a digital services coordinator to apply the regulation to smaller platforms and coordinate among themselves through an advisory group, called the European Board for Digital Services. France, for instance, has revamped its regulatory structure, combining its traditional media regulator and its digital intellectual property watchdog with a new digital regulator and renaming the new entity Autorité de regulation de la communication audiovisuelle et numérique (Arcom). It has moved ahead of other European regulators in releasing a consultation in 2022 designed to implement the DSA's mandate for researcher access to data.[4]

In competition policy reform, the United Kingdom and the European Union have taken the lead in developing a new ex-ante regulatory regime for digital markets. But they differ in institutional implementation. The United Kingdom has proposed the creation of a new Digital Markets Unit with regulatory authority to implement a procompetition regime for digital markets, and it intends to house the new digital unit within the existing Competition and Markets Authority. The European Union's finalized Digital Market Act would authorize the European Commission to monitor, implement, and enforce special competition rules for digital gatekeepers, but it creates no new institutional structures. Enforcement is housed in the commission's traditional directorate general for competition. In a related area of digital regulation, the European Commission's proposed AI regulation would require member states to designate national supervisory authorities to conduct market surveillance of AI products but would not mandate the creation of new, specialized AI regulatory authorities.[5]

In summary, the rest of the world has gone in several directions in terms of institutional implementation. Some jurisdictions move toward the creation of new institutions, while others seek to build upon existing regulatory structures.

All these legislative measures to address competition and content moderation concerns need to develop some mechanism for regulatory coordination. The United Kingdom's emerging regulatory structure for digital industries has the most well-developed system for regulatory coordination. To approach online regulation in a uniform and harmonized way, the United Kingdom has created a nonstatutory digital regulation cooperation forum, consisting of the Digital Markets Unit in the CMA, the traditional privacy regulator (the Information Commissioner's Office), and the content moderation regulator (Ofcom), as well as the financial regulator, the Financial Conduct Authority. It has named an executive director to guide the coordination process—an indication that it intends this interagency cooperation mechanism to endure. One of the first products of this cooperation was a joint statement from the privacy regulator and the competition regulator on how to craft a common approach on privacy and competition issues, identifying both areas of synergy and tension.[6]

The United States can learn a lot from these institutional designs, in particular from the innovative approach in the United Kingdom of creating a digital regulation cooperation forum. But ultimately it must craft its own way, one that responds best to its own traditions and political culture and reflects the realities of its own institutions.

The uniform approach of other countries is to house the responsibilities for competition, privacy, and content moderation in different administrative agencies. But this separation of regulatory responsibilities into separate institutions will not work for a regulatory regime that is focused on the unique problems of digital industries. The UK scheme for cooperation among separate regulators is innovative and forward looking, but it is unlikely to be able to deal effectively with the synergies and tensions among competition, privacy, and content moderation. These overlaps in digital industries are likely to be commonplace, rather than rare or isolated corner cases. In terms of the Venn diagram with three intersecting circles that is our visual model of the policy spaces in digital industries, most of the policy tools would fall into areas of overlap. Almost any measure that promotes competition implicates privacy and content moderation. And the same is true for all the other policy tools—they all implicate the other policy areas. As a result, a coordinating mechanism that relies on consultations among independent regulators with no common decision maker would be less likely to result in balanced measures that give each policy area its due. It would be far more likely to descend into an empty exercise of checking the consultation box. A common administrative structure would avoid this tendency.

Surprisingly the United States has almost accidently arrived at this result that avoids this defect in the approaches taken in the rest of the world. US policymakers are handicapped in arriving at a thoughtful answer to this question of regulatory structure by the fragmented way in which public policy is developed in the United States. Policy development occurs through legislative procedures that rely on discrete institutional silos. Legislative committees in Congress are set up according to agency and policy jurisdictional lines. The Commerce Committees in the House and Senate, for example, deal with privacy and content moderation issues, but not with antitrust issues, which are considered in the Judiciary Committees. This is a natural and sensible division of tasks, since the only way legislation can be processed is through a limitation on which subdivision of the legislature can begin and manage the process.

Fortunately, in the case of the regulation of digital industries, legislation to reform competition and privacy law and to establish a content moderation framework has converged on a common institutional structure. The competition reform bills passed out of the House and Senate in 2021 and 2022 lodge rulemaking and enforcement authority for the new procompetition regime for digital companies with the traditional competition authorities, the Department of Justice, and the FTC. Most proposed national privacy laws, including the one that advanced out of the House Commerce Committee in August 2022, establish rulemaking and enforcement with the FTC. Content moderation bills under consideration in both House and Senate all put implementation and enforcement responsibilities with the FTC.

Taken together, these separate measures amount to a collective decision to make the FTC the new digital regulator, with responsibility for new competition rules, new privacy rules, and a new content moderation regime. The FTC can avoid regulatory fragmentation through in-house administrative processes. It is vital to house all three missions in the same administrative structure with authority to balance the sometimes-conflicting demands of each policy area. Lodging authority for new privacy, competition, and content moderation rules in the FTC accomplishes that.

Moreover, given the current dynamic leadership under the agency's new chair Lina Khan, the FTC might be a wise choice for the digital regulator. If anyone can effectively take advantage of new authorities and responsibilities to protect the public from competition, privacy, and content moderation abuse, she and her new team can do it. Such an opportunity to get the new digital regime off to a good start might not come again for many years.

So, the default toward which the policy process in the United States is almost unconsciously tending might be a workable, even attractive result. This accidental achievement in institutional design should not be undervalued. But long-term institutional questions should not be decided by accident or by an assessment of the capabilities of current leaders. Policymakers should rethink the organizational structure for a new digital regime from scratch in order to get it right from the beginning.

The key problem is that the FTC is an economywide regulator. This is a problem because, as we have seen in example after example in the previous chapters, the rules needed to address competition, privacy, and content moderation challenges in digital industries have to be specific to the digital industries themselves in order to be effective. Competition rules must define discriminatory practices, for instance, and this can be done only for specific digital lines of business; data protection rules must specify fiduciary duties, abusive app, or website design, for instance, and this too means specific practices for specific digital sectors; content moderation due process protections need to be written for social media, not for traditional media companies or digital firms generally.

There is no reason in principle why an economywide regulator such as the FTC cannot take on such industry-specific tasks, but it is an awkward fit with its existing economywide missions. A clumsy bifurcation of responsibilities would inevitably develop with some staff or bureaus focusing on digital activities for at least some of their time and becoming more and more disconnected from the agency's broader functions as the need to develop and maintain industry expertise increased over time.

Moreover, the new digital regulator has to be a rulemaking agency. Much of the detail in the procompetition, privacy, and content moderation legislation cannot be specified in the legislation itself. It must be delegated to an expert agency to make judgments determined by industry facts and contexts.

But the FTC has never fully embraced the role of a rulemaking agency. Despite its existing rulemaking authority, it has largely been an enforcement agency focused on applying its statute to particular cases rather than developing and implementing ex-ante rules. It lacks the institutional expertise that other rule-writing agencies have developed over time and has a reflexive preference for case-by-case adjudications. This might be changing under new leadership, especially in the area of privacy where the agency has launched an ambitious attempt to adopt data protection rules after an extended rulemaking process, but it would be an institutional revamping of considerable magnitude.[7]

The alternative, which has been raised repeatedly in the discussion in the previous chapters, would be an industry-specific regulator with authority only over companies engaged in digital lines of business and with a mandate to pursue and balance the policy goals of promoting competition, protecting privacy, and enforcing effective and fair content moderation practices. This is the recommendation from, among others, a group of reformers clustered around former FCC chair Tom Wheeler—a group that includes, in addition to Wheeler, former antitrust enforcer Phil Verveer, veteran consumer activist and former head of the public interest group Public Knowledge Gene Kimmelman and Harold Feld, who is Public Knowledge's current senior vice president. The heart of their insight is that the separate information and communications technologies used in digital industries play complementary roles in a larger network of what could be viewed as a single industrial sector. A separate agency for this sector makes sense, just as a single agency for the emerging "communications industry" made sense in 1934 when Congress established the FCC putting the disparate technologies of telephone, telegraph, and radio under a single agency.[8]

The proposal in this book for a digital regulator is modeled on sector-specific regulatory agencies that operate to protect the public interest in discrete segments of the economy. Sector-specific agencies regulate media firms, communications carriers, energy companies, pharmaceutical firms, and financial services firms, among others. The agencies are authorized to do this because these firms provide recognizably discrete services that are central to public life and are unavoidable for citizens seeking to participate fully in the economic, social, political, and cultural life of their country.

Often these agencies have subject matter jurisdiction that spans several policy areas, since their ultimate responsibility is to ensure that these essential businesses operate in the public interest. Financial regulators are sector-specific in their focus, but with multiple missions. They aim to preserve safety and soundness of financial institutions, mitigate systemic risk, and protect investors and financial consumers. They also have responsibilities for information security and financial privacy. A similar model might be the FCC. It has broad authority to promote competition, protect privacy, and write rules promoting source and content diversity for the telephone, broadcasting, and cable companies under its jurisdiction.

In short, an attractive model for digital industry regulation might be the sector-specific comprehensive regulatory approach of the FCC rather than the generalist enforcement approach of the FTC. In 2022, Senator Michael Bennet introduced legislation setting up a new digital platform commission mirroring the recommendations from Wheeler, Public Knowledge, and other commentators. In 2023, Senator Bennet reaffirmed his commitment to a digital platform agency by reintroducing the Digital Platform Commission Act. Senator Peter Welch, who had sponsored the earlier House version of the bill, had been elected to the Senate and joined Senator Bennet as co-sponsor.[9]

Of course, no fundamental reform is ever accomplished in one single legislative act, and often the development of a specialized regulator takes place after an experiment of turning the regulatory responsibility over to an existing regulator or agency. This is what happened in telecommunications. The first attempt at federal regulation of telecommunications companies came in 1910 with the passage of the Mann-Elkins Act, which reformed railroad rate regulation at the Interstate Commerce

Commission (ICC). Almost as an add-on, this law designated "telegraph, telephone, and cable companies" as common carriers and assigned the jurisdiction over interstate rates charged by these companies to the ICC. In 1920 the Esch-Cummins Act gave the ICC added jurisdiction over "the transmission of intelligence by wire or wireless," apparently in an attempt to create a regulatory regime for the emerging radio industry. The agency did not know what to do with its communications industry jurisdiction, and its oversight authority languished unused for twenty-four years until in 1934 Congress created a new agency, the FCC, to protect the public interest in telecommunications.[10]

Congress treated radio with the same procedure. In 1912, it passed the Radio Act, which gave some regulatory authority over radio to the Commerce Department. When that authority was insufficient to deal with the explosion of broadcast stations in the 1920s, Congress passed the Radio Act of 1927, giving a new agency the Federal Radio Commission (FRC) wide licensing and regulatory powers. Congress transferred this authority to the FCC in 1934, creating a single agency covering both telephone service and broadcasting and authorized to regulate to protect the public interest in electronic communications whether by wire or wireless.[11]

Following these historical examples, it might be politically more realistic to create a sector-specific digital regulator in a two-step process. In the first step, the FTC would take on the tasks of the digital regulator, with all the awkwardness that would be entailed by trying to embody a rule-writing sectoral regulator inside a generalist enforcement agency. As the agency develops over time, however, and the needs of the digital part of its responsibilities become more and more divorced from its generalist mission, Congress could revisit the institutional structure and separate off the digital responsibilities to a new agency.

This is essentially what happened with the creation of the CFPB. The consumer protection function had previously been lodged within the traditional financial regulators, but because those agencies were by custom and tradition inclined to favor the safety and soundness of the financial institutions themselves over the interests of financial consumers, the consumer protection function was always the junior partner in the combination of regulatory goals within the same institution. As the Senate Report accompanying the Dodd-Frank Wall Street Reform and Consumer Protection Act, the law that created the CFPB, noted, "Placing consumer protection regulation and enforcement within safety and soundness regulators does not lead to better coordination of the two functions . . . when these two functions are put in the same agency, consumer protection fails to get the attention or focus it needs. Protecting consumers is not the banking agencies' priority, nor should it be." As a result, the consumer protection function was removed from the prudential regulators and lodged with a separate agency focused solely on protecting consumers from unfair, deceptive, and abusive acts and practices by financial institutions.[12]

This history shows something similar might happen if the digital regulator were initially housed in a generalist enforcement agency. The digital issues might not get the attention or focus they need at the generalist FTC. Only a digital agency can make these digital issues its priority. Ideally, Congress would create a digital regulator from scratch, but a second-best (and perhaps politically more realistic) alternative is to get to a digital regulator in a two-step process.

The remainder of this chapter deals with important issues that should be addressed if the digital regulator is to do its job.

Defining Digital Industries

Statutes often provide broad regulatory authority over a general business sector or technology and then identify specific lines of business that an agency is explicitly authorized to regulate. The Communications Act of 1934, for instance, provided the FCC with regulatory authority over "all interstate and foreign communication by wire or radio."[13] In addition, it explicitly authorizes the commission to regulate broadcasting, which it defines as "the dissemination of radio communications intended to be received by the public, directly or by the intermediary of relay stations."[14] The 1934 statute likewise defined key concepts in the provision of telephone service such as telephone exchange service and toll service.[15]

Many times since its founding in 1934, the FCC has had to extend its authority to new lines of business to keep up with rapid developments in the communications industry. The agency extended its rules from broadcast stations to broadcast networks, a decision upheld by the Supreme Court in its 1943 case *National Broadcasting Co., Inc. v. United States* decision.[16] Later, the FCC struggled to find a basis to regulate cable companies when they first emerged in the 1950s and 1960s since this retransmission service for broadcasting was not explicitly mentioned in the 1934 Communications Act. At last, the agency settled on regulating cable as "ancillary to broadcasting." This authority was confirmed by Congress in the 1984 Cable Communications Act. In its Computer Inquiries in the 1970s and 1980s, the FCC wrestled with the question of its authority over information services and computer processing services. Over a twenty-year period starting in 2000 as part of its attempt to establish policy on network neutrality rules, the agency went back and forth on defining internet access service as a regulated telecommunications service or an unregulated information service.

These examples from the communications industry show that the difficulty of applying regulatory categories to shifting technology and business models is nothing new. The legislation setting up the digital regulator should provide clear authority over specific digital sectors that are the source of the greatest concern in connection with competition, privacy, and content moderation, and it should also create a fair and efficient procedure and standard for expanding that authority to new digital sectors to keep up with changing business models and technology.

Digital industries are particularly in need of a regulatory agency with clear authority to regulate specific enumerated lines of business. As we have discussed throughout this book the core digital industries that are of greatest policy concern are electronic commerce, search, social media services, mobile app infrastructure, and the complex of digital ad technology services. Leaving out any one of these digital services will continue to expose users and the public competition, privacy, and content moderation abuses. The digital regulator should have immediate and unquestionable authority to take action in each of these digital services.

Enabling legislation should also authorize the agency to regulate more broadly. Digital companies have shown repeatedly that they can invent and rapidly dominate new digital services that almost overnight become integral to the conduct of daily life. It makes little sense to require the digital agency to return to Congress whenever technological and economic developments create a new digital line of business that presents the significant risks of harm to competition, consumer privacy, and fair and effective content moderation.

The history of public utility regulation shows the futility of relying on legislatures to ensure a timely growth and consolidation of regulatory jurisdiction as technology and business models change. It took almost fifty years (from 1871 to 1919) for the legislature to grant the Massachusetts Department of Public Utilities responsibilities over railroads, gas and electricity, telephones, street railways, and steamships. At the national level, Congress had to act to grant the ICC, established in 1887, the additional authority to deal with interstate trucking in 1935 and to regulate domestic water carriers in 1940, thereby bringing the different transportation modes under a single regulatory umbrella. These legislative delays suggest the need for a regulatory agency to have discretion to expand its authority to respond rapidly to today's rapidly changing digital environment.[17] But the agency should not have the authority to extend its own jurisdiction without limit. The outer bounds of the lines of business over which the digital regulator may exercise authority should be set by the legislation itself.

Many proposals limit the digital regulator to have authority only over digital platforms. Public interest advocate Harold Feld, Jason Furman's report on digital markets, and the Stigler Center report on digital competition all focus on platforms as the key business structure to regulate.[18] These reports define their subject matter in terms of very general economic and technical characteristics, including usage of the internet or other information and communications technologies, the provision of service to two or more sides of a multisided market, the presence of significant network effects, and (sometimes) other barriers to entry.

This notion of digital platform will not work as a way to limit the jurisdiction of the digital regulator. It is both too broad and too narrow. In one sense of the word, platforms with network effects seem to be everywhere. Newspapers, broadcasters, cable companies, social media companies, and search engines link advertisers to an audience. Taxi companies and Uber both link drivers to riders. Communications networks link senders to receivers of messages. Record companies and streaming music services link artists to listeners. Multiple listing services connect housing buyers to sellers. E-prescription companies link doctors to pharmacies. Payment companies link merchants to cardholders. Retail outlets link manufacturers to final customers. Bookstores link book publishers to readers. Once they go online, they are all digital platforms. Moreover, all these businesses exhibit the classic indirect network effect where many people on one side of the market (such as suppliers) creates demand for many people on the other (such as buyers). A digital regulator will not be properly cabined if it can extend its jurisdiction (with the right showing) to all these industries and services.[19]

The notion of platform also has the opposite problem that, in some usages at least, it is potentially too narrow. As some analysts use the word, a company is a platform only when it provides a way for independent third parties to transact business or exchange content. The platform connects them but is not a party to the transaction or the exchange. In this way of thinking about a platform, a marketplace like eBay is a platform, but an online retail store like Walmart.com is not. When I buy from Walmart.com, the store sells me something. In contrast, when I buy from a merchant on eBay, the merchant sells me something. When I take an Uber, I pay the driver, who turns over part of the payment to the company; in contrast, when I take a cab, I pay the taxicab company that, in turn, pays the driver a salary based on a percentage of the fare. Uber is a platform that links independent contractors and riders, but a taxicab company is not because its drivers are employees. In this way of thinking, Airbnb is a platform, but a hotel is not. As a guest of an Airbnb host, you pay the host, and Airbnb collects a 3 percent cut. YouTube is a platform where you directly access the video content creators provide, but Netflix curates the content for you and lets you see only the content it has selected or produced itself. Facebook is a platform, but the online news site BuzzFeed is not because Facebook doesn't produce its own content or select it, while Buzzfeed produces original news reports and commentary for your consumption.

This obscurity in the notion of a platform, especially in electronic commerce, affects the scope of the House Judiciary Committee antitrust reform bills that passed the committee in June 2021. Press reports at the time suggested the only thing that would prevent Walmart from being covered by the bills is its size.[20] But this might not be the case. The definition of a "covered platform" in the bills seems to suggest that no matter how big Walmart's online retail store gets it will not be covered. This is because it does not "facilitate" transactions between consumers and "businesses not controlled by the platform." The consumer transacts with Walmart, not Walmart's vendors. Walmart's online retail store acts as the final link in the vertical distribution chain, taking possession of goods obtained from a supplier at wholesale prices and reselling them at a retail rate. Its main retail business does not provide a service to separate retail merchants seeking to reach their own customers.

Amazon, too, might be able to circumvent coverage under these bills. If it were forced to separate commerce and platform, and it sold off its marketplace and returned to the "everything store" it previously was before it opened itself to third-party merchants, it would no longer "facilitate" transactions between consumers and "businesses not controlled by the platform." As a result, it would no longer be covered by the law and would be beyond the reach of the digital regulator. The agency would be unable to regulate the contracts that Amazon might sign with its formerly owned marketplace to recreate the self-preferencing that motivated the separation to begin with.

Amazon has discovered that this distinction between store and marketplace has collapsed in the context of product liability claims. Two court cases from 2020 and 2021, *Bolger v. Amazon* and *Loomis v. Amazon*, for instance, have interpreted Amazon's position as a platform operator to provide no immunity from product liability suits. The court found the company has a "pivotal" place in the "chain of distribution" between customer and third-party merchants, regardless of whether it is called a "retailer," "distributor," or merely "facilitator."[21] Recognizing the changed legal reality, Amazon switched and supported a California bill, which died in 2020 in the California Senate, that would have codified these rulings, provided that the bill included "all online marketplaces regardless of their business models."[22]

The distinction between retailer and marketplace might not be so crucial for competition policy, either. Walmart has only 6 percent of the online retail market, but it unquestionably provides some online competition to Amazon from the point of view of retail customers. It should not be excluded simply from digital regulation because its business model is not primarily that of a platform.

Competition, privacy, and content moderation issues can arise regardless of the form the business adopts in its relationship with its suppliers. Narrowing the possible scope of the digital regulator to include just business platforms might leave important problems unaddressed.

The UK government recognized this problem when it rejected the concept of a digital platform in its competition reform legislation. It noted the "risks associated with narrowing the scope of the regime to 'digital platform activities' as this could rule out circumstances where there are competition concerns that would best be addressed by this regime."[23]

This is not the first time the notion of a platform has arisen in connection with attempts to rein in the behavior of corporations. The 2018 Supreme Court case concerning Amex's anti-steering business rules for merchants pitted those who thought two-sided platform businesses required a special, and weaker, set of antitrust rules—and therefore wanted to permit the Amex rule—against those businesses that deserved no special antitrust treatment and that therefore wanted to strike down the rules as anticompetitive.[24]

A group of legal academics headed by the acknowledged leading scholar in the antitrust field, Herbert Hovenkamp, argued strongly against special antitrust status for companies that linked two sides of a market. They insisted that "two-sidedness is ultimately a description of *a business model*, not a 'market' at all." Uber and regular taxi drivers operate in the same market, they noted, even though one uses a two-sided business model and the other does not. There shouldn't be one set of antitrust rules for Uber and another for ordinary taxi drivers.[25]

In its Amex filing, the Open Markets Institute—a progressive antitrust advocacy group—also rejected the idea that platforms deserve special antitrust treatment, noting that businesses can choose their preferred business model:

> *Whether a firm gets characterized as a "two-sided" platform may also come to depend on its chosen business model. For example, Netflix charges consumers for content without also seeking advertising revenue, and so would likely be considered "one-sided." . . . But a service like Hulu that charges both consumers and advertisers would be "two-sided." The distinction here would be based not on the market in which these firms operate, but on the specific business strategy they adopt.*[26]

In the end, the Supreme Court sided with Amex, ruling that the antitrust laws should give special treatment to simultaneous, two-sided "transactions" markets. The effect of this ruling for other two-sided markets is unclear since the Court created substantial uncertainty by appearing to exclude from this special treatment two-sided markets like advertising markets where indirect network effects are not very strong.

Opponents of the Amex decision pointed out that a special and weaker antitrust rule for two-sided markets would give businesses facing antitrust liability an incentive to re-describe themselves as two-sided. Given the ubiquity of businesses that fit the economic model of two-sidedness, this might be a real danger.

Defining the jurisdiction of the new regulatory agency as a subset of companies with a two-sided business model creates opportunities for the opposite kind of mischief. Companies seeking to avoid regulation would no longer characterize themselves as two-sided platforms and would thereby slip out from under digital regulation. It would allow digital companies to use the same kind of redescription of its business that Uber uses to evade labor laws by insisting it is a technology platform, not a taxi company.

Advocates for greater regulatory controls on tech companies cannot be opportunistic on the utility of the concept of multisided market platforms. If the concept is so opaque and slippery that it cannot be used as the basis for a special antitrust rule, then it surely cannot be the basis for an entirely new competition regime.

Still, either the notion of two-sidedness is clear enough for use in competition policy or it is not. It cannot be embraced when the issue is expanding regulatory controls to combat the pernicious consequences of strong network effects and rejected as hopelessly unclear when it is a question of a weakening competition policy tools aiming to deal with the same problem.

In the case of social media, however, the notion of a platform is crucial. Social media companies, by definition, provide a platform for users to communicate with an indefinitely large group of other users. They provide a forum for the speech of others. It is this promise of openness to all speakers that justifies the requirements of due process and transparency, and the implicit limited right to carriage that these requirements create. Under the legislation proposed here, other online entities such as online news sites have no such obligations because they restrict speakers to a specially chosen group of employees or contractors.

It would only make sense to apply due process and transparency rules to platforms that hold themselves out as forums for the speech of others. This, however, is not a limitation on the jurisdiction of the digital regulator, but a limitation on the proper and sensible application of the regulator's authority. It would be bad policy, perhaps even arbitrary and capricious, to extend due process and transparency requirements to an online news site because the public has no expectation of being able to contribute to the news stories and so no implicit right to speak there if it follows the site's content rules—but that is not because a digital news site is forever outside the reach of the digital regulator.

The United Kingdom adopted the right approach to defining digital industries in its proposed new procompetition regime for digital markets. This proposal would limit the scope of the regime to activities where digital technologies are a "core component" of the products and services provided as part of that activity. The idea is to "rule out of scope activities which have a digital component but are essentially non-digital, while preserving flexibility to respond to new digital business models where firms with [strategic market status] could emerge."[27]

The UK government rejected a suggestion from its digital task force to cover all activities where digital technologies are "material to" the activity. This suggestion cast the regulatory net too wide and would cover businesses where the use of digital technologies was not essential to the service it was providing. The use of digital technology must be an essential, core part of the business. For instance, a brick-and-mortar store that opened an ancillary online presence would not be covered under this definition of a digital industry because its use of digital technology was only incidental to its main business. Some companies use digital technologies to facilitate certain aspects of business operations such as airlines offering online booking for flights or companies that use websites to provide information about their services. But this should not be enough to bring them within scope. The requirement that the use of digital technologies must be a "core component" of the business serves to exclude them.

The legislation for a US digital regulator should adopt this approach toward expanding the scope of its jurisdiction beyond the digital industries specifically enumerated in the law. The notion of a digital industry as an industry that uses digital technologies as a core or essential component of the service it provides should be written into the law as a limit on the agency's ability to expand its jurisdiction.

In light of some concerns about the workability of the "core component" definition of digital activities, the UK government indicated in May 2022 that it was considering alternative ways of defining the "digital activities" at which the new competition regime is targeted. The legislation ultimately introduced in April 2023 uses instead the notion of a service provided "by means of the internet" or the provision of one or more pieces of "digital content." However, this overly broad notion is even less workable than the "core component" idea. The US approach should stay with the "core component" idea.[28]

It is worth listing some examples of digital activities that might be within scope under this definition of digital industries as ones where the use of digital technologies is a core component of the service. This list should be incorporated into the statute or its legislative history as a nonexclusive list of digital activities that are potentially within the jurisdiction of the digital agency. It could include video conferencing services like Zoom, Teams, and WebEx; TV operating systems like Roku; home assistants like Alexa; door monitoring security services like Ring; streaming TV services like Netflix, Prime Video, and Hulu; online music streaming services like Spotify, Apple Music, and SiriusXM; grocery delivery services such as Instacart, DoorDash, and Uber Eats; taxi services such as Uber and Lyft; house and apartment rental services such as Airbnb and Vrbo; online video gaming services like Xbox, PlayStation, and Nintendo; and connected virtual reality platforms like Oculus, Sony VR, and HTC VIVE. As Facebook moves into the metaverse, the digital regulator should be able to follow the company there if its new activities present substantial risks to competition, privacy, and content moderation.

The metaverse is a good example of how such a flexible system might work. Digital legislation in Europe and the United Kingdom has broad definitions of the activities their digital laws cover. In both cases, the definitions are broad enough so that the metaverse would be covered. In October 2022, the head of Ofcom, the UK agency that would implement the proposed Online Safety Act, said the agency was "in good stead" to regulate the metaverse. When asked by the European Parliament whether the Digital Markets Act and the Digital Services Act covered the metaverse, a European Commission official replied in June 2022 that these laws "provide the appropriate framework and the necessary tools to tackle issues concerning metaverse." In contrast, the United States tried to get at the metaverse through a long-shot antitrust case that failed to block Meta's acquisition of a virtual app provider.[29]

In a flexible digital regulatory system in the United States, the digital regulator would not be able to regulate the metaverse as a matter of statutory authority. The only lines of business immediately under its jurisdiction would be social media, e-commerce, search, ad tech, and mobile apps. The metaverse does not fit there. It does, however, use digital technology as an essential core part of the service it provides. As a result, the digital agency could reach out and cover the metaverse, provided it follows the appropriate process and makes the necessary findings.

Due process safeguards would be essential to ensure that the interests of the affected firms are protected as the agency seeks to expand its scope. The process for expanding jurisdiction would require a full Administrative Procedure Act rulemaking, with the possibility of judicial review, thereby providing protections against arbitrary or capricious agency action or action that extends beyond the agency's statutory authority.

In addition, Congress could require the filing of initial reports or delays on the effective date of any final action to allow Congress the opportunity to review the decision and take action under the Congressional Review Act to disapprove the decision.

When should the digital regulator reach out to bring a segment of the digital world within its regulatory scope? Two conditions need to be satisfied. The first is a finding that the service provided is central to a large range of activities in contemporary life. The second is that there has been a failure of the normal mechanisms of competition and the emergence of companies that dominate the industrial segment. I turn now to a discussion of those criteria.

Defining Dominance and Centrality

In proposed UK legislation for a new digital competition regime, the standard of strategic market status emerged as a trigger for applying the new procompetitive rules.[30] The idea is that a company will be designated as having strategic market status when it has "substantial and entrenched market power" in at least one digital activity, giving it a strategic position. A company's market power would be considered "substantial" when users of a firm's product or service lack good alternatives to that product or service and there is a limited threat of entry or expansion by other suppliers. A company's market power would be "entrenched" when it is not merely transitory and likely to be competed away so that the likelihood of a rival emerging and taking a substantial share of the market is low. In addition, the firm's substantial and entrenched market power must provide it with a "strategic position" in which the effects of its market power are likely to be particularly widespread or significant.

Under the UK approach, once each of these three necessary conditions is satisfied—substantial and entrenched market power leading to a strategic position—the digital regulator could designate a company as having strategic market status and bring it within scope of the new competition regime. The UK government is also considering a minimum revenue threshold to ensure that smaller firms are not within scope.[31]

The legislation creating the digital regulator in the United States should adapt this notion of strategic market status as a way to define dominance in the core digital industries under its jurisdiction. Assessing substantial and entrenched market power would involve the usual antitrust tools, including measuring firm size and market share, but without the need to define a precise antitrust market. The digital regulator would look at, for instance, whether consumers or businesses could "credibly switch to an alternative service offered by another company without losing out, and the ease with which other firms could enter and expand." The agency would also need to determine that the market power is not likely to be eroded through competitive entry or expansion so that it is likely to persist.

The digital regulator would also have to assess whether a firm had strategic position—that is, the ability to use its market power in a significant way across a range of activities. Based on the UK approach, the new law could require the US digital regulator to assess strategic position looking at five criteria: whether the size or scale of the firm's activity is significant, whether the firm is a gateway for a diverse range of other activities, whether the firm can use its activity to entrench its market power or extend it to other activities, whether the firm can impose rules or business practices on other firms, and whether the activity has significant impacts on markets that may have broader social and cultural impact.

The UK government rejected this last cultural criterion that had been proposed by the digital markets task force because it wanted to focus its new digital markets unit on competition issues. But the US digital regulator would have a broader mandate to cover privacy and content moderation issues, and so a criterion that looks at the broader social and cultural impacts would be appropriate.

Once a company is designated as having strategic market status, the full regime of procompetition tools, digital privacy rules, and content moderation regulations would apply. The digital regulator would have authority to forbear from applying some or all these rules for companies in core digital industries lacking strategic market status.

For the digital regulator to extend its authority to a new digital sector, it must do more than show that there is a failure of competition through the emergence of a dominant company. The notion of a public utility in US law and policy can help to focus this test of centrality.

The legal history of public utility regulation begins with the 1877 Supreme Court case of *Munn v. Illinois*, which held that government could regulate private enterprise when "such regulation becomes necessary for the public good." In particular, the court held that the state is justified in imposing regulation when "property is affected with a public interest." The court further specified that "property does become clothed with a public interest when used in a manner to make it of public consequence and affect the community at large."[32]

As legal scholar William Novak has noted, in its original meaning as part of the progressive movement in the early twentieth century, the idea of a public utility covered broad swaths of the nation's economic life, including from urban transportation to ice plants. Progressive reformers such as Rexford Tugwell thought the sphere of public service regulation included railways, water companies, hotels, telephone companies, bridges, stockyards, stock exchanges. creameries, news distributors, rental housing, banking, and fire insurance.[33]

The Supreme Court rejected the idea that public utility status was a requirement for the state to exercise regulatory authority in the 1934 ruling that legislatures could regulate any business so long as they had a rational basis for doing so, requiring not special status as affected with the public interest. It required only that the regulation was not "unreasonable, arbitrary or capricious, and that the means selected shall have a real and substantial relation to the object sought to be attained."[34]

Despite its originally very broad usage, the term "public utility" has come to be associated with monopoly providers of service in a rather restricted range of industries such as water, electricity, and gas. These companies are thought to be natural monopolies, where single firms are the most efficient provider of a service. But this common conception is too narrow.

As the former president of the public interest group Demo and law professor K. Sabeel Rahman notes, the notion of public utility is useful as a line dividing businesses that need enhanced, industry-specific regulation versus companies that are subject only to generally applicable rules.[35] In particular, Rahman says, businesses are thought of as public utilities when the products or services they supply are essential to the ordinary business of life, and there is some kind of failure of competition in the marketplace in which they operate.

Drawing on Louis Brandeis's dissent in *New State Ice Co. v. Liebmann*, Rahman separates public utilities from other companies because they "provided necessities of life" such as companies that produce ice, and so "could be regulated more stringently as public utilities to ensure that the production and distribution of these goods were managed in accordance with the public good."

Rahman adds, however, a monopoly condition, but that is not key to the idea of a public utility. The key is the industries exhibit "a moral or social importance that made the industries too vital to be left to the whims of the market or the control of a handful of private actors." They are "vital industries that provided foundational goods and services on which the rest of society depended."

The essence of the notion of a public utility is centrality of economic role, the fact that many people depend on the service to live their lives or play their own economic role. Orla Lynskey helpfully crystalizes the public utility idea as "a business that furnishes an everyday necessity to the public at large."[36] The products or services provided by such businesses are needed by large numbers of people to engage in the ordinary business of life.

The history of public service regulation reflects this focus on centrality. Economic historian Thomas K. McCraw records the basis for Charles Adams's administration of the Massachusetts Board of Railroad Commissioners as "the centrality of the railroad industry to the people of the state, most of whom encountered railroads in their daily lives."[37] The fact that a company fulfilling such a role was a monopoly provider might affect the nature of the economic regulation, but a company fulfilling that role without holding a monopoly position would not automatically escape the need for some special enhanced level of social control of its activities. The key was social need. In an almost contemporary account of the Mann-Elkins Act of 1910 that strengthened the ICC's authority in railroad regulation, an economist remarked that the new law responded to "the demand of the people of the country, constantly becoming more insistent, for genuine regulation of the industry upon which their very life depends."[38]

This focus on social necessity, on the centrality or criticality of economic function, rather than just on monopoly, was evident, for instance, in the early movement for railroad regulation. To be sure, "captive shippers" complained about monopoly railroads extorting high prices on short-haul lines. But customers of long-haul service (such as between New York and Chicago), which was often provided by competing railroads, complained it was the very competition between railroads that produced a bewildering pattern of preferential rates, rebates, and discounts that favored some customers over others and made it impossible for consumers to rationally choose, driving a demand for standardized nondiscriminatory rates set by tariff, even in the presence of competition.[39]

In some parts of the country, the railroad problem was excessive competition, not uncontrolled monopoly. McCraw says, "In the East, the major regulatory issue often had to do with excessive competition: too many railroads handled too little freight." He adds that pricing was a regulatory issue not just because it was set at monopoly levels but also because of the rate structure, in which different classes of shippers were charged different rates for the same service "often violated deep-seated popular conceptions of fairness."[40]

Law professor Brett M. Frischmann has developed a modern version of the notion of public utility with his concept of an infrastructure resource. He says that infrastructure resources "satisfy the following criteria: (1) The resource may be consumed nonrivalrously for some appreciable range of demand. (2) Social demand for the resource is driven primarily by downstream productive activity that requires the resource as an input. (3) The resource may be used as an input into a wide range of goods and services, which may include private goods, public goods, and social goods." While he mentions such supply-side issues as production externalities, his real concern is demand-side—that is, the fact that infrastructural resources are "basic inputs into a wide variety of productive activities . . . [that] often produce public and social goods that generate spillovers that benefit society as a whole." The structure of the market or the economic dominance of the suppliers are not the key considerations for Frischmann. His policy recommendation is that "we should share infrastructure resources in an open, nondiscriminatory manner when it is feasible to do so."[41]

Drawing on Frischmann's work, Rahman developed the notion of an "infrastructure" company and then further refines that notion into the conception of an "information infrastructure company. He first defines "infrastructure" as "those goods and services which (i) have scale effects in their production or provision suggesting the need for some degree of market or firm concentration; (ii) unlock and enable a wide variety of downstream economic and social activities for those with access to the good or service; and (iii) place users in a position of potential subordination, exploitation, or vulnerability if their access to these goods or services is curtailed in some way."[42]

This notion of infrastructure adds the notion of potential abuse to the traditional public utility concept of an essential service provided by a company facing limited competition. But it is still an economywide notion, encompassing companies that provide a vast array of products and services in both the digital and the nondigital environment.

Rahman further refines this general notion of infrastructure into a more specific notion of informational infrastructure as a basis for regulation of digital companies like Facebook and Google.[43] In that framework a company becomes an informational infrastructure firm when it operates at scale, it enables "widespread 'downstream uses' as inputs into a plethora of economic and social uses and activities," and its users are vulnerable to abuse. In addition, information infrastructure companies exercise gatekeeper power over their users, whereby they control access to the infrastructure itself, and they hold transmission power, whereby they control the flow of information and activity among the users.

Crucially, an informational infrastructure company is to be distinguished from a regular infrastructure company because it is essentially involved in the transmission and processing of information among its users. Rahman says, "As these platforms become more widely used, they become more necessary for access to information." Rahman also notes that "these platform companies can structure—and manipulate—the flows of information and activity among participants once they enter into the platform or network."

Rahman's notion of an information infrastructure aligns very closely with the UK standard of a firm with strategic market status and helps to elaborate the standard of a "strategic" position. For the US law setting up the digital regulatory agency, it provides a factor that the digital regulator should take into account in assessing whether a digital service has a central position in the life of the community.

The notion of unavoidability also helps illuminate the idea of centrality as a condition for extending the regulatory reach of the digital agency. Law professor Lauren Scholz notes, "Five companies in particular—Amazon, Apple, Facebook, Google, and Microsoft—are virtually impossible for the average American consumer to avoid."[44] In 2019, tech reporter Kashmir Hill tried to stay away from Google, Apple, Facebook, Microsoft, and Amazon for six weeks and found the experience to be "hell."[45] The fact that certain people with heroic efforts can isolate themselves from the services provided by ubiquitous technology companies does not demonstrate that these services are avoidable in any realistic sense. Ordinary people using reasonable methods of self-help simply cannot escape the reach of these vital technologies.

Privacy scholar Laura Moy has tried to develop this notion of unavoidability in the context of information sharing. She notes, "People do not have much of a choice when it comes to sharing information with healthcare providers, education providers, and financial providers. These are essential services—they are necessary and unavoidable parts of participating fully in modern society."[46]

Her notion of unavoidability is the idea that information sharing is unavoidable when it is necessary for the receipt of essential services. The notion thus incorporates both the necessity of providing information in order to get a service and the necessity of the service itself as elements of unavoidability. Patients, for instance, cannot avoid giving information to doctors to receive service, and receiving medical care is itself an essential service. When these two conditions hold then, Moy maintains, information sharing is unavoidable and special privacy rules are needed.

In her conception, the presence of many alternative suppliers does not mitigate the unavoidability. If a patient is to get medical care, he or she would have to provide information to any of the thousands of doctors who could provide it. Moy is going beyond monopoly and competition issues and dealing with what services are essential and what information is needed to provide that service. The lack of consumer alternatives doesn't seem to be the heart of what her notion of unavoidability is aiming to capture. The lack of consumer alternatives, in her view, exacerbates the unavoidability, but is not essential to it.

This idea of centrality of a service is also illustrated in Harold Feld's notion of the cost of exclusion.[47] As part of his comprehensive legislative proposal to promote competition and other social values in digital platform markets, he describes a new measure of platform dominance called the cost of exclusion. He proposes that a company be considered dominant when the cost of exclusion from the company's service is too high. The paradigm case is exclusion from a communications network.[48]

Cost of exclusion is more applicable as a measure of the centrality of a service than to dominance of a firm. As a new technological innovation becomes more and more embedded in the everyday lives of people, it increases in the intrinsic value it provides to users. Its growing ubiquity means that complementary goods and services are gradually built up around it. The introduction of cars and electricity and telephones had this feature that, as they spread more and more of everyday life, came to depend on having access to these products and services in order for people to work, play, feed themselves, and obtain ordinary goods and services. Conversely, the lack of a car, electricity, or telephone service became more and more costly as the use of these infrastructure products increased.

Still this notion of rising costs of exclusion does not always apply at the level of the firm providing a new technology. When there is only one provider, as essentially there was during much of the history of the telephone network, the technology and the provider of the technology become the same. But if there are many providers of the new technology, it is less clear that the cost of exclusion from the technology is under the control of any one provider. With even three car manufacturers, it would be hard to maintain that any one of them had the power to exclude people from the use of cars. Cost of exclusion therefore measures in an intuitive way when the value of a new technology has increased to the point that it is a central element in a country's way of life.

These notions of an information infrastructure, unavoidable information sharing, and costs of exclusion should be considered when the digital agency wants to extend its authority to new digital lines of business. They can help to define the necessary condition of centrality of digital service. It is not enough that a sector be digital. It is not enough that it is dominated by a single firm or a small number of firms. In addition, the service must have a central position in the everyday life of the community for the digital regulator to extend its reach to cover it.

Agency Structure and Jurisdiction

This section discusses a range of important issues in setting up a digital regulatory agency, including whether it will have exclusive jurisdiction over competition, privacy, and content moderation for digital industries; provisions for independence, or limited authority and accountability; its internal organization; and the resources needed to carry out its responsibilities.

Exclusive Jurisdiction

An agency able to do the job of regulating today's digital industry and flexible enough to keep up with tomorrow's challenges must be a new sector-specific institution with policy mandates in all three policy areas of competition, privacy, and content moderation. As an interim measure, the FTC can play this role, with only limited adjustments to its mandate and jurisdiction. This seems to be the likeliest path for Congress to take in establishing a digital regulator. Ultimately, however, this role will have to be assigned to a new rulemaking agency, focused solely on digital industries. This choice, then, raises the question concerning the relationship between the authority of the new agency and that of existing antitrust agencies.

This is not a question of whether the old antitrust laws should be repealed for digital industries and replaced with the new procompetitive measures. The new digital requirements should build on the strictures in traditional antitrust law against unreasonable restraints on competition and monopolization, except with mergers where the new more stringent review standard should replace the old one.

The question is which agency should have authority to enforce the old antitrust laws. Should the new digital regulator also be the enforcer of traditional antitrust law for digital industries? Or should the existing antitrust authorities retain their old jurisdiction over digital industries? For reasons outlined in this section, the better course is to transfer all antitrust authority to the new digital agency.

The enabling legislation setting up a new digital agency could leave the existing authority of the antitrust agencies unchanged through a savings clause. The 1996 Telecommunications Act, for instance, set up a comprehensive, procompetitive regime for the industry through the FCC but explicitly said, "Nothing in this Act or the amendments made by this Act shall be construed to modify, impair, or supersede the applicability of any of the antitrust laws."[49] This savings clause meant that the new FCC regulatory regime did not displace existing antitrust authority; more important, it left antitrust enforcement authority with the traditional agencies. The FCC would enforce the new procompetition measures, but the Department of Justice and the FTC would retain their traditional authority over the antitrust laws.

As applied to the new digital regulator, this approach would mean that the new digital agency would leave existing antitrust law intact but go beyond the old antitrust limitations in the case of digital industries. It would supplement and reinforce the antitrust laws rather than replace them or contradict them. It would not repeal the old antitrust laws with respect to digital industries but supplement them with new, more powerful procompetitive tools. This is the approach recommended in the Shorenstein Center's report, for instance.[50]

This approach, however, risks creating exactly the kind of unresolvable conflict among policy objectives that the choice of a single agency was designed to avoid. In its 2000 *Trinko* decision, the Supreme Court examined a refusal to deal complaint involving the 1996 Telecommunications Act. The Court warned against "the real possibility of [antitrust] judgments conflicting with the agency's regulatory scheme." The Court was thinking of the possibility that conduct permitted, or even encouraged, by the regulator might be the target of antitrust activity.

This could happen in the case of the digital regulator. The digital agency might require a company to withhold certain personal data from competitors to protect privacy while an independent antitrust agency, thinking information was vital to spur competition and the privacy claim was merely pretextual, might file a complaint seeking to override the digital agency's judgment. We have already seen how this potential conflict could be made real in the ad-tech industry, where UK competition authorities have indicated concerns about efforts to restrict the use of cookies, and in the news business where the Australian competition authority has encouraged tech companies like Google and Facebook to share users' personal information with news sites to enable them to provide more accurately targeted ads.

The downside of a savings clause leaving antitrust authority in the hands of traditional enforcers is a considerable risk of regulatory incoherence. However, there is not much to be gained from leaving antitrust authority for digital industries in the hands of the traditional enforcement agencies. The *Trinko* Court also noted that, in analyzing whether a firm has a duty to deal, "one factor of particular importance is the existence of a regulatory structure designed to deter and remedy anticompetitive harm. Where such a structure exists, the additional benefit to competition provided by antitrust enforcement will tend to be small." This is especially true when the digital regulatory structure is deliberately designed to replace the ineffective ex-post regime of antitrust enforcement with a more robust scheme of ex-ante procompetitive rules. For instance, the procompetitive regulatory structure explicitly sets up a duty to deal for digital companies with strategic market status, which again, according to the *Trinko* decision, is largely beyond the reach of antitrust law.

Law professor Samuel Weinstein notes this advantage of encouraging competition through regulation, rather than traditional antitrust. He remarks in connection with structural regulation of financial markets, "The difficulty of prevailing on the sorts of antitrust claims that arise in markets involving competitive bottlenecks suggests that structural regulation indeed may do a better job safeguarding competition than antitrust enforcers or private plaintiffs suing under the antitrust laws can do under current law."[51]

Alternatively, the new procompetitive measures could be assigned to the old competition authority. This approach is adopted in the legislation that passed the House Judiciary Committee in June 2021. It authorized the existing antirust agencies to take the additional steps outlined in the bill to promote competition in digital industries.[52]

This would resolve any possible conflict between the demands of the old antitrust laws and the new procompetitive measures. And if privacy and content moderation were also assigned to an antitrust agency like the FTC, this would resolve the potential conflicts. As indicated earlier, however, this is best thought of as an interim measure not a permanent solution.

Alternatively, the enabling legislation could remain silent on the question of the assignment of regulatory jurisdiction and leave the matter up to the vagarics of court application of the doctrine of implied immunity. Under this doctrine of implied immunity, regulated companies can sometimes gain immunity from enforcement actions by the antitrust agencies. The courts rarely endorse implied immunity and then only when there is a conflict between antitrust and the regulatory scheme, and immunity is needed to make the regulatory scheme work. In the case of securities law, for instance, the Supreme Court in *Credit Suisse* laid out four factors that could lead to a conclusion of implied antitrust immunity in a particular case, including (1) the existence of regulatory authority (2) that a responsible agency is exercising and (3) a risk of conflict between antitrust and regulatory requirements that is (4) within the area of the regulatory authority's jurisdiction.[53]

This course of kicking the issue to the courts is unsatisfactory. For one thing, it leaves the immunity question open for each new case of potential conflict and would require an extensive court review to determine in each of these cases which agency has ultimate authority—the antitrust enforcer or the digital regulator. Remaining silent on the question in the legislation authorizing the digital regulator would do more harm than good by prolonging uncertainty. It would just turn the question over to endless litigation rather than have Congress answer it.

Finally, the enabling legislation could expressly reserve exclusive antitrust authority to the new digital agency. The need to avoid policy conflicts among competition, privacy, and content moderation favors this last alternative as the best way to prevent competition authorities from acting at cross-purposes with the new digital agency.

The same issue of whether a generalist antitrust enforcer should regulate digital industries arises in the case of privacy enforcement. A new comprehensive privacy law might assign enforcement to an economywide privacy regulator. But a digital regulator with expertise in the line of business it is regulating would be a better job of finding areas of privacy abuse in those lines of business than an economywide regulator. A digital privacy regulator would also be able to apply comprehensive privacy requirements to digital companies and enforce them in nuanced and flexible ways to meet the needs of digital companies and users. It makes no sense to have two privacy regulators for a digital company, especially if they are seeking to enforce the same general standards. But these considerations suggest that the comprehensive privacy law should assign enforcement to a digital regulator.

In practice, these issues of exclusive jurisdiction would not arise immediately. As noted in the introduction to this chapter, Congress appears to be legislating separately in competition, privacy, and content moderation, but it seems to be assigning enforcement authority in each of these areas to the FTC. At least for a transition period, then, the FTC is likely to be the digital regulator, with authority to enforce traditional antitrust law, the new procompetition measures, the new privacy requirements, and the new content moderation rules. This approach would resolve the issue of exclusive jurisdiction during this transition.

When Congress transfers the FTC's authority over digital industries to the new digital agency, it can address the question of exclusive jurisdiction at that point. It would make sense to transfer the authority to enforce the old competition laws and the new procompetitive measures to the new agency. It would also make sense to allow the new digital regulator full authority to enforce the privacy requirement for digital industries.

Another jurisdictional question arises in connection with state law. The laws creating digital responsibilities in competition, privacy, and content moderation should preempt inconsistent state laws in the areas of privacy and content moderation to make sure the country has a single, uniform national policy in this vital area. It is true that the FTC and the state attorneys general share authority to enforce the antitrust laws, and this has had the healthy effect of enlarging the resources needed to protect competition. But this should change for the new digital procompetitive measures. A centralization of regulation and enforcement for the procompetitive measures is needed to jump-start competition in the digital industries and to protect dependent users. No one would benefit from multiple interpretations of an interoperability requirement, for instance, that could arise if each state had its own jurisdiction over the new competition tools. Similar confusion would arise if fifty states had their own versions of transparency requirements. A single uniform national policy in digital competition, privacy and content moderation is needed.

Independence

The enabling legislation that establishes a new sectoral agency for digital industries must also provide for independence, restricted authority, and accountability. It is urgent to get these details of administrative structure right because the agency will be making decisions closely related to the content and diversity of information distributed to the public through digital outlets. Its authority must be properly cabined to prevent partisan abuse of this power.

The digital agency should be independent in its operation, finances, and leadership. Operational independence would ensure that agency decisions are not reviewable or subject to modification or repeal by other parts of the current government. Financial independence would provide that the agency budget would not be subject to the control of another administrative agency in the government. Finances would come from legislative authorizations and appropriations, or from industry service fees.

Congress should avoid the financing structure it established for the CFPB, which is designed to avoid the need for regular congressional appropriations. The CFPB receives its funding through requests made by the CFPB director to the Federal Reserve, which is itself funded outside the appropriations process through interest on the securities it owns. Congress decreed that the CFPB budget could not exceed 12 percent of the Federal Reserve's own budget, required the Federal Reserve to fund CFPB at any requested amount below this cap, and otherwise placed no limit on the funds that could be made available to the Bureau.

This funding mechanism provides financial independence, but too much of it. Congress should always retain control over the activities of regulatory agencies. They are to a great degree "creatures of Congress" designed to carry out quasi-legislative tasks, relying on specific policy and industry expertise that cannot be developed and maintained in a generalist legislative body. One way to ensure this power is exercised in a way consistent with congressional intent is through the power of the purse. The CFPB funding mechanism might also face constitutional obstacles. In October 2022, the Court of Appeals for the Fifth Circuit ruled that CFPB's double-insulated funding mechanism violated the separation of powers.[54]

Leadership independence is perhaps the most crucial form of independence. It would ensure that agency leaders could not be removed by the existing government, except for cause, including inefficiency, neglect of duty, or malfeasance in office. Leadership independence is especially needed to prevent each administration from directly influencing in a partisan way agency action connected to digital content, which it would be more easily able to do if it could remove and replace its director at will.

Instituting such leadership independence is complicated by the *Seila Law v. Consumer Financial Protection Bureau* case, once again involving the CFPB. In this case, the Supreme Court ruled that the head of a single-administrator agency must be subject to executive branch authority.

The head of CPFB, the Court said, must be subject to the president's authority to fire executive branch officials at will. The agency cannot have the leadership independence of an independent multimember commission.[55]

The *Seila* case is consistent with the traditional Supreme Court approval of independent regulatory agencies. In the 1935 *Humphrey's* case involving the FTC, the Court generally upheld the constitutionality of independent regulatory agencies, ruling that Congress had the authority to create expert agencies led by a group of principal officers protected from the president's unrestricted removal power and removable by the president only for good cause.[56] Under this decision, the president would not be free to remove an officer of an independent agency based on disagreements about agency policy or its decisions in particular cases. The Court held that the structure of independent agencies justified this limitation on the president's unrestricted removal authority. The FTC was composed of five members—no more than three from the same political party—and was designed to be "nonpartisan" and to "act with entire impartiality." The FTC's duties were "neither political nor executive" but instead called for "the trained judgment of a body of experts" "informed by experience."

In the *Seila* case, the Court determined that *only* the structure of an independent commission justified the limitation on the president's power to remove agency heads. But in an opinion concurring in part, Justice Thomas joined by Justice Brett Kavanaugh would remove this limitation on presidential removal authority, even for agencies with a commission structure because, in their view, it would create an unaccountable institution. It would have regulatory power, the concurring opinion said, that cannot be checked by the executive branch through the removal of its leaders for policy disagreements. These two justices would repudiate the *Humphrey's* precedent and eliminate the independence of independent agencies. Only time will tell whether the full Court takes this position in a future case.

As a result of this decision, a trade-off now exists in administrative law between a multimember commission whose members can be removed only for cause and a single-administrator agency, whose leader serves at the will of the president. Multimember commissions are less agile and less efficient but more independent than single-administrator agencies. The ideal might be the efficiency of a single administrator and the independence of a multimember commission, which is how the CFPB was originally organized. But the court case rules out this possibility.

Which structure should Congress choose for the digital regulator: single administrator or multimember commission? The fact that the agency will be so close to the content decisions of digital companies prioritizes the need for independence to minimize the risk that the agency could be used to impose a partisan bias on the content judgments of digital companies. Given the court-imposed trade-off, this means that the digital agency would have to be structured as a commission, like the FTC or the FCC. As a traditional regulatory commission, the agency would be led by five commissioners, each nominated by the president and confirmed by the Senate, with no more than three from the same political party.

To help to ensure independence, as well as to mitigate the risk of agency capture as discussed later in this chapter, the term of the agency's commissioners could be extended from its current seven years in the case of an agency like the FTC or five years in the case of the FCC to ten years, with the terms staggered so that a term expires in each even-numbered year. This approach would give the digital agency an extra degree of independence from the current administration.

Limited Authority

The agency would have standard rulemaking authority as provided for under the Administrative Procedure Act.[57] This would require them to publish notices of proposed regulatory action and allow time for interested parties to comment before taking a final action. It would also have authority to make decisions in specific cases using adjudicatory procedures under the APA.[58] All agency actions would be subject to court review to ensure due process, consistency with statutory authority, and a rational relationship between the measure adopted and the policy objectives sought. The agency should be empowered to issue injunctions, assess financial penalties up to a statutory limit, and seek judicial enforcement.

It should also possess the authority to inspect books and records as necessary to carry out its responsibilities under the act.

These authorities should not be unlimited. Operational, leadership, and financial independence provide a firewall, protecting digital companies from partisan abuse by an incumbent administration, but even with these measures in place, the danger of partisan abuse is significant, and the consequences of this abuse would be enormously harmful to our system of political governance. As an extra precaution to prevent this abuse, the authorizing legislation must restrict agency authority. Restricted authority means that even if the agency wanted to improperly influence social media content or other activities of digital companies to pursue a partisan agenda, it would not have the capacity to do so.

One model for ensuring limited authority is a key provision of a proposed social media bill making it clear that the bill would not authorize the regulatory agency to "review any action or decision" by a social media company related to the application of its content standards.[59] Such an anticensorship provision would keep the digital regulator from second-guessing the content decisions of companies in the digital industries.

Under this no-censorship provision, the digital regulator would not be able to act as an external dispute resolution agent, and that is part of its purpose. But the digital regulator would still be able require social media companies to participate in an external dispute resolution service such as the one run by the Financial Industry Regulatory Authority, the self-regulatory organization for the broker-dealer industry. The digital agency would retain supervisory powers without substituting its judgment for that of the privately run dispute resolution system.

The digital regulator would still be able to enforce transparency requirements and other regulatory measures through pattern or practice investigations, similar to enforcement of fair lending laws by financial regulators, rather than through individual determinations of fairness in particular cases. Financial regulators can ensure equal opportunity lending without making individual judgments about creditworthiness or prescribing standards of creditworthiness. If it decides that a formula for determining creditworthiness is discriminatory, it need not prescribe a new formula. Instead, it could simply demand that the financial institution develop a less discriminatory formula. In the same way, a digital regulator can ensure a general practice of fair procedures without making individual content judgments or mandating that companies follow specific procedures.[60]

An anticensorship provision prohibiting content judgments by the digital regulator would provide protection from partisan abuse, even if the courts later strike down the independence of regulatory agencies. A digital agency ordered by the president to engage in partisan content moderation rulings can do so only if Congress gives the agency this power. Prudence strongly suggests Congress should not do so.

Accountability

Agency independence is assured to some degree through operational and financial independence and through the commission structure that provides for leadership independence. But too much independence would mean that the agency could become a law unto itself. This is the fear that motivates Justice Thomas and Justice Gorsuch in *Seila* to seek to end the institution of independent agencies. Despite this concern, an independent commission structure allows for sufficient accountability to the president, Congress, the courts, and the public.

In a commission structure, the president still nominates the commissioners and can remove any of them for cause. Even though the president cannot remove sitting commissioners from office for a policy disagreement, he or she still has powers to hold them accountable. He or she can, for instance, refuse to renominate them to the commission and they will be forced to leave the commission after their term expires. The president also chooses the administrative head of the agency by selecting the chair and can change chairs at will. With authority to remove an agency head at will, the president can direct the regulatory and enforcement focus of the agency and enforce these directions, if necessary, by removing any chair who tries to pursue an independent course. This power cannot direct the outcome of any specific agency action since this depends on a vote of all the commissioners, and the president is powerless to remove any commissioner from the commission itself based on a policy disagreement. This combination of powers thereby balances the need for decisional independence with overall accountability to the president for agency performance.

The agency would be accountable to the legislature as well. Congress must approve the agency's budget and personnel levels. This is why the CFPB's funding mechanism is suspect—it removes this element of accountability. The Senate must approve the leadership and withhold this approval if it lacks confidence in a nominated commissioner. Congressional committees conduct public oversight highlighting potential abuses or agency failures and communicating congressional views on the proper direction of agency activities and priorities. In the extreme, Congress can withdraw authority from the agency in certain areas and can override decisions in particular cases.

In addition, the Congressional Review Act requires agencies to report their rulemaking activities to Congress and provides expedited procedures for Congress to overrule agency action. Once an agency action is overruled, the agency loses authority to reinstate the overruled measure or anything substantially similar to it. Congress has used the power to overturn agency rules in twenty cases since its passage in 1996. Prominent examples include the congressional rejection of the FCC's broadband privacy rule in 2017 and CFPB's auto loan rule in 2018.[61]

The courts also provide a further measure of external accountability. They would have substantial authority over agency procedures and decisions. As we have seen, courts can review decisions for procedural fairness and to prevent arbitrary or capricious actions. It can override agency interpretations of ambiguous provisions in its enabling statute, and in extreme cases it can withdraw agency authority to act in certain areas as unconstitutional delegation of legislative authority. As discussed later in this chapter, the courts are seeking to tighten these measures of control over regulatory agencies.

Additionally, policymakers drafting digital reform legislation can ensure that the public has access to agency decision making by requiring the agency to hold public meetings to discuss and make major, consequential agency determinations and rules. Some agencies such as the FCC have a tradition of holding monthly open meetings to discuss and decide major items. Others such as the FTC never developed such a tradition of public meetings. It was an innovation on the part of Khan, President Biden's FTC head, to begin to hold public FTC meetings in an attempt to promote transparency and accountability to the public.[62]

Co-Regulation

The United Kingdom's initiative to establish new procompetition rules for digital markets relies on consultation with the affected industry. It proposes the creation of enforceable codes of conduct for digital companies with strategic market status. The codes would incorporate statutory objectives of fair trading, open choices, and trust and transparency. These code objectives would be made more precise through legally binding code principles derived from the objectives. For instance, a code principle might be to trade on fair and reasonable terms. Under the government's proposal, these code principles would be set out in statute, but the new digital markets unit in the Competition and Market Authority would have authority to update these code principles. In a key institutional nod to the interests of the affected industry, the CMA would be required to "consult with stakeholders" in constructing the codes and before updating them.[63]

The United States is considering a similar consultative approach in the proposed ACCESS Act that passed the House Judiciary Committee in June 2021. It calls for a "technical committee" to advise the FTC on constructing standards for data portability and interoperability. This committee would be composed of representatives of (1) businesses that utilize or compete with a digital platform, (2) competition or privacy advocates and independent academics, (3) the National Institute of Standards and Technology, and (4) the affected digital platforms. The committee's recommendations are advisory, but the FTC is required to give "strong consideration" to its recommendations. It retains, however, the ultimate authority to issue the recommended implementation standards or to reject them.[64]

It is worth going beyond this consultative approach toward a true co-regulatory engagement with the affected industry. The Shorenstein report calls for a "New Cooperative Industry-Government Regulatory

Model." This model would create "a Code Council composed of industry and public representatives." The Council would create codes of conduct that implement the requirements of the digital legislation. The digital regulator in this model would become "a supervisor of code development and enforcer of the results of a joint public-private effort to establish behavioral codes that carry out the purposes of the statute." The initial agency approach should be to favor "cooperatively developed and enforceable behavioral codes." However, the digital regulator makes the final call. "Where such cooperative activity does not produce results acceptable to the [digital regulator]," the report concludes, "the agency will act on its own."[65]

Congress should build on this suggestion in the Shorenstein report that the rules of the digital road should be developed in concert with the industry itself. This is one way to ensure the agility and flexibility needed to adapt rules to the rapidly changing nature of digital companies. The competition, privacy, and content moderation laws that establish the digital regulator should provide ample authority for the agency to work cooperatively with the industry in setting up enforceable codes of conduct that implement the requirements in the statutes. Enabling legislation should authorize the digital industries to form self-regulatory organizations to work with the digital regulator on the development and enforcement of these codes.

This would mean that the agency would actively encourage digital industry segments to organize themselves into associations that could then propose binding codes for their own conduct consistent with the requirements of the competition, privacy, and content moderation laws. The agency's approval of these codes would transform them into binding rules. For instance, a social media self-regulatory organization could propose common content moderation standards and enforcement measures. The digital agency's approval of these standards would not extend to the content itself but would be restricted to assuring that the organization is properly constituted to represent the industry and has followed appropriate procedures in gaining industry consensus for the standards. As discussed in the chapter on content moderation, enforcement of the content rules themselves would continue to be with the social media firms, with appeal rights to the industry association's arbitration panel.[66]

The models for this co-regulatory approach are the private sector associations that regulate stock exchanges and the broker-dealer industry. The 1934 Securities Act authorized the SEC to recognize these self-regulatory organizations and to work with them to devise rules and regulations to govern the conduct of exchanges and broker dealers. The agency supervises and approves and can modify any of the rules of self-regulatory organizations.[67]

Other countries have embraced this co-regulation approach in the digital space. Australia's 2021 online safety law authorized the eSafety Commissioner to guide the development of new industry codes to regulate harmful online content. These codes are aimed at stopping the online distribution of child sexual abuse material, pro-terror content, and to limit children's exposure to pornography and other harmful material. In September 2021, the eSafety Commissioner announced guidance for the industry in drafting these codes and specified that they will apply to "eight industry sections, including social media services, websites, search engines, app stores, internet service providers, device manufacturers, hosting services, and electronic services, including email, messaging, gaming and dating services." The guidance outlines ways the codes could be enforced including "through technology such as proactive human and machine monitoring, account suspensions and deactivations, deindexing of search results, and the use of forms of age assurance or parental controls." And it insisted that "the responsibility then falls to industry in offering solutions."

Despite this deference to the industry, ultimately the eSafety Commissioner is in charge. It approves the codes it finds acceptable, and if the industry is unable to establish appropriate codes, it has the power to establish binding industry standards. The guidance makes it clear that the agency enforces the codes noting that the commissioner "will be able to receive complaints and investigate potential breaches of the codes or standards, and they will be enforceable by civil penalties, enforceable undertakings and injunctions to ensure compliance."[68]

The digital regulator should be authorized to go beyond the consultative approach and utilize the more participative co-regulatory approach. The idea that the industry itself should help to shape the rules of the road for their industry is sound. At the end of the day, the regulatory agency is responsible for approving and adding to any recommendations from the industry. But the involvement of the industry assures that the digital regulator will have the flexibility to adapt to technical and business developments in the fast-changing digital world.

Internal Organization

The logic of focusing on the industry segment, not the policy space, motivates the choice of a digital regulator focusing on policy issues of competition, privacy, and content moderation solely within the digital industries. The regulator would be an industry-specific regulator, not a policy specialist regulator. This is the only way the policy issues could be handled in a flexible, efficient way based upon expert knowledge of the industry segment.

Applying this reasoning about the sectoral jurisdiction of the regulator to the agency's internal organization, it might seem best to organize the agency internally along digital lines of business. In this approach to the agency's internal organization, the agency would house separate bureaus for social media, search, electronic commerce, mobile app infrastructure, and ad tech. Within each bureau there would be separate policy divisions for competition and privacy and, in the case of social media, content moderation. The staff in the social media bureau, for instance, would develop policy expertise in competition, privacy, and content moderation focused primarily on how these issues arise for social media companies.

The need to pay close attention to the details of industry context in putting in place procompetition and pro-privacy measures favors an internal agency organization based on line of business. It would facilitate reaching a balanced result to have the sometimes-competing policy agendas housed in the same bureau where compromises can be developed within the same internal organizational substructure. This industry-focused internal organization would mimic, to some degree, the internal structure of the FCC, which in its heyday had a common carrier bureau, a broadcasting bureau, and a cable bureau to address issues that arose in the three major industry segments it regulated.

Alternatively, it is clearly possible to organize internally by policy area, to have separate bureaus for competition, privacy, and social media, and then to have specific industry divisions within each policy area as needed. The advantage in this arrangement would be to prioritize the development of relevant policy expertise over the development of expertise within a single industrial context. But it might make the development of flexible balance policy outcomes more difficult to the extent that the different policy bureaus failed to communicate and coordinate well. This internal structure would more closely match that of the FTC, which has a bureau of competition and a separate bureau of consumer protection.

The decision on this question might be answered initially by the way in which Congress is most likely to create a digital regulator. As discussed earlier, it appears that different legislative vehicles will address digital competition, privacy, and content moderation, but each bill seems likely to assign rulemaking and enforcement responsibilities to the FTC.

As a result, the most likely structure for the digital regulator in its initial incarnation within the FTC would be structure according to policy area. Congress seemed to be moving in that direction as well in 2021, with a directive included in the Build Back Better Act to the FTC to set up a privacy bureau and an allocation of $500 million over a nine-year period.

This decision might be revisited when Congress takes steps to spin off the digital functions it initially assigned to the FTC. Congress and the new digital agency would work together to set up the internal structure that looked most likely to achieve the agency's three policy missions of promoting competition, privacy, and good content moderation and to do so in a coherent way that accommodates the different policy goals in an overall balance.

Looking further into the future, it is not unreasonable to anticipate that the need to focus resources on specific digital lines of business might require the digital agency itself break up into smaller units. Electronic commerce, for instance, has a very different business model and industry characteristics than search or social media. The digital agency will naturally experience substantial difficulties in gaining relevant expertise in that line of business and learning how data portability and interoperability might work for different electronic commerce companies. At some point, what the electronic commerce specialists have in common with other experts in search or social media might diminish so much that the advantages of a common administrative structure no longer outweigh the benefits. A new electronic commerce agency might then be born.

This kind of fragmented regulatory structure arose in financial services, where specialist regulators have come to deal separately with different industry segments. The Federal Reserve Board regulates bank holding companies. The Office of the Comptroller of the Currency regulates national commercial banks and federal savings associations. The Federal Deposit Insurance Corporation (FDIC) ensures savings at US banks and savings associations. State bank regulators such as the New York State Department of Financial Services supervise and regulate state-chartered banks that are domiciled in their state. State insurance regulators oversee insurance companies operating in their state. The Commodity Futures Trading Commission regulates commodity futures and options and other related derivatives markets. The SEC regulates the US stock exchanges, the broker-dealer industry, and investment advisors. It has delegated regulatory authority to and supervises FINRA, a self-regulatory organization for the broker-dealer industry. State securities regulators require investment advisors in their states that are not registered with the SEC to register with them.[69]

Such detailed and bewildering regulatory specialization need not arise in the digital industries. Still, the example of the financial industry regulatory structure shows that diversification and regulatory focus are possible and to some degree desirable. Some spinning off of regulatory duties from a digital regulator might make sense in the future after Congress and the regulator have some experience in detailed industry regulation and compliance efforts.

Resources

The digital agency would have a budget and staffing needed to accomplish its missions. The best way to think about the needed resources is to examine the budgets and personnel of agencies with comparable missions. As with other key questions, Congress might need to make an initial estimate of needed resources when it houses the digital regulator within the FTC and then revisit the question when it moves the digital missions to a stand-alone agency.

Some examples indicate the likely range of resources needed. The new federal privacy agency proposed by Representatives Anna Eshoo and Zoe Lofgren has a $550 million yearly budget with about 1,600 employees. The 2021 proposed budget of the FTC is $390 million and 1,250 employees; the Department of Justice's Antitrust Division has a proposed budget of $188.5 million with 782 employees; the FCC's proposed budget is $389 million with 1,550 employees; and the CFPB, a comparable sector-specific federal agency, has a proposed budget of $618 million and 1,560 employees.[70] The Build Back Better Act, passed by the House of Representatives on November 19, 2021, would provide $500 million to the FTC over a nine-year period to "create and operate a bureau, including by hiring and retaining technologists, user experience designers, and other experts," that focuses on "unfair or deceptive acts or practices" relating to "privacy, data security, identity theft, data abuses, and related matters."[71] Senator Michael Bennet funds his Digital Platform Commission at $500 million starting in 2027.[72]

An initial estimate of the agency's proposed size would therefore be roughly the same as the size of the proposed privacy agency—$550 million and 1,600 employees. The actual resources needed to do the job will depend on experience with the agency's efforts to supervise digital companies. The sticker shock of new federal outlays might be mitigated to the extent that the industry's self-regulatory organization can take on much of the regulatory work and fund itself through service fees on industry members.

Other Policy Issues

The digital agency's jurisdiction is limited to competition, privacy, and content moderation, but many other policy issues affect digital industries. The Venn diagram of three intersecting circles that has been our guide to the digital policy issues actually has many more overlapping circles. Digital industries are vectors for information security attacks, national security threats, and discriminatory treatment of protected classes to name just a few of the other policy challenges. How should the digital agency deal with these other issues?

The short answer is that to the extent it needs to address these other policy issues, it should rely on the determinations of other agencies. For instance, if another agency of government has determined that a company has lax information security practices in that it has repeatedly failed security audits designed to detect whether it has established and maintained a security program reasonably designed to detect and mitigate security vulnerabilities, the agency should be allowed to deny that company the benefits of some of the procompetition measures such as data portability and interoperability.

In the transition, where the FTC is the digital agency, this determination of compliance with information security requirements could be carried out by the agency itself. This is because as currently constituted, the FTC has information security authority for certain financial services companies and has acted under its unfairness authority to impose information security programs on nonfinancial services companies when they have failed to maintain reasonable security practices.

If Congress decides to create a new digital agency, it will have to face the question of whether to transfer rulemaking and enforcement authority for information security to the new agency as well as the competition, privacy, and content moderation jurisdiction. In creating the CFPB, Congress transferred the authority of the banking agencies for privacy rulemaking and enforcement authority to the new agency, but not their information security responsibilities. Congress might follow a similar path in spinning off a new digital agency from the FTC and choose to leave information security with the FTC and transfer the remaining responsibilities to the new agency.[73]

In connection with national security, the digital agency should be constrained. It should act solely based on determinations made by other agencies of government including executive branch interagency bodies, the Department of Commerce, the Department of Homeland Security, the Department of Defense, the Office of the Director of National Intelligence, the National Security Agency, the Federal Bureau of Investigation. This is the procedure Congress adopted in instructing the FCC not to grant licenses to communications equipment provided by companies posing a significant threat to national security.[74] The digital agency could be instructed not to grant companies on such a national security threat list the benefits of the procompetitive measures such as interoperability or data portability.

Some national security decisions would continue to take place outside the digital agency's purview. The FCC's license review mission would operate independently of the digital agency. The Committee of Foreign Investment in the United States (CFIUS) would continue its work of reviewing transactions for consistency with US national security incidents without the need to consult with the digital agency, and its decisions might block mergers that the agency would be inclined to approve on competition grounds. The Department of Commerce would continue to administer its export controls and to restrict the ability of US companies to furnish goods and services to companies deemed national security risks. The president would continue to be able to exercise his broad authority under the International Emergency Economic Powers Act (IEEPA) to restrict economic activity in the United States after declaring a national emergency because of "any unusual and extraordinary threat, which has its source in whole or substantial part outside the United States, to the national security, foreign policy, or economy of the United States."[75] The digital agency would have only a limited role in these separate national security decisions.

Discrimination based on protected class status is also beyond the purview of the digital agency. In the future, this might change if Congress passes legislation outlawing discrimination in the provision of digital services the way it has for lending, housing, and employment. Search engines have produced many famous examples of discrimination against African Americans that have been documented in careful studies of the industry, including in Safiya Noble's research on biased search results for "black girls" and Latanya Sweeney's work on discriminatory search results for black-sounding names like "Trevon Jones."[76] Content moderation at Facebook routinely treats content from minorities more harshly than similar content from whites, and its efforts at "race-neutral" content moderation result in hate speech directed at whites accounting for 90 percent of material removed for violation of its hate speech rules.[77]

Even though these biases in search and content moderation are harmful, they are not illegal under current US discrimination law. That could change if Congress passed new legislation extending protection to protected classes in the context of search or social media. If this were to happen, it would make sense to provide enforcement authority to the digital agency. This is how the antidiscrimination laws work in housing, where the law assigns enforcement authority to the Department of Housing and Urban Development, and lending, where the law assigns enforcement authority to the banking agencies.

There would naturally be some overlap and jurisdictional issues to work out if this were to happen. Under current law, for example, the Department of Housing and Urban Development has brought a discrimination case against Facebook for discrimination in housing, since it allowed its "ethnic affinities" advertising category to be used for housing ads.[78] This would be an example of the intersection of housing discrimination law and a new digital discrimination law, and the agencies would have to work out which one had jurisdiction. The case also shows, however, that to some degree existing discrimination law, administered by existing agencies, can address some of the biases in digital industries.

The Digital Regulator and Artificial Intelligence

In the wake of the blizzard of publicity and use of Open AI's ChatGPT in late 2022 and early 2023, calls for regulation of artificial intelligence in general and AI-generated content in particular dramatically increased. This attention from policymakers was a welcome development and is a demonstration of the fact that the long forty-year policymaker deference to innovators to deploy new technology without regulatory controls was drawing to an end.

It is important to disentangle the issues of digital regulation and regulation of artificial intelligence. The digital agency would regulate AI as it appears in the industries under its jurisdiction, much the same as any sectoral regulator would. It would not be in charge of regulating AI as such or general-purpose providers of AI systems.

The US sectoral approach to regulating AI was on full display in April 2023 when, speaking for a group of federal regulatory agencies, FTC chair Lina Khan observed tartly, "There is no AI exception to the laws on the books." Civil rights law, employment law, and consumer protection law, among others, all apply to activities conducted with the use of AI systems.[79]

There has also been a lively debate about regulating general purpose AI, systems that can be used in a wide range of specific economic and social contexts. Some commentators such as Brookings scholar Anton Korinek have thought that a key element in regulating AI is designating an agency to focus on these issues that crosscut the jurisdiction of the specialized agencies. A new crosscutting agency would be needed, the thinking goes, to oversee the transparency, risk assessments, audits, and mitigation requirements appropriate for general purpose AI systems. The designated AI agency would also be a reservoir of technical knowledge that could be shared with business or policy regulators at specialized agencies and ensure a consistent technical approach across agencies.[80]

Regardless of how that debate turns out, the role of a digital regulator is not to regulate providers of general AI services. The digital regulator would not be the designated AI agency if the United States were to move in that direction. The digital agency should be fully authorized to prevent the companies in the specific digital industries under its jurisdiction from using AI systems in ways that threaten competition, invade privacy, or encourage information disorder on their systems. Concerns, for instance, about using algorithmic pricing models to fix prices in digital industries would fall under the digital regulator's purview. So would the use of AI in online marketing and advertising, as well as the use of AI content generation systems such as ChatGPT for creating social media content.

These examples are purely illustrative, but they make the point that the digital regulator is like the other specialized agencies dealing with AI in the areas under their jurisdiction. The digital regulator is not an economy-wide agency seeking out the use of AI wherever it appears and endeavoring to ensure that it operates in a safe and trustworthy manner.[81]

Regulatory Capture

In a famous critique of the idea that specialist regulators advance the public interest, economist George Stigler argued instead that "regulation is acquired by the industry and is designed and operated primarily for its benefit."[82] Progressive critics agreed with this assessment, concluding that "class-conscious corporate elites successfully used the state to stabilize modern capitalism and co-opt radical policy demands from below."[83] This critique led in the 1970s to the regulatory goal of promoting competition to the regulated industry as a way to minimize regulation that simply entrenched the dominant position of regulated companies.

The mechanism that transforms regulation in the public interest into regulation in the industry's interest is the lure of post-service employment in the regulated industry, which distorts the judgment of regulators in office and gives them an incentive to favor the regulated industry in the hopes of securing lucrative private sector posts after their government service.[84]

As widespread as this critique is, in its general form, it is simply too broad. If it is true that specialist regulators simply serve the regulated industry and not the public interest, then reformers and policymakers should be in the business of dismantling the array of specialist regulatory agencies that currently oversee the conduct of specific industries. The FDA, according to this critique, should be abolished since it protects not the public interest in safe and effective drugs but the interest of the pharmaceutical industry in selling drugs. The nation's experience during the COVID-19 pandemic with the urgent need for safe and effective vaccines and treatments demonstrates the extent to which the criticism of regulatory capture is overstated.

Going forward, it simply strains credulity to believe that all regulatory agencies so completely disserve the public interest that no reform should ever contemplate setting up a similar regulatory structure for digital industries. The fear of regulatory capture certainly did not dissuade financial services reformers from seeking to establish the CFPB in 2010 against industry opposition and to defend it against determined attempts by the industry and its allies to dismantle and hobble it.[85]

It is often said that sector regulators are prone to regulatory capture in a way that antitrust agencies are not.[86] It follows from this supposed fact that policymakers should rely on generalist antitrust and not on industry regulation to promote competition. Agency regulators, being more prone to capture by the industry, will simply secure the dominance of the digital industries instead of regulating them to promote competition.

As we have seen throughout the book, however, the only effective strategy for promoting digital competition is through a regulatory structure that can interpret and apply measures such as interoperability that are simply beyond the capacity of generalist antitrust officials and judges. So, measures to control regulatory capture rather than abandonment of the regulatory approach are the better way to proceed, despite the risks of regulatory capture.

It is worth questioning the premise that antitrust officials are beyond capture by industry. It is true that judges do not often go to work for the companies that appear before them. They do, however, attend industry-sponsored seminars instructing them on how to interpret and apply competition law, and these events almost always endorse the idea of lax antitrust enforcement.[87] Moreover, judges do not bring antitrust cases. In the absence of agency action, there is nothing even the most concerned judge can do to enforce the antitrust laws.

So the real issue is whether officials at the antitrust agencies are any more or less prone to regulatory capture than officials at sector agencies. But there is simply no evidence for that. Officials at antitrust agencies regularly leave to work for companies and law firms and often represent companies that are being sued by their former agencies. No study shows that antitrust officials do this less often than do officials at specialist regulatory agencies such as the SEC or the FCC.

The oft-repeated worry about regulatory capture of specialist agencies is less an empirically grounded research finding and more a talking point regularly trotted out whenever the threat of regulation seems to raise its head again. Nevertheless, it should be an important purpose of the legislation that sets up or transfers authority to a new digital agency to structure the agency so as to minimize the chances of regulatory capture.

Some specific measures might minimize these risks. Post-service employment restrictions would be needed and should include not working post-service on behalf of the regulated industry on any matter before the agency in any capacity whatsoever. In addition, the agency's pay structure should reward long and productive service with substantial pay raises and bonus and increasing levels of responsibility to allow for professional development and advancement. Agency management might be placed more fully in the hands of highly paid long-term civil servants who would have a career interest in a stable and well-managed institution.

The terms of agency commissioners might be extended beyond the five to seven years typical in regulatory commissions to something closer to the term of fourteen years enjoyed by each of the seven members of the Federal Reserve Board of Governors. Each member of the Board of Governors is appointed for a fourteen-year term; the terms are staggered so that one term expires on January 31 of each even-numbered year.[88] This arrangement gives a president only limited control of the board.

In a similar way, each digital regulatory commissioner could be appointed for a ten-year term with the terms staggered so that a term expires in each even-numbered year. As noted earlier, this would give the agency an extra degree of independence from the current administration. It also would provide the opportunity for the agency commissioners to develop detailed expertise in the industries they regulate. Moreover, the financial rewards of a high-status government position with a decade-long tenure should make the job sufficiently attractive to qualified and dedicated officials so that the limitations on post-office employment would not be a serious disincentive.

Public Knowledge Senior Vice President Harold Feld notes that because the "agency capture" theory has been "deployed with the single end of eliminating public oversight of the private sector," it "has been elevated from caution to dogma." He nevertheless recognizes that the system of digital regulation he advocates must be designed with "appropriate limits and appropriate safeguards."[89] This balanced judgment gets it just about right.

Balancing Agency Missions

The movement for regulation of digital industries would likely impel Congress to pass different statutes that reform competition policy for digital companies, create privacy rights that protect users of digital services, and vindicate rights to seek, receive, and impart receive information on social media platforms. These different statutes would authorize a regulatory agency, likely the FTC, to pursue the objectives set out in the statutes.

Digital competition reform statutes would aim to promote competition and protect dependent businesses from abuse by dominant companies. As Vaheesan, the legal director at the Open Markets Institute urges, the statute should also adopt a fair competition philosophy and aim to promote not competition for the sake of competition but only business rivalry that eschews unfair methods of competition in digital industries.[90]

A national privacy statute would aim to protect the right to data privacy in digital industries and define this right as the protection from the harmful use of information by digital companies. It would authorize the regulator to impose various ex-ante rules on digital companies to implement this statutory right.

A content moderation statute for social media companies would aim to vindicate the information rights of social media users as laid out in international human rights instruments. In particular, it would authorize the regulator to implement rules to ensure that social media users can enjoy the rights laid out in Article 19 of the Universal Declaration of Human Rights to "seek, receive, and impart information and ideas" through the medium of social media.[91] It would also enshrine as a statutory objective for social media the diversity principle articulated in the Supreme Court's *Associated Press* call for "the widest possible dissemination of information from diverse and antagonistic sources."[92]

Policymakers are on course to assign enforcement and implementation of these different statutes to the same regulatory agency, the FTC. This common administrative structure to administer the different statutes would be a natural and attractive way to accommodate the different objectives. This is particularly so, since as we have seen repeatedly throughout this book, these policy objectives overlap, sometimes reinforcing each other and other times in tension. As legal scholar Erika Douglas puts it succinctly in the case of antitrust and privacy, "Competition may be enhanced by data access, while data privacy is eroded by it."[93]

Without guidance from Congress, however, the agency will have a free hand to balance the competing objectives in whatever way seems best to it. If Congress does not provide guidance, the courts will step in to fill the void left by Congress and substitute its judgment for the proper balance in place of the agency's. But leaving the balancing to court review of agency action might very well privilege competition law over privacy and content moderation law. For example, in the 2019 *HiQ v. LinkedIn* case pitting data access and against privacy, the US Court of Appeals for the Ninth Circuit held that LinkedIn could not stop a competitor from overriding user privacy preferences to access information that would be helpful to the rival company in competing with LinkedIn.[94] Even if congressional lawmakers think this was the right result in this particular case, they would be well advised to provide some guidance to the agency rather than turning over the balancing decision to whatever principles courts develop on their own in the absence of clear guidance from the legislature.

This guidance, however, should not take the form of a systematic preference for the goals of one policy sphere over the goals of the others. Systematic reconciliations are possible in principle, but they are unwise. A systematic preference could be established allowing measures needed to promote competition to override all consumer privacy interests. Or the opposite preference could be made systematic by exempting private data from disclosure as an antitrust remedy. It might seem possible to blend the two policy objectives by requiring that an antitrust remedy of data access for competitors be subject to the data subject's consent. This consent-to-remedy approach, however, is just another way of privileging privacy interests over competition interests, since obtaining consent would be next to impossible in practice.

The only way forward is through a case-by-case approach, not through a systematic reconciliation that could be enshrined in legislation. Douglas describes this case-by-approach as "accommodative" in that it "grants equal billing to both areas of law. It automatically prefers neither."[95]

The same concerns apply to the conflicts between social media content moderation and privacy and competition policy. Would an interoperability requirement force social media companies with good content moderation policies to share access to their user base with social media companies that have few or no content controls? There is no systematic solution to the tensions. They must be addressed one at a time and balanced through an assessment of the context and strength of factors that needed to be considered in reaching a coherent result.

Nevertheless, the legislation can guide the agency's case-by-case assessment by specifying a required framework for the agency to use as it seeks to resolve policy tensions in specific cases. Certain factors need to be considered such as the extent to which the disclosure of private data is really needed to accomplish the procompetitive or content moderation purpose and whether less privacy-intrusive measures might accomplish the procompetitive purpose equally well. It could lay out a cost-benefit balancing standard with certain factor required to be taken into account in reaching a judgment.

Some guidance for legislators crafting an appropriate framework for the regulator to apply in making these case-by-case judgments can be found in the work done in Europe on defining and implementing the legitimate interests basis for data processing, particularly the guidance provided by the Article 29 Data Protection Working Party.[96]

The GDPR allows companies to collect and use personal data beyond what is needed to provide service to consumers without user consent when they can show that doing so would be necessary to serve a legitimate interest. Applying this framework to the task of the regulator seeking to balance privacy against competition and content moderation goals in effect treats aiming to achieve these other goals as a legitimate interest that can override user privacy interests.

According to the regulatory guidance, the balancing test comparing the legitimate interest of the data processor and the rights and interests of the data subjects is qualitative but scaled. A "minor and not very compelling" legitimate interest may only override "even more trivial" rights and interests of the data subject, while "important and compelling legitimate interests" could "justify even significant intrusion into privacy or other significant impact on the interests or rights of the data subjects."

When there is "legal and cultural/societal recognition of the legitimacy of the interests" invoked by a company to justify its data use, that weighs "more heavily" in the balancing test against the rights and interests of the data subjects.

The assessment of the impact on the data subjects borrows from the methodology of risk assessment. It assesses the size and likelihood of both positive and negative impacts on the data subject and depends on "the nature of personal data, the way the information is being processed, the reasonable expectations of the data subjects and the status of the controller and data subject."

As mentioned earlier, the United Kingdom suggests that companies conduct a "legitimate interests assessment" (LIA) as a best practice when they are basing their data practices on that legal justification.[97] This methodology might also be a basis for congressional guidance to regulatory officials in how to balance competition, privacy, and content moderation. These assessments would start with a consideration of three tests for legitimate interests—namely, the "purpose test (identify the legitimate interest); the necessity test (consider if the processing is necessary); and the balancing test (consider the individual's interests)." The assessments would consider "the nature of the personal data you want to process; the reasonable expectations of the individual; and the likely impact of the processing on the individual and whether any safeguards can be put in place to mitigate negative impacts." To find a balance, the company must "weigh up all the factors identified . . . for and against the processing, and decide whether you still think your interests should take priority over any risk to individuals." This balancing is not "a mathematical exercise and there is an element of subjectivity involved, but you should be as objective as possible."

Other guidance for congressional policymakers on how the agency should balance competition, privacy, and content moderation can be gleaned from the work of the United Kingdom's ICO and CMA on privacy and antitrust. The 2020 joint statement from the ICO and CMA recognized the areas of tension between competition and data protection but was confident that they "can be overcome through careful consideration of the issues on a case-by-case basis." On resolving these tensions, the ICO commented that if data access interventions are an appropriate remedy for competition problems, then "any perceived tensions can be resolved through designing them carefully, such that they are limited to what is necessary and proportionate."[98]

These tests of necessity and proportionality are a good model for congressional guidance to the digital regulator. They are widely used in European law and bear a certain relationship to the tests for constitutionality under US law. For instance, under European case law, the right of privacy in EU law is protected by a three-part proportionality test. First, measures that infringe on privacy may "not exceed the limits of what is appropriate and necessary in order to attain the objectives legitimately pursued by the legislation in question." Second, "when there is a choice between several appropriate measures recourse must be had to the least onerous." Third, "the disadvantages caused must not be disproportionate to the aims pursued."[99]

When a fundamental right is at stake, the judicial review will be more "strict" and the discretion of the legislature more limited than with measures not involving a fundamental right.[100] In Europe, the right of privacy is subject to strict review: "According to settled case-law, the protection of the fundamental right to privacy requires that derogations and limitations in relation to the protection of personal data must apply only in so far as is strictly necessary."[101]

But these necessity and proportionality tests are typically used in cases where a fundamental right conflicts with a government policy goal. They are meant to privilege the fundamental right against the government policy goal and force policymakers to invade the fundamental right only when absolutely necessary, and there is a clear balance of advantages to achieving the policy goal.

Using the tools of necessity and proportionality, the analysis of a typical case of a conflict between a fundamental right and a government interest proceeds in four stages. First, the policy interfering with the right must pursue or serve a legitimate aim or public policy goal. Second, there must be a rational connection between the policy and the achievement of the goal. The means must suit the end sought. Third, the law must be necessary in that there is no less intrusive or less onerous but equally effective alternative. At this stage, alternatives must be considered, and recourse must be had to the least onerous alternative. Fourth and finally, the benefits of achieving the legitimate aim must not be disproportionate to the encroachment into the fundamental right concerned. The restriction must not impose an unacceptably harsh burden on the individuals involved.[102]

This test is aimed at minimizing the interference with the fundamental right in question, which seems appropriate when seeking to protect individual human rights from infringement by governments. This prioritization of rights over interest is accomplished crucially at the third stage of the test, where it must be shown that the restriction on the fundamental right is no more than is necessary to achieve the legitimate aim. Rights generally trump interests, and this four-stage test implements this ideal.

When the question is the conflict of human rights, such as the right of privacy and the right of free speech, a single application of the proportionality test could provide the wrong answer. When fundamental rights conflict, the question is reconciling this conflict between the two fundamental rights when neither of them as such has priority over the other. If one is treated as the subordinate "government interest," it will automatically lose out to the one treated as the more important "human right."

A framework has been developed for resolving these cases of conflict of rights. The framework involves a double proportionality test in which decisionmakers conduct parallel analyses to unearth all the relevant considerations while giving neither side of the conflict an intrinsic preference.

This framework was set out in a series of court decisions in the United Kingdom and described by Andrew Cheung, permanent judge of the Hong Kong Court of Final Appeal.[103] This framework is useful when there is a need to protect two fundamental rights that can be qualified when it is necessary and proportionate to do so in order to accommodate other interests and rights. The method is "one of parallel analysis in which the starting point is presumptive parity, in that neither [right] has precedence over or 'trumps' the other. The exercise of parallel analysis requires the court to examine the justification for interfering with each right, and the issue of necessity should be considered in respect of each. It is not a mechanical exercise to be decided upon the basis of rival generalities. An intense focus on the comparative importance of the specific rights being claimed in the individual case is necessary before the ultimate balancing test in terms of proportionality is carried out."[104]

The legislation authorizing the digital regulator can instruct the agency to apply a version of this framework to assess conflicts and tensions among competition, privacy, and content moderation. The key idea is that the above necessity and proportionality test must be applied to each of the issues in conflict in a particular case.

To see how this analysis would work in practice, consider the question of whether the digital regulator should grant data access to competitors of a dominant digital company. On the one hand, this would advance competition interests, but it would also infringe on privacy rights. The above framework for resolving this kind of conflict would start by noting that mandating data access to a dominant digital company's competitors would be a prima facie privacy violation and so must be analyzed using the four steps needed to protect privacy rights. First, does data access aim to serve a legitimate interest? Yes. The legitimate interest intended is the promotion of competition. Second, is there a rational connection between data access and the promotion of competition? Yes. If competitors have access to this data, they will be able to compete more effectively. Third, is mandated data access no more than is necessary to achieve the goal of promoting competition? Is there a less intrusive or less onerous but equally effective alternative? This question is not so clear. Other measures, such as voluntary data sharing with the consent of the data subject, might do the procompetitive job just as effectively. Or perhaps anonymized data would be just as useful to the rival companies. Finally, is the gain to competition from data access disproportionate to the harm done to privacy rights? Perhaps. Access to the data might not be the key thing that would jump-start competition. It would help a little, but by itself it might not enable anyone to compete fully with the dominant company. The analysis thus leads to a consideration of other mechanisms for promoting competition.

That is not the end of the assessment, however. A parallel analysis must be undertaken as well. If a dominant company is allowed to prevent rivals from accessing the data they need to compete, this can be seen as a violation of their rights to fair competition and a level competitive playing field. This refusal to grant access must be analyzed in the four steps needed to justify an infringement on these competition rights. First, does blocking data access serve a legitimate aim? Yes. The legitimate interest aimed at is the protection of privacy rights. Second, is there a rational connection between the refusal to deal with competitors and the protection of privacy? Yes. The lack of data access means that fewer companies will be able to collect use user information, and this will protect privacy. Third, is a complete lack of data access necessary to protect privacy? Are there other measures that are less restrictive of competition rights that are equally protective of privacy? Here is the heart of the question. Data subjects could be offered a choice about whether they wanted to share data with competitors, perhaps even an opt-out choice that would require action on their part to block the flow of data to competitors. Or competitors could be allowed to use the information solely for the purposes of competing with the data collector and for no other purpose. These measures might be equally protective of privacy but allow some degree of data competition. Finally, if there is no equally effective alternative, is the gain to privacy disproportionate to the harm done to the promotion of privacy? Here the analysis could assess how much harm data subjects might experience from the mandated data access. Also relevant would be the extent to which the privacy interest has the backing of strong and entrenched social consensus.

This mode of analysis would be applicable to all the conflicts among competition, privacy, and content moderation. In effect, this balancing framework would allow measures that override privacy rights only if it is essential and proportionate to achieving competition or good content moderation. Additionally, it would allow measures to override competition goals only if it is essential and proportionate to protecting privacy and content moderation. It would countenance overriding speech rights that are vindicated by fair and effective content moderation only if it essential and proportionate to protecting privacy or competition. Each policy domain would respect each other's domain by intruding into it to the smallest extent necessary and only when the balance of gains over losses is clearly positive.

Judicial Review

When Congress writes legislation authorizing a digital regulator to interpret the statute it administers and to write rules implementing and enforcing its provisions through fines, injunctions, and other penalties, it clearly intends that the agency will have substantial power. One check against agency abuse of this power is judicial review of agency actions. In light of that point, Congress must craft that legislation carefully to ensure that courts do not strip the agency of the authority it needs to apply the statute and update it regularly considering changed industry and technological conditions. This section describes two developments in judicial review jurisprudence that Congress had to bear in mind as it crafts digital regulatory statutes.

Chevron Deference

The current attacks on the Chevron deference doctrine and the strong possibility that the Supreme Court might significantly water it down or eliminate it entirely raise consequential issues for Congress in drafting the new digital laws. The Chevron deference doctrine instructs courts to defer to an agency's reasonable interpretation of ambiguous statutes. Constricting or eliminating it could diminish the flexibility of agencies to adopt old statutes to new business and economic circumstances, an especially important capability for digital industries still in the throes of rapid evolution.

In its traditional form, the doctrine is based on a two-step test. "When a court reviews an agency's construction of the statute which it administers," the *Chevron* Court ruled in 1984, "it is confronted with two questions." The first is "whether Congress has directly spoken to the precise question at issue. If the intent of Congress is clear, that is the end of the matter; for the court, as well as the agency, must give effect to the unambiguously expressed intent of Congress." This is a question of whether the statutory meaning is plain on its face. According to the now-famous footnote 9, courts are to "apply all the tools of statutory interpretation" when they determine whether a statute is ambiguous. But "if the statute is silent or ambiguous with respect to the specific issue, the question for the court is whether the agency's answer is based on a permissible construction of the statute." In reviewing an agency's interpretation of a statute that it administers, "a court may not substitute its own construction of a statutory provision for a reasonable interpretation made by the administrator of an agency."[105]

A background assumption, sometimes called Chevron Step Zero by law professors, is a "presumption that Congress, when it left ambiguity in a statute meant for implementation by an agency, understood that the ambiguity would be resolved, first and foremost, by the agency, and desired the agency (rather than the courts) to possess whatever degree of discretion the ambiguity allows."[106]

After this, Chevron Step One is whether a term or statutory provision is ambiguous. In Chevron Step Two, courts defer to the agency's interpretation provided that this interpretation and the resulting policy is reasonable. As summarized by Justice Antonin Scalia in the 2013 case of *City of Arlington v. FCC*, "Chevron thus provides a stable background rule against which Congress can legislate: Statutory ambiguities will be resolved, within the bounds of reasonable interpretation, not by the courts but by the administering agency."[107]

In 2000, the Supreme Court articulated an important aspect of Chevron deference in rejecting the FDA's attempt to regulate cigarettes. The case turned on the interpretation of the terms "drugs" and "devices."

The FDA regulates both drugs and medical devices, and it asserted that nicotine was a "drug" and cigarettes and smokeless tobacco were "devices" that deliver nicotine to the body. But the court refused to defer to the agency's interpretation of these statutory terms. It said that Chevron deference "is premised on the theory that a statute's ambiguity constitutes an implicit delegation from Congress to the agency to fill in the statutory gaps." It granted that this implicit delegation should be understood to apply in "ordinary" cases. But it added that in "extraordinary cases . . . there may be reason to hesitate before concluding that Congress has intended such an implicit delegation." The application of an extensive regulatory regime to the tobacco industry was just such an extraordinary case. Would Congress really have delegated authority to the FDA to regulate the tobacco industry through the indirect method of ambiguity in the terms "drug" and "devices"? The Court rejected this idea, ruling that it was "confident that Congress could not have intended to delegate a decision of such economic and political significance to an agency in so cryptic a fashion."[108]

The Supreme Court reiterated this major policy doctrine in its 2001 decision concerning whether the Environmental Protection Agency (EPA) had authority from Congress to consider costs in setting national air quality standards. In several sections of the Clean Air Act, Congress expressly granted the EPA the authority to consider costs, but it does not provide this authority clearly in the section of the act that authorized the EPA to set national air quality standards. Congress, said the Court in refusing to allow the agency to consider costs, "does not alter the fundamental details of a regulatory scheme in vague terms or ancillary provisions—it does not, one might say, hide elephants in mouseholes."[109]

Several years later, in its 2005 *Brand X* decision, the Supreme Court upheld the FCC's decision to classify internet access as an information service as that term is defined in the 1996 Telecommunications Act.[110] Alternatively, the agency could have classified cable internet access as a telecommunications service, another term in the act that would have triggered treating cable internet access service as a common carrier service subject to substantial non-discrimination requirements. Following the Chevron procedure, the Court said there was ambiguity in whether cable internet access was properly classified as an information service or a telecommunications service, and upheld FCC's discretionary classification as reasonable, even though it thought a better interpretation would be that cable internet access is a telecommunications common carrier service.

Curiously, the majority opinion did not address the question of whether this reclassification decision was an ordinary or an extraordinary case with major economic and political significance. In his dissent, Justice Scalia implicitly raised the major policy issue that the majority opinion ignored. He said the commission had "attempted to establish a whole new regime of non-regulation . . . an implausible reading of the statute and has thus exceeded the authority given it by Congress." He said the terms "information service" and "telecommunications service" in the act were not ambiguous at all. They unambiguously meant that cable internet access was a telecommunications service, and so, in his view, Chevron deference should not come into play at all. The commission had simply exceeded its authority by misreading the statutory text. The plain language of the text did not have the ambiguity that would justify deferring to the agency's interpretation.

After *Brand X*, the Supreme Court again refused to apply Chevron deference in cases involving major policy decisions. In a 2015 case involving tax credits in the Affordable Care Act, the Court refused to defer to an IRS interpretation. It ruled that "the tax credits are one of the Act's key reforms and whether they are available on Federal Exchanges is a question of deep 'economic and political significance'; had Congress wished to assign that question to an agency, it surely would have done so expressly." The court conducted its own analysis de novo, substituting its own interpretation of the act.[111]

After this case that reasserted the major policy doctrine, the courts again considered the issue of deferring to the FCC on the question classifying internet access as an information service or as a telecommunications service, and this time directly confronted the major policy doctrine. In 2015, the FCC had reversed its earlier decision to classify internet service as an information service and adopted a net neutrality order that treated internet service as a telecommunications service. In 2017, a three-judge panel of the US Court of Appeals for the District of Columbia upheld the FCC's new interpretation, and the full court rejected petitions for a rehearing.[112] However, in a dissent to the rejection of the petitions for rehearing, Justice Kavanaugh asserted that Chevron deference did not apply to statutory interpretations involving a major policy decision, citing the 2000 *Brown & Williamson* tobacco case and the 2015 Affordable Care Act case *King v. Burwell*, among others. He added that the decision to impose common carrier-like obligations on internet service providers was a matter of major economic and political importance and concluded that Chevron deference should not apply. He had his own view of what Congress had intended in the 1996 Telecommunications Act. He thought the correct interpretation of the statutory terms was that internet access service is an information service, since this involves less regulation and is consistent with what he took to be the deregulatory purpose of the 1996 Telecommunications Act.

After the 2016 election, a different FCC rescinded the previous FCC's open internet order that had been under review in the DC Court of Appeals. The Supreme Court denied a petition for certiorari, although Justice Thomas, Justice Alito, and Justice Gorsuch would have granted the petitions and vacated the judgment of the lower court.[113]

The result seems to be that in cases of ambiguity the courts should defer to reasonable agency interpretations of statutory terms unless the interpretation involves a major policy decision, in which case the court should interpret the statute afresh with no deference to the agency opinion. It is not clear what the Supreme Court itself would rule on this question of the FCC's authority to require net neutrality if the matter ever got to them again, but it is likely that they would not give the agency deference.

The threat to broad agency discretion is even greater than this current doctrine suggests, however. In 2020, Justice Thomas, who wrote the 2005 *Brand X* decision, deferring to the FCC on the internet access question, recanted. In a 2020 dissent from a refusal to grant certiorari, he wrote that the deference scheme used in *Brand X* "appears to be inconsistent with the Constitution, the Administrative Procedure Act (APA), and traditional tools of statutory interpretation."[114] Chevron deference, he wrote, "undermines the ability of the Judiciary to perform its checking function on the other branches . . . when the Executive is free to dictate the outcome of cases through erroneous interpretations, the courts cannot check the Executive by applying the correct interpretation of the law." Under Justice Thomas's new view, instead of deference to reasonable agency interpretations of statutory ambiguity, the courts should reject "erroneous" interpretations and apply the "correct" ones.

It is not clear there is a majority on the Supreme Court for the complete dismissal of Chevron deference. There are some signs that Justice Gorsuch and Justice Kavanaugh might be willing to go beyond curtailing Chevron deference and repudiate it entirely.[115] But that would not constitute a majority of the court, and the views of the remaining Justices are not known. But complete elimination is a distinct possibility.

It is also possible that the Court will whittle down rather than eliminate Chevron deference. There is some ground between Chevron deference and de novo review. One such middle ground is represented by the intermediate standard of Skidmore deference. Under this standard, the courts would start with an agency's interpretation of a statute it administers and defer to it if the agency's interpretation demonstrates persuasive reasoning. Under Skidmore deference, agency interpretations are "entitled to respect," but only to the extent that they are persuasive. In the 2000 case of *Christensen v. Harris County*, the Court applied this standard to agency interpretations contained in policy statements, agency manuals, and enforcement guidelines, which do not deserve Chevron-like deference to any reasonable agency interpretation, since they do not have the force of law.[116] It is possible that the Supreme Court would carve back Chevron deference to this less deferential Skidmore standard for agency interpretations of the statute it administers rather than eliminate it entirely.

Some members of the Court seek to get to the Chevron deference question whenever it seems to be within reach. In the argument in November 2021 before the Court in *American Hospital Association v. Becerra*, Justices Gorsuch, Kavanaugh, Thomas, Alito, and Amy Coney Barrett raised the question of whether overturning Chevron deference was needed to reach a decision on whether Medicare had the authority to "adjust" hospital reimbursement rates as it had done. In its decision, however, the Court did not so much overrule Chevron as ignore it. Once again in May 2023, the court accepted a case, this time *Loper Bright Enterprises v. Raimondo*, in which it could overturn or narrow Chevron if it wanted to. This case turned on whether the National Marine Fisheries Service has the authority to require the fishing industry to pay for the costs of observers who monitor compliance with fishery management plans. In accepting the case, the Court seemed to set up a definitive ruling on the issue.[117]

The real enemy of some members of the Supreme Court in their long-running attempt to rein in Chevron deference is agency discretion. Courts have always scrutinized agency actions to determine whether they have clear statutory authority to do what they are seeking to do. In the future, they will examine agency action much more carefully to see whether its interpretation of ambiguous provisions of the statute it administers provides them with clear statutory authority to regulate.

This issue of whether the judiciary or the agency interprets ambiguous statutory language might have substantial importance for the effective operation of the digital agency. As many have pointed out, the loss or significant retrenchment of Chevron deference means no agency interpretation of ambiguous statutory language is final until the courts have blessed it. It would allow the judiciary to substitute its judgment on regulatory policy for that of the agency.[118]

The interaction of Chevron deference and the major questions doctrine are unclear, but at a minimum, legislators seeking to provide the digital agency with authority to act in promoting competition, privacy, and good content moderation must do so clearly. The Congressional Research Service summed up the implications of Supreme Court rulings as follows: "If Congress wants an agency to decide issues in an area courts would likely consider to be of vast economic and political significance, Congress should clearly specify that intention in the relevant underlying statute as opposed to relying on vague or imprecise statutory language."[119]

It is not clear what reformers interested in writing legislation authorizing a digital agency can do to clearly grant the rulemaking authority it wants the agency to have. Avoiding ambiguity might be a good tactic. It has always been a good idea to be as clear as possible in statutes, but it will be more important than ever going forward. Some statutory ambiguities result from careless drafting and can be avoided by skillful legislative counsel. Drafters must ensure that they construct statutory text so that it clearly and expressly grants the agency the authority they want it to have.

Sometimes, however, ambiguity is a deliberate choice, a stratagem to obtain congressional consensus that would not be possible if the statute were crystal clear. Congress tends to punt difficult issues to agencies to resolve when legislators themselves cannot reach a common policy choice. When this is so, as a practical matter, ambiguity cannot be avoided if the bill is going to become law at all. Some other institution—agency or court—will have to clear up the ambiguity. In the future, legislators will need to reduce this tendency to evade hard choices through strategic ambiguity, unless they are comfortable with the courts, not the agencies, making these choices.

Statutory ambiguity is very often the natural result of changed circumstances and unforeseen business and technological developments. Congress cannot anticipate all future developments in the industries it wants to regulate. The most it can do is indicate that when ambiguity develops because of unforeseen circumstances, the agency is authorized to resolve the ambiguity in the best way possible, considering the context and purposes of the statute. The digital laws assigning an agency responsibility for competition, privacy, and content moderation should clearly provide agencies with this authority. If courts choose to disregard this congressional instruction and impose their own version of proper policy through its preferred statutory interpretation, there is nothing Congress can do in advance to remedy that. Its sole recourse might be to legislate again to correct what it perceives as bad policy adopted by the courts in its interpretation of a statute rendered ambiguous by time and changed circumstances.

Non-Delegation

The issue of Chevron deference backs up into the question of when Congress is permitted under the Constitution to delegate authority to a regulatory agency. Under Chevron doctrine, Congress cannot delegate a major policy choice to an agency through ambiguity. But can it delegate the authority to decide a major policy issue to an agency at all?

It is generally agreed that Congress has some power to delegate authority to an agency. Congress simply cannot make all regulatory decisions itself, but this authority to delegate to agencies must be limited. The current Supreme Court seems poised to deny Congress the authority to delegate major policy choices to agencies, even if it does so not implicitly through ambiguity but clearly and expressly in unambiguous statutory language.

Twice in 1935, but only in that year, the Supreme Court has ruled that Congress overstepped its limits in delegating authority to agencies. In the key *Schechter* case, it overturned the National Industrial Recovery Act for unconstitutional delegation of essential legislative powers. The NIRA provided authority to the executive branch to approve industry-developed "codes of fair competition" for each sector of the economy or to prescribe codes it had developed itself. A violation of these codes would be deemed an unfair method of competition within the meaning of the FTC Act and would be enforced by an injunction from a federal court.

Congress determined these codes should fulfill certain purposes, including "to remove obstructions to the free flow of interstate and foreign commerce," to promote "cooperative action among trade groups . . . to induce and maintain united action of labor and management . . . to eliminate unfair competitive practices, to promote the fullest possible utilization of the present productive capacity of industries, to avoid undue restriction of production . . . to increase the consumption of industrial and agricultural products by increasing purchasing power, to reduce and relieve unemployment, to improve standards of labor, and otherwise to rehabilitate industry and to conserve natural resources." The court summarized these purposes as providing for the "rehabilitation, correction and development" of trade and industry.

The authority to carry out these purposes was not further cabined in the statute. The court concluded that "Congress cannot delegate legislative power to the President to exercise an unfettered discretion to make whatever laws he thinks may be needed or advisable for the rehabilitation and expansion of trade or industry." The principle the Court used was that Congress may delegate to agencies "the making of subordinate rules within prescribed limits, and the determination of facts to which the policy, as declared by Congress, is to apply; but it must itself lay down the policies and establish standards."

The court was not attempting to eliminate all authority of agencies to regulate in the public interest. In the *Schechter* decision, the Court referred to and reaffirmed the power of Congress to delegate authority to the ICC and to the Radio Commission (the predecessor of today's FCC) to regulate in the public interest, even though these statutes left substantial power in the hands of regulators to set rules for the industries under their jurisdiction. The *Schechter* decision also referred approvingly to the authority of the FTC to determine unfair methods of competition.[120]

In the 1932 ICC case that the Supreme Court reaffirmed in its *Schechter* decision, the Court upheld the authority of the ICC to approve railroad consolidations when they are in the public interest. It ruled that the "public interest" criterion of the ICC's authority "is not the public welfare in general, but the public interest in the adequate transportation service sought to be secured by the Act." The criterion is not "a mere general reference to public welfare, without any standard to guide determinations"; it is not "a concept without ascertainable criteria"; it "has direct relation to adequacy of transportation service, to its essential conditions of economy and efficiency, and to appropriate provision and best use of transportation facilities." It therefore is not problematic "so far as constitutional delegation of authority is concerned."[121]

In *Schechter*, the Court did not repudiate this reasoning it used in the earlier ICC case. The Court relied on this ICC case as a precedent in the 1943 *NBC v. United States* case, upholding the public interest standard in the 1934 Communications Act.[122] It rejected a claim that this public interest criterion was so vague and indefinite that the delegation of legislative authority was unconstitutional. Looked at in the context of the statute and its purposes, it was clear to the Court in 1943 that the public interest in question is not the general welfare but was cabined by the need "to secure the maximum benefits of radio to all the people of the United States." Hence the statute limited the agency in its licensing and regulatory powers to "generally encourage the larger and more effective use of radio in the public interest."

In the years since *Schechter*, the Court has never overturned a single statute for non-delegation reasons. In 2000, Cass Sunstein memorably said that the "conventional" version of the non-delegation doctrine "has had one good year and 211 bad ones (and counting)."[123] In continuing to uphold regulatory authority in the years since 1935, the Court has relied on a 1928 Supreme Court decision upholding the authority of the executive branch to set tariffs. In that case the Court ruled, "If Congress shall lay down by legislative act an intelligible principle to which the person or body authorized to fix such rates is directed to conform, such legislative action is not a forbidden delegation of legislative power." In the tariffing case, Congress had specified the rule to be used to set rates and left to the executive branch the responsibility of fixing the rates according to this rule.[124]

This "intelligible principle" test has been the touchstone of non-delegation doctrine ever since. Even *Schechter* apparently relied on it, since the Court referred approvingly in *Schechter* to this earlier tariff decision based on the intelligible principle test in distinguishing unconstitutional grants of authority from constitutional ones.

The current judicial landscape, however, is very different. In a dissent in the 2019 *Gundy* case, Justice Gorsuch articulated an alternative non-delegation standard.[125] The Gorsuch standard would limit Congress's ability to delegate authority to three circumstances. First, to fill in the details of a major policy choice made by Congress. The language used by Congress must be "sufficiently definite and precise" to determine whether this congressional policy choice had been followed. Second, Congress can make the major policy choice that a certain rule applies if certain conditions are satisfied and then assign to the agency the job of ascertaining the facts. Third, Congress can assign non-legislative duties to the executive branch covering matters that are already within its purview.

This contrast is often summarized as a difference between an expansive "intelligible principle" standard and a more limiting "sufficiently definite and precise" standard to determine whether delegation is constitutional.

To be clear, my own view is with the "intelligible principle" status quo. It is summarized succinctly by law professors Sunstein and Adrian Vermeule:

> *There are constitutional limits on the power of Congress to grant open-ended authority to the executive branch . . . the intelligible principle test is a good way of identifying the constitutional limits . . . even with apparently open-ended statutory wording, courts are generally able to investigate both text and context to identify an intelligible principle. Because courts can do that, and because judges are appropriately deferential to Congress in this domain, the current state of the nondelegation doctrine—not enforced, but available for truly extreme cases—is nothing to lament . . . courts should not understand Article I, Section 1 of the Constitution to require Congress to legislate with specificity.*[126]

However, my own view and that of Sunstein and Vermeule might be beside the point. It looks as if there is a majority on the current Supreme Court to use something like the Gorsuch test for non-delegation. Chief Justice John Roberts and Justice Thomas joined Gorsuch's dissent in the *Gundy* case. Justice Alito did not join the dissent but indicated he would support a wholesale revision of the non-delegation doctrine. Justice Kavanaugh has indicated that he agrees with Justice Gorsuch's position, and his vote would provide the fifth to reform the current non-delegation doctrine.[127]

Justice Kavanaugh would formulate the restrictions on delegated authority somewhat differently from Justice Gorsuch. He thinks the judicial status quo is that an agency can exercise regulatory authority over "a major policy question of great economic and political importance" only if Congress "expressly and specifically decides the major policy question itself," and delegates to the agency the authority to regulate and enforce, or Congress can "expressly and specifically" delegate to the agency the authority both to decide the major policy question and to regulate and enforce it. His preferred reform, which he also attributes to Justice Gorsuch, would bar Congress from delegating authority to agencies to decide major policy questions, even if Congress does it expressly and specifically. The result for Justice Kavanaugh would be that agencies could only fill in the details or make "less-than-major" policy decisions. This might or might not be consistent with the test established by Justice Gorsuch for policy choices in statute "sufficiently definite and precise" for a court to determine whether an agency was acting within its guidelines.

It might be that, even under the revised or reinterpreted principle of non-delegation, a digital agency can be set up in a way that meets the criteria. In October 2022, the Court of Appeals for the Fifth Circuit upheld the grant of rulemaking authority to the Consumer Financial Protection Bureau. The CFPB has broad authority to "to prescribe rules . . . identifying as unlawful unfair, deceptive, or abusive acts or practices." The Fifth Circuit affirmed this rulemaking authority, saying it was "accompanied by a specific purpose, objectives, and definitions to guide the Bureau's discretion."[128]

The Supreme Court has used the major questions doctrine to rule that agencies lack rulemaking authority they sought to exercise. In *Alabama Association of Realtors v. HHS*, the Court explained that the eviction moratorium established by the Centers for Disease Control (CDC) during the COVID-19 pandemic was of major national significance but was beyond the agency's power since it lacked a clear statutory basis. In *National Federation of Independent Business v. OSHA*, the Court considered OSHA's emergency temporary standard requiring workplace precautions against COVID to be of major economic and political significance. It, too, was outside the agency's power because Congress did not provide authority for the agency to regulate hazards that also occurred in ordinary life outside the workplace. The dissent by Justices Gorsuch, Thomas, and Alito held that if Congress had clearly conferred on OSHA this power to regulate public health, it would be an unconstitutional delegation of authority.[129]

In *West Virginia v. EPA*, the Supreme Court ruled that the Environmental Protection Agency lacked the authority to regulate greenhouse gas emissions in industry, even though it considered cost, non-air impacts, and energy requirements. In its opinion, the Court's majority referred to the "major questions doctrine" for the first time. It said that regulating greenhouse gases is one of the "extraordinary cases" where the "economic and political significance" of authority asserted requires "clear congressional authorization." EPA lacks regulatory authority in this area because the statute does not clearly grant it to the agency.[130]

Implications for the Digital Regulator

In light of this likely judicial development on non-delegation doctrine, a major concern for legislation authorizing an agency to establish and enforce rules for digital industries that promote competition, protect privacy, and provide for effective and fair content moderation is to insulate it insofar as possible from being stricken down in whole or in part for an unconstitutional delegation of legislative power. The best way to do this is to show how Congress has decided the major policy questions itself and has delegated to the agency only the authority to decide subsidiary questions and has done so in a manner that is sufficiently definite and precise to determine whether the congressional policy choice has been followed.

This section identifies the areas in the statutes authorizing the digital regulator to adopt, implement, and enforce rules that might pose non-delegation issues and shows how they can and should be cabined in anticipation of a potential challenge under the new more restricted non-delegation judicial regime.

In the legislation assigning competition, privacy, and content moderation responsibilities to a digital regulator, an important delegated decision is the determination of market power. When a company has market power, certain competition, privacy, and content moderation rules apply. When it does not, certain other competition, privacy, and content moderation rules apply. Congress describes certain factors to consider when making that determination, including market share, firm size, and barriers to entry. The agency does not have further discretion in deciding which rules apply. It might be possible for Congress to devise a more tiered approach. For instance, circumstances of moderate market power might trigger certain intermediate standards. Congress might decide that a company with moderate market power should not be subjected to the full range of regulations appropriate for companies with substantial market power but should instead face rules of intermediate stringency, more protective of the public than the standards applicable to digital companies with no or only minimal market power.

The key point for passing the non-delegation test is that Congress delegates this determination of substantial, moderate, or minimal market power to the agency with a list of factors to consider in making that determination. But it reserves for itself the policy choice of what rules apply consequent upon a determination of a company's market position.

Congress might, in addition, instruct the agency to review economic, business, and technological conditions from time to time to determine whether the market position of industry participants has changed, and to make appropriate changes in their regulatory classification. The key though is that Congress has predetermined the policy changes consequent upon changed circumstance, regardless of whether it has only two levels of regulatory stringency or a more nuanced, tiered approach.

A generalized forbearance authority might prove valuable in aiding the regulator to respond more flexibly to changing market conditions and is something for Congress to consider. The FCC has such authority and has used it extensively, most notably in its now-repealed 2015 open internet order.[131] But that level of discretion might also run into challenges on the grounds that it authorizes the regulator to depart from statutory requirements based on considerations other than changed circumstances or factual determinations. Court reviews of the FCC's open internet order revealed some concerns in that area.[132] Congress will have to consider the wisdom of providing that level of regulatory flexibility, considering the potential risk that it might be invalidated on non-delegation grounds.

The laws regulating digital competition, privacy, and content moderation limit the implementing agency initially to the core digital industries of search, social media, electronic commerce, and the mobile app distribution infrastructure. Congress could reserve for itself any authority to extend the scope of the agency's jurisdiction beyond these enumerated core digital industries. But it might also determine that this would create an unacceptable delay in responding to developments in the rapidly evolving digital world. As discussed elsewhere in this chapter, Congress could also require the agency to extend regulation to other digital lines of business upon making findings of centrality and lack of competition.

The law could define a centrally important service as one essential for full participation in contemporary social, economic, cultural, and political life, and provide a list of factors to consider in making a determination of centrality such as the cost of exclusion. The law could give the regulator several measures of lack of competition, including market shares, firm size, existence of strong barriers to entry from supply-side scale or demand-side network effects. It could define a digital line of business as an activity that uses digital technologies, including the internet as a core component of the service or product it is offering. To guide agency judgment, it could provide in the statute a nonexclusive list of lines of business satisfying the definition of a digital business.

The way such a system would work is laid out in the section of this chapter on defining the digital sector. This delegation of authority reserves the major decision to Congress and allows the agency only to make subsidiary choices. Congress makes the major policy decision that regulation should be extended to companies in a digital line of business that are central to contemporary life and where competition has failed. The agency makes the factual determinations of centrality and impoverished competition that trigger this policy choice.

The Supreme Court might very well endorse this approach. It has repeatedly upheld the authority of the FCC to define its own jurisdiction. In the 2013 *City of Arlington* case, the Court upheld the agency's decision to require local regulatory action on a petition for a cell tower siting within 90–150 days against a challenge that the agency had no authority in the area. The court's opinion, written by Justice Scalia, was not only that the agency could determine its statutory authority when it was clearly specified in statute how to extend its jurisdiction but also that, in the case of ambiguous statutory language, the court should apply Chevron deference to "an agency's determination of its own jurisdiction."[133]

However, other considerations might lead policymakers in a different direction. Surely it is a major question whether a company in an unregulated digital line of business is brought under a comprehensive system of regulation designed to promote competition, privacy, and effective and fair content moderation. In the 1990s, the Supreme Court struck down an attempt by the FCC to deregulate parts of the telecommunications industry on the grounds that "it is highly unlikely that Congress would leave the determination of whether an industry will be entirely, or even substantially, rate-regulated to agency discretion."[134] How much more concerned would the court be if an agency used, even explicitly granted, discretion to bring an industry under regulation?

Congress might decide that granting an agency discretion to modify its own jurisdiction and thereby determine on its own whether an industry will be entirely or substantially subject to regulation would be a step too far. If so, measures to allow the agency to respond rapidly to the evolving tech industry are still possible. Congress might provide itself with an opportunity to review the agency's recommendation for extending regulation. It could decide that if it fails to act within a set period, then the recommendation would become effective. Failure to act in the face of this previous congressional judgment might be seen by the courts as implicit approval. This is what Congress did in the case of enacting the medical privacy laws. It assigned the Department of Health and Human Service the job of writing draft privacy regulations and determined these regulations would become effective unless Congress acted to the contrary within a set period.[135]

Alternatively, Congress could require the agency to assess annually the state of centrality and competition in digital industries and to report any recommendations for extending regulation to Congress. If Congress fails to act, however, then the recommendation lapses and does not become effective. This is the option Ireland is proposing in its 2021 Online Safety bill.[136]

Other delegated decisions in the proposed laws seem on firm ground. Congress would make the major decision in statute to outlaw the practice of favoritism on dominant electronic commerce platforms. The agency retains the subordinate choice to use nondiscrimination rules or separation requirements to accomplish this purpose. The statute clearly defines the prohibition as preventing a digital company with strategic market position from using its dominant market position to favor its own services and disfavor those of competing dependent businesses. It would specifically authorize an agency to write, implement, and enforce non-discrimination rules that define self-dealing and prohibit it in these circumstances. It would further require the agency to assess the effectiveness of these rules and to impose a stronger measure if it finds that they are not effective. Specifically, it authorizes the agency to separate a company controlling a platform with strategic market position from any ownership of a company offering products or services on that platform if it finds that such a structural separation requirement is needed to accomplish the statutory purpose of controlling prohibited self-dealing. The agency is further instructed to write rules and adjudicate cases to determine whether contracts between separate companies have the same purpose or effect as prohibited self-dealing. In this way, the prohibition on self-dealing could be made sufficiently precise so that the courts could tell whether the congressional purpose has been attained and the congressional guidance followed.

Congress also makes the major choices in a definite and specific way in the digital privacy statute assigning responsibilities to the regulator to protect user privacy. For instance, the statute imposes fiduciary duties on digital companies. It would require the agency to write and implement rules defining these duties based on the common law. But it restricts these duties to those connected to the use of user personal information and instructs the agency to modify them to consider the special characteristics of digital companies. These duties are sufficiently similar to existing common law duties so that the agency's actions are cabined and subject to sufficient clarity so a reviewing court could determine whether the agency had exceeded its authority.

Similarly, the digital privacy statute prohibits deceptive, abusive, or dangerous design in digital industries, and requires the agency to write rules implementing this prohibition. This prohibition draws on existing precedents in product liability law and consumer protection law, including the FTC's notion of consumer harm in the use of their personal information. This policy goal is sufficiently definite and precise so that it can be determined whether the agency is furthering this policy goal in the subsidiary policy decisions it makes to implement the statutory prohibition.

The statute's requirement to demonstrate a legal basis for data use also constrains agency discretion. This requirement is essentially a demand that companies protect users from harm in the use of their personal information by showing either that they need to use the information to provide the service the user has requested or that it serves a legitimate interest that is not overridden by the need to protect user privacy or that they have obtained affirmative user consent. The agency has the subordinate task of ascertaining in particular cases, or by rule in classes of cases, whether the digital companies have satisfied at least one of these requirements.

The legislation establishing content moderation duties for social media companies also properly cabins the authority it delegates to the digital regulator. The requirement for due process and related disclosures is narrowly defined to achieve the interest of the user in obtaining the service that they thought they were getting based on the representations of the company. The policy choice is made by Congress that social media companies must have in place publicly disclosed content rules, appropriate notification procedures, enforcement techniques, explanations for violations of the rules, procedures for complaints, and the like. The agency is assigned the subsidiary tasks of determining which disclosure methods, enforcement techniques, and so on satisfy these general objectives.

Similarly, Congress makes the judgment that the larger social media companies providing for candidate political ads must disclose certain information in connection with these ads. It lists the types of information the social media companies must disclose. It assigns the agency only the subordinate tasks of determining the manner of these disclosures and enforcing them.

Congress also made the major policy decision to require companies to disclose sufficient information to the digital regulator to enable it to enforce the law. The agency must have discretion to access all books and records needed for that purpose. The law constrains the agency to respect privacy and the confidentiality of business information in doing this.

Congress also requires the agency to assess the effect of social media company technologies and business practices on various social problems, including cyberbullying, psychological harm to children, hate speech, and health and political disinformation that might have a material impact on public health or the effective operation and integrity of elections and the extent to which the operation of content moderation systems and algorithmic amplification serves the goal of political pluralism. Congress also requires the agency to investigate various matters in connection with political ads, including the extent to which social media companies distributed candidate ads, any limits imposed on targeting or frequency, and whether and the extent to which social media companies limited the content of political ads pursuant to their content moderation policies. Congress authorizes the agency to access company information needed to carry out these investigations and to authorize and vet independent researchers to access company information for these purposes.

Congress did not authorize the agency to take any regulatory measures on its own to address these issues. Instead, it was required to report back to Congress any legislative measures it recommended to address the problems found, including any measures to implement and enforce a requirement for political pluralism for dominant social media companies and other rules such as mandatory carriage of political ads, a no-censorship rule, and a right of reply. Congress reserved these additional major policy decisions to itself and instructed the agency only to act as fact finder and recommender of legislative measures.

As this summary indicates, under the content moderation bill as proposed, Congress would make all the major policy decisions and would delegate to the agency only the means and methods of carrying them out. These policy choices are sufficiently definite and precise to allow a determination of whether the agency is furthering them, and the subsidiary policy decisions the agency would have to make to carry out its duties are necessary but minor choices of methods to use in pursuit of these general policy goals.

It is only realistic to note that under the emerging doctrine of non-delegation and major policy questions the digital regulator would be substantially more constrained than under the generalized public interest standard that governs the conduct of other agencies, including the FCC. The digital agency would be authorized to act only in the three defined policy areas of competition, privacy, and content moderation. The FCC was able to develop subsidiary policy goals needed to advance the public interest in the communications industry. It used this discretion to adopt policies aiming at competition, diversity, and localism in broadcasting. The digital regulator would have no such authority to invent subsidiary goals.

Under the public interest standard, the FCC was able to devise and impose broadcast ownership rules without a specific mention of that policy tool in the 1934 Communications Act. The digital regulator would not have this flexibility. It would have no authority to invent new policy tools beyond those mentioned in the stature. If Congress wants the agency to impose a measure such as general horizontal ownership limits similar to those in broadcasting and banking, it will have to specifically authorize the agency to do this.

Policymakers might lament these constraints. There is a significant risk that they would hobble the effective operation of the agency in light of the rapidly evolving changes in the digital industries. It is only realistic, however, to recognize the changed judicial landscape and accommodate it in the drafting the new digital statutes.

Coda

The considerations that lead to the need for a digital regulator are compelling, but they do not dictate many of the parameters that must be set before the digital regulator can effectively do its job. This chapter has attempted a first cut at how to set those parameters in legislation. It charts the development of the digital regulator in two stages where Congress first assigns authority to regulate competition, privacy, and content moderation to the FTC and then later spins off these duties to a separate digital regulator. This digital regulator would then have exclusive jurisdiction over competition, privacy, and content moderation in digital industries.

The limits of the agency's authority would be defined in statute by enumerating the industries covered. The list includes search, social media, electronic commerce, mobile app infrastructure, and ad tech. The agency, however, would have authority to extend its jurisdiction to any digital activity that is central to contemporary life and where the presence of dominant companies limits the effectiveness of competition in protecting the public interest. The authorizing legislation must then define these key notions of digital activity, dominance, and centrality. Following the lead of the United Kingdom in setting up its digital markets unit, the legislation would limit the scope of the agency to activities where digital technologies are a "core component" of the products and services provided as part of that activity, and it would define dominance according to the notion of strategic market status. A company would be dominant when it has "substantial and entrenched market power" in at least one digital activity, providing it with a strategic position, where the effects of its market power are likely to be particularly widespread or significant. The notion of centrality is defined through reference to the history of public utility regulation in the United States as a service that people cannot avoid using if they are to fully participate in the nation's social, political, cultural, and economic life.

To prevent partisan abuse of the agency's power over digital industries, the regulator would have independence from the executive branch and no authority to second-guess content decisions made by the companies it regulates. This independence requires that the regulator should have the institutional form of an independent regulatory commission, composed of five members, no more than three of whom would be from the same political party. The agency would be accountable to the president indirectly through his or her ability to nominate commissioners and designate the commission's chair. In addition, its actions would be subject to court and congressional review.

The agency should be authorized to engage the industries it regulates through self-regulatory organizations that have some ability to develop and enforce industry rules. It should have an efficient internal structure organized around the industry segment regulated rather than the policy areas of competition, privacy, and content moderation, and it should have sufficient resources to attract and hold expert staff. Constraints on post-service employment and other mechanisms should be imposed by statute to control the risk of regulatory capture by the regulated industry.

While other policy areas impinge on the functioning of digital industries, the digital agency is authorized only to carry out missions to promote competition, protect privacy, and vindicate fundamental information rights through regulation of social media content moderation practices. It would not be a national security agency or an AI regulator. It must balance the tensions among these policy areas following a statutory framework that does not privilege any one policy domain over the others. The legislation would require the agency to adopt competition policy, privacy, and content moderation measures that achieve their goals in ways that interfere with conflicting goals to the smallest extent necessary and only when the balance of gains over losses is clearly positive.

Legislators must take seriously the likelihood that courts will limit the Chevron deference they have traditionally accorded to agency interpretation of any ambiguities in statutory language and seek the greatest possible precision in legislative drafting. In view of the likely return of the non-delegation doctrine to active use by the courts, legislators must also delegate only limited authority to the digital regulator by making the major policy decisions itself and assigning to the agency responsibility for fact-finding and subsidiary policy choices made with clear guidelines.

The choices made on these issues in this chapter are not the last word. Others might reach different judgments on how to define the key notions of dominance and centrality or how to limit the agency's jurisdiction to just digital industries. Some might think the agency should not be granted exclusive jurisdiction over competition, privacy, and social media content moderation or have different views on whether co-regulation should be allowed. Questions of internal organization and needed resources are always subject to debate and reconsideration. Some might think the measures to guard against regulatory capture are draconian and would drain the agency of needed expertise or that the framework outlined here for balancing tensions in achieving the agency's three missions is one-sided or cumbersome. Still others might think my concerns about losing Chevron deference or undue constraints on regulatory flexibility arising from the return of the non-delegation doctrine are overstated.

My hope in the is chapter is to have flagged many, if not all, the key issues and to have indicated in a rough way how they could be addressed, not to have definitely solved them. Policymakers, industry representatives, advocates for privacy, competition, and content moderation reform, civil society organizations, and academics, especially specialists in administrative law, must weigh in as Congress considers the shape and functions of the digital regulator.

Notes

1. McCraw, *Prophets of Regulation*, Kindle location 2817.

2. William James, *Pragmatism and Other Writings* (New York: Penguin Publishing Group, 2000), 64.

3. Online Safety Bill 2021, Parliament of Australia; "The Government's Proposed Approach," Government of Canada; "Culture, Arts, Gaeltacht, Sport and Media," Republic of Ireland; UK DCMS, "Draft Online Safety Bill."

4. Regulation (EU) 2022/2065 of the European Parliament; "Actor's Views: Roch-Olivier Maistre," Renaissance Numerique, October 17, 2022, https://www.renaissancenumerique.org/en/news/actors-views-roch-olivier-maistre; Peter O'Brien, "France Taps Tech Researchers to Police Social Media," *Politico*, May 25, 2022, https://www.politico.eu/article/france-regulator-work-global-network-researcher-police-social-media-tech.

5. Regulation (EU) 2022/1925 of the European Parliament; UK DCMS and BEIS, "A New Pro-Competition Regime"; European Commission, "Proposal for a Regulation Laying Down Harmonised Rules on Artificial Intelligence," April 21, 2021, https://digital-strategy.ec.europa.eu/en/library/proposal-regulation-laying-down-harmonised-rules-artificial-intelligence; MacCarthy and Propp, "Machines Learn that Brussels Writes the Rules."

6. UK Competition and Markets Authority, "The Digital Regulation Cooperation Forum"; Damien Geradin, "The Need for Coordination Among Digital Regulators: The Example of the UK Digital Regulation Cooperation Forum," *Platform Law Blog*, May 5, 2021, https://theplatformlaw.blog/2021/05/05/the-need-for-coordination-among-digital-regulators-the-example-of-the-uk-digital-regulation-cooperation-forum; "Gill Whitehead Appointed Chief Executive of Digital Regulators Forum," Ofcom, November 1, 2021, https://www.ofcom.org.uk/news-centre/2021/gill-whitehead-appointed-digital-regulators-forum-chief-executive; CMA & ICO Joint Statement on Competition and Data Protection Law, May 19, 2021, https://www.gov.uk/government/publications/cma-ico-joint-statement-on-competition-and-data-protection-law.

7. FTC, "Trade Regulation Rule on Commercial Surveillance and Data Security."

8. Feld, "The Case for the Digital Platform Act"; Wheeler et al., "New Digital Realities."

9. Digital Platform Commission Act, S. 4201, 117th Cong. (2022); Office of Senator Michael Bennet, "Bennet-Welch Reintroduce Landmark Legislation to Establish Federal Commission to Oversee Digital Platforms," press release, May 18, 2023, https://www.bennet.senate.gov/public/index.cfm/2023/5/bennet-welch-reintroduce-landmark-legislation-to-establish-federal-commission-to-oversee-digital-platforms.

10. G. Hamilton Loeb, "The Communications Act Policy Toward Communication: A Failure to Communicate," *Duke Law Journal* 1978, no. 1 (March 1978): 6–9, https://scholarship.law.duke.edu/cgi/viewcontent.cgi?article=2650&context=dlj.

11. National Broadcasting Co. Inc. v. United States, 319 US 190 (1943), https://supreme.justia.com/cases/federal/us/319/190.

12. Senate Report 111–176, April 30, 2010, 10, https://www.congress.gov/111/crpt/srpt176/CRPT-111srpt176.pdf.

13. Communications Act of 1934, 47 U.S.C. § 152(a).

14. Communications Act of 1934, 47 U.S.C. § 153(7).

15. Communications Act of 1934, 47 U.S.C. § 153(53) and (54).

16. National Broadcasting Co., Inc. v. United States, 319 U.S. 190 (1943), https://supreme.justia.com/cases/federal/us/319/190/.

17. McCraw, *Prophets of Regulation*, Kindle location 797–808, 864.

18. Feld, "The Case for the Digital Platform Act," 30; Furman et al., "Unlocking Digital Competition," 21–22; Scott Morton et al., "Stigler Committee on Digital Platforms," 29.

19. See Jean-Charles Rochet and Jean Tirole, "Platform Competition in Two-Sided Markets," *Journal of the European Economic Association* 1, no. 4 (June 2003): 990, and David S. Evans and Richard Schmalensee, "The Antitrust Analysis of Multi-Sided Platform Businesses" in *Oxford Handbook on International Antitrust Economics*, edited by Roger Blair and Daniel Sokol (New York: Oxford University Press, 2014); also available at https://ssrn.com/abstract=2185373.

20. Dana Mattioli and Ryan Tracy, "House Bills Seek to Break Up Amazon and Other Big Tech Companies," *Wall Street Journal*, June 11, 2021, https://www.wsj.com/articles/amazon-other-tech-giants-could-be-forced-to-shed-assets-under-house-bill-11623423248.

21. Bolger v. Amazon.com, LLC, (2020), https://law.justia.com/cases/california/court-of-appeal/2020/d075738.html; Loomis v. Amazon.com LLC (2021), https://law.justia.com/cases/california/court-of-appeal/2021/b297995.html.

22. Annie Palmer and Megan Graham, "Controversial E-Commerce Bill Criticized by Amazon Rivals Such as Etsy Won't Move Forward for Now," CNBC, August 31, 2021, https://www.cnbc.com/2020/08/31/controversial-ca-consumer-bill-will-not-advance-in-its-present-form.html.

23. UK DCMS and BEIS, "A New Pro-Competition Regime," 21.

24. Ohio v. American Express Co., 585 US __ (2018), https://supreme.justia.com/cases/federal/us/585/16-1454.

25. Ohio v. American Express Co., brief of 28 Professors of Antitrust Law as Amici Curiae Supporting Petitioners, December 14, 2017, https://www.supremecourt.gov/DocketPDF/16/16-1454/23982/20171215114926870_16-1454%20TS%20AC%2028%20Profs.pdf.

26. Ohio v. American Express Co., brief.

27. UK DCMS and BEIS, "A New Pro-Competition Regime," 20.

28. UK DCMS and BEIS, "Government Response to the Consultation on a New Pro-Competition Regime," 17; United Kingdom, Department for Business and Trade, Digital Markets, Competition and Consumers Bill, April 26, 2023, p. 2, https://publications.parliament.uk/pa/bills/cbill/58-03/0294/220294.pdf.

29. Ryan Browne, "Meta and Microsoft Can't Self-Regulate Their Metaverses, UK Regulator Warns," CNBC, October 26 2022, https://www.cnbc.com/2022/10/26/meta

-and-microsoft-cant-self-regulate-their-metaverses-ofcom-warns.html; European Parliament, answer given by Mr. Breton on behalf of the European Commission, June 1, 2022, https://www.europarl.europa.eu/doceo/document/E-9-2022-000656-ASW_EN.pdf; MacCarthy, "FTC's Case Against Meta's Acquisition of Within."

30. UK DCMS and BEIS, "Government Response to the Consultation on a New Pro-Competition Regime."

31. UK DCMS and BEIS, "Government Response to the Consultation on a New Pro-Competition Regime," 17.

32. Munn v. Illinois, 94 US 113 (1877), https://supreme.justia.com/cases/federal/us/94/113, Id. at 126.

33. William J. Novak, "Law and the Social Control of American Capitalism," *Emory Law Journal* 60, nos. 377, 386, 400 (2010), https://scholarlycommons.law.emory.edu/elj/vol60/iss2/4.

34. Nebbia v. New York, 291 US 502, 525 (1934), https://supreme.justia.com/cases/federal/us/291/502.

35. K. Sabeel Rahman, "The New Utilities," *Cardozo Law Review* 39, no. 1621 (2018), http://cardozolawreview.com/wp-content/uploads/2018/07/RAHMAN.39.5.2.pdf.

36. Orla Lynskey, "Grappling with 'Data Power': Normative Nudges from Data Protection and Privacy," *Theoretical Inquiries in Law* 20, no. 189 (2019): 211, https://www7.tau.ac.il/ojs/index.php/til/article/view/1613/1714.

37. McCraw, *Prophets of Regulation*, Kindle locations 367–68.

38. Frank Haigh Dixon, "The Mann-Elkins Act, Amending the Act to Regulate Commerce," *The Quarterly Journal of Economics* 24, no. 4 (August 1910): 622, https://www.jstor.org/stable/pdf/1883490.pdf.

39. Kearney and Merrill, "The Great Transformation of Regulated Industries Law."

40. McCraw, *Prophets of Regulation*, Kindle locations 835, 838.

41. Brett M. Frischmann, *Infrastructure: The Social Value of Shared Resources* (New York: Oxford University Press, 2012), xiv, xii.

42. Rahman, "The New Utilities."

43. K. Sabeel Rahman, "Regulating Informational Infrastructure: Internet Platforms as The New Public Utilities," *Georgetown Law Technology Review* 2, no. 234 (2018), https://georgetownlawtechreview.org/wp-content/uploads/2018/07/2.2-Rahman-pp-234-51.pdf.

44. Lauren Scholz, "Fiduciary Boilerplate" *Journal of Corporation Law* 46 (June 5, 2020), https://ssrn.com/abstract=3620164.

45. Kashmir Hill, "I Cut the 'Big Five' Tech Giants from My Life. It Was Hell," *Gizmodo*, February 8, 2019, https://gizmodo.com/i-cut-the-big-five-tech-giants-from-my-life- it-was-hel-1831304194.

46. Laura Moy, "The Underappreciated Role of Avoidability in Privacy Law," unpublished manuscript, May 2020, 2.

47. Feld, "The Case for the Digital Platform Act," 41–45.

48. Rahul Tongia and Ernest J. Wilson III, "The Flip Side of Metcalfe's Law," *International Journal of Communications* 5 (2011): 665–81, https://ijoc.org/index.php/ijoc/article/view/873/549.

49. Communications Act of 1934, 47 U.S.C. § 152, https://www.law.cornell.edu/uscode/text/47/152.

50. Wheeler et al., "New Digital Realities."

51. Samuel Weinstein, "Financial Regulation in the (Receding) Shadow of Antitrust," *Temple Law Review* 91, no. 447 (2019), Cardozo Legal Studies Research Paper No. 573, https://ssrn.com/abstract=3356737.

52. American Choice and Innovation Online Act, H.R. 3816, 117th Cong. (2021), Section 7.

53. Credit Suisse Sec. v. Billing, 551 US 264, 275 (2007), https://supreme.justia.com/cases/federal/us/551/264.

54. Community Financial Services Ass'n of Am. v. CFPB, 2022 WL 11054082 (5th Cir. Oct. 19, 2022), https://www.ca5.uscourts.gov/opinions/pub/21/21-50826-CV0.pdf.

55. Seila Law LLC v. Consumer Financial Protection Bureau.

56. Humphrey's Executor v. United States, 295 US 602 (1935), https://supreme.justia.com/cases/federal/us/295/602.

57. Administrative Procedure Act, 5 U.S.C. § 553, https://www.law.cornell.edu/uscode/text/5/553.

58. Administrative Procedure Act, 5 U.S.C. § 554, https://www.law.cornell.edu/uscode/text/5/554.

59. PACT Act, S. 797, 117th Cong. (2021).

60. "Fair Lending Laws and Regulation," FDIC, https://www.fdic.gov/resources/supervision-and-examinations/consumer-compliance-examination-manual/documents/4/iv-1-1.pdf.

61. Congressional Review Act of 1996, 5 U.S.C. § 802, https://www.law.cornell.edu/uscode/text/5/802; Congressional Research Service, Congressional Review Act (CRA): Frequently Asked Questions, November 12, 2021, https://sgp.fas.org/crs/misc/R43992.pdf; Public Law 115–22, April 3, 2017, https://www.congress.gov/115/plaws/publ22/PLAW-115publ22.pdf; Public Law 115–172, May 21, 2018, https://www.congress.gov/115/plaws/publ172/PLAW-115publ172.pdf.

62. Ephrat Livni, "The First Open Meeting of the F.T.C. under Lina Khan Starts with Political Sparks," *New York Times*, July 1, 2021, https://www.nytimes.com/2021/07/01/business/ftc-lina-khan.html.

63. UK DCMS and BEIS, "A New Pro-Competition Regime."

64. ACCESS Act of 2021, H.R. 3849, 117th Cong. (2021).

65. Wheeler et al., "New Digital Realities."

66. See MacCarthy, "A Dispute Resolution Program for Social Media Companies."

67. Securities Exchange Act of 1934, Section 19, https://www.nyse.com/publicdocs/nyse/regulation/nyse/sea34.pdf.

68. "Development of New Industry Codes to Better Protect Australians Online," eSafety Commissioner, September 29, 2021, https://www.esafety.gov.au/newsroom/media-releases/development-new-industry-codes-better-protect-australians-online.

69. "Who Regulates Whom? An Overview of the U.S. Financial Regulatory Framework," Congressional Research Service, August 17, 2017–March 10, 2020, https://www.everycrsreport.com/reports/R44918.html.

70. See budget proposals for the FTC, FCC, CFPB, Antitrust Division, and the Eshoo-Lofgren proposal for a Digital Privacy Agency.

71. Build Back Better Act, H.R. 5376, 117th Cong. (2021).

72. Digital Platform Commission Act, S. 4201, 117th Cong. (2022).

73. Dodd-Frank Act, 12 U.S.C. § 5481(12)(J), https://www.law.cornell.edu/uscode/text/12/5481.

74. Secure and Trusted Communications Networks Act of 2019, 47 U.S.C. § 1601, https://www.law.cornell.edu/uscode/text/47/1601.

75. International Emergency Economic Powers Act, 50 U.S.C. § 1701–1702, https://www.law.cornell.edu/uscode/text/50/chapter-35.

76. Safiya Noble, "Google Has a Striking History of Bias Against Black Girls," *Time*, March 26, 2018, https://time.com/5209144/google-search-engine-algorithm-bias-racism; Safiya Noble, *Algorithms of Oppression: How Search Engines Reinforce Oppression* (NY: New York University Press, 2018); Latanya Sweeney, "Discrimination in Online Ad Delivery" (January 28, 2013), https://ssrn.com/abstract=2208240.

77. Shirin Ghaffary, "The Algorithms that Detect Hate Speech Online Are Biased Against Black People," *Vox/Recode*, August 15, 2019, https://www.vox.com/recode/2019/8/15/20806384/social-media-hate-speech-bias-black-african-american-facebook-twitter; Elizabeth Dwoskin, Nitasha Tiku, and Craig Timberg, "Facebook's Race-Blind Practices Around Hate Speech Came at the Expense of Black Users, New Documents Show," *Washington Post*, November 21, 2021, https://www.washingtonpost.com/technology/2021/11/21/facebook-algorithm-biased-race.

78. HUD v. Facebook, HUD ALJ No. FHEO No. 01-18-0323-8, March 28, 2019, https://www.hud.gov/sites/dfiles/Main/documents/HUD_v_Facebook.pdf; Tracy Jan and Elizabeth Dwoskin, "HUD Is Reviewing Twitter's and Google's Ad Practices as Part of Housing Discrimination Probe," *Washington Post*, March 28, 2019, https://www.washingtonpost.com/business/2019/03/28/hud-charges-facebook-with-housing-discrimination.

79. Cat Zakrzewski, "Federal Regulators Call AI Discrimination a 'New Civil Rights Frontier,'" *Washington Post*, April 25, 2023, https://www.washingtonpost.com/technology/2023/04/25/artificial-intelligence-bias-eeoc/.

80. Anton Korinek, "Why We Need a New Agency to Regulate Advanced Artificial Intelligence Systems," Brookings Report, December 8, 2021, https://www.brookings.edu/research/why-we-need-a-new-agency-to-regulate-advanced-artificial-intelligence-lessons-on-ai-control-from-the-facebook-files/.

81. Mark MacCarthy, "A Digital Regulator Must Be Empowered to Address AI Issues," *Lawfare Blog*, May 9, 2023, https://www.lawfareblog.com/a-digital-regulator-must-be-empowered-to-address-ai-issues.

82. George J. Stigler, "The Theory of Economic Regulation," *The Bell Journal of Economics and Management Science* 2, no. 1 (Spring 1971): 3–21.

83. Gerald Berk, "Corporate Liberalism Reconsidered: A Review Essay," *Journal of Policy History* 3, no. 1 (1991): 70–84.

84. Kearney and Merrill, "The Great Transformation of Regulated Industries Law."

85. Dodd-Frank Wall Street Reform and Consumer Protection Act, 12 U.S.C. § 5491 (2010).

86. Samuel Weinstein, "Financial Regulation in the (Receding) Shadow of Antitrust," *Temple Law Review* 91, no. 447 (2019), https://ssrn.com/abstract=3356737.

87. Chris Young, Reity O'Brien, and Andrea Fuller, "Corporations, Probusiness Nonprofits Foot Bill for Judicial Seminars," Center for Public Integrity, March 2014, https://publicintegrity.org/politics/corporations-pro-business-nonprofits-foot-bill-for-judicial-seminars.

88. Board of Governors of the Federal Reserve System, Structure of the Federal Reserve System, https://www.federalreserve.gov/aboutthefed/structure-federal-reserve-board.htm.

89. Feld, "The Case for the Digital Platform Act," 15–16.

90. Vaheesan, "Fair Competition Policy."

91. "Universal Declaration of Human Rights."

92. Associated Press v. United States, 326 US 1 (1945).

93. Douglas, "The New Antitrust/Data Privacy Law Interface," 683.

94. HiQ Labs, Inc. v. LinkedIn Corp., 938 F.3d 985 (9th Cir. 2019), https://cdn.ca9.uscourts.gov/datastore/opinions/2019/09/09/17-16783.pdf.

95. Erika Douglas, "Monopolization Remedies and Data Privacy," *Virginia Journal of Law and Technology* 24, no. 2 (2020), https://ssrn.com/abstract=3694607; Douglas, "The New Antitrust/Data Privacy Law Interface," 683.

96. Article 29 Data Protection Working Party, Opinion 06/2014 on the Notion of Legitimate Interests of the Data Controller Under Article 7 of Directive 95/46/EC, 2014, https://www.huntonprivacyblog.com/wp-content/uploads/sites/28/2014/04/wp217_en.pdf.

97. Information Commissioner's Office, "How Do We Apply Legitimate Interest in Practice?"

98. UK Competition & Markets Authority, "Competition and Data Protection in Digital Markets," Information Commissioner's Office, May 19, 2021, https://ico.org.uk/media/about-the-ico/documents/2619797/cma-ico-public-statement-20210518.pdf.

99. See, for instance, Case CC-331/88 Fedesa and Others (1990) ECR 1–4023, Par. 13, http://eur-lex.europa.eu/resource.html?uri=cellar:ffd72601-c072-4215-83f8-ed59f5af0d03.0002.06/DOC_2&format=PDF.

100. "Judgment of the ECJ in Digital Rights Ireland data retention challenge," *Official Journal of the European Union*, April 8, 2014, http://eur-lex.europa.eu/legal-content/EN/TXT/HTML/?uri=CELEX:62012CJ0293&from=EN, "With regard to judicial review of compliance with those conditions, where interferences with fundamental rights are at issue, the extent of the EU legislature's discretion may prove to be limited, depending on a number of factors, including, in particular, the area concerned, the nature of the right at issue guaranteed by the Charter, the nature and seriousness of the interference and the object pursued by the interference."

101. Case C-473/12 IPI EU:C:2013:715, paragraph 39, http://curia.europa.eu/juris/document/document.jsf?text=&docid=144217&pageIndex=0&doclang=EN&mode=lst&dir=&occ=first&part=1&cid=159802.

102. Kai Möller, "Proportionality: Challenging the Critics," *I•CON* 10, no. 3 (2012): 710–31, https://www.corteidh.or.cr/tablas/r30064.pdf.

103. Andrew Cheung, "Conflict of Fundamental Rights and the Double Proportionality Test," a lecture in the Common Law Lecture Series 2019, delivered at the University of Hong Kong, September 17, 2019, https://www.hkcfa.hk/filemanager/speech/en/upload/2236/Common%20Law%20Lecture%20(Final%20Version).pdf.

104. [2005] EWHC 1564 (Fam), paragraph 53, https://www.5rb.com/wp-content/uploads/2013/10/Re-W-Fam-14-July-2005.pdf.

105. Chevron U.S.A. Inc. v. NRDC, 467 US 837 (1984), https://supreme.justia.com/cases/federal/us/467/837; Cass R. Sunstein and Adrian Vermeule, *Law and Leviathan* (Cambridge, MA: Harvard University Press, 2020), 131–37.

106. Smiley v. Citibank (South Dakota), N. A., 517 US 735 (1996), https://supreme.justia.com/cases/federal/us/517/735.

107. City of Arlington v. Federal Communications Commission, 569 US 290 (2013), https://supreme.justia.com/cases/federal/us/569/290.

108. FDA v. Brown & Williamson Tobacco Corp., 529 US 120, 159 (2000), https://supreme.justia.com/cases/federal/us/529/120; see also "The Major Questions Doctrine," Congressional Research Service, November 2, 2022, https://crsreports.congress.gov/product/pdf/IF/IF12077.

109. Whitman v. American Trucking Assns. Inc., 531 US 457 (2001), https://supreme.justia.com/cases/federal/us/531/457.

110. National Cable & Telecommunications Assn. v. Brand X Internet Services, 545 US 967 (2005), https://supreme.justia.com/cases/federal/us/545/967.

111. King v. Burwell, 576 US 473 (2015), https://www.supremecourt.gov/opinions/14pdf/14-114_qol1.pdf.

112. United States Telecom Assoc. v. FCC, No. 15-1063 (D.C. Cir. 2016), https://cases.justia.com/federal/appellate-courts/cadc/15-1063/15-1063-2016-06-14.pdf?ts=1465916544; United States Telecom Association v. FCC, No. 15-1063, On Petitions for Rehearing En Banc, Court of Appeals for the District of Columbia, Case, May 1, 2017, https://www.cadc.uscourts.gov/internet/opinions.nsf/06F8BFD079A89E13852581130053C3F8/$file/15-1063-1673357.pdf.

113. Supreme Court, Order list 586 US, Monday, November 5, 2018, https://www.supremecourt.gov/orders/courtorders/110518zor_o759.pdf.

114. Baldwin v. United States, 140 S. Ct. 690 (2020) https://www.law.cornell.edu/supremecourt/text/19-402.

115. Kristin E. Hickman, "To Repudiate or Merely Curtail? Justice Gorsuch and Chevron Deference," *Alabama Law Review* 70, no. 3 (2019), https://ssrn.com/abstract=3396667; Brett M. Kavanaugh, "Fixing Statutory Interpretation," *Harvard Law Review* 129, no. 2118 (June 10, 2016), https://harvardlawreview.org/2016/06/fixing-statutory-interpretation.

116. Christensen v. Harris County, 529 US 576 (2000), https://supreme.justia.com/cases/federal/us/529/576; Skidmore v. Swift & Co., 323 US 134 (1944), https://supreme.justia.com/cases/federal/us/323/134.

117. Nicholas Bagley, "Justices Mull Chevron and Voice Skepticism of Medicare's Rate Cut for Hospital Drugs," *SCOTUSblog*, November 30, 2021, https://www.scotusblog.com/2021/11/justices-mull-chevron-and-voice-skepticism-of-medicares-rate-cut-for-hospital-drugs; James Romoser, "In an Opinion that Shuns Chevron, the Court Rejects a Medicare Cut for Hospital Drugs," *SCOTUSblog*, June 15, 2022, https://www.scotusblog.com/2022/06/in-an-opinion-that-shuns-chevron-the-court-rejects-a-medicare-cut-for-hospital-drugs; Amy Howe, "Supreme Court Will Consider Major Case on Power of Federal Regulatory Agencies," *SCOTUSblog*, May 1, 2023, https://www.scotusblog.com/2023/05/supreme-court-will-consider-major-case-on-power-of-federal-regulatory-agencies.

118. Blair Levin, "NSR Policy: Lawsuit Aims at the Heart of FCC (and All Administrative) Authority," NewStreet Research, October 11, 2012, https://www.newstreetresearch.com/download-page/nsr-policy-lawsuit-aims-at-the-heart-of-fcc-and-all-administrative-authority.

119. Congressional Research Service, Congressional Review Act (CRA): Frequently Asked Questions, https://crsreports.congress.gov/product/pdf/R/R43992.

120. A.L.A. Schechter Poultry Corp. v. United States, 295 US 495 (1935), https://supreme.justia.com/cases/federal/us/295/495.

121. New York Central Securities Corp. v. United States, 287 US 12 (1932), https://supreme.justia.com/cases/federal/us/287/12.

122. National Broadcasting Co. Inc. v. United States, 319 US 190 (1943), https://supreme.justia.com/cases/federal/us/319/190.

123. Cass Sunstein, "Nondelegation Canons," *University of Chicago Law Review* 67, nos. 315 and 322 (2000), https://chicagounbound.uchicago.edu/uclrev/vol67/iss2/1.

124. JW Hampton, Jr & Co. v. US, 276 US 395, 409 (1928), https://supreme.justia.com/cases/federal/us/276/394.

125. Gundy v. United States, 588 US __ (2019), https://supreme.justia.com/cases/federal/us/588/17-6086.

126. Sunstein and Vermeule, *Law and Leviathan*, 122.

127. Paul v. United States, 140 S. Ct. 342, 342 (2019), https://www.law.cornell.edu/supremecourt/text/17-8830.

128. Community Financial Services Ass'n of Am. v. CFPB.

129. Alabama Association of Realtors v. HHS, 594 US __ (2021), https://www.supremecourt.gov/opinions/20pdf/21a23_ap6c.pdf; National Federation of Independent Business v. Department of Labor, Occupational Safety and Health Administration, 595 US __ (2022), https://www.supremecourt.gov/opinions/21pdf/21a244_hgci.pdf.

130. West Virginia v. EPA, 597 US __ (2022), https://www.supremecourt.gov/opinions/21pdf/20-1530_n758.pdf.

131. Telecommunications Act of 1996, 47 U.S.C. § 160, https://www.law.cornell.edu/uscode/text/47/160; FCC, "Open Internet Report and Order," February 26, 2015, para. 51, https://www.fcc.gov/document/fcc-releases-open-internet-order.

132. US Telecom Association v. FCC, No. 15-1063, on Petitions for Rehearing En Banc, Court of Appeals for the District of Columbia, Case, Dissenting Opinion of Circuit Judge Brown, and Dissenting Opinion of Circuit Judge Kavanaugh, May 1, 2017,

https://www.cadc.uscourts.gov/internet/opinions.nsf/06F8BFD079A89E138525811300 53C3F8/$file/15-1063-1673357.pdf.

133. City of Arlington v. FCC, 569 US 290 (2013), https://supreme.justia.com/cases /federal/us/569/290.

134. MCI Telecommunications Corp. v. American Telephone & Telegraph Co., 512 US 218, 231 (1994), https://supreme.justia.com/cases/federal/us/512/218.

135. Department of Health and Human Service, 45 CFR Parts 160 and 164, "Standards for Privacy of Individually Identifiable Health Information; Final Rule," *Federal Register* 65, no. 250 (Thursday, December 28, 2000), 82469–70, https://www.hhs.gov/sites /default/files/ocr/privacy/hipaa/administrative/privacyrule/prdecember2000all8parts.pdf.

136. Republic of Ireland, Department of Tourism, Culture, Arts, Gaeltacht, Sport and Media, Online Safety and Media Regulation Bill, updated June 2, 2021, https://www.gov .ie/en/publication/d8e4c-online-safety-and-media-regulation-bill/#.

Chapter 6

Where Do We Go from Here?

"The corporation is the creature of the people; and it must not be allowed to become the ruler of the people."

—Theodore Roosevelt[1]

Introduction

The lack of competition in digital industries, the abusive exploitation of personal information by digital companies, and the information disorder in digital platforms feed on each other to produce social harms that seem to be greater than the sum of their individual injuries. In a similar way, but in reverse, the remedies to these problems can reinforce each other to protect digital users and the public from these harms.

Competition reform seeks to strengthen the government's ability to constrain the ability of dominant digital companies to abuse their rivals and dependent businesses. But it might also help in the fight against privacy invasions and unfair content moderation. New privacy rules would give government the tools to protect the users of digital services from harm in the use of their personal information. They might also enable rivals to compete more effectively against the digital giants. Content moderation measures would protect the rights of users to seek out and receive information on social media services without being subject to abusive hate speech, misinformation, and propaganda from other users and from the social media companies themselves. But they might also prevent unfair competition from social media companies who provide no content moderation services at all.

Not all measures will work well together. Data portability or data access might help competitors but at the expense of user privacy. Conversely, consumer rights to opt out of mandated data access might frustrate their procompetitive purpose. Strong privacy rights might also interfere with the monitoring necessary for good content moderation on social media. Similarly, interoperability for competitive purposes might reduce the efficiency of content moderation efforts on social media.

Balanced implementation of these measures by a digital regulator would improve the lives of digital users and allow innovative digital businesses to flourish as never before. Perhaps the major contribution in this book is the recommendation that policymakers should consider these separate policy areas together as one coherent system of regulation. Competition, privacy, and content moderation are not separate silos. They are overlapping policy areas where measures to promote any one policy objective interact with the others in ways that could reinforce each other (if done right) or interfere with each other (if done wrong). To recall again the central image of our policy discussions, competition, privacy, and content moderation form a Venn diagram of intersecting circles, where almost the entire space overlaps. Because of these synergies and tensions, the most effective way to make sure the different elements of competition, privacy, and content moderation regulation work together is to have a digital regulator implement them under a common administrative structure.

The United States is not alone in facing these challenges. In Europe and the United Kingdom, lawmakers are moving forward to enshrine new regulations to promote competition and good content moderation. Australia, New Zealand, Canada, and Ireland also have new content moderation systems in place or proposed.

The European Union finalized the Digital Services Act and the Digital Markets Act in 2021. The DSA sets out a framework of notice liability for illegal material on social media and other platforms. It also creates obligations for user transparency, mandated public reports, risk assessments, audits, and access to data for researchers. It requires companies to document their risk mitigation processes and procedures, and it empowers the European Commission in conjunction with member country regulators to instruct social media companies to improve unsatisfactory risk mitigation measures.

The DMA applies ex-ante procompetitive obligations and prohibitions to the larger digital platform gatekeepers. The duties include allowing third-party interoperability, business user access to platform information about their users, verification tools for online advertisers, and permitting business users to access customers off the platform. The prohibitions include a ban on favoring their own services over similar services offered by the platform's business users, forbidding rules that prevent users from linking with businesses outside their platforms, barring practices that prevent users from uninstalling software or apps, and an interdiction on tracking user activity off the platform without effective consent.

Europe's new digital regulations are far more developed than anything in the United States. Many of their provisions are models for proposed digital laws under consideration in the United States and are reflected in many of the recommendations in this book. But both the DSA and the DMA suffer from a lack of an effective system to implement and enforce the new measures. They treat the new content moderation and procompetition obligations as largely self-enforcing. Companies are required to present plans to implement the new requirements, and then the enforcing agency at the Commission or in the member country determines whether they are good enough. If they come up short, the agencies tell them to try again. Enforcing agencies are largely not empowered to write implementing rules that specify what the statutory obligations mean in practice. They allow the industry to interpret the new duties and then object if they think that interpretation is unsatisfactory. This retreat from implementing regulation is likely to cripple effective enforcement.[2]

The United Kingdom's competition and content moderation proposed laws provide for much more robust regulatory enforcement. The Online Safety Bill mandates disclosure of content rules, due process protections, transparency reports, risk assessments, and mitigation measures for harmful content. It lodges enforcement authority in the traditional media regulator Ofcom, and it gives the agency extensive regulatory powers, although not the licensing authority and ability to review particular programming that the agency has for traditional media. The proposed Digital Markets, Competition, and Consumers Bill would establish a digital markets unit inside the existing Competition and Markets Authority. It would ensure that the larger platforms (those with "strategic market status") do not apply discriminatory terms to their users, do not bundle their platform services with other services, and provide clear, relevant, accurate, and accessible information to users. The digital markets unit would be required to develop binding specific guidance on how these requirements would work in practice.

Many of these proposed measures served as guideposts for the recommendations developed in this book. The definitions of "strategic market status" and "digital activity" in the legislation that sets up the United Kingdom's digital markets unit DMU bill drove the similar concepts of dominance and centrality in digital industries in our recommendations. The Online Safety Bill's focus on systems regulation and its prohibition on Ofcom reviewing specific pieces of online content are in line with similar recommendations in earlier chapters. Lodging enforcement in empowered regulators with rule-writing capacity and calling for cooperation among the regulators to deal with synergies and tensions among the different policy missions are also lessons from the Online Safety Bill for US policymakers.[3]

There is good reason for optimism over the prospects of creating a new regulatory structure for digital industries in the United States. Policymakers and the public are at a tipping point in the conversation about regulating digital industries. Over a decade ago, in 2011, internet companies in the United States thoroughly routed the once powerful recording, movie, and publishing lobbies that were seeking to impose additional copyright enforcement responsibilities on tech companies. This fight over the Stop Online Piracy Act (SOPA) was the high point of influence for digital industries, and for years afterward they used their influence to block all attempts at digital regulation.[4]

By 2021, however, the climate of opinion had changed dramatically. Over the last several years, policymakers across the political spectrum have proposed competition policy, privacy, and content moderation measures aimed at setting guardrails for digital industries. In late 2021, former Facebook analyst turned whistleblower Frances Haugen turbocharged the pro-regulatory movement among policymakers with revelations that Facebook's own research showed its services caused substantial psychological harm to vulnerable teenagers.[5] Congressional hearings produced a bipartisan consensus to regulate. By late 2021, even the pro-business *Financial Times* was calling for Congress to rein in big tech in the same way it regulated the robber barons in the nineteenth century through a "Cyberspace Commerce Commission" that would "start setting some boundaries."[6]

The urge to do something should never be stronger than the urge to do something intelligent. In addition to its key recommendation for the creation of a strong digital regulator, this book sets out competition, privacy, and content moderation measures that will be practical, effective, politically feasible, and able to pass judicial scrutiny.

The intellectual forces calling for little or no action are still strong. In a 2021 discussion of the shift from traditional antitrust enforcement to regulation sponsored in part by the tech industry group the Computer and Communications Industry Association, many of the most respected antitrust experts condemned the move to regulation.[7] Even those who support controlling big tech hope that traditional antitrust alone can do the job. This is not a new idea. Conservative economist George Stigler, writing in 1952, said, "The dissolution of big businesses is . . . a part of the program necessary to increase the support for a private, competitive enterprise economy, and reverse the drift toward government control."[8]

This is an illusion. The dissolution of the power of big tech, as we have seen throughout this book, will require more, not less government control of business. Powerful companies holding commanding positions in their digital lines of business cannot be brought under social control by a weak state. It is a chimera to think that the economic power of today's digital giants can be dismantled by one or two big antitrust enforcement cases. It will take ongoing regulatory supervision to develop, foster, and maintain competition in the digital economy, if indeed it can be sustained in these industries at all.

Some contemporary antitrust reformers such as Senator Elizabeth Warren put their faith in structural remedies that break up companies and hope, thereby, to avoid a commitment to ongoing regulation. In defending her call for a breakup of digital companies, Senator Warren said, "When you've just got a bright-line rule, you don't need the regulators. At that point, the market will discipline itself."[9]

This proposed strategy of break up and walk away is a triumph of hope over experience. The standard examples of successful structural separations in the electric utility and financial services world took place against a backdrop of pervasive state and federal regulation. In telecommunications, Judge Harold Greene did nothing for twelve years but supervise the line-of-business restrictions on the spun-off Regional Bell Holding Companies that were contained in the 1982 decree, breaking up AT&T's integrated telephone monopoly. He functioned as a de facto industry regulator, and he was assisted in this effort by the Antitrust Division of the Department of Justice, an active and energetic FCC, and state public utility regulators all over the country. The proposed breakup of Microsoft into a software company and an operating system company was based on this telephone experience. The proposal was sought by the Antitrust Division, approved by the trial court, but rejected by the appeals court. Making such a breakup order effective in the face of a rapidly evolving computer industry would have required the creation of a new Federal Software Commission or the transformation of the Antitrust Division into its equivalent.

There is no way around a digital regulator if the objective is competition in digital industries. The digital regulator needs to do more than promote competition, however. One of the biggest fallacies in the current debate over tech power is the notion that promoting competition will solve all tech industry ills. This sometimes arises in discussions of privacy, but it is most frequently heard in discussions of content moderation. For example, consider this remark from the Electronic Freedom Foundation urging the courts to strike down the Texas social media law that provides for viewpoint neutrality and transparency: "Of course, it's true that moderation decisions by large platforms can silence legitimate speech and stifle debate online. But as EFF has repeatedly argued, the way to address the concentration of a handful of large services is by reducing their power and giving consumers more choices. This includes renewed antitrust reforms, allowing interoperability, and taking other steps to increase competition between services."[10]

As we have seen, unrestricted interoperability that would promote competition between rival social media services would also make it much more difficult to engage in good content moderation, as people from poorly moderated platforms use their interconnection rights to lob hate speech, lies, and disinformation to users on other platforms. Moreover, there are some things that are beyond competition policy. As antitrust practitioner Carl Shapiro has said, antitrust is not equipped to handle the challenges of privacy and information disorder on social media, and its push to encourage competition might make these problems worse.[11]

An empowered digital regulator must pursue three policy objectives at once: the promotion of digital competition, the protection of digital user privacy, and the maintenance of effective and fair content moderation on social media platforms. Let's summarize what needs to be done in each of the policy areas and how it might be accomplished through legislative action.

Competition Policy

A series of bills passed by the US House Judiciary Committee in June 2021 would provide an interlocking set of tools designed to jump-start and sustain competition in the tech industry. The Ending Platform Monopolies Act would separate platform and commerce, prohibiting a large platform from owning a line of business that utilizes the platform "for the sale or provision of products or services."[12] The ACCESS Act of 2021 would impose data portability and interoperability requirements on these platforms.[13] The American Choice and Innovation Online Act would impose various nondiscrimination and access requirements on platforms.[14] Similar nondiscrimination measures are contained in the bill that passed the Senate Judiciary Committee in January 2022, with a bipartisan vote of 16–6. A revised version was prepared for Senate floor action.[15] The Platform Competition and Opportunity Act of 2021 would prohibit the largest online platforms from engaging in mergers that would eliminate competitors or potential competitors.[16] In addition, the Senate's Open App Markets App would establish a regulatory structure for app stores. On February 3, 2022, the Senate Judiciary Committee approved this bill, with an impressive bipartisan vote of 20–2.[17]

These five competition reform bills provide a good model for what needs to be done. Ideally, Congress would combine them into a single legislative package and move this comprehensive digital competition reform measure through the legislative process. Congress made some progress in 2022, moving bills through both the Senate and the House Judiciary Committees, but it was not able to pass these reform bills.

The key policy objectives of this digital competition reform legislation should be (1) to instill competition in the core digital industries of search, electronic commerce, social media, mobile app infrastructure, and ad tech, and (2) to protect dependent businesses that rely on dominant providers in these industries from anticompetitive abuses. Congress should authorize a regulatory agency to use specified procompetitive policy tools when necessary to achieve these objectives. These tools should include data portability, interoperability, restrictions on data use, data sharing, nondiscrimination rules, structural separation measures, and line-of-business restrictions. In addition, the agency should be required to follow a new, more stringent standard for reviewing tech mergers as outlined in Senator Amy Klobuchar's 2021 reform bill.[18] This new standard would shift the burden of proof to the merging party to show that a proposed merger is legal and would forbid mergers that "create an appreciable risk of materially lessening competition." The agency would have broad and clear authority to interpret these requirements, to write rules implementing them under the procedures of the Administrative Procedure Act, and to enforce them through fines, injunctions, and other penalties.

Ideally, the implementing agency for these new competition rules for digital industries would be a new independent digital regulator. But realistically, Congress is highly likely to lodge enforcement authority with the FTC and transfer authority to a sector-specific digital regulator in a second step, if at all. This is not an unusual process in the history of regulation. In 1933, Congress authorized the FTC to supervise disclosure rules for the securities industry and transferred this authority to the newly formed SEC in 1934. Institutional change, says antitrust activist Matt Stoller, "takes time."[19]

The legislation should enumerate the digital lines of business covered and include search, electronic commerce, social media, mobile app infrastructure, and ad tech. The agency should have authority to extend its jurisdiction to cover additional digital lines of business. But it should be able to do this only upon a finding that these digital services are essential, central to full participation in the nation's social, cultural, economic, and political life, and that there has been a substantial failure of competition in that industry. A substantial failure of competition would occur upon the emergence in the industry of companies with durable strategic market position.

In line with the definition in the United Kingdom's draft digital markets unit proposal, the legislation should define a digital industry as one where digital technology is a "core component" of the products and services provided as part of that activity. The definition would rule out of scope activities that have a digital component, or even use digital technologies in a material way, but which are essentially nondigital. But it would preserve flexibility for the regulator to respond to new business models where digital technology is an essential, core part of the business.

The legislation or its legislative history should contain a nonexclusive list of additional digital lines of business that might be subject to the agency's regulatory jurisdiction. A likely list would include video conferencing services like Zoom, Teams, and WebEx; TV operating systems like Roku; home assistants like Alexa; door monitoring security services like Ring; streaming TV services like Netflix, Prime Video, and Hulu; online music streaming services like Spotify, Apple Music, and SiriusXM; grocery delivery services such as Instacart, DoorDash, and Uber Eats; taxi services such as Uber and Lyft; house and apartment rental services such as Airbnb and Vrbo; online video gaming services like Xbox, PlayStation, and Nintendo; and connected virtual reality platforms like Oculus, Sony VR, and HTC Vive.

The legislation should set up two or more tiers of competition regulation for digital companies depending on whether their market power is substantial, moderate, or minimal. Some procompetition requirements might have to apply to all companies in a digital line of business if they are to be effective such as data portability and interoperability. Others, such as nondiscrimination rules, structural separations, or line-of-business restrictions, should apply only to dominant companies with substantial market power and a strategic position within the industry. Modeled again on the UK digital markets unit proposal, the legislation should require the regulatory agency to use a series of tests for determining strategic market position including market share, number of users, revenue, assets, and ability to make rules or decisions that substantially affect the ability of other companies to provide their service.

For the moment, the constellation of forces is evenly balanced between the bipartisan push for digital competition reform and the equally bipartisan resistance to these reforms. The change to Republican control of the House in the 2022 midterm elections might stall movement toward legislation in the immediate future, but the pressure toward amending competition law to deal with digit concentration will continue. No major reforms are ever enacted in a single congressional session. The prospect for immediate reform might not be bright in 2023, but in the long term it is not a question of if but when.

Privacy

Congress has been considering national privacy legislation for several years. In 2021, however, only one comprehensive national privacy law was introduced—the Information Transparency and Personal Data Control Act, sponsored by Representative Suzan DelBene.[20] Moreover, legislative movement on a national privacy bill has been elusive. Surprisingly, the difficulties do not concern finding bipartisan agreement on the substance of privacy protections but on resolving long-standing partisan differences in connection with private rights of action and preemption of inconsistent state laws.

Progress was made on a national privacy law in 2022 with the American Data Privacy and Protection Act. It was introduced on June 21, 2022, by Representative Frank Pallone. The House Energy and Commerce Committee adopted this compromise bill that addressed the twin challenges of private rights of action and state preemption that had been preventing forward movement of the legislation. But leading privacy advocates criticized the House bill as inadequate compared to the California privacy law it would preempt. Partly as a result, the House and the Senate failed to act. Into this vacuum stepped the FTC, which opened a privacy rulemaking proceeding that could go a long way toward establishing a national policy, without however creating the uniform approach that pre-empting state laws would allow.[21]

This inaction at the federal level has allowed the initiative on privacy legislation to pass to the states. In 2021, two states—Virginia and Colorado—joined California in enacting comprehensive privacy legislation, expanding rights for consumers and obligations for businesses in all segments of the economy that are not already covered by sectoral privacy laws. Still, federal legislation represents the best hope for a coherent national privacy policy.

The major elements of the proposed national privacy bills introduced over the past several years track to some degree the privacy measures proposed in this book for digital industries. The way forward might be for Congress to pass national privacy legislation applicable to all companies and then assign implementation and enforcement in connection with digital industries to a digital regulator.

The key policy objective of needed national privacy legislation should be to protect people from the harmful use of their personal information. The new privacy law should require companies to have a legal basis for their data practices that involve the collection, sharing, and use of personal information. This legal basis could be the consent of the data subject, the necessity of providing service to customers, or the legitimate interest of the company or a third party. The legislation should also require companies to follow the principles of data minimization and purpose specification in their data practices. Companies would be subject to "prohibitions on unreasonably deceptive, abusive, and dangerous design" as outlined in the work of privacy scholar Woodrow Hartzog and should be required to act as information fiduciaries obliged to advance the informational interests of their users in their collection and use of personal information that pertains to them, as suggested in the work of legal scholar Jack Balkin.[22]

National privacy legislation should also provide an agency with broad and clear authority to write and enforce implementing regulations that would specify what these privacy requirements mean in the context of digital lines of business. The enforcing agency should also have the authority to prohibit certain data uses if needed to protect user privacy interests.

Congress should also require the enforcing agency to establish a two-or-more-tiered regulatory structure for privacy. For the large companies with substantial market power, the full panoply of privacy regulations would be in order. For companies with moderate or minimal market positions, the risk of privacy harms is less, and the digital regulator should be allowed to forbear from privacy regulations that are not needed to protect user privacy in these market conditions. The extent of informational fiduciary duties, for instance, might be narrower or the form of consent involved might allow opt-in or take-it-or-leave-it conditions when digital users can easily avoid companies with minimal market power.

Ideally, the implementing agency for digital privacy rules would be a digital regulator. This sectoral approach is consistent with the sectoral approach taken in other areas of privacy law, including financial services, health care, and education. Realistically, Congress is highly likely to lodge enforcement authority for a comprehensive national privacy law with the FTC. In late 2021, Congress indicated its consensus in favor of FTC privacy enforcement by passing legislation in the House that funds the creation of a bureau of privacy at the agency, which would be responsible for developing enhanced regulatory expertise in privacy. At the same time, a group of key Democratic senators also urged the FTC to use its current authority to develop ex-ante privacy rules, which the agency did in launching a privacy rulemaking in 2022.[23]

This choice of the FTC to implement the national privacy rule means that if Congress succeeds in passing both digital competition reform and privacy legislation, the FTC would be responsible for administering both new laws. This would accomplish one of the major advantages of a digital regulator—namely, lodging the implementation of privacy measures and procompetition measures in the hands of a single regulator. This single regulatory structure creates the best chance of avoiding regulatory incoherence and finding the areas where privacy and competition measures reinforce each other rather than work at cross-purposes.

If I am right that the digital regulator is ill housed inside a generalist enforcement agency, it will become clear over time, and Congress can take steps at a future point to remedy the situation. At that point, Congress can and should transfer the responsibility for measures promoting both privacy and competition into the hands of a digital regulator.

Content Moderation

Content moderation is the trickiest digital policy area because it impinges on questions of free expression and political pluralism. In no other area is the mismatch as great between the scale of the problems and the practical, politically feasible, and constitutional remedies. Information disorder does not threaten the well-being of competitive rivals to the digital giants, nor does it violate the personal privacy of digital users. It imposes damages on the country that in many ways might be far worse. It degrades the very ability of the country to govern itself and deal with national emergencies such as COVID-19. It threatens the mental health of the nation's children. And yet the feasible solutions will largely relate to due process, transparency, and data access for further research.

Between 2020 and 2023, Congress was extraordinarily active in producing draft legislation and holding investigative hearings on the problems of information disorder on social media platforms. There was a bipartisan consensus to do something but little agreement on exactly what that might be. In general, Republicans wanted to ensure equal opportunity for conservative speech on social media, while Democrats wanted increased content moderation to reduce the amount of lies, disinformation, and hate speech on social media. Both seem determined to take steps to control the distribution of harmful material to children.

The most attractive vehicle for improving content moderation to emerge from this period of legislative ferment appears to be the Platform Accountability and Transparency Act of 2021 (PACT Act), introduced by Democratic Senator Brian Schatz and Republican Senator John

Thune. This bill would require social media companies to publish an acceptable use policy that outlines what content is out of bounds on the system, what the company does to enforce the policy, and how users can notify the company of material violating its policy. Social media companies must publish biannual reports on the operation of their content moderation system, and they must also establish a complaint system and process complaints within fourteen days. To protect against partisan abuse of this regulatory power, the bill specified that the FTC has no authority to "review any action or decision by a [social media company] related to the application of the acceptable use policy of the provider."[24]

A content moderation statute for social media companies should aim to vindicate the information rights of social media users as laid out in international human rights instruments. In particular, it would authorize the regulator to implement rules to ensure that social media users can enjoy the rights laid out in Article 19 of the Universal Declaration of Human Rights to "to seek, receive and impart information and ideas" through the medium of social media.[25] It should also enshrine as a statutory objective for social media the diversity principle articulated in the Supreme Court's *Associated Press* ruling calling for "the widest possible dissemination of information from diverse and antagonistic sources."[26]

To carry out these objectives, Congress should establish due process measures and associated transparency and reporting requirements modeled on the provisions of the PACT Act to make sure content moderation programs are effective and fair. To further improve fairness and accountability, Congress should establish an external dispute resolution mechanism empowered to override a social media company's particular content moderation decisions. To insulate this system from partisan abuse, it should be run not by the regulator but by an industry self-regulatory organization modeled after FINRA.

Congress should go beyond this to require social media companies to do risk assessments that catalog the ways in which their amplification systems contribute to the spread of harmful material online. The risk assessments must also outline the measures the companies are taking to counteract the reach this material has on their systems. Such assessment studies are required in legislation proposed by Senator Ron Wyden, as well as in the European Commission's proposed Digital Services Act and in its proposed AI regulation of high-risk algorithms.[27] Congress came close to enacting the Kids Online Safety Act (KOSA) at the end of 2022. It should move ahead with it or a similar measure to mandate design changes in online platforms to protect children from harmful material online.

Policymakers must determine the extent to which social media companies are liable for the illegal material posted on their systems by their users, which involves reform of Section 230. One approach might be a liability system modeled after the notice and take down safe harbor system for online copyright violations established in the United States under the Digital Millennium Copyright Act and the similar notice liability system developed in Europe under the Electronic Commerce Directive. Policymakers should recognize, however, what a small part of the information disorder problem Section 230 reform would address, since most of the harmful information circulated and amplified on social media is perfectly legal.

Congress should adopt one further measure to improve the current system. It should pass legislation modeled on the Honest Ads Act.[28] This proposal would apply to the larger social media companies updated and improved disclosure rules for political ads modeled on those that govern the broadcast industry and provide needed transparency into the opaque world of online political advertising.

As in the other policy areas, a two-tiered system of regulation makes the most sense. All social media companies should live up to due process and associated transparency rules and participate in the industry dispute resolution program, but the requirements for reports and systemic risk assessments might be relaxed for smaller social media companies that fall below a certain threshold of average monthly users. The political ad disclosures need not apply at all to smaller social media firms.

Other commonly discussed measures are not ready for prime time. Measures to discourage algorithmic amplification of harmful content are poorly defined and lack any proof of effectiveness. Risk assessments, content moderation reports, and access to data for researchers might reveal effective methods to control the spread of disinformation and hate speech, but until they do, Congress should refrain from mandating any specific measures. Moreover, mandating the use of effective techniques to limit the spread of harmful but legal speech might also raise constitutional questions, since burdening legal speech is as much a free speech violation as banning it.

The widely discussed common carriage requirement to force social media companies to carry all legal content would be a step in the wrong direction since it would deprive social media companies of the means to keep their systems free of harmful hate speech and disinformation, which are largely legally protected under US free speech jurisprudence.

Many think social media companies should be allowed and even encouraged to engage in extensive content moderation to control harmful speech on their platforms, but they should not be politically biased. Many commentators think they should have a duty to provide a broad diversity of political views to their users, parallel to the now-repealed Fairness Doctrine for broadcasters. This ideal of political pluralism is appealing for social media companies since it would work against the tendency of social media algorithms to create filter bubbles and guard against the immense power of social media companies to improperly influence the directions and salience of political discussions and activity.

It is hard, though, to define the key notions involved in this duty for political pluralism. What counts as a political perspective as opposed to objectionable hate speech? Under US law, racism is a legally protected point of view, and yet social media companies ban white nationalist emanations as hate speech. Should they be required to distribute hate speech under the banner of political pluralism? The appealing ideal, moreover, is hard to measure. What would a fair or proportionate distribution of political perspectives look like in social media?

Requirements for access to social media platforms for candidates for federal office are also appealing. Broadcasters must provide equal access to their airwaves for candidates and refrain from censoring them. Why not impose digital analogues of these duties for social media companies? Attractive as that would be to constrain the power of social media to pick and choose among political candidates, it is not entirely clear what such broadcast-based duties would amount to in the very different world of social media.

The best thing to do with these attractive but premature regulatory ideas is to study them further. As part of legislation imposing other content moderation duties on social media companies, Congress should establish a congressional advisory commission to conduct further research and assessment of the ideal of political pluralism and how it might be implemented in practice by social media platforms. The advisory commission should work together with the digital regulator to explore these issues and report back to Congress with their findings and legislative recommendations.

In sum, Congress should require public interest responsibilities for social media companies that include due process, transparency, reporting, risk assessment, and political ad disclosure. The legislation should assign implementation and enforcement of these public interest responsibilities to a digital regulator. As with digital competition and digital privacy rules, that regulator would almost certainly be the FTC. And as with the other policy areas, responsibility for administering content moderation rules could eventually be moved to a sector-specific digital regulator.

If Congress passed all three laws, all the competition, privacy, and content moderation measures for the digital world would be under the control of a single regulator. This result would be a highly desirable way to bring about the key recommendation in the book, which is to establish a digital regulator with authority over competition, privacy, and content moderation. Over time, Congress could transition these responsibilities away from the FTC and to a separate independent agency.

While content moderation is the trickiest of the three policy areas, it is also the most likely to produce a legislative outcome in the near future. This might seem counterintuitive to those who follow congressional matters, since it seems evident that Republicans want social media companies to take down less content associated with the conservative cause while Democrats want social media companies to take down or downplay more content, including misinformation, hate speech, incitements to violence, and material harmful to children.

Eventually the different sides may recognize that due process, transparency, and access to data for researchers will serve all their interests and that the other issues will have to be put off until another day. The due process, transparency, and reporting duties in the federal bipartisan PACT Act mirror those in the partisan social media bills passed in Texas and Florida. If they could be separated from the more controversial carriage requirements in those bills, they would almost certainly receive bipartisan support in Congress. Access to data is another broadly shared concern. The level of anger about the failure of Facebook to act on secret research that only it knew about is leading both Republicans and Democrats to strongly back legislation to provide access to data such as the draft bill circulated in late 2021 by Nathaniel Persily, professor of law at Stanford Law School and director of the Stanford Cyber Policy Center.[29]

In addition, the likely outcome of Supreme Court review of the state social media laws in Texas and Florida is to approve transparency measures and to cast doubt on their further measures to regulate content as violations of the editorial rights of social media companies. It might also, however, leave the constitutional door open to other measures to achieve political pluralism. In that case, Congress then might be able to agree on social media transparency requirements and set up a process for considering these further political pluralism measures.

Coda

Policymakers face the same dilemma today that the nation did in the 1912 presidential campaign that pitted Woodrow Wilson's New Freedom against Theodore Roosevelt's New Nationalism. Wilson wanted to destroy concentrated economic power in part out of fear of the size and power of the national government that would be powerful enough to control large corporations on an ongoing basis. Roosevelt accepted the reality of large private companies as an economic necessity in the modern world but insisted government would have to grow in power and size to bring these private companies under public control.

Wilson won the election, and his branch of the progressive movement has prevailed ever since. It beat back a short-lived effort to establish an associational model of business-government cooperation in the codes of fair competition administered by President Franklin Roosevelt's Depression-era National Recovery Administration. The NRA's statute authorizing these codes was invalidated as an unconstitutional delegation of legislative power by a unanimous Supreme Court that included Wilson's mentor Louis Brandeis. After the decision, Justice Brandeis remarked to one of President Franklin Roosevelt's advisors, "This is the end of this business of centralization, and I want you to go back and tell the president that we're not going to let this government centralize everything."[30]

Despite his suspicion of bigness in both business and government, Brandeis recognized that the agency charged with breaking up the giant corporations would not be able to do it once and then disband itself. The FTC that was his brainchild was supposed to police business practices on an ongoing basis to detect and root out any "unfair methods of competition." He was convinced that this permanent agency role was needed to regulate competition. It would supervise business practices to prevent companies from using anticompetitive tactics to win business rivalries and establish a dominant position of power within an industry.

Brandeis sold this idea of an agency to promote competition to Wilson who made it a centerpiece of his presidential campaign against Theodore Roosevelt. Wilson's embrace of a regulatory agency to promote competition meant that his difference with Roosevelt was not over the need for a powerful government agency to supervise business but whether this agency would regulate competition or monopoly.

With the benefit of more than one hundred years of regulatory experience, especially the experiment by the FCC to introduce competition into the telecommunications industry, it is possible to see today that this choice between regulating competition or regulating monopoly is a false dichotomy. It is possible to do both.

The divided branches of the progressive movement can come together over the need for a digital regulator with a mission both to promote competition *and* to prevent digital companies from abusing a dominant position to harm their rivals and dependent business users. The same digital regulator must also prevent digital companies from using their dominant position to invade their users' privacy rights. The digital agency's third mission is to require dominant social media companies to respect the paramount rights of their users to seek, receive, and send information and ideas.

Choosing regulation as the method to promote competition in key industries means government cannot simply create competitors out of nothing. At some point, businesses must determine whether there is money to be made by challenging a dominant digital company, and if there is not a sufficient incentive, they will go elsewhere with their investment dollars. Competition cannot be compelled by government fiat.

This means that the project of promoting competition through regulation might fail. At that point, as Lina Khan and others have pointed out, the mission of the digital competition regulator collapses into its second prong of defending dependent business users from abuse. The digital agency's competition role becomes primarily one of supervising the conduct of a monopolist to ensure that it treats its business customers fairly.

A key message of this book is that a digital agency must do this, and it must do much more. Existing and perhaps permanent dominance of companies in digital lines of business means the existing and perhaps permanent possibility that these companies will abuse their users' personal information in ways that do them tangible and measurable harm. The digital regulator must be the cop on the beat to prevent that privacy abuse from happening, requiring digital companies to respect their users' privacy rights.

Dominant social media companies do not provide fair and effective content moderation services today. They do not provide adequate reports on the functioning of these systems. They do not do adequate risk assessments of the harms caused by the operation of their algorithmic amplification systems. They do not describe their mitigation efforts for review by the public. They refuse to provide independent researchers with adequate access to data that would allow independent assessments of their content moderation, algorithmic recommendation, and ranking systems. They are not transparent about the opaque world of candidate political ads, and their ad archives of political ads are woefully inadequate for genuine and timely research.

The digital regulator must require dominant social media to do all these things they are not doing today. Perhaps these requirements will not be enough to control the wave of disinformation and hate speech on these platforms today, but they are a good start, and they will be a source of vital information that can inform what other measures might need to be taken.

A digital regulator able to all this will be a very powerful organization. Small government defenders are right to worry that it might become too powerful. The dangers of an overreaching state are real, especially when it attempts to determine for citizens the purpose and meaning of individual life. Harvard Law professor Adrian Vermeule's common-good constitutionalism has a lot going for it in its celebration of the use of government power to produce a just and well-ordered society that brings us together in a common purpose. He is not alone in thinking that the project of protecting individual rights and autonomy is too thin a purpose for government and has led to alienation, indifference, and hostility to the exercise of legitimate and necessary government authority. Communitarian philosophers such as Harvard University professor Michael Sandel have been making this point for several generations. But Vermeule goes over the edge in seeking a governmental definition of the "concept of existence, of meaning, of the universe, and of the mystery of human life."[31] His casual willingness to let an intrusive government decide these most fundamental questions of human existence warns us clearly that government can go too far in seeking the common good.

Congress must respond to this danger in setting up a digital regulator. The power of a digital regulator can be constrained by limits on its authority to second-guess company content decisions. Congress should limit the resources available to the agency and require measures to ensure accountability to the public, the president, Congress, and the courts. But the agency must nevertheless be powerful enough to control the very large and powerful companies that control today's digital world. In the end, setting up such a strong digital regulator is a risk.

The dire state of today's digital world counsels taking the risk. US policymakers cannot allow the digital status quo to persist. Perhaps it was not a good idea to allow digital companies to be unregulated for as long as the United States did. What's done is done, however, and there is no going back to revisit that choice. But laissez-faire cannot be the choice for the future. The question now is whether the country will control the digital companies or whether digital companies will continue to exercise undue influence over the country. Policymakers must act now to create a strong, flexible, and accountable regulatory regime for the digital companies that dominate so many aspects of the nation's social, cultural, economic, and political life.

Notes

1. Quoted in Sandel, *Democracy's Discontent*, 248.
2. Regulation (EU) 2022/2065 of the European Parliament; Regulation (EU) 2022/1925 of the European Parliament.
3. UK DCMS, "Online Safety Bill"; Secretary of State for DCMS and the Secretary of State for BEIS, "Government Response to the Consultation on a New Pro-Competition Regime"; Mark MacCarthy, "What U.S. Policymakers Can Learn from the U.K.'s Online Safety Bill," *TechTank*, Brookings Institution, May 19, 2022, https://www.brookings.edu/blog/techtank/2022/05/19/what-u-s-policymakers-can-learn-from-the-u-k-s-online-safety-bill.
4. "The Untold Story of SOPA/PIPA," Public Knowledge, March 18, 2021, https://www.youtube.com/watch?v=Wo8heHlNRnc.
5. Frances Haugen's statement before the US Senate Committee on Commerce, Science and Transportation, Sub-Committee on Consumer Protection, Product Safety, and Data Security, October 4, 2021, is available at https://www.commerce.senate.gov/services/files/FC8A558E-824E-4914-BEDB-3A7B1190BD49.
6. Brooke Masters, "Apple Has Too Much Power over Its Rivals," *Financial Times*, October 31, 2021, https://www.ft.com/content/94d9f964-10d8-4ff3-9781-821f3fc9ee3a.
7. Competition Policy International in collaboration with CCIA, Antitrust Brainstorming Board, August–September 2021, https://www.competitionpolicyinternational.com/antitrust-brainstorming-sessions.
8. Quoted in Wu, *The Curse of Bigness*, 84.
9. Patel, "Elizabeth Warren Wants to Break Up Apple, Too."
10. Karen Gullo, "Court's Decision Upholding Disastrous Texas Social Media Law Puts The State, Rather Than Internet Users, in Control of Everyone's Speech Online," Electronic Frontier Foundation, October 6, 2022, https://www.eff.org/deeplinks/2022/10/courts-decision-upholding-disastrous-texas-social-media-law-puts-state-rather.
11. Shapiro, "Protecting Competition in the American Economy," 9.
12. Ending Platform Monopolies Act, H.R. 3825, 117th Cong. (2021).
13. ACCESS Act of 2021, H.R. 3849, 117th Cong. (2021).
14. American Choice and Innovation Online Act, H.R. 3816, 117th Cong. (2021), https://www.congress.gov/117/bills/hr3816/BILLS-117hr3816ih.pdf.

15. American Innovation and Choice Online Act, S. 2992, 117th Cong. (2021), Amendment in the nature of a substitute, 2022, https://www.klobuchar.senate.gov/public/_cache/files/b/9/b90b9806-cecf-4796-89fb-561e5322531c/B1F51354E81BEFF3EB96956A7A5E1D6A.sil22713.pdf.

16. Platform Competition and Opportunity Act, H.R. 3826, 117th Cong. (2021).

17. "Blumenthal, Blackburn & Klobuchar Introduce Bipartisan Antitrust Legislation"; S.2710—Open App Markets Act; "Ranking Member Buck, Congressman Johnson Introduce Bipartisan Plan to Rein in App Store Monopolies"; Mark MacCarthy, "The Open App Markets Bill Moves Out of the Senate Judiciary Committee," *Lawfare Blog*, March 8, 2022, https://www.lawfareblog.com/open-app-markets-bill-moves-out-senate-judiciary-committee.

18. Competition and Antitrust Law Enforcement Reform Act, S. 225, 117th Cong. (2021).

19. McCraw, *Prophets of Regulation*, Kindle location 2,250; Matt Stoller, "Why Didn't the Government Stop the Crypto Scam?" *BIG*, November 11, 2022, https://mattstoller.substack.com/p/why-didnt-the-government-stop-the.

20. Information Transparency and Personal Data Control Act, H.R. 1816, 117th Cong. (2021), https://www.congress.gov/bill/117th-congress/house-bill/1816.

21. American Data Privacy and Protection Act, H.R. 8152, 117th Cong. (2022); Bryan, "Passage of Federal Privacy Bill Remains Possible This Year"; FTC, "Trade Regulation Rule on Commercial Surveillance and Data Security"; Mark MacCarthy, "Why the FTC Should Proceed with a Privacy Rulemaking," *TechTank*, Brookings Institution, June 29, 2022, https://www.brookings.edu/blog/techtank/2022/06/29/why-the-ftc-should-proceed-with-a-privacy-rulemaking.

22. Hartzog, *Privacy's Blueprint*; Balkin, "Lecture, Information Fiduciaries and the First Amendment."

23. Build Back Better Act, H.R. 5376, 117th Cong. (2021); "Democrats Urge FTC to Begin Privacy Rulemaking," IAPP News, September 21, 2021, https://iapp.org/news/a/democrats-urge-ftc-to-begin-privacy-rulemaking.

24. The Platform Accountability and Transparency Act of 2021.

25. "Universal Declaration of Human Rights."

26. Associated Press v. United States, 326 US 1 (1945).

27. Algorithmic Accountability Act, S. 1108, 116th Cong. (2019); European Commission, "The Digital Services Act: Ensuring a Safe and Accountable Online Environment," December 15, 2020, https://ec.europa.eu/info/strategy/priorities-2019-2024/europe-fit-digital-age/digital-services-act-ensuring-safe-and-accountable-online-environment_en; European Commission, "Proposal for a Regulation of the European Parliament and of the Council Laying Down Harmonized Rules on Artificial Intelligence (Artificial Intelligence Act) and Amending Certain Union Legislative Acts," April 21, 2021, https://eur-lex.europa.eu/legal-content/EN/TXT/?qid=1623335154975&uri=CELEX%3A52021PC0206.

28. Honest Ads Act, S. 1356, 116th Cong. (2019).

29. Persily, "Facebook Hides Data Showing It Harms Users"; Persily, "Platform Accountability and Transparency Act."

30. Harry Hopkins, "Statement to Me by Thomas Corcoran Giving His Recollections of the Genesis of the Supreme Court Fight," April 3, 1939, typescript in Harry Hopkins Papers, quoted in A.L.A. Schechter Poultry Corp. v. United States, Wikipedia, https://en.wikipedia.org/wiki/A.L.A._Schechter_Poultry_Corp._v._United_States.

31. Adrian Vermeule, "Beyond Originalism," *The Atlantic*, March 31, 2020, https://www.theatlantic.com/ideas/archive/2020/03/common-good-constitutionalism/609037; Sandel, *Democracy's Discontent*.

Index

About the Author

Mark MacCarthy is adjunct professor at Georgetown University's Communication, Culture, & Technology Program, a nonresident senior fellow at the Brookings Institution, and a nonresident fellow at the Institute for Technology Law and Policy at Georgetown Law. He was formerly a public policy advocate for Capital Cities/ABC, the Wexler/Walker Group, Visa, and the Software & Information Industry Association. In the 1980s, he served as professional staff member of the Committee on Energy and Commerce of the US House of Representatives under the chairmanship of Representative John D. Dingell Jr. of Michigan. A prolific writer and researcher, he publishes commentary regularly on tech policy issues with Brookings, *Lawfare*, *The Hill*, *Forbes*, and the Centre for International Governance Innovation. He lives in Bethesda, Maryland, with his wife, Ana Maria Espinoza.